"会计基础设施"助推
"一带一路"

李扣庆　王　鹏　白　容　曾顺福　主编

中国财经出版传媒集团

经济科学出版社
Economic Science Press

图书在版编目（CIP）数据

"会计基础设施"助推"一带一路"／李扣庆主编 .
—北京：经济科学出版社，2017. 11
ISBN 978 - 7 - 5141 - 8709 - 0

Ⅰ. ①会… Ⅱ. ①李… Ⅲ. ①会计学 - 研究 Ⅳ. ①F230

中国版本图书馆 CIP 数据核字（2017）第 286737 号

责任编辑：程新月
责任校对：徐领柱
责任印制：李 鹏

"会计基础设施"助推"一带一路"
李扣庆 王 鹏 白 容 曾顺福 主编
经济科学出版社出版、发行 新华书店经销
社址：北京市海淀区阜成路甲 28 号 邮编：100142
教材分社电话：010 - 88191309 发行部电话：010 - 88191522
网址：www. esp. com. cn
电子邮件：esp@ esp. com. cn
天猫网店：经济科学出版社旗舰店
网址：http://jjkxcbs. tmall. com
北京密兴印刷有限公司印装
710 × 1000 16 开 28. 25 印张 450000 字
2017 年 11 月第 1 版 2017 年 11 月第 1 次印刷
ISBN 978 - 7 - 5141 - 8709 - 0 定价：80. 00 元
（图书出现印装问题，本社负责调换。电话：010 - 88191510）
（版权所有 侵权必究 举报电话：010 - 88191586
电子邮箱：dbts@esp. com. cn）

目　　录

序

加强"会计基础设施"建设，助推"一带一路"

赵鸣骥[*]

2013 年，习近平主席提出"丝绸之路经济带"和"21 世纪海上丝绸之路"的重大倡议，得到海内外的广泛关注和积极响应。经过近 4 年的发展，在中国的积极推动和各国的共同努力下，"一带一路"建设在政策沟通、设施联通、贸易畅通、资金融通、民心相通等方面都取得了丰硕成果。2017 年 5 月，举世瞩目的"一带一路"国际合作高峰论坛在北京成功举办，对外发出了各方合力推动"一带一路"国际合作、携手共建人类命运共同体的积极信号，对世界、对中国都有着十分重要的意义。

近年来，按照中央部署，中国财政部积极发挥职能作用，从政策和资金两个方面推动"一带一路"建设，促进"五通"顺利实施，取得了积极成效。加强政策沟通是推动"一带一路"建设的重要保障，财政部本着求同存异的原则，积极通过国际对话机制深化政府间宏观政策沟通交流，推动区域经济融合。与此同时，紧紧围绕"避免双重征税"和"落实自由贸易区战略"两个重点开展工作，在促进贸易畅通方面发挥积极作用。资金融通是"一带一路"建设的重要支撑，中国政府倡议成立了亚洲基础设施投资银行、丝路基金等机构，并深化同世界银行等传统多边开发机构的合作，推动形成层次清晰、初具规模的"一带一路"融资网络。民心相通是"一带一路"建设的社会根基，近年来，中央财政大力支持开展与"一带一路"沿线国家的各种交流活动，为深化多双边合作奠定了坚实的民意基础。财政部为落实习近平主席在"一带一路"国际合作高峰论坛上的倡议，成

---

* 本文作者为财政部部长助理、党组成员。

立了"一带一路"财经发展研究中心，努力打造服务"一带一路"建设的财经智库和合作交流平台。财政作为国家治理的基础和重要支柱，将进一步在"一带一路"建设中发挥积极作用，推动"一带一路"建设行稳致远。

作为互联互通基础的商业语言，会计是现代社会经济活动开展的重要基础。一个经济体内部会计工作的质量直接关系到宏观和微观运行的效率，而不同经济体之间会计准则或制度的差异则会直接影响到贸易往来和资金融通。可以这样认为，会计是推动国际经济往来和经济发展的重要基础设施。而会计准则、会计人才、会计监管体系等又是决定一国会计工作质量与效率的重要基础。

"一带一路"沿线国家和地区具有不同的民族文化，使用50多种官方语言、10余种会计制度。面对会计体系的差异，包括准则、制度以及会计人才等方面的差异，如何采取有效措施，推动沿线各国会计体系的互联互通，进而实现共同发展、包容发展、绿色发展是我们必须面对的一个重要问题。财政部部长肖捷在"促进资金融通"平行主题会议上明确指出，推动"一带一路"建设行稳致远，是资金融通的重要使命。而要实现高效、安全的资金融通，要求各国相关机构之间加强会计、税收、金融等方面的协调和合作，从而为区域内的货物流通和资金融通提供便利的条件。在这样的一个背景下，在全社会都凝心聚力推动"一带一路"倡议实施之时，会计界积极响应，集体研究推动"一带一路"倡议的"会计基础设施"问题，我感到今天的论坛主题很好，非常贴切，恰逢其时，也很有必要。

要实现"一带一路"建设的伟大构想，"会计基础设施"建设意义重大，同时也任重道远。

第一，持续推进准则、制度的趋同或协调，降低资金融通和贸易畅通的交易成本

推进会计准则的国际趋同，加强各国间会计制度方面的沟通协调，是全球化的必然要求，"一带一路"倡议的推进对此提出了更加紧迫的要求。自70年代末启动改革开放以来，作为推动社会主义市场经济建设的重要举措之一，中国政府高度重视会计制度体系建设，积极推动中国会计准则与国际会计准则的趋同。"一带一路"沿线国家会计准则建设的路径不同，有些全面采用国际会计准则，有些则沿用本国独特的准则体系。我认为，各国之间应加强会计准则体系建设方面经验与教训的交流，找到适合国情差异巨大的"一带一路"沿线国家之间会计准则趋同或协调的最佳路径，降低跨境交易成本，促进相互间的贸易往来和资金融通。

第二，加强国际化会计人才培养以及"一带一路"沿线国家会计人才培养方面的合作

中国北宋思想家胡瑗有一句名言："致天下之治者在人才，成天下之才者在教化"。"一带一路"倡议提出了建立人类命运共同体的美好构想，这一美好构想实现的关键之一在于我们要能够培养出足够多的适应"一带一路"倡议实施需要的优秀人才。近年来，中国和很多"一带一路"沿线国家在高端人才培养方面都推出了一系列举措。中国财政部自 2005 年起启动全国会计领军人才培养工程，取得了显著的成效。由国家会计学院具体承担的全国会计领军（后备）人才培养工程实施十余年来，累计招收 38 个班，1587 名学员，先后有 601 名学员顺利毕业，并招收特殊支持计划三期共 27 名学员。此外，全国各地方财政部门因地制宜，也开展了各具特色的地方会计领军人才培养工作。上海国家会计学院（亚太财经与发展学院）培养了首届发展中国家会计专业硕士研究生，这些工作取得了显著成效，为"一带一路"倡议人才培养积累了宝贵经验。

尽管我们已经在人才培养方面做了很多努力，但是相较于"一带一路"倡议以及我们参与全球经济治理的人才需求而言，国际化高级会计人才的供给还有较大缺口，我们还需要在培养适应"一带一路"倡议所需要的人才方面做出更大的努力。为此，要把"一带一路"倡议需求纳入各自人才培养框架，要加强各自对人才培养的投入，同时也应加强各国之间在会计人才培养方面的合作。我也希望国家会计学院等机构能在这方面有更加积极的探索，为会计人才培养做出更大的贡献。

第三，加强"一带一路"沿线国家会计界，包括学术界、政府部门、注册会计师行业的沟通交流

习近平主席强调，推进"一带一路"建设，要努力形成政府、市场、社会有机结合的合作模式，形成政府主导、企业参与、民间促进的立体格局。真正要建成"一带一路"，必须在沿线国家民众中形成一个相互欣赏、相互理解、相互尊重的人文格局。要形成这样的格局，会计界要做出自己的贡献，需要持续努力，建立全方位、多渠道的沟通机制和平台，不断地增进理解，凝聚共识。论坛就是一个很好的平台，论坛的嘉宾都很有代表性，既有来自政府部门的官员，也有来自学界的专家，还有来自国际机构的代表，以及积极投身"一带一路"倡议的代表性企业。今后期待会计界有更多类似的沟通平台，积极回应、践行"一带一路"倡议。在此特别提议，"一带一路"沿线国家的学术界、中介机构、企业界等加强对"一带一路"倡议推进进程中会计、税收、金融等相关问题的合作研究，及时发现战略推进过程中的问题，回应社会关切，提出可行的解决方案，贡献会计新智慧，贡献会计好声音，为加强政策协调出谋划策。

建设"一带一路"，是福泽全球的重大战略决策。"会计基础设施"是一个重要的命题，在现代社会中，经济越发展，对"会计基础设施"的要求越高。完善的"会计基础设施"对加速社会经济活动，促进国家间的经贸往来起着巨大的推动作用。此次论坛的作用在于破题，相信也会是一个很好的开始，希望各方继续研究、完善"会计基础设施"的内涵，共同推动"一带一路"倡议实施过程中的"会计基础设施"建设，充分发挥会计作为通用商业语言的作用，为推进"一带一路"建设的伟大实践增添新的助力。

前　　言

　　鉴于会计基础设施在推动"一带一路"合作中的重要性，2016年底，上海国家会计学院与ACCA、德勤中国联合组建了课题组，对"一带一路"沿线国家的会计准则建设、会计人才培养及税收制度问题进行专题研究。2017年7月，三方又携手中国会计学会、浪潮集团等联合主办了"会计基础设施助推'一带一路'"高层研讨会，现在奉献在大家面前的就是中、英文两个版本的研究报告和研讨会专家演讲文稿。

　　课题研究报告及专家演讲从不同视角分析研究了"一带一路"倡议推进中的会计准则协同、税收风险监管及跨境资本合作等问题，希望能为所有有志于研究相关问题的朋友们提供有益的参考。"一带一路"是一项规模宏大、影响深远的重大工程，我们也衷心希望本书的出版能对"一带一路"建设中会计及相关问题的研究起到积极的推动作用，为"一带一路"建设奠定更为坚实的会计基础设施。

本书编辑组

什么是会计基础设施?

李扣庆　葛玉御[*]

一、问题的提出

作为经济社会领域的重要概念,"基础设施"最早由发展经济学家 Paul Rosenstein-Rodan 于 1943 年提出,他将一国或一地区的社会总投资分为两类:社会分摊资本和私人资本,前者即基础设施。这一分类为后世所承袭。伴随着社会发展,基础设施的内涵不断丰富。根据世界银行发布的《世界发展报告(1994)》,基础设施可以划分为经济基础设施(Economic Infrastructure)和社会基础设施(Social Infrastructure)两大类。经济基础设施是指长期使用的工程构筑设备设施及其为经济生产和家庭所提供的服务,具体包括公共设施(如电力、通信、管道煤气、自来水、排污、固体垃圾收集与处理)、公共工程(如大坝、水利工程、道路)以及其他交通部门(如铁路、城市、交通、港口、河道和机场)等三种类型,经济基础设施也称"硬基础设施"。而社会基础设施则主要包含教育、卫生保健、法律体系、规章制度和金融体系等,也称"软基础设施"。

基础设施具有先行性和基础性,即基础设施所包含的公共服务内容是其他社会生产和人民生活顺利开展的必不可少的前提和基础,因此,基础设施对于经济社会的发展具有重要意义。从理论研究来看,国内外研究文献从不同层面证明基础设施建设可提高经济效率,降低交易成本,进而带

* 本文作者:1. 李扣庆为上海国家会计学院党委书记、院长、教授;2. 葛玉御为上海国家会计学院教研部讲师,硕士生导师。本文在写作过程中得到了佟成生、叶小杰、宋航、赵敏、王蕾等的大力支持。

动经济增长（Easterly & Rebelo, 1993；Gramlich, 1994；刘生龙和胡鞍钢, 2010；张光南和宋冉, 2013）。从国家实践来看, 世界各国的经济增长都伴随着大规模的基础设施投资和建设, 尤其新兴市场国家在近些年的高速发展正是得益于此。理论和实践均证明基础设施建设对于经济发展的重要性。亚洲开发银行（2017）的报告明确指出, 为促进亚洲经济增长, 亚洲基础设施投资在 2016~2030 年间需达到 26 万亿美元, 平均每年 1.7 万亿美元, 这一需求远超亚洲开发银行当前提供投资贷款的能力。因此, 在中国首倡、多国共同参与下, 于 2015 年 12 月成立了亚洲基础设施投资银行, 重点支持基础设施建设, 促进亚洲区域互联互通和经济一体化。

显然, 各国在基础设施建设方面不遗余力, 甚至在经济全球化的背景下开展了卓有成效的跨国集体行动。然而, 当前基础设施建设的重点集中于交通、能源、通信等"硬基础设施", 而对保障经济活动顺利运转的会计、税收、金融、法律等"软基础设施"关注不够。事实上, "硬基础设施"在建设过程中很大程度上离不开"软基础设施"的支持。更进一步而言, 如果"软基础设施"严重滞后, 交通、能源等"硬基础设施"对经济发展的推动作用也将面临严重掣肘。黄亚生（2005）的研究发现, "软基础设施"会产生长期发展的动力, 应更加重视。会计作为"软基础设施"的重要内容, 也是国际通用的商业语言, 经济越发展, 会计越重要。对国家内部的商业活动和资金融通来说是如此, 对国际间商品、服务贸易和资金融通来说也是如此。因此, 有必要明确提出"会计基础设施", 并深入研究。

二、会计基础设施的内涵

中共十八届三中全会明确提出"财政是国家治理的基础和重要支柱", 财政在现代国家治理和经济发展中的基础性作用毋庸置疑, 而会计则是财政乃至整个财经工作的重要基础, 扮演着为基础奠基的角色。从微观层面看, 会计信息的质量, 包括会计信息的准确性、及时性、充分性、相关性等直接关系到引导资源配置的价格信号的合理性, 对微观主体的投融资决策等有重大影响。从宏观层面看, 会计信息的质量则会影响到宏观数据的准确性, 影响到财政、税收、货币等宏观经济政策的制定及其运作效果。

从更广泛的国际视角来看，由于不同经济体会计准则（制度）可能存在差异，会计监管水平及会计从业人员的水平也参差不齐，会计信息还可能存在着无法直接对接的问题。商业语言不通用，必然加大跨境经贸活动的交易成本，影响到多个层面的跨境经贸合作。

结合对基础设施的定义，本文认为，会计基础设施是指为一国经济运行和国际经济交往提供计量信息支持的基础设施。具体而言，会计基础设施主要包括三要素：会计准则体系、会计监管体系和会计人才体系。首先，会计准则是会计实践发展到一定阶段后，对会计核算和财务报告进行的规范，其目的在于提高会计核算和财务报告的统一性、真实性和可比性，为信息使用者提供决策有用的财务信息。一国会计准则的完备程度，在很大程度上决定了其会计基础设施的完备程度。没有科学合理的会计准则体系，会计计量和核算就失去了统一的依归。其次，会计信息作为一种稀缺资源，在现代企业制度两权分离的背景下，由于信息不对称，为保障会计工作平稳进行，需提供完善的会计监管体系。张以宽（2003）认为会计监管的目的是防止会计信息失真，保证经营管理决策以及投资决策所需的正确信息。会计准则与会计监管具有理论上的统一性，会计准则是会计监管的基础，高质量的会计准则能够加强市场约束；会计监管必须以会计信息为基础，会计准则质量的高低直接关系到监管指标的效用。而良好的会计监管则确保会计准则得到严格落实，防范会计风险。最后，准则的制订、完善、执行及会计监管都需要由处于各类机构中的人去实施。会计人才的数量、水平及其结构是决定一国会计基础设施能否支持其经济健康运行的关键。准则、监管及人才构成支撑经济运行的会计基础设施的核心架构。总之，从内在逻辑来看，会计准则体系是基础，会计监管体系是保障，会计人才体系是关键。以此三者为核心，又可衍生出一国会计体系的若干相关联的要素，如会计教育和人才培养、各类会计服务和监管机构设置等。

许多国家的经济发展实践都表明，加强会计基础设施建设，是经济发展水平提升不可或缺的前提。一个健全的会计基础设施体系能在很大程度上促使一国经济行稳致远。改革开放以来，我国政府高度重视会计基础设施建设，为经济高速增长保驾护航。1995年6月，在研究注册会计师培训中心（国家会计学院前身）建设的现场办公会上，时任国务院副总理朱镕基同志就指出："这是千秋万代的事业，是为社会主义市场经济奠基，是极为重要的事情之一。"2006年，我国建成了与国际财务报告准则趋同的中国企业会计准则体系，并自2007年1月1日起开始实施，大幅提升了我国企业的会计信息质量，促进了资本市场的健康发展。我国企业会计准则体系已经与香港地区财务报告准则、欧盟所采用的国际财务报告准则实现等效。政府有关部门还在持续针对国际、国内新形势的变化，继续研究完善我国企业会计准则体系，使中国企业会计准则与国际财务报告准则持续趋同。在会计监管方面，我国逐步建立了以政府监管为主、行业自律为辅的会计监管模式，不断完善政府监管的体制和运行机制，厘清会计监管思路，明确各监管机构之间的权责范围，避免重复监管，以有效降低监管成本和会计风险。在人才培养方面，通过建设国家会计学院等多种举措，整合全社会资源，建立了完整的会计人才培养体系。财政部于2010年出台了《会计行业中长期人才发展规划（2010～2020年）》，指导会计人才培养实践，对会计人才梯队建设进行了系统、长期的谋划。综合来看，我国在会计基础设施的建设和完善等方面进行了有益的探索，取得了显著的成绩，对社会主义市场经济的持续快速发展起到了重要的支撑作用。

三、"一带一路"倡议下的"会计基础设施"建设

自2013年以来，"一带一路"建设在"政策沟通、设施联通、贸易畅通、资金融通、民心相通"等方面都取得了丰硕成果，其中，"设施联通"作为五大抓手之一，既是"一带一路"建设的核心工作，又是"贸易畅通""资金融通"的基础前提。而"会计基础设施"作为"设施联通"的重要内容，直接关系到"一带一路"建设的成效。从现实来看，"一带一路"沿线国家的"会计基础设施"建设存在两点不足。第一，部分国家在会计准则、人才和监管等方面严重不足，基础设施薄弱；第二，不同国家之间因国情差异，"会计基础设施"情况差别巨大，沿线国家使用多种不同的会计准则、制度，联通性较差，增加了交易成本。

考虑到"一带一路"沿线各国国情的复杂性和加强"一带一路"倡议下的"会计基础设施"建设的重要意义，应从会计准则、会计监管和会计人才三方面入手，多国协作配合，加强"会计基础设施"建设，助力"一带一路"倡议取得更加丰硕的成果。首先，要开展深入研究。对"会计基

础设施"的内涵与外延，对"一带一路"倡议实施进程中的重大会计及相关的税收、金融等问题进行深入研究，要整合"一带一路"沿线国家、相关国际机构的力量，研究推进"一带一路"沿线国家"会计基础设施"提升和联通的有效路径。其次，合作开展"一带一路"会计人才培养。要积极推动"一带一路"沿线国家在会计人才培养上的合作，通过实施各类跨境合作人才培养项目、鼓励会计人才跨境流动等举措，促使"会计基础设施"较为薄弱的国家会计体系的跨越式提升。最后，要建立多渠道、多层次的沟通机制，加强沿线国家会计监管方面的协调，防范会计风险，积极推进"一带一路"国家间会计准则的趋同或等效、联通，降低跨境交易成本，为"一带一路"建设保驾护航。

参考文献

1. 郭永清. 论我国高级会计人才培养体系的构建，会计研究，2008（10）.

2. 黄亚生. 经济增长中的软硬基础设施比较：中国应不应该向印度学习？世界经济与政治，2005（1）.

3. 金戈. 中国基础设施资本存量估算，经济研究，2012（4）.

4. 刘生龙，胡鞍钢. 基础设施的外部性在中国的检验：1988—2007，经济研究，2010（3）.

5. 张光南，宋冉. 中国交通对"中国制造"的要素投入影响研究，经济研究，2013（7）.

6. 张以宽. 论有中国特色的会计监管体系，审计与经济研究，2003（1）.

7. Easterly, W. and Rebelo, S. "Fiscal Policy and Economic Growth：An Empirical Investigation." *Journal of Monetary Economics*, 1993, 32（3）.

8. Gramlich, E. "Infrastructure Investment：A Review Essay." *Journal of Economic Literature*, 1994（32）.

9. World Bank, World Development Report 1994：Infrastructure for Development, Oxford：Oxford University Press, 1994.

"会计基础设施"助推
"一带一路"倡议

白 容[*]

我已经和中国打了很多年交道。在此过程中，我很荣幸地目睹了中国财会行业的不断发展和壮大。对于近三十年来特许公认会计师公会（简称ACCA）中国会员在构建该行业声誉过程中发挥的重要作用，我深感自豪。

财会行业在中国之所以享有很高的声誉，很大程度上归功于中国国家会计学院的巨大贡献。ACCA 和上海国家会计学院保持着长期且富有成效的合作伙伴关系，我们很高兴再次与他们合作举办此次论坛，并借此机会发布 ACCA 携手上海国家会计学院与德勤共同完成的"一带一路"最新报告。

在这份研究报告中，我们共同探讨了专业会计师在"一带一路"倡议发展过程中所需扮演的重要角色。"一带一路"是富有远见的国际化贸易路线，其成功离不开沿线经济体的通力协作与参与。ACCA 一直是全球标准的积极支持者和倡导者，我们认为这不仅有助资本的跨境流动，还将为该行业的人才创造巨大机遇。

该报告凝聚了我们"会计基础设施"系列的最新研究成果，围绕如何实现会计准则国际化、如何协调国际税收政策以及如何培养国际化财会人才等热点议题，集大家之所成，全面展示了各方看法与意见。我们也很荣幸能有机会听到来自欧盟议会和中巴研究所各位代表的观点。

为了实现这一目标，我们从实际出发，广泛收集了"一带一路"沿线20 多个国家的会计师事务所中相关会计和税务专家的真知灼见。通过筛选和分析，本报告汇集了其中 14 个国家相关专家的看法与意见，并得出初步结论。其他更具意义的深入洞察研究将进一步在未来的洞察报告中陆续

---

* 本文作者为特许公认会计师公会（ACCA）行政总裁。

呈现。

　　ACCA 高度关注"一带一路"为会员和财会行业所带来的机遇。作为专业会计师机构，我们始终致力于连接全球，促进全球网络构建，创造可持续增长。在全球 101 家 ACCA 办事处和中心的支持下，我们已拥有 19.8 万名会员和 48.6 万名学员，遍布全球 180 个国家。ACCA 已在全球 52 个国家开展业务，其中 21 个为"一带一路"沿线国家。因此，ACCA 与"一带一路"倡议高度契合。在 ACCA 多元化的会员基础上，他们年轻、灵活且在财务管理领域有着较强的专业水准，同时辅以专业的职业道德，可以说 AC-CA 会员是当今高度互联、日益复杂的商业环境中最为理想的人才储备。

　　作为凝聚全球会员的纽带，ACCA 期待能够连接各专业会计师团体，共同致力于推动新"丝绸之路"的不断前行。今天发布的报告进一步阐明了我们致力于支持"一带一路"这一倡议的雄心壮志。在此过程中，我们也衷心感谢上海国家会计学院和德勤会计师事务所的通力协作和给予的大力支持。ACCA 将一如既往地支持和帮助我们的会员实现"一带一路"的美好愿景。让我们一同继续这场激动人心的征程。

德勤中国助力"一带一路"

曾顺福[*]

2013 年的秋天,习近平主席提出共建"丝绸之路"经济带和 21 世纪"海上丝绸之路"的倡议,得到国际社会的广泛关注和积极响应。三年来,各项工作取得了丰硕的成果。事实证明"一带一路"倡议顺应了和平与发展的时代要求,符合各国加快发展的内在愿望,有助于促进沿线经济建设和全球经济繁荣。据商务部公布的数据显示,2016 年中国境内投资者全年共对全球 164 个国家和地区的 7900 多家境外企业进行了非金融类直接投资,创下 1700 亿美元的历史新高;海外并购交易也增长迅猛,2016 年中资企业共发起了 729 宗海外并购交易,共计约 3300 亿美元。同时,借力全球化经营,2016 年进入世界 500 强的中国公司数量由 2006 年的 23 家增加至 110 家。更为突出的是,中国企业开展国际化业务的方式方法正在转变。从最初的工程承包转变为开始探索采用跨国并购、绿地投资、PPP 等多种模式投资开发大型基础设施、资源矿产与工业园区等,使得企业可以在价值链高端获得更高的收益。同时,带动制造、设计、运营甚至是技术、标准全产业链"走出去",从单纯的承包商转型升级为投资商及服务商。

可以看出,中国企业"走出去"的国际化进程是不可逆转的趋势,怀揣着中国企业势将引领全球化新进程的信念以及帮助中国企业参与国际合作与竞争的使命感,在过去多年来德勤始终关注中国企业"走出去",走得稳不稳,走得好不好。我们曾经对 54 家中央和地方国企的中高层管理人员进行了问卷调查。在被问及企业国际化或参与"一带一路"项目,最需要加强的能力时,60% 的受访企业选择了国际化战略的制定,54% 选择了需要政府、金融机构或社会资本对企业国际化的融资支持,46% 选择了需加强对

* 本文作者为德勤中国首席执行官。

投资/建设目的地的政治、法律、税务、文化（宗教）等各类风险评估能力、防范能力和应对能力，还有 33% 选择了需要储备懂得当地法律法规和文化又懂管理运营的国际化人才。不难看出，今天我们论坛所关注的会计体系的差异与协调、税收风险的识别与规避、资本市场的融合与发展以及融汇在所有问题之中的国际化专业人才的培养都是大家非常需要了解和探讨的话题。

毋庸置疑，会计信息在企业国际化的进程中起着举足轻重的作用，会计作为一项国际通用的商业语言，是各类投资规划、决策、管理、控制、评价的依据。经济越发展，会计越重要，完善的会计基础设施对加速社会经济活动，促进国家间经贸往来起着巨大的推动作用。感谢上海国家会计学院牵头组织——会计基础设施助推 "一带一路" 论坛，为各国财会类专业人士以及政界、商界、学界的朋友，提供了一个相互交流、沟通互鉴、加强合作的平台。愿各位朋友能在这个平台上畅所欲言，发表真知灼见，进行思维碰撞，就企业参与 "一带一路" 建设中取得的成功经验、获得的机遇、面临的困难挑战进行探讨，从而为后来者提供经验借鉴，为决策者提供参考依据，为会计行业推动 "一带一路" 发展献计献策。而德勤——作为世界一流的专业机构，拥有多种专业服务能力和遍布逾 150 个国家的全球网络，一贯也将继续竭力为中国企业参与 "一带一路" 提供全方位的专业服务支持。

希望在座各位携手并肩，传播 "一带一路" 声音，续写 "一带一路" 建设的新篇章。

"一带一路"中国企业国际化会计体系——差异与协调

傅俊元*

在推动"一带一路"倡议的过程中,中国的"硬实力"走出去了,但我们的"软实力",尤其是在会计领域的"软实力",如何在"一带一路"推动过程中发挥应有的作用,这是一个值得深入研究的重要问题。在"一带一路"倡议实施过程中,许多项目比较重大,备受当地老百姓和当地政府关注(包括执政党和反对党),会计处理稍有不慎就可能引发一些风险和问题,所以非常有必要对此问题进行研究。

一、会计准则的差异:"一带一路"沿线国家的六大会计体系

中国交通建设股份有限公司(以下简称中国交建)是"一带一路"的先行者,"一带一路"沿线 66 个国家主要分布在亚洲和非洲,2017 年"一带一路"峰会有 130 多个国家参会,所以"一带一路"的外延已扩展到全球大多数国家,这与中国交建的业务非常吻合:中国交建产品和业务遍布150 多个国家,在 103 个国家设立了 193 个驻外机构,与大部分国家的会计体系、业务都有密切的关系,所以今天进行讨论的一个基础问题,就是与中国交建有业务活动的这些国家的会计准则。

近年来,中国的会计准则和国际会计准则趋同越来越明显,中国交建在香港 H 股上市,也在上海 A 股上市。公司既需要按国际会计准则进行披露,也需要按中国会计准则披露。根据中国交建上市 10 年来的实践,两个准则间需要调整的内容越来越少,进一步说明中国会计准则和国际会计准

---

* 本文作者为中国交通建设股份有限公司执行董事。

则大部分趋同，只在计量、列报披露方面有些差异。因此，这两个准则不是今天所要讲的重点。

今天的重点是研究"一带一路"沿线国家也包括全球其他国家的会计准则。每个国家的会计准则都具有自身特点，各不相同，但是根据多年来的实践，相当一部分国家的会计准则有一些共同属性，按照这些共性我们进行适当分类。我们借鉴了国际上通用的国际会计模式分类，特别是美国会计学会将国际会计模式分为英联邦会计模式、法国会计模式、德国会计模式、美国会计模式、共产主义国家会计模式。在此，结合中国交建主要业务国家情况，我们将会计模式分为六大类，包括法语系、葡语系、西班牙语系、美国系、英语系、俄语系等六大会计体系。

六大会计体系的划分主要考虑了我们有业务的 150 多个国家的基本情况，也考虑相同宗主国、殖民地情况。比如说英语系就是过去所谓的英联邦国家，过去都是英国的殖民地，这些国家自然而然形成了一定的会计环境和共同会计准则。俄语系主要是原苏联地区，后来分解成 15 个加盟共和国，也包括南斯拉夫地区。美国系主要就是过去以美国为核心的一些会计体系。葡语系主要是在南美的一些国家，比如说巴西等等。西班牙语系是过去西班牙的一些殖民地，包括南美的哥伦比亚、委内瑞拉等一些国家。

法语系主要包括刚果布、赤道几内亚、塞内加尔等中西非国家，从它的会计体制、会计管理规范、会计监督机构以及国际趋同的现状来看，有一些共同点。1993 年在毛里求斯的路易港，16 个中西非财政部长签订了《非洲商法协调条约》。以条约为基础，统一了一系列的法律，包括会计统一法，对成员国会计立法、会计准则等都做出了一些统一的规定和要求。有 17 个国家（西非 7 个、中非 10 个）的会计体系主要受到法国的影响。法语系会计准则主要是借鉴法国的会计法案，基本上趋同于国际会计准则。

二、会计准则的协调：思路和原则

会计协调与处理的思路和原则有三个方面。首先，需要满足所在国的税务申报和稽查。很多非洲国家并不关注企业披露，也不关注上市与否，重点关注的是企业纳税情况，企业会计处理是否合理、符不符合所在国的会计法案，特别是一些大项目会计处理，所有的调整必须满足所在国的税务申报。其次，需要满足中国政府的税务申报和稽查以及上市公司信息披露要求。最后，需要满足中国会计准则和政府审计的要求。

在实际账务处理模式上有两种：一种是一套账处理模式，就是说把所有的经济业务，按照所在国会计准则的要求，或者按照中国会计准则的要求，形成财务报告。但是报告如果按照所在国的会计准则处理，那必须要调整符合中国会计准则。一套账有其优势，同时也存在一些问题，优势在于工作量比较少，做些调整就可以，大的业务没有太大差别，目前很多语系的会计准则要求与国际财务报告体系趋同，调整的量越来越少。但这种调整是在企业对所在国和对中国会计准则差异非常了解的基础上才能进行，这有可能出现"挂一漏万"的情况，容易出现遗漏和差错，一旦出现遗漏和差错，有可能造成很多失误，这一点我们深有体会。

另一种是两套账模式，即一套外账，按照所在国会计准则进行处理；一套内账，按照中国会计准则处理。外账按照所在国会计准则处理，可以满足企业当地的税务申报要求，内账符合中国会计准则要求。两套账的处理模式也有优缺点，优点就是外账和内账都是独立的，可以最大限度地规避会计和税务的风险，不存在差错问题，不足是成本相对较高，耗费比较大。

海外外账处理大体有三种模式，一是内部财务人员具备了对所在国会计准则全面了解的能力，自身就可以进行外账处理；二是聘请专业机构进行处理，在有些国家情况比较复杂、业务又相对比较简单的情形下可以聘请所在国比较好的会计师事务所进行会计处理，比如说在非洲国家我们可能请普华永道，也可能请德勤来进行一些外账处理；三是聘请当地的会计人员，作为公司的正式员工专门处理外账，按照国际化要求进行属地化管理，在部分国家具备会计人才的基础上此方法可以执行。从某种意义上看，这种办法成本也比较低，因为中国的人口红利在逐渐消失，外派财务人员成本比当地聘请财务人员成本要高得多，所以这种模式现在已经比较普遍。中国交通建设股份有限公司部分驻外机构的外账是聘请当地的会计员工进行处理，从实际推行效果来看非常好。

三、总结与展望

一是"一带一路"沿线大部分国家会计准则与中国会计准则区别仍比较大。特别是一些非洲国家，自身经济业务发展不是非常发达，市场化程度也比较弱。在苏联的一些国家计划经济色彩还比较浓厚，这几年中国会计准则已经与国际会计准则趋同，但还是有一部分国家，这方面的趋同仍然有些缓慢，尤其在法语和俄语系国家。

二是大部分中国企业在海外没有编制完整的满足所在国要求的财务报告。这实际上存在很大风险。中国交通建设股份有限公司是走出去比较早的企业，经过二三十年的发展，公司财务体系相对比较完整。但随着近年来"一带一路"的兴起，有相当一部分企业刚刚走出去，还没有经验，而"一带一路"沿线国家政治形势、经济形势千差万别，稍有不慎就可能会给我们带来很大的风险。

三是在现有状态下，最好还是按照两套账的模式进行会计处理。一套账处理的方法很可能会带来很大问题，因为我们的能力、水平还有差距。当然对于有些与国际会计准则体系比较接近的国家，可以按一套账模式处理，关键是要密切地跟踪所在国会计准则的趋同进展，与时俱进，适时调整。

"金砖国家"会计监管与国际趋同

王　鹏[*]

　　财政部会计司、中国会计学会对"金砖国家"会计监管与国际趋同这一主题的有关研究成果，要从"新要求、新定位、新出发"三方面进行分析。这三者之间的内在逻辑是，中国会计学会作为财政部主管的国家级会计学术组织，要适应新形势，把新形势提出的这些新要求落实在我们的工作之中。因此，就要求中国会计学会确定新的定位，在新的定位下，中国会计学会应该有新的作为，新的出发。

一、新要求

　　首先，我们现在面临的新要求。党的十八大以来，党中央提出了全面深化改革的总体要求，财政部会计司、中国会计学会也一直在落实这些新要求。习近平主席2017年5月14日出席"一带一路"国际合作高峰论坛开幕式，作了题为《携手推进"一带一路"建设》的重要讲话，他强调，4年来，全球100多个国家和国际组织积极支持和参与"一带一路"建设，联合国大会、联合国安理会等重要决议也纳入"一带一路"建设内容。"一带一路"建设逐渐从理念转化为行动，从愿景转变为现实，建设成果丰硕。这是政策沟通不断深化的4年；这是设施联通不断加强的4年；这是贸易畅通不断提升的4年；这是资金融通不断扩大的4年；这是民心相通不断促进的4年。我们欢迎各国结合自身国情，积极发展开放型经济，参与全球治理和公共产品供给，携手构建广泛的利益共同体。要发挥智库作用，建设好智库联盟和合作网络。"一带一路"建设植根于"丝绸之路"的历史土壤，

14

＊本文作者为财政部会计司副巡视员、中国会计学会秘书长。

重点面向亚欧非大陆，同时向所有朋友开放。

我们今天研究"一带一路"的会计趋同、会计的发展战略问题，也包括"金砖国家"的会计趋同问题，实际上习近平总书记的重要讲话已经给我们提出了很多新的课题。比如说，他要求我们要参与到全球的治理和公共产品的供给中来，他要求我们要携手构建广泛的利益共同体。可以说企业会计准则本质上就是一种公共产品，尤其是在当今全球经济一体化和"一带一路"倡议实施的大背景下，企业会计准则更是一种国际公共产品。那么，企业会计准则的国际趋同，实际上就是参与全球经济治理的重要组成内容和重要体现方式。再如他要求我们要发挥好智库的作用，强调"一带一路"建设植根于丝绸之路的历史土壤，重点面向亚非欧大陆，同时向所有国家开放。因此，我们研究的视野也应该是有国际化的视野。

二、新定位

其次，在新的要求下，中国会计学会提出了新的定位。中国会计学会的新的定位是"三位一体"，主要是三个方面：第一，要把中国会计学会建设成财政部的高端智库，要围绕国家的重大战略和财政部的重大课题做研究。第二，要把中国会计学会建设成为国家品牌性社会组织。第三，要把中国会计学会建设成彰显国际影响力的中国会计学术组织。这三个方面是中国会计学会下一步发展的一个新定位。在新定位下，中国会计学会要有新作为，就是要做到"有声有色"，有"声"就是要发出声音，中国会计学会要向上、向中间、向下三个方向发出会计的声音；有"色"就是要有形象，要突出中国会计学会的品牌性、主导性、引导性和凝聚性的特色。无论是新定位还是新作为，这其中重要的一个方面就是智库建设。在智库建设上，我们要充分发挥好中国会计学会的服务和联络功能，要搭建平台，把政府、社会、市场，也包括高校等其他方面的作用联系在一起，要构架桥梁，做到"上情下达、下情上传"，共同努力为国家重大战略的实施发挥我们应有的作用。

围绕今天研讨会的"会计基础设施"助推"一带一路"，我们前期也做了有关会计趋同的研究工作。因为"一带一路"的会计趋同、会计战略，实际上是一个非常大的题目，因此，我们采取了"分步走"的策略。首先围绕"金砖国家"来进行研究，提出的工作部署是"竞争同步、全部覆盖、虚实结合"。

所谓"竞争同步"，就是中国会计学会同时组建了五个团队，同时研究"金砖国家"的会计趋同问题。"全部覆盖"，就是"金砖国家"的会计趋同问题要覆盖到这些国家与会计相关的所有方面，如企业会计准则的制定机构、企业会计准则的发布机构、企业会计准则的监管机构，以及这些国家的企业会计准则法规体系等方面都要进行研究。"虚实结合"，就是理论界和实务界同时研究同一个问题，从组织上保证我们的课题研究的高质量。在这样一个考虑下，中国会计学会组建了"4＋1"团队，有上海大学、西南财经大学、重庆大学、浙江财经大学，也包括今天参加会议的中兴通讯公司。组建的"4＋1"团队即4个理论界团队再加上1个实务界团队，最后形成"1＋5"的工作成果。我们5个团队形成的5份独立研究报告都提交给了财政部会计司，由财政部会计司形成了金砖国家会计趋同的1份总体研究报告，因此，我们说形成了"一份总体报告，再加上五份独立报告"的工作成果形式。

三、新出发

新出发具体包括以下五个方面：

一是"金砖国家"企业会计准则的制定、发布、批准和监管的基本情况。

二是"金砖国家"企业会计准则的法规体系。

三是"金砖国家"企业会计准则的实施安排。

四是"金砖国家"企业会计准则的趋同情况。

五是"金砖国家"企业会计准则趋同的最新进展与个人思考。

（一）"金砖国家"企业会计准则制定、发布、批准和监管的基本情况

下面，分别围绕巴西、印度、俄罗斯和南非四个国家介绍"金砖国家"企业会计准则的制定、发布和监管的基本情况。

1. 巴西

巴西企业会计准则制定机构是会计公告委员会（CPC），这是一个非营利性组织，不属于政府组织。这个机构除负责制定巴西本国企业会计准则外，还负责批准巴西采用国际财务报告准则。因此，这个机构既是巴西企业会计准则的制定机构，也是批准机构。对于巴西企业会计准则的实施监管来讲，巴西的主要监管机构包括三个方面：一是巴西证券交易委员会（CVM），二是巴西中央银行，三是保险监管机构，这些机构负责巴西企业会计准则的实施与监管工作。

2. 印度

印度特许会计师协会（ICAI）负责制定印度本国会计准则，其下设的会计准则理事会（ASB）负责具体的起草工作。印度特许会计师协会是1949年依据《印度特许会计师法》成立的一个法定机构。印度企业会计准则的批准机构是由印度公司事务部（MCA）成立的国家会计准则顾问委员会（NACAS），该委员会具体负责印度企业会计准则的审核，审核后经公司事务部批准和发布后生效。这样的制度安排是由印度《公司法》规定的，它要求印度特许会计师协会制定的企业会计准则必须经中央政府认定和公告。在印度，企业会计准则的监管机构主要有印度公司事务部、印度储备银行（RBI）等金融保险监管当局，印度证券交易委员会（SEBI）负责对上市公司实施企业会计准则进行监管。

3. 俄罗斯

俄罗斯在企业会计准则制定机构方面情况比较复杂，其中，俄罗斯联邦财政部（MFRF）负责制定和发布俄罗斯本国企业会计准则；俄罗斯联邦中央银行（CBR）负责制定适用于中央银行和其他金融机构的会计准则，其他有关政府部门也可以结合各自的行业特点，制定行业企业会计准则。俄罗斯联邦财政部负责制定和发布俄罗斯本国企业会计准则，俄罗斯如果要采用国际财务报告准则需要经过联邦财政部指定的独立机构——国家财务会计组织（NOFA）进行技术评估，通过其评估的企业会计准则，由俄罗斯联邦财政部、联邦中央银行和联邦司法部联合发布后生效。从监管机构来讲，俄罗斯联邦财政部、俄罗斯联邦中央银行、俄罗斯联邦证券市场委员会（FCSM）都在负责监管企业会计准则的实施工作。

4. 南非

南非的企业会计准则制定机构是南非财务报告准则委员会（FRSC），该机构是由南非贸工部（DTI）依据 2006 年新修订的《公司法》组建的独立机构，其运作资金来自于国家拨款。南非会计准则理事会（SAASB）是南非财务报告准则委员会下设的一个职能部门，具体负责起草企业会计准则公告和解释。在监管机构上，南非贸工部和约翰内斯堡证券交易所（JSE）负责监管企业会计准则的实施工作。

（二）"金砖国家" 企业会计准则法规体系

在企业会计准则法规体系方面，这四个国家也很有特点。巴西、印度和南非这三个国家的企业会计准则制定机构均为非营利性组织，不直接隶属于政府部门。这些国家的《公司法》都对企业财务报告的编制作出了一定的要求。但是，对于俄罗斯来讲，则有系统的关于企业会计准则制定和会计行业管理的法律法规，主要有三部：第一部是《俄罗斯联邦会计法》，类似于我国的《会计法》。第二部是《合并财务报表法》，规定了企业编制合并财务报表的主体范围及基本要求。第三部是有关俄罗斯采用国际财务报告准则的程序法，具体规定了俄罗斯采用国际财务报告准则的评估过程和审计程序。

（三）"金砖国家" 企业会计准则的实施安排

这个方面主要是总结在这些国家企业会计准则到底是如何去实施的。这四个国家在企业会计准则的实施安排既有共同点，也有各自的特点。

1. 巴西

目前巴西上市公司和大部分金融机构的合并财务报表层面采用国际财务报告准则，在个别财务报表层面则采用与国际财务报告准则趋同的巴西企业会计准则。但是，巴西企业会计准则与国际财务报告准则相比，仍然还存在着个别差异。比如说，资产重估、利润表列报等方面还存在差异。

2. 印度

印度上市公司和大企业的合并财务报表层面和个别财务报表层面，均采用与国际财务报告准则趋同的新印度企业会计准则，较小规模公司采用印度本土企业会计准则。新印度企业会计准则尽管与国际财务报告准则实现了趋同，但是与国际财务报告准则相比，还是存在诸多差异，比如说外币计价可转换债券、企业合并、投资性房地产、综合收益表等方面都存在差异。

3. 俄罗斯

目前，俄罗斯上市公司和金融机构的合并财务报表层面采用国际财务报告准则，但是，所有公司的个别财务报表层面都必须采用俄罗斯企业会计准则。俄罗斯目前仍存在多项行业企业会计准则，并且俄罗斯企业会计准则还主要服务于税收目的。

俄罗斯企业会计准则与国际财务报告准则存在诸多差异，比如说，俄罗斯企业会计准则没有引入公允价值概念，租赁、存货等会计准则还存在很多差异。再比如，俄罗斯企业会计准则没有关于资产减值、衍生金融工具、套期会计、投资性房地产等方面的规定。

4. 南非

目前，南非上市公司和金融机构，无论是合并财务报表，还是个别财务报表层面，都直接采用国际财务报告准则。南非的中小企业也直接采用中小企业国际财务报告准则。南非财务报告准则委员会的主要工作是仅仅就个别业务发布解释公告。

（四）"金砖国家"企业会计准则的趋同情况

这四个国家在企业会计准则与国际财务报告准则趋同方面存在两种情形：一是南非因为历史和语言等原因，全面直接采用了国际财务报告准则。二是其他"金砖国家"在企业会计准则国际趋同的过程中，因为法律、文化、语言等因素的影响，其趋同的范围和程度各有特点。巴西和俄罗斯仅在上市公司和部分金融机构的合并财务报表层面采用国际财务报告准则，其本国企业会计准则与国际财务报告准则仍然存在或多或少的差异。印度采用的是趋同模式，尽管已经宣称与国际财务报告准则实现了趋同，但是差异仍然较大。

（五）"金砖国家"企业会计准则国际趋同的最新进展与思考

新华社上海6月19日电，中国担任"金砖国家"主席国期间的第二次"金砖国家"财长和央行行长会议19日在上海成功举行，"金砖国家"就财金合作成果文件达成共识，承诺在九大领域加强合作，为"金砖国家"领导人厦门会晤做好了财金领域政策和成果准备。其中，第五个方面即是，"金砖国家"同意就会计准则趋同和审计监管等效开展合作，为"金砖国家"债券市场互联互通提供制度保障。因此，"金砖国家"企业会计准则趋同，实际上已经取得了阶段性成果。

第一，"金砖国家"都提出来要建立全球统一的高质量的企业会计准则。这个目标是G20峰会提出来的，五个国家都是G20的成员国，都支持建立全球统一的高质量的企业会计准则。

第二，"金砖国家"都是新兴经济体，客观上都有在国际财务报告准则上增强话语权，维护新兴经济体的利益的要求。

第三，从当前的现实需要来讲，"金砖国家"债券市场的互联互通已经提到了议事日程。因此，企业会计准则的国际趋同，要为"金砖国家"债券市场的互联互通提供制度保障。

第四，"一带一路"倡议的实施与企业会计准则国际趋同的关系问题，实际上就是新形势下为企业会计准则的国际趋同提出的新课题。我国企业会计准则国际趋同战略实质上是在2006年就已提出来，并且到今天为止，与国际财务报告准则实现了实质性趋同的企业会计准则在我国已经有10年时间的实施实践，但是，2006年企业会计准则国际趋同的背景跟今天实施"一带一路"倡议的新形势不完全一样。因此，要求我们结合新的形势、适应新的形势，来思考进一步完善我国企业会计准则国际趋同的战略、趋同的方式。

第五，企业会计准则国际趋同与审计监管等效的关系问题。企业会计准则的国际趋同，实际上是实现了企业会计标准的统一，是"会计语言的互联互通"，由此必然带来的下一个问题是标准的实施和标准实施的监管问题，其中，就政府层面而言，主要是审计监管等效问题。因此，可以讲企业会计准则的国际趋同和审计监管等效是"一枚硬币的两面"，需要一同安排、一同协商、一同推进。

第六，企业会计准则的多层次和分类别实施的关系问题。通过上述比较分析，我们可以清晰地看到，金砖国家都共同存在企业会计准则多层次的特点，也都共同存在企业会计准则实施的分类别的特点。比如说，本国企业和外国企业、上市公司和非上市公司、个别财务报表和合并财务报表、大中型企业和小型企业，事实上都在采用不同的企业会计准则、会计标准。财政部已经将修订《会计法》列入 2017 年会计工作重点，希望我们在座的各位能够结合我国会计工作的新实践，也包括结合实施"一带一路"倡议新的大背景，来思考我国《会计法》相关问题的修订工作。

"走出去"企业全球财务管理的"中兴经验"

陈 虎*

一、国际化为企业财务管理带来重大挑战

中兴通讯股份有限公司于 1985 年成立，1995 年走出中国国门。从刚开始的一个人带着通讯设备参加日内瓦电讯展，发展到今天有接近 50% 的销售收入来源于中国大陆以外地区，中兴通讯在全球 107 个国家设有分支机构，产品销往全球 160 多个国家和地区，可以这么说——全球百万以上人口的国家，都有中兴通讯的通讯设备在其国土上服务。在"一带一路"60 多个国家中间，中兴通讯也在 53 个国家拥有自己的常设机构。

企业的国际化给财务带来重大挑战。本杰明·富兰克林有句名言："对于个人来说，只有税收和死亡是无法避免的。"对于企业来说，只有财务和法务是不可避免的，从企业诞生开始，财务部门和法务部门将一直伴随企业直至消亡。

在中国大陆地区做生意就像在内河里行船，一旦走出国门，则如同在茫茫大海中航行，会面临很多问题。那么从财务的角度来看，目前存在五方面问题。第一，因为时差、距离的影响，公司运营成本数量级增加，总部的监管极其困难。第二，全球监管造成合规的管控更加困难，海外人才日益流失。第三，会计核算也存在全球会计准则不统一的情况，由准则引起的会计政策会有巨大变动，会计科目设置是随意的，会计核算混乱，整个全球的会计信息系统多种多样。第四，资金安全失控，具有外汇管控的

---

* 本文作者为中兴通讯股份有限公司副总裁。

风险和税率损益的风险，汇率也面临巨大波动。第五，税制和税务，税收环境有巨大差异，纳税的遵从，常设机构的设立以及 TP、PE 等等风险都会造成巨大影响。还有语言和文化的差异，法律环境的差异，战局、自然环境、员工安全、时差、网络等等，这些都会对企业的财务管理和企业日常运营产生巨大影响。这仅仅是我们一个企业目前遇到的事情。

对财务人员来说，在中国仅仅是一个会计，但到了海外就将扮演 CFO 的角色。一个"国家 CFO"需要了解的事项，至少需要懂得本地核算，需要知道给公司出具管理报告，需要知道商务、税务、资金、外汇、库存、业绩、经营分析、收款、预算、项目、财务投资、语言、人员管理。而企业培养这样一个财务人员需要多长时间呢？中国著名高校硕士毕业生，至少在所在国家工作 5 年时间，才有可能建立这套知识体系。如果在尼日利亚、在南非、在巴西工作 5 年，员工想回国了，换个人则又要重新开始。所以当企业面对这么多风险、这么多事项，面对这么困难的人才培养时应该怎么办？中兴集团（以下简称中兴）在探索中建立了一套全球财经管理体系。

二、中兴探索建立全球财经管理体系

全球财经管理体系，要保证全球的财务管理能够支持公司运营，要能够保证公司合规，要能够及时地反馈信息。它包括四大部分：第一，如何建立起一个全球的财务组织和培养全球化、国际化财务人才；第二，要有完整的业务解决方案，从基础的 ATT，即核算、资金和税务，再加上风险，到支持公司运营管理的战略、经营、项目管理和风控这些扩展性的职能，再到有一个完整的信息系统解决方案。我们在海外的 107 个国家的分支机构，简略统计约使用了五六十种信息系统。那么，如何搭建起一个完整的信息系统平台呢？这就要求我们建立一个全球财务共享的组织体系。

（一）全球财务共享的组织体系

这个全球财务共享的组织体系，意味着一个全球化的财政组织，可称做"三三制"。第一个"三"，全球的财务架构要以公司总部的财务为核心，它是我们的参谋中枢，是大脑。要有遍布全球各地的财务部门，它是我们的传感器、执行机构，再通过设立云端的财务共享服务中心，来实现基础业务的集中，实现"三足鼎立"的格局。第二个"三"是在本地，在本地有中方CFO外派的团队，在当地支持业务经营、做管理决策、帮助辅助管理决策。同时，也要有本地的财务团队。本地的财务团队是眼睛向外的，要尽可能使我们的财务本地化，因为从国际化发展的层次来说，不能本地化的企业不能够真正成为当地的企业公民，它不是一个真正意义上的国际化企业。建立起本地的财务团队，可以使我们当地国家的财务人员能够面对银行、面对客户、面对事务所和面对我们的税务机关及当地的监管机构。总之，一切可以坐房间里工作的都是可以被远程的，一切可以远程的都是可以云化的，一切云化的都可以智能化。因而中心思想是：建立起一个全球"三"位一体的架构，来支撑企业本地"三"位一体的架构。

（二）全球化人才的培养

全球化人才培养，首先要实现中方人才的国际化。首先，希望更多的中国高校培养国际化的财务人才。目前，因为中国的会计人才主要按照财政部的规则来培养，已经越来越难以适应企业走出国门的需要。其次，海外人才本地化，要建立一支本地化的财务队伍。熟悉中国的文化将有助于中国企业在海外做生意。希望中国高校未来不仅要培养中国的本地化国际人才，也应该培养外国人中国化的人才，并鼓励更多外国留学生在中国工作。

（三）会计核算体系的搭建

会计核算体系的搭建，从业务角度看，会计财务体系、资金管理、税务管理、风控的管理非常重要。中兴建立了"五个统一""两种核算维度""一体化应对"。五个统一是指：统一会计政策、统一会计科目、统一会计流程、统一信息系统、统一数据标准。在五个统一基础上，还要面对两种核算维度。第一是本地化的账务处理，第二是集团账务处理的要求，其实还需要加上管理会计报告。一体化应对，是指运用一套核算规则来建立起三种核算要求。我们对财务的要求是"数出同源、管算结合"。即，数据要来源于原点，按照不同的处理规则，出具相关财务情况的数据反映，或者按照财务报告的要求，但是它一定来源于原点。另外，管算结合是指管理和结算是相结合的，"算为管用"。

（四）全球税务管理

全球税务的管理，首先绝不仅仅指申报这一环节。纳税筹划、全球税务政策研究、海外常设机构、集团内部转移定价、国家商业模式、全球纳税遵从和具体国别的税务风险控制等各个方面的工作，都应从企业还没有进入到这个国家开始，在业务开展之前，就要有税务筹划的相关安排。第二，建立起税务核算的体系。在海外我们有很多分支机构，中兴通讯除了在中国内地和香港上市以外，在海外的大部分国家暂时都没有谋求上市的需求。所以目前的主要任务是当地的税务遵从问题。满足税务申报的相关要求，同时还须建立起税务稽查的应对方案。

从集团税务到本地税务，再到全球的税务核算平台，要进行一体化运作，才能够很好地控制全球税务风险。全球的资金管理是指要完成全球银行账户的统一管理工作，我们在全球共享中心中管理着全球110个国家和地区的上千个银行账户，每一笔资金流动都要经过中国地区，都要经过共享中心来完成资金的收付，保证所有的内部管理是可控的；同时建立全球的分资金池，就像航空公司的区域点一样，分布在主要的航路中间完成区域的交会，建立起全球的汇率机制，保证资金是"可回来"的，同时降低对财务报表和资金风险的影响。

全球风险管理是财务面临的重大课题，在走到海外以后的风险，国家的风险、运营的风险、合规的风险和财务的风险都会反映到最终的运作结果中，那么如何建立起一个完整的风险防控机制呢？这些内容组合在一起，才是一套全球的财经管理体系。这套全球的财经管理体系可以支撑中国企业的全球化运作。

三、中兴全球化经营的"知识体系"

财务是公司重要的信息系统和管理支持系统。财务的信息系统在中国国内应该说是树状结构，走向全球化以后则是一个神经网络结构。我们要搭建起财务面对的所有会计、税务、资金、贸易、风险等等"神经元"，为此中兴建立起一整套知识结构来支持全球化运作，包括国际的财经知识、具体国家的国别指南，同时又把它分解为全球国际核算支持体系，包括管理层、国别层；分解为税务管理知识体系，包括国际税收、国际重复征税的积极减除、避税和反避税、税收协定、国际税务发展趋势；再分解为税收的生命周期，包括税收优惠、国际税收争议、税收筹划、跨国税收风险，全球税务政策的数据库，以及全球税务管理的趋势；具体到每个国家，按避税和税务与会计的差异，建立起全球财务知识的管理体系，建立起各个国家的对外贸易知识体系，希望能够有机地支撑全球化的运作。

国别指南方面，前期已完成四个金砖国家，内容丰富（每国约 100～200 页），目前正在将"一带一路"沿线国家全部进行整理。中国企业"走出去"是一条非常艰辛的道路，但是只有中国企业"走出去"才有中国的复兴，才有中华民族的复兴。

跨国企业税务管理介绍

吴莉敏[*]

联合利华在全球有四个业务单元：家用清洁、个人护理、食品及冰淇淋饮料业务。而在中国为大家所熟知的是力士洗发水、沐浴露、奥妙洗衣粉、清扬洗发水和路雪冰淇淋等品牌。联合利华的全球业务规模约为500亿欧元，拥有17万名员工，其中大约60%来自于发展中国家，业务覆盖了约190个国家和地区，并在多地建立了财务共享中心。

联合利华的一个重要使命，就是致力于长期的可持续发展，在业务增长的同时降低对环境的负担。我们确保100%的农产品通过可持续发展的方式来采购，以保护当地的生态环境。联合利华也和当地的政府、相关社会机构以及本地的农民和厂商携手一起以一种可持续的方式来提高生产力。我们全球的工厂和仓库，完全符合安全、环保、节能和卫生的建设要求。我们通过一些品牌和产品，比如，布鲁雅尔的空气净化器和沁园水净化器的业务，来改善当地民生，加强卫生和健康方面的建设。之所以强调这一点，是因为在国际化进程中，企业会不断进入新的市场。当地的消费者和政府关心的并不仅仅是简单的经济增长、产品开发和就业等。在全球化的环境中，特别是互联网、信息化的时代，非常多的消费者、政府和社团，都会关注企业到底对本地民生和环保创造了什么价值，企业的发展是否可持续，生意对环境有积极的帮助还是负面的影响。所以，这是企业全球化战略不可分割的一部分。

作为一家历史悠久的企业，联合利华100多年前发源于荷兰和英国。联合利华经历了"走出去"的过程，慢慢地扩展到今天的全球业务。开展全球业务，有几点需要关注。第一，了解所在国家和文化。第二，发展合适

---

　*　本文作者为联合利华北亚区财务副总裁。

的当地人才。第三，以长远的视角去制定战略。第四，以国际标准来要求企业。尤其强调两点：一是培养本地合适的人才。执行业务并不仅仅需要对公司本身或者业务模块的专业知识，同样也需要对本地环境、文化、沟通方式和业务伙伴之间如何合作有一个深刻的了解。这些了解和知识很多是本地人才所具有的。如何在外派人员和本地人员之间达到一个合理的平衡，从初创阶段到以后的成熟阶段，有相应、系统的项目来培养本地人才，非常重要。二是国际标准。各个国家会采取不同的国家产品标准。在一些国家可能国标并不成熟，或者要求相对比较低。对于企业而言，采取当地标准，明显会有一个短期的成本优势。但是如果放眼企业中长期的发展，消费者有多种渠道了解什么是更好的标准、更好的产品。联合利华会在所有的国家采取我们能够做到的最高标准，这样的做法虽然会有一定成本压力，但是有利于中长期发展，建立品牌和确立消费者信心。

接下来从四个方面分享关于国际企业税务管理的体会：第一，了解当地环境、法规和管理体系。第二，建立专业的税务团队。第三，关联交易的合规体系建设。第四，提高应对改变的能力。

一、了解当地环境、法规和管理体系

进入一个国家，要对当地的税收环境、税收文化、税收法规和税收监管体制的情况，有深入、彻底的了解。有很多相关的当地资料可以参考，但更重要的是掌握市场、经济环境的一些动态，以及在这些动态当中如何遵从税收法规。一些发展中国家的税收法规相对比较宽泛，在具体的执行操作中不够具体。面对实际遇到的税务问题如何解决，哪些方面需要相应的税务主管机关的参与，这是对公司税务部门的一个挑战。通过和当地的企业、商会和税务主管机关的合作，掌握大环境的变化，了解各类本地案例的执行情况，对企业建立自己的税收合规体系非常有帮助。

二、建立专业的税收团队

联合利华在190个国家和地区开展业务，所以面临的税收环境非常复杂。公司把税务团队分成地方税务部门和税务专业团队，地方税务部门不仅做日常税务申报、税务报表的工作，更要负责当地的税务策划、风险管理和与当地税务机关沟通、及时了解税务政策的发展趋势和法规更新。而税务专业团队则负责处理跨国交易中一些比较复杂的问题，比如关联交易、跨国并购。这些方面需要的知识比较专业，涉及的法规比较复杂，对于这些税收业务，需要在区域或者全球的范围内设立税务专员。

三、建设关联交易的合规体系

对于跨国企业而言，有两个挑战。第一个挑战是如何在每个国家遵循税务合规，第二个是避免双重征税。2015 年 60 多个国家参与了 BEPS 行动计划，在 BEPS 的框架下要求企业有清晰的价值链分析，纳税和实质发生地与价值产生的紧密联系。BEPS 行动计划中有具体的要求，比如价值链分析、三层的同期资料等，以增强在国际税务征管上的透明性和确定性。中国作为 G20 的领导国，在 BEPS 行动计划的执行上起到了积极领头的作用。

跨国企业的价值链很长，业务发生地遍布于世界各地，如何去避免双重征税？申请预约定价是比较有效的方案之一，公司和主管税务局通过单边或者双边磋商，对未来转让定价的方法和策略，确定一个比较明确的方案。预约定价的优势在于避免双重征税，对未来关联交易转让定价有确定性的安排，也加强了主管税务机关和企业之间的合作。当然，这也需要投入相关的人力和各方面资源，对改善税收透明度和合规性都非常有帮助。

四、提高应对改变的能力

目前，一些国家的税收体制也在改革之中，比如 2017 年 7 月 1 日刚刚发生的印度货物与劳务税改革。货物与劳务税的改革不仅影响相关企业的税负，也会对业务的上下游产生影响，比如影响企业的利润、消费者的价格、客户的库存等，这是对业务的挑战。也因为这样一个改变，对存货的估价、IT 系统的变化和会计准则的处理方式都可能造成变化，这是对财务团队的巨大挑战。在这种情况下，税务团队需要领导整个企业的相关部门来应对改变。

"一带一路"企业"走出去"的税收风险

朱 青[*]

企业"走出去"和在国内从事经营投资,区别在于涉及国别比较多。国内最多是跨省,走出去至少涉及两个国家,中国作为居住国,以及目标国家,即东道国。更多的情况下,走出去企业会通过中国香港、新加坡等国家或地区,还涉及中介国或地区的税收问题。时间所限,本文从三个方面分享走出去企业的税收风险问题。

一、EPC 项目中面临的税收风险问题

EPC(engineering procurement construction)项目,即工程总承包,是很多建筑企业选择的模式,将设计、采购和建筑施工合在一起。如工程项目总价10亿元,其中设计费2亿元,中国设备的采购费6亿元,建筑安装费2亿元。总价 10 亿元中哪一部分利润需要在东道国征税?根据企业反映,EPC 项目中特别有纠纷、争议比较大的是 6 亿元的国内设备采购,这 6 亿元国内设备采购当中的利润要不要在东道国交税,是一个比较复杂的国际税收问题。假定现在没有 E(即设计),也没有 C(即施工),只有 P,也就是设备采购。这 6 亿元的设备从中国卖给东道国,东道国是否征税?如果只是一个 6 亿元的设备,从中国卖给东道国,按照国际税收的规定,特别是按照国际税收协定的要求,如果中国这家企业在东道国没有设立常设机构,并非通过东道国常设机构销售的设备,则东道国不征税。而现在问题的复杂性就在于,施工部分可能会构成常设机构。而施工部分是否构成常设机构,根据国际税

* 本文作者为国际税收专家、中国人民大学教授。

收协定和国际税收的规则，关键取决于设备安装调试的时间。

我国签订的税收协定过去基本上是按照 183 天或者半年来确定建筑安装是否构成常设机构，但现在很多协定签的时间是 9 个月或 12 个月，甚至跟俄罗斯、等一些国家签的是 18 个月，即一年半。一般而言，设备安装不到半年或一年，就不构成常设机构，但问题是一般大型设备，比如水电站、发电设备的安装可能要超过半年，所以中国企业"走出去"很多施工的部分就构成了常设机构。东道国可能据此对 6 亿元的设备价款产生的利润征税。很多企业因此跟东道国产生纠纷，其中有的胜诉，有的败诉。所以，这是企业"走出去"非常重要的税收风险。需要在签订合同的时候特别明确各个部分的功能和职责，防止东道国认为这个合同是由两方或者多方共同构成的，即把 E、P、C 看成一个共同体，由此导致被征税。作为应对，很多企业通过拆分防止设备采购的部分被征税。

二、转让定价过程中的税收风险

"一带一路"沿线国家的税负是"冰火两重天"，像某些国家税率都很低，例如土库曼斯坦税率仅 8%，哈萨克斯坦 9%，但是非洲国家的税率却相当高，例如赞比亚为 35%。中国企业"走出去"，无论是走到税负高的还是税负低的国家都会面临问题。如到低税国，面临的问题是低税区交完税以后，利润向中国母公司做分配，母公司要申报纳税。像前面提到的 8%、9% 的税率，中国企业所得税税率是 25%，回国要补十六七个点的税收。所以，走出去企业认为到低税国并没有得到好处。

这里涉及一个关键问题，即海外利润中国要不要征税。我在《国际税收》杂志 2015 年第四期上发表了一篇文章，呼吁中国要实行免税法，不要实行抵免法。现在大国当中对海外利润征税的国家就三个，美国、中国、爱尔兰。其他国家，如欧洲的国家全部对境外所得免税，特别是 2009 年日本和英国也开始对境外所得免税，加拿大同样免税。这次特朗普的税制改革，在宣传上只是强调公司税要由 35% 降到 15%，其实还有一个重要内容，对海外利润免税，即由抵免法变成免税法。中国有关部门，现在也要行动起来，考虑如何应对特朗普的税制改革。有关部门考虑两点：第一，企业所得税 25% 的税率是否要降；第二，对海外利润是否也给予免税。对于那些高税国而言，比如非洲国家，无法改变其税率，企业要想减少税收负担，只有通过转让定价，把利润转出高税国。但问题在于，利用转让定价转移利润的行为属于避税，东道国要实施反避税。在 BEPS 的环境下，各国全都加强了转让定价的税务管理。现在很多国家对转让定价、转移利润不仅要补税，还要加收滞纳金，甚至还要处罚。比如印度最高罚补税金额的 3 倍；越南还加收 35% 滞纳金。而我们国家只对偷税加收滞纳金，对避税只收利息。还有些国家将滥用转让定价行为视同偷税进行处罚。中国对外商投资企业利用转让定价避税的处理较轻，学界曾向全国人大和财政部建议对外商投资企业利用转让定价进行避税的行为进行处罚，但考虑到吸引外资，短期内无法实现。因此中国企业"走出去"要注意这一点，操作不当将面临罚款。

三、不合理架构的税收风险

走出去企业往往需要架构，即利用一个第三国的中介公司。如中国要到卢旺达投资，卢旺达和中国没有税收协定，所以卢旺达不仅要征 30% 的公司所得税，还要征 15% 的预提所得税。因此，中国企业"走出去"，往往通过一定的架构，比如通过比利时到卢旺达投资。卢比两国之间是有协定的，根据协定，卢旺达对本国居民向比利时居民支付的股息免征预提所得税；中国跟比利时也有协定，比利时的预提税可以降到 5%；这种做法就属于滥用税收协定避税。截至 2017 年 6 月 7 日，全世界已经有 70 多个国家签订了《实施税收协定相关措施以防止税基侵蚀和利润转移（BEPS）的多边公约》，这个公约一揽子修订了 1000 多个双边税收协定。中国现在有 102 个协定，另外内地同港、澳、台还有协议，一共 105 个。这个公约把 OECD 应对 BEPS 的 15 个行动计划中的反避税规定都加进税收协定中，其中包括第 6 个行动计划，即反协定滥用的部分。这部分有两种反滥用措施：一是 PPT（principal purpose test），即看签署协定和交易的目的是否为了避税；二是 LOB（limitation on benefits），即限制符合条件的第三国居民获得税收协定提供的税收利益。以上提到的卢旺达和比利时有两个协定，第三国企业就是中国的企业，限制第三国企业享受协定就是中国企业不能享受卢比两国税收协定的利益。所以，很多企业"走出去"是利用架构的形式，但在这个公约生效以后，很多办法都不可行，这对走出去企业会带来很大风险。

"走出去"企业海外并购的
税务风险管理

宋　宁[*]

2014 年是万达集团大踏步进行海外并购的鼎盛时期，包括耳熟能详的传奇影业、铁人三项等，也包括投资印度 100 亿美元的印度工业城项目。

万达可能跟中兴有非常大的差异，万达所有的海外投资都是以并购为主，很多项目根本没有时间去做准备，而是直接进场。很多时候不仅没有时间去做准备，而且在项目接手时就已经是一个既成事实的投资结构或一个海外实体，因此，就面临越来越多的压力和挑战。比如万达在美国的投资也是万达非常自豪的第一例院线项目，2012 年投资，当年就盈利，之后就面临大量税务上的问题。我们要接受这个既成事实的投资结构，当年考虑投资的时候没有人考虑到税务结构，不仅中国的民营企业在海外投资没有考虑到税务结构，中国很多国有企业在海外投资、海外并购的时候也根本不征求税务团队的意见，甚至很多国有企业到现在为止没有专门的税务总监。所以，中国企业在"一带一路"走出去的过程中，税务工作将面临非常大的挑战。

以下 18 个字：走得出、走得稳，长得大、长得快，拿得回、拿得多，把海外投资分成三个阶段：第一个阶段是并购阶段，第二个阶段是运营阶段，第三个阶段是投资回收阶段。

　＊　本文作者为中国国际商会税务专委会执行主席、前大连万达集团税务总监。

一、走得出、走得稳

（一）走得出

走得出是什么概念？要熟悉中国对于海外投资的国家政策导向，要保证项目的海外投资能够获批，因为很多时候中国政府的海外投资政策经常进行调整。企业在进行海外并购、或者前期在很多战略条款达成的情况下，在申请审批时反而会遇到问题。如果海外并购进行到一定阶段，尤其合同、契约都已经签署的情况下，结果"走不出去"就很有可能导致巨额的赔款。其实万达也为此交过很多"分手费"，这是我们在"走出去"时要避免的问题。在这一阶段，税务上不仅仅要考虑在并购投资或者说绿地投资的过程中是否能够取得政府的批准，而且当面临着投资不确定的情况下如何把沉没成本转化成企业的可扣除的税前费用等都是需要考虑的重要问题。

（二）走得稳

第二个周期的问题，就是走得稳，中国企业走出国门就跌大跟头的例子屡见不鲜，既包括民企也包括国企，这说明税务尽职调查或者税务筹划不到位。建议税务尽职调查一定要成为海外投资的一个非常重要的组成部分。2014 年在万达对所有的海外投资都开展了详尽的海外尽职调查，包括两个方面：第一是海外投资环境的尽职调查。比如，万达投资印度的工业城项目，在确定投资印度之前，董事长选择东南亚"一带一路"沿线上的 10 个国家进行全面的尽职调查，借助四家中介机构的力量；在包括建筑、经济金融环境、财税等方面，进行全方位的尽职调查。通过这 10 个国家全方位的尽职调查，再做出投资回收模型及投资决策。在这个基础上，投资风险就会相对小很多。第二是对投资标的企业的税务风险尽职调查。很多中国企业在海外并购的时候，比较重视法务和财务上的风险，很少重视税务上的风险。如中国一家国有企业并购了北欧一家石油公司，并购后第二年就曝出一个接近 10 亿美金的税务漏洞，最后通过中国国家税务总局动用双边国际磋商，协助去协调解决这个问题。作为普通的民营企业如何去面对这种税务风险？非常困难。所以，与其出门跌跟头不如把尽职调查做好。

二、长得大、长得快

如何让我们的海外企业能够长得大、长得快，税务合规是一个非常重要的方面。很多五百强企业是学习的榜样，通过调研 IBM、施奈德等很多外资企业，了解他们在全球税务管控方面的特点，同时拜访国内走出去的民营企业，分析他们海外税务管控的特点，博采众家之长，建立起万达海外税务的管控体系。

在海外税务管控的基础上，再利用集团内部的业务安排，根据业务特点做相应的税务筹划。当面临比较高的海外税负，或者一些税收协定的差异，要积极地去利用协定的优惠待遇。但是在利用协定优惠待遇的过程中，既要想办法降低企业的税负，又要规避税务的风险。税务筹划很重要，一定要有合理的商业目的、有真实的商业实质、有真实的商业受益人，基于这三个条件基础之上采取税务筹划。例如当时万达体育收购美国的铁人三项，同时收购了瑞士的盈方体育，毕竟美国、瑞士和中国之间的税收协定是有差异的，因此可以通过真实交易的安排和业务的安排，来实现税负的最低化。从而推动企业在当地发展壮大，来回报股东的投资。

三、拿得回、拿得多

第三阶段是回收环节，包括两个方面：第一是股息的回收，第二是股权转让退出的回收。很多中国企业"走出去"的时候，只是顾及如何把项目拿下，没有想到将来怎样处置。因此，税务结构一定要有一个弹性，即适应性。比如，如果老板希望持有这个公司，要考虑到股息分配的结果；如果老板希望企业在国内 IPO，要考虑到在国内 IPO 的税务架构如何安排。或者老板希望不在国内 IPO，而选择在香港 IPO，在海外发债或海外融资等等，所有的不确定性都需要事先有预案。因此，合理的税务筹划一定要在"走出去"的投资环节就要考虑到投资回收问题。

印度税制概览及税改动向

Rohan Solapurkar[*]

印度是一个很大的国家，而探讨印度的税制及其独特的优点和面临的挑战将耗费大量时间。鉴于印度企业同样高度重视"一带一路"倡议，分享一下印度税制存在的重大问题和机遇，以及印度的投资监督及其表现形式和在印度投资时将面临的主要问题。

一、印度的主要税种

印度由位于德里的中央政府管辖。全国有 29 个州，这些州就相当于中国设立的各个省份。印度的每个州都设有自己的州政府，州政府还负责征收该州的一些税（例如，财产税或印花税、增值税以及目前征收的商品及服务税）。因此，印度税制基本上分为两部分：一部分由中央政府负责管理（如所得税），另一部分由州政府负责管理。州政府主要负责征收增值税和商品及服务税。如今，增值税已纳入商品及服务税的范围，而商品及服务税现已遍及全印度。印度还有关税和其他间接税，关税同样由中央政府负责管理。除此之外，还有印花税以及由州政府负责征收的其他税种。以上是关于印度税制的简要介绍。

* 本文作者为德勤新加坡税务合伙人。

二、企业所得税概况

（一）基本情况

印度企业就全球范围内取得的收入缴纳企业所得税。对于设立境外机构并拥有境外子公司的印度企业而言，由境外子公司汇给印度母公司的股利亦须纳税。在印度设立"常设机构"或项目办公室的外国公司必须基于归属于该项目办公室或常设机构的利润或收入在印度纳税。外国公司按各种不同的税率纳税。印度征收股利分配税。在印度境内注册成立的企业（即在印度境内依法成立的企业）无论是否存在外国股东均须在向股东宣告股利之前在印度境内缴纳股利分配税，股利分配税必须由该印度公司负责缴纳。在向股东实际分配股利时无须代扣代缴所得税。

（二）税收减免规定

关于企业所得税减免的几种情况，首先，一般来说内部重组与合并均可免税，但必须满足某些条件。其次，如果在印度发生经营亏损，可将经营亏损向以后年度结转，结转年限不超过 8 年。第三，折旧方面的规定则为，一旦产生折旧损失，该项损失可无限期向以后年度结转。此外，2017年 2 月印度采用了一项新规定，根据此项规定，因向非居民关联方借债而支付利息时所享有的利息减免不得超过 EBITDA（利息、税项、折旧及摊销前利润）的 30%。这相当于在印度建立了资本弱化税务规定。

（三）实际税率及企业税负

印度企业所得税税负的基本情况如下。（1）如果企业在 2015～2016 财年的营业额低于 850 万美元且应纳税所得额低于 16 万美元，其实际税率应为 25.75%；如果应纳税所得额在 16 万～160 万美元，其实际税率应为 27.55%；如果应纳税所得额高于 160 万美元，其实际税率应为 28.84%。（2）如果企业在 2015～2016 财年的营业额高于 850 万美元且应纳税所得额低于 16 万美元，其实际税率应为 30.90%；如果应纳税所得额在 16 万～160 万美元，其实际税率应为 33.06%；如果应纳税所得额高于 160 万美元，其实际税率应为 34.61%。（3）对于小型企业而言，如果企业在 2014～2015 财年的营业额约低于 80 万美元且应纳税所得额低于 16 万美元，其实际税率应为 29.87%；如果应纳税所得额在 16 万～160 万美元，其实际税率应为 31.96%；如果应纳税所得额高于 160 万美元，其实际税率应为 33.45%。

假以时日，印度政府计划将企业所得税的名义税率降至 25%。考虑到折旧和税收减免的因素，实际税率可能介于 21%～22% 之间。

（四）其他规定

上文还提及了另一种税——股利分配税。向股东分配股利的企业必须缴纳股利分配税，其实际税率为 20.36%。由于股利分配税属于印度企业的应交税费，因此，外国公司不太可能有机会针对印度企业所缴纳的股利分配税申请税款抵减，股利分配税因而构成一项成本。对于外国公司而言（无论是分支机构还是常设机构），其实际税率均为 41.2%。因此，印度公司的最终税率和境外分支机构或常设机构的税率稍有不同。

印度还有一种适用于国内企业的所谓 "最低替代税"。最低替代税不适用于未在印度境内设立常设机构的外国公司。当根据正常的所得税规定计算得出的纳税义务不高于调整后的账面利润的 18.5% 时，应缴纳最低替代税。最低替代税的税率在 19.05%～21.34% 之间，具体情况视企业的收益而定。这跟美国的操作流程相类似，美国称为 "替代性最低税"。超出正常纳税义务之外的已缴纳最低替代税应作为税款抵减结转至以后年度并用来抵销未来年度的正常纳税义务。

代扣代缴所得税是针对符合条件的外债和长期基础设施债券的利息征收的。因此，它跟所有其他国家的代扣代缴所得税大同小异。

三、国际税收与转让定价

国际税收合作方面，印度拥有庞大的税收协定网络，该网络几乎涵盖了欧洲、非洲和亚洲地区的所有国家以及美国。印度的税务机关在转让定价方面一贯保持激进的姿态。在印度，大量的诉讼案均涉及转让定价。然而，印度现已针对转让定价推出了若干颇为有效的税收规定，而其他司法管辖区的税务监管机构亦对此类规定期待已久。印度针对大多数事项所采取的立场与税基侵蚀和利润转移（BEPS）报告一致。受到印度税务机关密切关注并已成为印度诉讼焦点的事项如下：广告、跨境服务、成本补偿、特许权使用费以及地方性节税。

四、商品及服务税改革

印度近期发生了一项重大税制改革——开征商品及服务税。印度自2017 年 7 月 1 日启用商品及服务税，这将给印度带来巨变。从计算商品及服务税的角度来看，如今整个印度变成了一个司法管辖区。此前，各个州都有自己的增值税，因此从东部到西部必须缴纳各种不同的税。现在，这些税都被一个统一的商品及服务税所取代。商品及服务税存在多档税率：5%、12%、18% 和 28%。5% 适用于一般商品，而 28% 则适用于奢侈品。在实行商品及服务税以后，我们必须重点关注某些领域：首先，ERP 系统必须作出变更以减少系统中断的发生率。其次，在某些情况下可能会增加对营运资本的需求。我们必须对这种情况加以考虑。最后，就合同而言——我们可能必须针对相关合同进行重新谈判。这是由于法律条文发生了上述变化，因此，可能必须进行重新谈判。可以说，这是自 1947 年印度独立以来，印度税制发生的最大的变化之一，这一举措将对印度的经济产生深远的影响。同时，我们认为由于采用了商品及服务税将导致印度在未来出现 8%～8.5% 的经济增长率。

五、其他需要注意的涉税事项

关于印度的商业实体类型。一旦成立了非公司实体、公司实体或合伙企业就可以开始经营业务。既可以设立代表处、联络处或分支机构，也可以设立项目办公室。就公司实体而言，可以设立子公司、合资企业，现在还可以设立有限责任公司。因此，可以在印度成立多种类型的商业实体。

除了以上提及的税种以外，印度还有一些法规与税务处理息息相关。比如，印度的《外汇管理条例》用来管理外汇的流入和流出，但这并不意味着禁止支付外汇。相反，这将更加便于我们支付外汇（但必须向银行提交相关文件）。此外，印度还有《公司法》，《公司法》就企业如何运作进行了规范。当然，印度还制定了行业法规和其他法律（例如，必须遵循的各类环境保护法）。如果您要在海边建一家酒店就必须考虑——这样做是否违反了环境保护法，这家酒店将对环境造成哪些影响等等。又如，上市公司或计划上市的公司均须遵循SEBI（印度证券交易委员会）的规定，此类规定针对上市公司和投资者保护事宜作出了规范。印度还制定了与雇佣有关的法规来规范最低工资等事项。

目前，印度政府正致力于推动"在印度制造"的倡议并有意吸引投资者来印度投资制造业，从而重振印度制造业并将GDP（国内生产总值）从16%提升至25%。印度的一些主要行业（例如，防护设备、纺织品和服装）有意吸引更多外资。国家制造业投资区将提供税收优惠，印度政府专门针对某些相关行业提供了更多的投资支持。此外，印度还为上述基础设施企业和制造企业提供了一系列税收激励政策。而且，印度还针对科研和雇佣新员工等事项推出了各类税收激励政策。同时，与中国类似，在印度经济特区中的企业还可享受税收减免期优惠。

最后，简要介绍印度涉税争议的处理情况。印度的税务诉讼案很多，但客观而言印度的税制和相应的争议解决程序是比较完善的。纳税人和相关的税务机关遇到问题均可诉诸上级主管部门，直至最高法院为止。事实上，由印度各级法院做出的大量裁决已获得国际上的赞许，尽管印度的司法体系在做出裁决时速度稍嫌缓慢，但此类裁决却相当公正。

资本市场：一体化与发展

赤松范隆[*]

在"一带一路"倡议下资本市场的融合与发展中，重点是将"亚洲债券市场倡议"作为"一带一路"融资的支持方式。

一、区域资市市场一体化

资金融通是"一带一路"的目标之一，与政策沟通、设施联通、贸易畅通、民心相通共同构成了"五通"。对任何国家而言，发展金融市场都是长期以来面临的一大挑战，因此资本市场的合作与融合更具挑战性。"一带一路"倡议下的金融一体化旨在促进沿线国家之间的金融监管合作与协同，面向各国政府和蓝筹公司建设人民币债券市场，针对银行和债务市场建立信用信息系统。

目前，"一带一路"倡议融资协议由亚洲基础设施投资银行、金砖国家新开发银行、上海合作组织融资机构、丝路基金以及亚洲开发银行共同构建。其中，亚洲地区在区域一体化，特别是金融一体化方面积累了丰富的经验。赤松先生详细阐述了"东盟10＋3"金融合作过程中的亚洲债券市场倡议（ABMI）。该倡议于2002年首次发起，旨在应对亚洲金融危机的根本原因，即双重不匹配问题。"东盟10＋3"制定了亚洲债券市场倡议路线图，并在其后建立了四个工作组来负责实施事宜，分别为：第一工作组，工作重点为本币（LCY）债券供应；第二工作组，工作重点为本币债券需求；第三工作组，旨在加强和协调监管框架；第四工作组，负责处理区域结算基础设施方面的问题。

＊ 本文作者为亚洲开发银行金融合作与一体化高级顾问。

二、区域资本市场的发展

随着亚洲债券市场倡议的推出，"东盟10＋3"本币债券市场近年来实现了稳步增长。然而，该地区的发展并不平衡。由于各国在经济及金融发展水平上存在巨大差异，一些东盟国家在发展本币债券市场时遭遇了一系列障碍和挑战，在跨境债券发行、投资和交易方面表现得尤为突出。为了解决这些问题，"东盟10＋3"多币种债券发行框架（AMBIF）应运而生，通过关注该地区的专业细分市场，制定了各国彼此间互认的发行通用准则。同时，大额支付系统和中央托管机构互联（CSD－RTGS Linkage）被选定为实施"东盟10＋3"区域结算基础设施的范式。该模式将协助本币债券交易货银对付（DVP）结算与中央银行货币实现对接，从而确保结算安全，符合国际标准，同时具有成本效益。

"一带一路"倡议融资还面临着其他方面的挑战，譬如在人口密度不大的地区为陆路基础设施提供融资、网络沿线安全保障、参与国政府债务管理能力（包括或有负债管理）等问题。最后必须强调的一点是，贸易和投资畅通对于"一带一路"倡议下的资金融通也至关重要。

"一带一路"倡议之中国与欧盟

Anna Saarela[*]

　　资本流动不仅是"一带一路"倡议中的重要事项，对欧洲整体而言也非常重要。在这一背景下，各国更要大力吸引外国直接投资。当前各国监管机构正在针对会计、会计准则、税务以及金融政策等多个领域的监管框架开展合作，这对资本流动起着至关重要的作用。全球化时代不仅可以使资本在"一带一路"沿线国家相互流动，也能在欧洲畅行无阻，将整个世界连为一体。

　　我将首先介绍欧盟和中国关系的几个要素，从双边关系来看，中欧是关系非常密切的盟友，然后联系"一带一路"倡议，分析"一带一路"倡议与欧洲在这一领域及其他领域的各项计划和方案之间的相互关系。

一、欧盟与中国的关系

　　互联互通非常重要，这种重要性不仅体现在道路建设上，也包括相互沟通和民间交往。2017 年是欧盟成立 60 周年，一路走来，从关税联盟到统一市场（资本、商品、服务和人员自由流动），这是一个漫长的过程，也是一个逐步发展的过程。恰逢德国汉堡举行 20 国集团峰会，有必要分享一下多边合作的重要性。在峰会上，欧盟和中国再一次展现了他们在全球层面上对共同发展目标的决心和承诺。

（一）中欧关系

　　中欧关系历时已久，而且从彼此身上受益良多。随着战略伙伴关系的

建立，中国和欧盟正在多个贸易和经济领域开展紧密合作。2017年6月2日，我们在布鲁塞尔举办了第19届中欧峰会，峰会主题是"建立更加稳固的伙伴关系"。在这一年度政治峰会的指导下，中欧双边合作逐年增长，如今已经在很多实质性的领域开展了大约60场不同部门间的对话。一年一度的第12次中欧商业峰会将在中欧峰会后举行，它为经贸界人士提供与中国和欧盟领导人直接对话的机会，交换他们关于双边经济关系的挑战和其他问题的意见。

2017年4月份"第七次中欧战略对话"在中国举行，它为中欧峰会奠定了基础。2016年10月我们举办了第六届中欧经贸高层年度对话，2017年末我们即将举行新一轮中欧经贸高层对话。为了奠定稳固根基，我们还建立了中欧贸易投资联合委员会。所有这些不同层面的互动和不同领域的合作与协作都有利于强化中国与欧盟之间的双边关系。

"中欧合作2020战略规划"是中欧关系的基石，这是中欧签署的级别最高的联合文件，为多个领域的合作提供了战略指导，为年度峰会注入了实质内容。这一战略规划于2013年共同采纳，同年中国也提出了"一带一路"倡议。由此至今，中国和欧盟已经发生了翻天覆地的变化，因此，2016年欧盟也更新了其对中国的战略，并以欧盟联合通讯的方式发表了《欧盟对华新战略要素》。

在探讨投资的同时，我们也提到了资本流动的重要性。我们应该鼓励投资者，为他们创造自信的环境，例如制定双方互认的会计准则，保护投资者和投资项目。中国和欧盟目前正在全力协商，旨在达成一项全面的中欧投资协议。2017年5月份我们举行了第十三轮谈判，加快协商进程并达成一致意见是我们的优先事项。这份双边协定将会促进中欧之间的投资流动，推动"一带一路"倡议发展。

（二）中国仍是全球增长的重要驱动力

虽然中国经济正在放缓，溢出效应预计也将会出现。但就2017年的全球经济增长而言，中国预计仍将成为最大的贡献者。这是基于国际货币基金组织以及欧洲议会的研究，对2017年数据预测得出的结论。中国和欧盟在全球经济中都非常重要，如果把中国和欧盟加起来，两者对2016年全球GDP的贡献率超过37%。中国目前正在进行从投资向消费，从制造业向服务业的经济转型。根据 2017 年经合组织《经济展望》报告，经济转型预计将会使中国的 GDP 增长从 2017 年的 6.6% 下降到 2018 年的 6.4%。即便如此，将中国的 GDP 增长与欧元区和美国进行比较就会一目了然，欧元区 2017 年和 2018 年的 GDP 预计将呈现稳定增长之势，达到 1.8%，美国 2017 年的 GDP 增长预计为 2.1%，2018 年是 2.4%。所以，中国不仅在现在，而且在未来都是全球经济发展中的一支重要力量。

二、"一带一路"倡议与欧盟投资计划

欧盟投资计划早在 2015 年就已提出，中国和欧盟同意继续探索欧盟投资计划和"一带一路"倡议之间的互惠互利协同效应。事实上中国已经同意向欧盟投资计划出资。欧洲战略投资基金是欧洲投资计划的一个重要基石。2017 年 6 月份在中欧峰会上我们又签署了新的合作备忘录。

目前欧盟是中国最大的贸易伙伴，中国是欧盟的第二大贸易伙伴，仅次于美国。因此，在中国和欧盟之间建立交通网络至关重要。基础设施的建设不是孤立的，"一带一路"倡议也需要与已经建立的网络形成补充，例如欧盟内部建立的泛欧交通网络。事实上，泛欧交通网络也是中欧互联互通平台投融资专家组所推进的一项重要内容，不管通过海上还是陆上丝绸之路，它展示了中国和欧洲之间以及内部的紧密合作和互联互通关系。

（一）欧洲战略投资基金

欧洲战略投资基金是欧洲投资计划的核心和基石，在欧洲投资银行集团旗下运营。欧洲战略投资基金不仅为基础设施，也为教育、研究、可再生创新能源和能源效率提供资金。事实上，它所涉及的领域与"一带一路"倡议正好相同。2015 年中国承诺将会寻找机遇推动欧盟投资计划发展，之后在中欧峰会间隙，隶属于欧洲投资银行集团的欧洲投资基金（EIF）与中国"一带一路"投资基金签署了合作备忘录。该合作备忘录旨在共同投资私募股权和风险资本基金，再通过这些基金反哺主要位于欧洲的中小型企业。总投资额预计将达到 5 亿欧元，由中国和欧盟共同分担。此外，中欧联合投资基金的设立也会进一步提升中国"一带一路"倡议和欧盟投资计划之间的协同效应。

中国和欧盟在亚洲和欧洲的互联互通合作不仅体现在公路、铁路和机场上，还包括能源合作（通过中欧能源高层对话）。双方也在信息与通信技术（ICT）领域建立了合作关系，中兴集团通过逐步渐进的方法已经在 ICT 领域取得了成功。中国和欧洲都认识到了信息技术合作对数字经济的重要性，双方已在 2015 年联合宣布在第五代移动通信技术领域进行合作。中国和欧盟加深 ICT 领域的合作，旨在加强欧洲数字议程与中国"互联网＋"战略之间的协同效应，使中国和欧盟的 11 亿网民从中获益。

（二）区域融合

如前所述，2017 年是欧盟建立 60 周年，也是东盟成立 50 周年。区域融合不是一蹴而就的事情，而是一个循序渐进的过程。中国的"一带一路"倡议是一个区域融合性质的项目，它的成功也需要一定的时间。这一倡议如果想要取得成功，就必须让所有参与方都能从中受益，包括第三方国家。它要求所有人的平等参与，最重要的是各方共同认可"游戏的规则"。我们生活在一个全球化的世界，贸易和投资以及各国人民都是相互连接的。当下已经认识到了全球价值链的重要性，还要通过其他"道路"实现更深层次的区域融合。这些都能够促进产能、效率和资源管理，为所有人造福，使所有人从中获益，从而进一步减轻贫困。同时也需要积极参与全球治理，协力应对区域和全球挑战。G20 峰会上提到了气候变化问题，以巴黎气候协定为例，主办国德国等欧洲各国领导人将携手中国以及沙特阿拉伯等能源生产国在 G20 框架下共同努力，推动气候议程的发展。因为这不仅是为了我们的未来，还有我们的子孙后代。

（三）多边主义

2016 年中国在杭州成功举办了 G20 峰会，2017 年的德国汉堡峰会正是在 2016 年的基础上进行的。联合国框架非常重要，不仅可以缓解环境变化，也可以帮助实现 2030 年发展目标，确保人类生存的安全性。我们将和其他国家一起在这些框架下通力合作。世界贸易组织是以规则为基础的国际贸易体系的基石。通过这一平台，各国可以开展深入合作，进一步强化多边贸易规则在所有 WTO 成员方中的透明实施和有效迅速执行。特别强调一下《税基侵蚀和利润转移行动计划》（BEPS），在 2017 年 6 月份举行的经合组织论坛上，76 个国家和地区签署了（或者说正式表达了他们签署的意愿）实施税收协定相关措施以防止税基侵蚀和利润转移的新多边公约，这表明我们将共同迈上一个新的跨国论坛。

最后要强调的是"一带一路"倡议一定会成功，但前提是它必须使各方从中受益，不仅是中国和欧洲，还有其他参与这一项目的第三方国家。同时我们还必须建立各方认可的"游戏规则"，创造一个公平的竞争场所。一个公平的竞争场所、透明度和可预测性，这些都是欧洲企业和投资者极其看重的因素，对中国企业和投资者来说也是如此。欧盟是中国最重要的对外投资目的地，2016 年投资额达到 400 亿欧元，而欧盟在中国的投资却只有 80 亿欧元，比 2015 年减少了 23%。所以，需要寻找一个共同的立场，探索和发掘贸易投资潜力，在"一带一路"倡议下在多个领域和部门开展合作，在中国和欧盟已经开展共同对话的领域再接再厉。只要齐心协力，就一定能取得成功！

我国企业投资"一带一路"沿线国家基本情况

——基于晨哨平台的数据分析

王云帆[*]

一、企业跨境投资的"信息基础设施"

跨境投资并购领域是晨哨集团专注的业务方向。今天论坛的关键词之一是"基础设施",而目前提供基础设施的单位主要有两类:一是政府;二是互联网公司。这是由于基础设施有三个显著特征:第一,前期投入特别巨大;第二,产出的周期、回报期特别长;第三,直接的经济溢出效应或许不明显,但是它的带动效应则可能比较明显。

互联网公司为何有提供基础设施的意愿?第一,由于风险资本介入较多,所以互联网公司前期有特殊的融资能力。第二,互联网公司尤其是平台型公司,多数为长周期的投资过程。第三,互联网公司的商业模式业内常戏称为"羊毛出在猪身上,狗来买单",所以它通常不太计较前期投入的直接回报。因而,现在有许多互联网公司乐于成为基础设施的提供方。

晨哨在跨境投资并购领域是国内比较有名的互联网平台,它专注于特定行业、专业化的"基础设施"服务——为中资机构跨境股权投资提供充分的市场信息。其主营业务是跨境股权投资交易撮合,自身定位是一级市场的交易撮合系统和服务商。

---

* 本文作者为晨哨集团创始人兼首席执行官。

二、晨哨集团的数据库及平台服务

过去 3 年，晨哨围绕跨境股权投资这一细分市场做了四件事，以下重点介绍两件：

一是数据库建设。每天监测全球 3000 余个信息源，抓取全球投资并购资讯，第一时间进行翻译和发布，此外每天会对市场发生的重大交易进行分析和研究。目前，已经形成比较庞大和完整的并购数据库，包括 1978 年至今中国所有 9000 余个对外投资案例。

二是 China Merger 平台。它是一个创新的股权交易撮合系统，可以把它理解成互联网上的全球"股交所"。该系统由两个库组成：一端是全球项目库。它是目前市场上最大的全球项目库，目前在线活跃的全球股权项目有13000 多个，主要来源于全球精品投行、律所、PE 以及各国投促机构。合作的全球精品投行数量超过 800 家，律所超过 200 家，PE 超过 100 家。另一端则为中国买家库。平台上有 5000 余个中国买家用户，背后是 2500 多家中国机构，其中有 365 家上市公司、1000 多家产业公司和 PE。这些用户会把海外投资股权的需求，按照一定的格式和规范发布在 China Merger 平台上。

一端是全球项目发布，另一端是中国国内买家需求发布，在 China Merger，每个月会签订 60~80 个保密协议。真实买方和卖方围绕真实股权资产进行交易，这些股权资产的规模通常在几千万美元到十多亿美元之间。这便是晨哨为跨境股权投资业务提供的基础设施服务。

围绕"一带一路"，晨哨也做了大量工作。首先，在平台建设方面，通过 China Merger 平台将"一带一路"沿线国家和地区的项目汇集起来，形成了"一带一路"投资项目库。其次，晨哨在 2016 年和 2017 年连续两年承担了上海市发改委"以上海自贸区为载体推进'一带一路'建设"和"以自贸试验区为桥头堡推进'一带一路'建设"的课题研究。通过走访和调研过去 3 年上海自贸区围绕"一带一路"倡议所开展的项目，分析研究自贸区如何建设成为走出去企业和"一带一路"建设桥头堡。第三，集团2017 年还成功中标了上海市商委"一带一路"合作课程的培训，系统化地对上海"一带一路"走出去企业进行培训。此外，每月组织线下投资促进沙龙和路演活动，其中就包含"一带一路"主题活动。晨哨在 6 月份还发布了《2014～2017 年中资"一带一路"沿线国家投资并购发展报告》，受到了市场的极大关注。

三、中国"一带一路"对外投资数据分析

中国"一带一路"建设可分为三个阶段，第一阶段为倡议提出（2013年）；第二阶段为愿景和行动计划制定（2015 年）；2017 年则是进入行动阶段的标志性一年，发生了两件大事：一是 2017 年 5 月份"一带一路"峰会召开，举世瞩目；二是 2017 年 6 月 20 日国家发改委和海洋局联合发布了"一带一路"海上合作设想，这是"一带一路"建设进入实操阶段的标志。

这就形成了"一带一路"投资的两大重点概念：一是陆上"丝绸之路"六大走廊，二是海上三条蓝色经济带。根据商务部提供的对外投资数据，我国对外投资可以分成三大类别：第一，对外商品输出，这是最大类别；第二，对外工程建设的输出；第三，非金融类直接投资，包括绿地投资和股权投资。进一步细分，可将股权直接投资按照性质分成三大不同类型：第一类是政府的发展援助，这是比较传统的，直接体现国家意志，并且由政府直接决策。第三类在近几年比较活跃，属于真正民间的对外直接投资。中间还有一个类型是第二类，也是现在比较新且发展较快的投资形式，我们叫"开发性金融投资"，在一定意义上体现了国家战略，不过采取的是市场化运作方式。第二类介于第一类和第三类之间，现在数量越来越多且体量很大，对民营资本的吸引力也越来越强，比如中国工商银行前董事长姜建清发起的中东欧基金，民企复星和很多海外资金能成为它的 LP，同以往相比是很大的变化。

（一）对外股权投资

晨哨统计了我国对外股权投资的数据。该数据口径与商务部的统计有所区别，商务部数据的统计对象为国内注册实体的出境资金数目，而晨哨的数据"刺破了面纱"——只要是实际控制的机构都涵盖在内。以复星集团为例，一年投资 100 多亿美元几乎均通过海外平台完成，所以复星的投资未被统计在商务部口径内，因此晨哨的数据值要大于商务部的统计结果。

此外，这个数据库将一个投资从传闻到交割分成五个阶段进行动态跟踪，因而总体数据量也大大增加。

由数据可见，2015～2017 年"一带一路"建设投资总数与金额占过去 3 年全部对外股权投资的 1/5（18%～19% 左右）。被纳入统计的交易有 303 宗，其中披露交易金额的 199 宗，总共披露了 1022 亿元的交易规模；没有披露的一般为交易规模相对较小者。

（二）热门投资标的及投资目的地

"一带一路"国家和地区的热门投资标的，与对外全球投资的总体格局类似。六大热门行业，分别是 TMT、能源矿产、基础设施公用事业、制造业、医疗健康和金融业。在 China Merger 平台上，"一带一路"沿线国家项目占总数的 20% 左右（平台共有 13000 余个项目，其中"一带一路"项目 2000 余个）。

"一带一路"热门投资目的地：新加坡第一，以色列第二。具体数据：新加坡 46 宗，以色列 44 宗，印度 39 宗，俄罗斯 24 宗，马来西亚 19 宗，印度尼西亚 10 宗。

（三）中国买方机构的特征和需求

纵观中国对"一带一路"投资的买方机构的特征和需求分析，一方面，从重点区域看，国内可分成八大区域。北京加上中央企业排在第一位，上海排在第二位，上海已真正成为"一带一路"对外投资的桥头堡，并且自贸区的拉动作用明显：上海买方机构有超过 65% 发生在自贸区。另一方面，从企业属性看，民营企业总数占 67%，但金额仅占 11%，而国有企业平均单个投资金额要大于民营企业。

据数据统计，上市公司在"一带一路"对外投资中占据绝对主体，在 303 宗案例中上市公司有 209 个，但非上市公司投资平均规模大于上市公司，这可能由于许多大型项目是由上市公司的集团公司、母公司进行投资的。

进一步关注投资者希望投资的方式，有 65% 的投资者选择股权投资，31% 选择建立合资企业，少量选择了绿地投资，约 30% 属于成熟的控股收购。在上海的 50 家企业当中，5000 万美元意向占 8.8%，1000 万～

5000万美元以上占26%，500万~1000万美元占29%左右，100万~500万美元占26%左右，100万美元以下占8.3%，呈现了比较明显的橄榄形。这与我们对市场的观察是一致的：中间规模的交易是市场主体，占整个市场交易的70%左右。

如何利用香港地区资本市场
搭建境外融资平台

陈永仁[*]

香港地区资本市场是很自由、国际化的市场。中国企业在"一带一路"中做并购和发展项目等，最终都会选择证券化，要么利用这个市场融资，要么就是在收购资产以后，推动再上市。这个事情在持续发生，比如，中铝在秘鲁收购铜矿，几年前我们协助它在香港地区上市。再比如，中国有色集团在非洲赞比亚收购铜矿，也在香港地区上市，因为从结构上说，不能直接在 A 股上市，只能在香港地区通过分拆的方式。此外，很多"一带一路"沿线国家的企业，跟香港地区签订协议的，也会选择来香港地区上市。比如，哈萨克斯坦铜业，作为哈萨克斯坦的两颗明珠之一，企业规模非常大，选择在香港地区二次上市。最早是俄罗斯铝业，由我们帮助在香港地区上市。另外还有很多中国企业在"一带一路"沿线的国家做并购，其实大量资金都是在香港地区这边组团完成。因此，下面介绍一下香港地区资本市场的动向，包括融资、发债、股本融资方面的趋势。

一、香港地区资本市场情况

就国际化市场的占比来说，内地企业已经占到港股市场的半壁江山，达 50.2%，市值也占到 64%。十大上市公司中九大都是中国企业，包括各大银行、互联网公司腾讯，以及从上海发家的汇丰。

香港地区分两个板块，一个主板，一个创业板，但创业板当年发展不是特别成功。两个板块加起来有 2000 多家公司，规模上跟上交所和深交所

---

* 本文作者为中金国际投资银行部董事总经理。

差不多。港股市场是一个以机构投资者为主的市场。价值股主要是一些行业龙头，包括上海的一些知名企业，如复星医药H股，价值股一般有比较高的估值溢价。一些行业龙头公司选择在香港地区上市，表现都非常不错。

香港地区市场历年IPO融资占到全球第一，除了阿里巴巴去美国上市的那一年，这也让香港地区联交所痛定思痛，决心改革。2010～2015年是牛市，IPO融资可以达到500多亿美元和300多亿美元，当然A股融资功能也不错，香港地区市场的竞争力非常强。每年中国企业最大的融资，包括2016年我们运作的邮储银行上市，都是当年的巨大发行。每年最大的发行基本上是中资企业，都是选择在香港地区市场完成。很多企业也选择两地挂牌，先在香港地区上市再回到内地。当下很重要的趋势，是香港地区市场跟内地互联互通，在港股通、深港通开通之后，每天有100多亿元人民币资金南下买香港地区股票，境外投资人也可以有100多亿元资金来A股市场买股票。

二、"一带一路"利用香港地区搭建平台

很多中资企业要"走出去"，在目前外汇管制比较严厉的前提下，外汇出境非常困难。所以，这些中资企业做境外并购，尤其对很多A股上市公司，有一个境内平台，可能选择去香港地区发H股。2016年我们协助上海老牌公司大众公用做了一个H股发行，它是上海很早上市的企业，后来去香港地区发行。由于香港地区目前没有融资管制上的要求，包括减持、再融资，这些规定总体比较灵活。整体的趋势是很多公司都纷纷选择发H股，包括上海网速科技，尤其在面临要发展国际化业务需要资金，而资金又出不了境的情况下。香港地区市场在根本上还是中国市场，更多企业要走向"一带一路"沿线国家，往往选择香港地区先搭建一个平台，要么有一个上市公司，要么有一个香港地区控股平台。

香港地区上市的要求，总体和境内差不多，但是它有多个标准，尤其是关于市值的标准。没有盈利的企业，也可以选择到香港地区上市。比如美图，市值达到几百亿元，但亏损十几亿元或几十亿元。还包括很多矿业公司，因为亏损而选择到香港地区上市。

对工程矿业公司而言，考虑到"一带一路"沿线多为欠发达地区和国

家，联交所专门针对这些企业上市有特别规定。比如，只要有这些工程项目特许权，包括道路、桥梁、铁路等，可以选择豁免盈利的要求，包括其他的财务标准。但是要证明管理层具有这方面的经验，而且联交所可以接受两个会计年度，因为香港地区上市和国内一样，也需要有三个完整的会计年度。这对于"一带一路"项目具有参照意义。

联交所在五六年前想把香港地区发展成澳洲、加拿大这样的矿业市场，所以出台了上市规则下的第十八章规定，不需要盈利，只需要有国际认可的储量报告，能够证明流动资金覆盖 12 个月的需求，且管理层有这方面的经验，也会允许在香港地区上市。但是，这些矿业公司在香港地区股价一般。因为尽职调查难以展开，这种公司投资者很难看明白，声称的储量万一挖不出来，可能就没法达到预期。

近期香港地区联交所在征询业内人士意见，推出创新主板和创新初板。创新初板是受国内新三板启发，希望吸引更多早期企业来香港地区上市，没有盈利，初创的公司都可以来。创新主板是给达到主板创业要求，但是部分不符合要求的企业，比如阿里的股权结构，以前接受不了，当然现在可以接受了。还有很多没有 3 年而只有一年业绩期的企业都会考虑。这类似于上海想推出的战略新兴板，不过上海已经叫停。整体来看，香港地区市场的改革力度很大，希望推动更多类似美图这种新兴经济的企业上市。对照国内创业板，2009 年推出到 2017 年，8 年的时间可以发展出大量龙头企业。而香港地区的创业板发展不足，希望通过这些吸引新兴经济的公司，在香港地区这边上市。

三、境外债券发行

最后分析一下香港地区市场作为中资企业的境外债券发行地问题。境内企业对外投资，需要通过 ODI 方式实现，而现在要求很严格，买足球队、电影院和地产等都比较难。即使现在买实业，审批进度也比较慢，很多企业通过直接平台，在香港地区发行美元债非常快，一般而言三四个月的时间。而且没有境内关于 40% 的净资产等规定，现在发改委和外管局都比较鼓励，资金发完债之后允许回流。结构上很灵活，有境内企业直接去境外发债，有境内母公司直接给境外子公司担保，通过这些结构，母公司不会放弃境外金额值,出任何问题,都负责把债赎回来。这些结构在香港地区都非常灵活,考虑企业各自在境外有无子公司,以及是否需要采用担保来增信这种方式确立。

担保方式最简单,但是会产生税收事项,境内投资者需要缴纳预提所得税,很多企业选择第二种方式,如果境内有平台,境外平台给境内做担保,境外平台直接发债,已经成为最主流的方式。

2014年、2015年中资发行人的债券发行量达1500多亿美元,2016年小幅下降,这是由于2016年国内公司特别火爆,很多企业选择境内上市。2017年趋势又回升,可能会接近2000亿美元,发行量非常大。现在很多企业考虑在欧洲和非洲的各种发行方式,可能先用美元债方式,借银行贷款,把它收购回来,再通过发行美元债来偿还。

总体来看,由于境外原因,香港地区各方面管制非常灵活。境内企业"走出去"做海外并购,香港地区投资市场的便利可以为"一带一路"项目投资提供很大的助力。

寻求"商业共同体":中国企业与全球市场的不断融合

钱毓益[*]

自从 2013 年习近平主席提出"一带一路"倡议以来,"一带一路"始终围绕五通,以点带面,从线到片,不断深入发展。越来越多的中国企业在"一带一路"沿线国家开展业务,通过工程总承包、投融资项目、供应链整合、技术转让等形式与当地企业开展合作,充分发挥各自优势。有些行业在短期内获得发展先机,成了"走出去"的排头兵,例如基础建设、金融服务、专业服务、通信技术、制造、物流等。随着"一带一路"的不断推进,预计电子商务、能源、生命科学、医疗保健等领域亦将不断发展,逐渐成为"走出去"的生力军。

ACCA 的研究报告《一带一路:全球价值链重塑》中指出中国企业在具体实施"一带一路"倡议时,也将面临多重挑战,例如当地政治、经济环境的不确定性、金融市场不成熟以及汇率波动和外币支付的风险、对包括税收在内的当地法律政策的变化和解读不足、当地劳动力市场的成熟度等影响因素。

为了帮助中国企业更好地借鉴"一带一路"的成熟经验和最佳实践,巴基斯坦中国学院、德勤中国、中国路桥集团和浪潮集团的专家都在此提出了各自宝贵的意见。三位中国专家分别从中国企业自身走出去的行业经验、专业服务机构服务于上百家跨国企业拓展"全球化战略"的全球视角以及数字丝绸之路助力"一带一路"政策落地这三个角度进行了分享。三位中国专家分享的共同之处在于,"中国企业做大做强,不仅仅是产品和服

---

* 本文作者为 ACCA 中国区政策主管。

务走出去，更是企业管理能力、品牌、影响力的对外输出，纵览全球，世界一流企业要想在全球市场获得优势，首先要学会的一件事：怎样与不同文化、不同信仰、不同风俗习惯的人合作交流。"巴基斯坦的参会嘉宾也对此深表赞同。他指出中国企业要想"赢得民心"，需要尊重当地文化习俗，增强环境保护意识，践行绿色发展理念，并注重维护良好的公共关系和公众形象。

中巴经济走廊介绍

Mustafa Hyder Sayed[*]

巴基斯坦中国学院在"一带一路"倡议中起着非常重要的先导作用，尤其是在中巴经济走廊这一背景下。中巴经济走廊是"一带一路"倡议的六大走廊之一，也是迄今为止"一带一路"倡议的旗舰项目。中巴经济走廊这一构想是于3年前提出，前巴基斯坦总理穆罕默德·纳瓦兹·谢里夫（Muhammad Nawaz Sharif）与中国国家主席习近平就此签署了合作备忘录。经济走廊的投资规模为460亿~620亿美元，包括能源、基础设施等项目。其中瓜达尔港不仅在中巴经济走廊，也在"一带一路"整个项目中占有中心地位。

（一）瓜达尔港的战略地位

为什么瓜达尔港具有如此重要的战略和经济地位？它与亚洲和中东地区的其他港口有何不同之处？瓜达尔港是丝绸之路经济带和海上丝绸之路的交汇点。这意味着海上贸易之路与陆上经济走廊在瓜达尔港会合，为瓜达尔港提供了得天独厚的贸易、战略和政治优势。瓜达尔港也是进入波斯湾的绝佳通道，同时它还是通往欧洲、非洲和中东地区的必经之地。

再回到陆上路线，来解释来自中国的商品如何通过陆上路线就近通过瓜达尔港。中国新疆维吾尔自治区与巴基斯坦的旁遮普省相邻。曾有一位来自中国路桥建设集团的人士表示，他们已经建成了喀喇昆仑公路，这条公路由新疆进入巴基斯坦，沿着中巴经济走廊，直达瓜达尔港，使从中国到巴基斯坦的贸易之路更加便捷高效。

从海上通道来看，从广州港和上海港两个港口通过马六甲海峡可以到

---

* 本文作者为巴基斯坦中国学院执行总监。

达中东。如果走这条路线，里程至少需要 11000～12000 公里，但是如果走瓜达尔港这条路线，只有大约 3600 公里。目前商品运输走的都是广东和上海港这条路线，穿过中国南海，进而经过周边所有国家。如果通过瓜达尔港，可以连接陆上通道和海上通道，这就是瓜达尔港的战略地位。这个港口目前由中国海外港口控股公司建设，该公司是中国交通建设集团旗下的子公司，目前，瓜达尔港已成为"一带一路"倡议的旗舰项目。

（二）中巴经济走廊的合作

中巴经济走廊最重要的意义在于其已经成为中巴两国之间，伊朗、阿富汗、土耳其和哈萨克斯坦等周边国家之间的区域合作框架机制典范。这些国家都表达了参与中巴经济走廊并从中获益的兴趣。他们将自动成为这一宏伟项目的受益人。巴基斯坦中国学院的主席也是中巴经济走廊议会委员会主席，他认为"一带一路"不只是能源基础设施建设，也包括文化互联。"一带一路"架起了各国人民之间的友谊桥梁，也是区域和国家之间的连接通道。这种互联互通性在中巴经济走廊中浑然天成，整个南亚地区也会从中受益，甚至可以产生一种泛区域主义，帮助整个区域培育许多出色的经济增长点，同时还会创造众多工作岗位，使巴基斯坦等发展中国家中成千上万的国民能够更好地就业。

巴基斯坦国家电网的发电力已经增加了 5000 兆瓦。这对巴基斯坦这样的国家而言是一个非常重要的成就，因为巴基斯坦曾经历过严重的电力危机，且其能源短缺。在中巴经济走廊的 460 亿美元投资中，超过 70% 的资金将投资到 BOT 模式（建设—运营—移交）的能源项目中，中国企业可以从中获得 17% 的保底收益。企业发电，然后将电按照区域协调关税价卖给政府，政府也能从中赚钱。巴基斯坦是受益者，因为这些项目为巴基斯坦生产了能源，同时中国企业也是受益者，因为他们能够从中获利，所以这就是双赢合作，大部分国家都能从中获益。

这个框架下的合作机制可以逐步扩展。先从能源开始，2016 年的发电量和 2013 年相比，有着令人不可思议的增幅。这是中巴经济走廊项目下的一部分能源项目，如今这一项目已经发展到了另一阶段：建立经济特区。

经济特区，即选择一些规划好的区域，巴基斯坦政府在这些区域中制定免税期、免费土地及其他激励政策。经济特区对"一带一路"倡议的长期发展非常重要。经济特区将由中国企业与地方政府以及地方和跨国企业联合开发。这些经济特区将会刺激生产，满足巴基斯坦和中国以及区域内其他国家和邻近国家市场的需求，进一步将会辐射到整个中亚地区，哈萨克斯坦、吉尔吉斯斯坦、乌兹别克斯坦、伊朗、阿富汗和印度等国。所有这些国家都会从中巴经济走廊上设立的经济特区中获益。

巴基斯坦每个省有两个经济特区，第一个经济特区建在瓜达尔港，因为这里是中巴经济走廊的中心，这一特区已经成立。特区的价值，可以以深圳为例。30年前，深圳只是一个小渔村，渔民只能勉强维持生计，并不富裕。如今的瓜达尔港就像30年前的深圳一样，走上了同样的发展道路，在这一点上非常相似。瓜达尔港除了渔业项目外，还引进了电力项目，并建设了一个独特的工业园区，从事生产制造活动。对其他专业组织中的会计和税务体系而言，"如果企业想从'一带一路'倡议中获益，实现盈利，如果企业想把自己的政策和愿景与'一带一路'倡议统一起来，企业必须看到'一带一路'项目如何落地"。将利益相关者集结在同一个屋檐下是迫切需求，同时也必须认清中巴经济走廊的模式，因为它可以复制到其他"一带一路"沿线国家的相关项目中。这是一个由中国国家发展和改革委员会与巴基斯坦和其他主办国政府制定的标准框架。因此，港口建设对"一带一路"倡议、能源开发、道路、铁路和管线互联非常重要。

中国财政部部长助理也提到所有"一带一路"沿线国家应该合作发展"一带一路"项目。国有企业、私人企业以及ACCA、德勤等其他专业组织也已经建立合作关系，共同开展工作，从而将"一带一路"项目的效益和红利最大化。

上述协同机制非常重要，左手知道右手在做什么，右手也知道左手在做什么，这是非常必要的。像中国交通建设集团这样的企业可以分享他们在巴基斯坦和其他"一带一路"沿线国家做得比较成熟的项目的经验，展示项目的时间框架、执行过程，他们所使用的会计和审计公司，以便其他公司、专业组织和会计师事务所从中借鉴，开展未来项目，把握未来机遇。

当然，关于"中巴经济走廊"，存在一个国家级的问题：安全。对于投资安全及保持投资不会断流的问题，巴基斯坦政府和军队采取了一个非常特别的措施——成立特别安全部，通过这支专门化的安全军队来保护中巴经济走廊项目、中国企业以及在巴基斯坦的中国工人的安全，确保项目得到全面保障，不会遭受任何灾祸和前所未有的安全问题。正是因为巴基斯坦的地位更加安全稳固，GDP增长率才会达到5.2%。阿里巴巴集团也选择到巴基斯坦投资，这对巴基斯坦而言是一个积极的信号。其他投资者也相继来到巴基斯坦，期望在政府制定的开放政策下，从巴基斯坦的政策和中巴经济走廊的红利中分"一杯羹"。如在水泥和钢铁行业，人们正在建设越来越多的钢铁和水泥厂，旨在满足中巴经济走廊项目的需求。

巴基斯坦在融资领域也有所提升。当前在巴基斯坦进行项目融资变得更加容易，根据MCIA指数，巴基斯坦已经是一个新兴市场，而2016年还只是边境市场。这表明，巴基斯坦当前的地位和俄罗斯、巴西、印度等国一样。人们对"中巴经济走廊"有许多期许和希望。巴基斯坦中国学院也邀请了许多ACCA的合作伙伴来到巴基斯坦，加入巴基斯坦中国学院的论坛，帮助人们更好地了解"中巴经济走廊"及其政策。

云计算与"一带一路"

王兴山[*]

　　作为云计算与大数据服务商，浪潮集团既是"一带一路"的参与者，也是中国企业"走出去"的合作伙伴。近年来，浪潮大力发展国际化项目，对外分享中国的信息化建设、互联网经济发展等经验，促进我国与"一带一路"沿线国家的数据互联互通，共建共赢共享。

　　国际化是浪潮的四大发展战略之一。目前浪潮全球业务已发展到全球108个国家和地区，重大项目覆盖了"一带一路"沿线一半的国家，比如与俄罗斯企业签约云计算中心，助力印度尼西亚、泰国、沙特阿拉伯建设智慧城市、教育云、椰枣基因研究等。

　　除了云计算、大数据服务，浪潮还积极开展"理念输出"，提供信息化人才的培养，并将成熟的"中国方案"推广到"一带一路"沿线国家。目前已在海外主办或承办了500多场技术培训和宣讲活动，为"一带一路"沿线国家培训了超过1万名的技术专家和官员，累计对外培训税务官员超过1000人次。以"税收风险"主题为例，"以票控税"是中国的税务治理理念，借助税务信息化服务项目，浪潮将这一理念分享到20多个沿线国家。2015年王军局长考察浪潮某国外信息化项目时，曾为浪潮点赞，表示浪潮的路径是正确的，鼓励要将中国的办税经验和税务信息化建设的先进经验在更多的国家和地区进行推广。2017年5月份"一带一路"高峰论坛之后，库拉索、埃塞俄比亚等国家领导人紧接着访问浪潮，也是对浪潮参与构建"数字丝绸之路"的肯定。

　　总结浪潮近年来自身走出去的过程，信息化发挥了关键性、支撑性作用。面对多语言、多币种、多时区、多会计准则等环境，企业需要的是将

统一标准、通用语言等固化到 IT 系统中，并利用云和共享模式，实现快速部署和简洁应用。因此，从"云与一带一路"方面，分享以下几点。

（一）互联互通，信息互通是支撑

现在全球进入数字经济时代，信息基础设施的互联互通的作用已经超过水电等基础设施，每个国家的每个人都离不开信息化，信息化建设已经成为企业的必选项。对浪潮而言，做更好的信息系统，必须在会计基础设施上加强学习、研究。比如，需要对"会计基础设施助推一带一路建设"课题进行全面、系统地培训。

云计算作为会计基础设施"走出去"的承载，是"一带一路"倡议落地的关键支撑。以财务为例，越来越多的企业通过"财务共享云"的方式为海外项目提供服务，做到管控与服务并重，中国交建正在依托在国内的共享中心经验，筹建东南亚财务共享中心，中交二航局和中交三航局已经完成了在马来西亚共享中心的建设，为马来西亚、越南、泰国、文莱、菲律宾等多个国家提供服务。

（二）推进"一带一路"，坚持"云优先"

推动"一带一路"建设，企业应采用"云优先"的策略，加快上云步伐，通过基础设施上"云"、业务上"云"、管理上"云"，搭上信息高速路快车，融入"数字丝绸之路"。当前，以云计算、大数据、物联网、人工智能为代表的新一代信息技术层出不穷，其中，云计算最早出现在公众视野，没有"云"就没有大数据，没有大数据就不会有人工智能，在这些技术中云是基础，应当坚持"云优先"。目前企业上"云"的大幕已经拉开，2017 年 4 月 12 日浙江省政府发布了十万企业上"云"的行动计划，紧接着江苏省、济南市政府也下文推进企业上"云"。昨天杭州市萧山区分配了4200 个企业上"云"指标，由省市一步步分解到各个乡镇。中国企业上"云"已经达到相当普及的程度。

为支持企业上云，浪潮于 5 月 26 日正式发布"浪潮企业云"，为大中小微企业提供包括"领域云""行业云"的全方位云服务，以"互联共享智能"的理念，帮助企业构建"智慧大脑"，助力数字化转型。在财务领域，浪潮和上海国家会计学院、德勤、ACCA 等密切合作，不断提升产品服务能力,就是希望浪潮"财务云",不仅在中国,而且在全球输出。"行业云"中的建筑云同样也是浪潮非常重视的,大型建筑企业是"一带一路"建设的先锋,所以,浪潮要进一步强化和中国交建、中国中铁等战略合作伙伴的合作,为更多的企业"走出去"提供 IT 支撑。

新发布的浪潮"企业云"具备云架构、业财税一体化、智能化、安全可靠、全新用户体验等五大特性。"云"架构上,支持多种"云"部署模式与付费模式,满足企业不同上"云"方式;对于业财税一体化,税和业务、财务互联互通,是未来管理软件、"企业云"发展的重要方向,浪潮要继续推进新一代信息技术与管理会计的融合,以端到端的流程,实现业财税一体化,推进产业链协同。除此之外,浪潮"企业云"还可以实现与京东、携程的无缝连接,将数据打通,提供人、财、物、客等全方位云服务,帮助企业构建企业云生态。

作为"一带一路"建设的积极践行者,浪潮已为中国交建、中广核、中国电建等众多"一带一路"排头兵提供信息化服务,未来将继续加强与战略客户协同创新,加强产学研合作,加大海外研发投入,为"一带一路"建设做出浪潮贡献。

企业参与"一带一路"
建设的基本情况

德勤参与"一带一路"建设的基本情况

蒋　颖

（德勤中国副 CEO）

德勤对走出去企业提供整合性的专业服务。德勤参与"一带一路"走出去的工作，已有十年之久，特别为很多中国建筑企业"走出去"做了大量 EPC（设计、采购、施工）项目的咨询工作。德勤作为专业服务机构的定位是：中国企业全球化，德勤伴您同行。助力中国企业"走出去"，参与"一带一路"建设，助力中国企业真正成为全球化的跨国公司，这是德勤的愿景。因此，德勤在 2003 年成立了德勤全球中国服务组，这个组当时是为了宣传推动引进外资到中国投资，而在过去的八九年中，德勤的主要工作则是帮助中国企业"走出去"。德勤在全世界 150 个国家，有 600 位能够说中文、懂中国，同时也具备当地经验的团队，在世界各地帮助中国企业在当地落户，助力走出去。

同时，德勤也协助很多政府机构，包括国资委和商务部，针对中国企业"走出去"面临的一些风险，合作出版研究分析报告。其中针对六七个热门行业，包括轨道交通、农业、生态、环保等做了具体的行业分析。总体来讲，德勤作为全球最大的专业服务机构，有能力也有责任帮助中国企业在走出去参与"一带一路"的过程当中，帮助企业做大做强，走出去、走进去和走上去。

中国路桥参与"一带一路"的基本情况

董付堂

（中国路桥工程有限责任公司总会计师，中国会计领军后备人才）

中国路桥于1958年走出去，当时代表中国政府开展经济援助业务，是最早走出去的四家中国企业之一。改革开放以后，中国路桥进行了公司化改制，发展到今天，中国路桥在全球63个国家和地区都有分支机构，是中国交建主要的海外平台公司之一。

目前，中国路桥在"一带一路"沿线多数国家实现了市场布局，跟踪推动了300多个项目，承建了一批互联互通的示范性工程。在东南亚地区，公司承揽了印度尼西亚泗水—马都拉海峡大桥、印度尼西亚梭罗路、柬埔寨57B号公路、老挝北本湄公河大桥、越南高岭桥等项目；在南亚地区，承建了巴基斯坦喀喇昆仑公路改扩建项目一期和二期、孟加拉国卡纳普里河底隧道；在中亚地区，公司承建了塔乌公路、中吉乌公路、塔中公路一期、沙赫里斯坦隧道等项目，累计公路里程超过2000公里；在东非地区，公司重点实施了肯尼亚蒙内铁路、内马铁路，铁路总里程超1000公里，合同额100多亿美元。中国路桥已形成了从施工建设到运营管理的铁路全产业链业务。同时，从内罗毕到马拉巴的内马铁路也已开工建设，通过东非第一大港蒙巴萨港，实现东非六国基础设施的互联互通；在中东欧地区，公司承揽了塞尔维亚泽蒙—博尔察大桥、塞尔维亚E763、匈塞铁路、黑山南北高速项目、白俄罗斯M5延长线等项目。这些项目的实施，进一步打通了所在国的发展瓶颈，提升了道路的通达水平，逐步完善了沿线国家和区域的交通运输网络。此外，公司还在阿富汗、伊朗、埃及、土耳其等重要节点国家开展了多个项目。除了传统业务以外，中国路桥现在在海外也在打造经济特区、自贸区、工业园，加强国际产能合作，包括蒙巴萨经济特区、塞尔维亚产业园、毛里塔尼亚产业园、马达加斯加产业园、印度尼西亚比通港产业园、巴基斯坦KPG省的两个产业园等。

"一带一路"走出去过程中
需要注意的问题

"一带一路"倡议中人文交流的重要性

Mustafa Hyder Sayed

（巴基斯坦中国学院执行总监）

巴基斯坦中国学院在与合作伙伴合作过程中，人文交流是重要的组成部分。文化交流始终是经济交流的基础，两者关系就像是硬币的两面，企业需要充分了解当地文化、语言、习俗等。正是基于这个原因，巴基斯坦中国学院专门为专业人士提供了中文课，巴基斯坦的工程师、教授、商人、知识分子等都可以在巴基斯坦中国学院的学堂里学习中文，也可以和巴基斯坦中国学院的合作伙伴机构进行交流，以加强对中国人文历史的了解。巴基斯坦中国学院还向中国企业派驻代表团，参观中国企业，了解中国机构。考虑到中国和巴基斯坦的文化、社会、政府治理都不相同，双方都需要不断地加深对对方的了解，从而进一步加深合作。跟中国人要先交朋友，再做生意，这种文化上面的交流，是"一带一路"重要的联通内容。以中国路桥公司为例，在合作过程中，人文交流即扮演着非常重要的角色。

"一带一路" 倡议中公共关系搭建的重要性

蒋　颖

（德勤中国副 CEO）

促进人文交流，增进彼此的互相理解，非常有意义，这样一种相互理解和相互融合、共赢是非常重要的主题。德勤一直在强调走出去，但德勤的理念是中国企业不仅仅是走出去，还应该是走进去和走上去，更多地融入当地文化和环境，从而能够达到长期可持续的发展，同时能够给当地带来价值的共赢状态。这才是从企业的角度长期发展的路径。公共关系和中国企业如何发声、如何发好声，从而使中国企业有影响力和竞争力常常被忽略。除了商业上的安排需要合规以外，文化的融合和整个公共关系的搭建也是德勤需要加强的地方。

"一带一路" 倡议中当地环境保护的重要性

董付堂

（中国路桥工程有限责任公司总会计师，中国会计领军后备人才）

在海外业务的拓展和合作上，要注重几个原则。

第一，价值引领原则。要以习近平总书记提出的"构建人类命运共同体"精神为指引，积极践行正确义利观，行大道、谋共赢，利他为先，舍得为上，打造"魂在中华、行在海外"的海外特色企业文化，在对外经济合作中开展人文交流，弘扬中华优秀传统文化，推进中外文化融合。在推进"一带一路"建设上，通过共赢、互补、共同发展，提高当地 GDP，提升人民福祉和收入水平，增加就业。通过他们的发展，中国企业也跟着发展，坚持合作共赢的发展模式。

第二，践行绿色发展理念，携手打造"绿色丝绸之路"。严格遵守当地环保法规，将环保理念创造性地融入工程设计、施工、管理等各个环节。比如，中国路桥承建的蒙内铁路项目，根据沿线的野生动物迁移路径和活动习性，设置一定数量的野生动物通道，引导动物安全穿过铁路；积极组织和参与各类环保公益和救助活动，如救援深陷泥潭的野生大象、组织国家公园垃圾清理活动等；在塞尔维亚，施工生产要符合欧洲标准，不能造成环境的二次污染等。中国的模式和发展理念在东南亚和非洲得到高度评价，当地很多学院都在研究中国的发展模式。为什么中国三十多年改革开放发展得这么好？中国路桥要把这种模式复制到海外，要特别注意在海外发展的可持续性，能够达到环境保护的要求。

第三，人文的融合。企业在海外面临的最大的困难是文化不同，必须要适应当地文化，遵守当地民族的人文习俗。这在中国人看起来可能是一件小事，而对于当地则是一件大事。比如，中国人喜欢吃狗肉，但在马达加斯加当地是不允许的，这些小事不注意就会带来误解。中国银监会的公司在海外，基本的用工比例是1∶10，一个中国路桥的人，可能要配10个当地人。这种大规模人员共同合作，难免会带来很多文化冲突。因此，文化融合非常重要，要跨文化的融合，彼此适应。许多走出去的企业容易忽视很多细节，如果这些方面都考虑到了，再加上在海外的合作，配合默契会越来越好，会提升中国的好声音和价值观，发展也会非常顺利。

"一带一路"倡议中当地技术培训及宣传的重要性

Mustafa Hyder Sayed

（巴基斯坦中国学院执行总监）

补充非常重要的两点：

第一，技术培训。对当地人的技术培训在"一带一路"中非常重要，特别是在发展中国家，为当地培训劳动力，培养就业人群，让他们能够获得更好的工作，更好地参与到"一带一路"建设当中。这能够真正推动企业的可持续发展，因为为当地进行职业培训和教育会为企业"走出去"带来更加有技能的劳动力，帮助的不仅仅是当地国家经济的提升和发展，也是为企业改善人力资源。

第二，宣传工作。企业真正需要做的，是向其他国家和地区的人民传递正确的信息。如何对自己做的善举进行宣传，如何来做公共关系是非常重要的。很多中国企业在不同的国家，包括在巴基斯坦做了很多公益活动，但是不知道如何宣传。其实宣传营销不是吹嘘，而是要让大家清楚我所做的事情，也是为当地人民和国家做的。中国企业做了很多很好的事情，一定要学会如何把善举进行宣传。

中国企业参与"一带一路"建设的发展机遇

基础设施建设带来的发展机遇

蒋　颖

（德勤中国副 CEO）

中国有句俗语"要致富先修路"。因此，在"一带一路"建设中，基础设施的建设，无论从项目的类型还是项目的大小来说，仍是最多的。对任何国家的经济发展而言，基础设施都非常重要。在整个基础设施建设的过程当中，中国企业可能刚开始走出去时只是单体，但现在已经是集成化，会全面负责从整体设计到整个建筑施工的所有过程。以大的燃料天然气项目为例，从项目开始到后期天然气的输送，已经是几个集团抱团走出去了。因为这些项目不仅仅是一个集团可以做的事情，它需要很多相关行业配合完成。进一步的发展机遇将会是电信和环保项目（如污水处理、垃圾处理、新能源等）。要相信随着沿线国家经济体的不断发展，市场将会越来越大。同样的，建筑企业、电信业走出去了，很多制造业的机器设备也会跟着一起走出去。因为从产业角度来看，这些企业都具有很多共通性。最后，从融资角度和中国的银行在当地发展的角度来看，金融业也会存在机遇。所以"一带一路"推动的是全产业链，而且是从企业的集群方面进行推动，是具有战略高度的一体化发展。

通常而言，企业"走出去"有四种方式，并购当地项目、EPC、绿地投资和贸易。目前而言,并购和 EPC 的基础设施建设投资量相对较大。

"一带一路"带来的发展机遇

董付堂

（中国路桥工程有限责任公司总会计师，中国会计领军后备人才）

第一，非洲处处是商机。改革开放以后，中国路桥在非洲项目三十多年，感觉处处是商机。关键是怎么抓住机会，要抓住对中国产业互补的机会更是重中之重。在基础设施部分，中国基础设施在全球的能力和技术水平数一数二，没有修不了的桥、路和港口，而"一带一路"对于基础设施的需求非常大。为什么中国要成立基础设施投资银行、中非基金和丝路基金？现在很多"一带一路"沿线国家的债务很大，超出了 IMF 的融资上限，很迫切需要中国提供新的融资方案。这在我们设计融资模式时要重点考虑。

第二，海外金融产业也有非常好的发展机遇。目前中资银行在非洲分支机构并不多，而中国企业在海外规模非常大，贸易融资、人民币互换和当地投融资需求强烈，包括当地银行对中间产品的需求明显，这意味着金融行业大有可为。

第三，电信通讯网络行业。现在中兴通讯和华为在海外布点比较广，而且提供的通讯网络很好，而没有他们的地方通讯网络往往很差。因此，只要当地有中兴或华为，就可以开展财务共享。对于财务基础设施的建设而言，通讯能力非常重要。

第四，最重要的是产业合作。现在中国企业要打造境外产业园，是非常好的发展理念。中国市场曾经走了很大的弯路，产业布局不好，比较分散。现在对于海外市场而言，不能把落后二三十年的产业布局带出去，因此要在国外打造产业园，让这些国家可以实现"弯道超车"。当然中国国内也做产业园，是把原来分散的产业布局聚集在一起。当前"一带一路"在海外建设的产业园，布局非常好，在所在国非常受欢迎。以塞尔维亚为例，当地的牛奶和蜂蜜很好，可以发展食品加工产业。中国企业就是要把优势产业带过去，跟他们的需求吻合。中国的优势产业，包括轻工、家居、家电、电子等都可以在海外建产业园。中国在海外一定要有一个比较高的起点，并且相信未来的非洲和东南亚发展潜力非常巨大。

信息产业国际化下的挑战和机会

王兴山

（浪潮集团执行总裁）

"一带一路"走出去需遵循合作共赢的理念，中国企业"走出去"要摒弃将低产能转出去，不顾当地资源和环境的做法。比如，瓜达尔港通过"一带一路"带动当地经济发展，让老百姓都富裕起来，这对中国和世界确实是很大的贡献。

"一带一路"推动中国企业"走出去"，也给国内企业带来了挑战。比如，人才和文化的挑战。以智慧粮库为例，中国多数智慧粮库都是浪潮做的，但在非洲或其他城市，粮库都不在大城市里面，而在偏僻地区，条件非常艰苦，因此缺乏熟悉当地文化的人才将成为很大的挑战。

当然，挑战也带来了机会，它倒逼中国的信息产业国际化，中国的企业管理软件和服务，不仅要支持中国企业"走出去"，还要随着中国企业"走出去"。当前，中国信息产业中管理软件进口很多，严重影响了我国的自主可控。为什么中国信息产业很难国际化，尤其在管理层面？因为管理里面有文化的问题、管理者思想的问题和习惯的问题，当然还有准则的一些问题。"一带一路"建设促使软件设计充分考虑税收和会计准则等问题，不断融合当地文化、管理思想和管理模式，倒逼中国软件国际化水平提升，中国交建海外财务共享中心正是例证。

企业参与"一带一路"建设的主要风险

企业"走出去"的尽职调查

Mustafa Hyder Sayed

（巴基斯坦中国学院执行总监）

当一个国家第一次走出去的时候，可能没有太多的经验，需要找到当地好的合作伙伴进行合作。这个合作伙伴要有经验，也要有关系。很多中国企业在其他国家进行投资，经常面临项目上的各种问题，如法务问题（诉讼、土地的纠纷等）。为防范风险，企业需要在投资前做好调研，而不是马上就进行投资。因此，要做好尽职调查，必须进行验证，深入研究。

调查结束之后，企业还需要循序渐进。此时，当地工程师非常重要，他会给企业提供建议，或者帮助企业找到合适的渠道等。可以通过寻找本地的合作伙伴，如果合作伙伴选择适宜，往往会事半功倍。因为不同国家习俗文化不同，所以要学会适应。比如，"一带一路"建设中可能很多的投资公司来自广州、山东这样不同的省份，而这些不同省份的公司虽然都在中国，但彼此之间可能存在很大的文化差异，所以需要和他们直接做咨询，了解如何进入当地新市场。

中国有些省份经济发展很快，企业也特别强，且很有投资海外的经验。但是，这些企业很可能没有"中巴经济走廊"的信息，甚至可能都不知道"中巴经济走廊"。此外，并不是所有企业都有海外投资经验。所以，作为巴基斯坦而言，巴基斯坦中国学院有义务跟他们交朋友，给中国企业提供正确的信息让他们感受到机遇在哪里，然后一步步来投资。

除此之外，需要选择合适的国家，并且这个国家跟中国关系良好，是中国政府支持的国家，然后在当地寻找合适的合作伙伴。有时候一个政府机关的发达程度并非特别理想，没有达到期望值；也有可能到一个国家投资，甚至拿不到任何有用的信息。这时候企业就需要自己做调查工作，同当地先搞好关系，再做生意。中国各省份之间经济存在差异，有些大省甚至比某些国家的经济还要发达。所以习总书记讲，"包容、理解、共赢、合作"，这是 "一带一路" 一个重要的指导思想。

中国企业 "走出去" 任重而道远

蒋 颖

（德勤中国副 CEO）

中国企业 "走出去" 主要从两个层面来看：

第一，像德勤这样全球化的专业服务机构，需要不断学习如何更好地了解和服务中国企业。除了德勤中国团队以外，其实国外团队也需要一个学习的过程。以巴基斯坦为例，由于 "中巴经济走廊" 的项目德勤参与很多，所以在过去五六年里，德勤在巴基斯坦有非常稳定且专门服务于中国项目的团队，他们对中国客户的需求、文化就有很多的了解。随之而来的是德勤在巴基斯坦项目的慢慢稳定，团队也越来越大，项目量也越来越多。这样才能够跟中国团队保持良好的合作来支持企业在当地的运作。德勤自身全球化过程当中也需要彼此磨合、慢慢了解。同样的，德勤在服务美国企业、欧洲企业和非洲企业都不一样，每个企业都有它独特的文化和特点。在整个磨合过程中，相互了解，先交朋友再做生意。

第二，从中国企业角度来讲，走出去和全球化还是任重而道远。德勤2016 年在北京做过一个调研，其中 90% 的调研对象是中央企业。里面有两组数据，一组数据是当时调研的 100 多家公司中大部分公司的海外业务收入占总体收入比重很低，甚至超过半数的公司海外业务量少于10%。这说明中国企业大多数业务还是在中国本土展开，缺乏国外运营经验。第二组数据关注海外业务量很大的企业如何管理海外业务，是否有专门集成化或者是分散化的组织来管理海外项目。数据表明，90%是有集中或分散的机构专门负责管理海外项目，而10%的企业则没有任何架构，完全根据项目进行管理。深入地了解这90%的企业，其在组织架构里的基础设施建设，比如整个组织架构管控、管理模式是否齐全等，德勤发现，大多数企业还处在摸索阶段。所以，从中国企业角度来说，企业整体管控模式的搭建、能力的培养，还有很长的路要走。

从专业服务机构角度来讲，企业有四个方面需要提升，不断加强企业的基础设施建设。第一，长期战略的制定和实施能力。很多企业"走出去"，并没有一个相对比较长期的战略，机会来了就抓住，这在刚开始开拓市场时也许可行，但是规模大了以后，肯定要有一个比较长期、稳定的战略。比如，去哪个领域投资？企业整个产业链搭建的整合价值等都需要考虑。第二，融资能力。融资能力不仅仅是融到钱，其中有各种各样复杂的情况。比如，企业如何在融资以后，能够有相对有效且稳定的项目或计划方案。这里面会有很多风险，特别是电站项目和天然气项目，对于融资的偿还，都会和储量及以后的产出相关。第三，整体风险管控能力。走出去企业的产业链里有很多风险，包括融资、财会、法务等，企业如何有相对比较稳定的管控体系，能够应对相关风险且保护自己，值得慎重考虑。第四，国际化人才。这个是最难的，因为人才培养需要时间，要自己组建并着力培育。如果这四点能力能够不断提升，那企业"走出去"的路，会更加平稳。

中国企业"走出去"所面临的各种风险

董付堂

（中国路桥工程有限责任公司总会计师，中国会计领军后备人才）

中国企业"走出去"主要面临以下几种风险：

第一，要关注在海外的政治和安全风险。国外环境和国内环境完全不同，很多非洲国家、东南亚国家政治不太稳定，安全形势堪忧，因此企业投资时一定要充分考虑。

第二，要考虑投资环境，尤其是否有双边投资保护协定。很多国家没有跟中国直接签订双边投资保护协定，要考虑能否在第三国设定一个股权架构，利用双边投资保护协定，获得更多的优惠政策，在法律层面上确保投资安全。

第三，对于财务而言，关注的重点是融资和汇率风险。在当地货币贬值速度比较大的情况下，汇率风险如何管控，是否采用套期保值和远期等方式。尤其当现在一些投资模式也发生改变的情况下，比如到海外做 PPP 项目，项目以后收取的都是当地货币，运营期的汇率风险非常大，是否需要在一开始就考虑财务模型，设计一个汇率风险锁定，或者一个汇率补偿机制，确保经营收入不贬值，这是非常重要的。

第四，BEPS 带来的税务风险。目前全球接近 70 个国家参与到 BEPS 行动中，BEPS 计划实施后，企业国别报告要上报给国际有关的组织，这种信息的交换，对于企业海外财务税务管理规范性的要求有所提高。企业要遵守当地法律，按照当地税法依法纳税，树立合规经营的理念。

第五，中资企业要合作共赢。中资企业在海外相互的竞争，前几年影响不太好，相互之间在海外直接竞争很多，这一点中国企业应该学习日本企业，日本企业"抱团"非常强，基本上没有看到日本企业在海外直接竞争的现象。这是走出去企业要特别关注的。

课题报告："会计基础设施"
助推"一带一路"

报告概述

"在国际经济交往中，会计应充分发挥国际通用商业语言的作用，在金融合作、境外投融资、经贸往来等方面成为规划、决策、控制和评价的依据。"

2013 年，习近平主席在出访中亚和东南亚国家期间先后提出"丝绸之路经济带"和"21 世纪海上丝绸之路"的重大倡议，得到海内外广泛关注和积极响应。该倡议不仅为中国与沿线国家优势互补、互利共赢开辟了广阔的空间，也为中国外向型经济跨越式发展和深度参与全球经济治理提供了历史机遇。经过近四年的发展，"一带一路"建设在政策沟通、设施联通、贸易畅通、资金融通、民心相通等方面都取得了丰硕成果。作为国际通用的商业语言，会计在"一带一路"的发展过程中如何发挥基础设施的作用？基于此目的，由上海国家会计学院、ACCA 和德勤中国的专家组成"一带一路"与会计基础设施课题组，研究"会计基础设施"如何助推"一带一路"的国家倡议。

基础设施是指为社会生产和居民生活提供公共服务的物质工程设施，是用于保证国家或地区社会经济活动正常进行的公共服务系统。它是社会赖以生存发展的一般物质条件。基础设施包括交通、邮电、供水供电、商业服务、科研与技术服务、园林绿化、环境保护、文化教育、卫生事业等市政公用工程设施和公共生活服务设施等。它们是国民经济各项事业发展的基础。我们认为"会计基础设施"是指在国际经济交往中，会计应充分发挥国际通用商业语言的作用，在金融合作、境外投融资、经贸往来等方面成为规划、决策、控制和评价的依据。政府可以根据会计报表的汇总信息进行有效的宏观调控，决定资源和利益的分配，使国家经济健康、有序的发展。投资者可以了解国家和企业的财务状况，确定能否取得相应的投资回报。在现代社会中，经济越发展，对会计基础设施的要求越高；完善的会计基础设施对加速社会经济活动，促进国家间的经贸往来起着巨大的推动作用。

"会计基础设施"是一个宏大的话题，"一带一路"沿线国家的会计发展状况差异又很大，所以会计基础设施的概念和范畴都有待研究。作为初期研究成果，课题组研究了沿线代表性国家的会计准则、税收风险和财会人才培养的经验和差异。首先，会计在资本市场上已经具有举足轻重的地位。会计通过对信息的收集、加工、总结，形成对经济决策和经济管理有效的信息系统，因此了解代表性国家的会计准则是非常重要的内容。其次，伴随着企业对外投资活动的愈发活跃，对外投资面临的税收风险也日益凸显，主要包括重复征税的风险、未充分享受税收协定待遇的风险、因转让定价和反避税问题导致的风险、海外并购标的企业的历史税收问题的风险和税收歧视等风险，如何规避和应对这些税收风险是企业走出国门的必修课。最后，无论是会计准则体系的协调与完善，还是税收风险的应对，都离不开国际化财会人才的培养，如何更好地培养具有全球化视野的专业财会人才，沿线国家是否有专门的机构或组织负责财会人才的培养、财会人才需要具备的能力有哪些、通过什么方式提升财会人才的胜任能力、不同国家的企业在培养模式上有哪些不同之处、有哪些经验值得互相借鉴等问题是各国、各企业非常关注的问题。关于代表性国家的选择，课题组借鉴了 ACCA、上海证券交易所以及国家"一带一路"信息中心等的研究成果，计算出沿线国家的国别合作度指数，按照指数排名，确立了新加坡、马来西亚、阿联酋、波兰、捷克、斯洛伐克、卡塔尔、匈牙利、泰国、越南、俄罗斯、印度尼西亚、哈萨克斯坦、印度和巴基斯坦等 14 国作为首批研究对象。课题组采用调查问卷的方式，针对 14 国的企业高管（包括本国企业和中资企业在这些国家的分支机构）于 2017 年 4～6 月之间进行了问卷调查分析。

第一部分 各国间会计政策的协调和统一

各国之间会计政策的协调是各经济体信息沟通的核心机制之一。研究表明，会计准则的差异被视为跨境投资的障碍。因此，会计准则的国际趋同将有助于帮助企业提供高质量、更具可比性、更透明的财务报告，弱化国别差异对会计信息可比性和透明度的不利影响；同时，促进跨境投资和资本市场的融通，提高市场的流动性；进一步来说，扩大企业的投资者范围，通过风险共担从而降低国际间交易成本，以实现更好的资本配置。

从发展趋势来看，中国的资本正在加速谋求海外市场。根据《2015年度中国对外直接投资统计公报》，2015年中国对外投资流量跃居全球第二，中国对外直接投资流量创下1456.7亿美元的历史新高，同比增长18.3%，超过日本成为全球第二大对外投资国。对"一带一路"相关国家的投资快速增长，高达189.3亿美元，同比增长38.6%，是对全球投资增幅的2倍。中国对外投资存量的八成以上（83.9%）分布在发展中经济体，在发达经济体的存量占比为14%，另有2.1%存量在转型经济体。

根据商务部《2016年"一带一路"沿线国家投资合作情况》报告，2016年，中国对"一带一路"沿线53个国家直接投资145.3亿美元，主要流向新加坡、印度尼西亚、印度、泰国、马来西亚等国家和地区。中国以工程承包为先导，辅以金融服务为支持，在"一带一路"沿线建设一系列合作园区与自贸区，并力争取得更多早期收获。这将成为中国海外投资的重要方向。

"一带一路"沿线国家采用的会计准则不尽相同。根据国际财务报告准则基金会于2017年3月发布的《国际财务报告准则指引：全球财务报告语言》（"指引"），IFRS的质量正在进一步提高，并在全球范围内得到越来多的采用。指引概述了在全球 150 个司法管辖区采用 IFRS 标准的进展情况，并包括有关标准和标准制定机构的信息。指引指出截止到指引发布日，在研究的 150 个司法管辖区中有 126 个（84%）已经要求所有或大多数国内上市公司和金融机构按照 IFRS 编制财务报表。按照指引，对"一带一路"沿线国家采用的会计准则的情况进行了汇总。在"一带一路"沿线的 65 个国家中，有 54 个（83%）国家已经要求所有或大多数国内上市公司和金融机构按照 IFRS 编制财务报表；有 3 个国家（越南、老挝、埃及）目前使用本国会计准则；有 2 个国家（印度、印度尼西亚）与 IFRS 持续趋同中；泰国正在直接采用 IFRS 过程之中；乌兹别克斯坦仅要求本国银行按照 IFRS 进行报告；另有 4 个国家（土库曼斯坦、吉尔吉斯斯坦、塔吉克斯坦、黎巴嫩）不在指南研究范围内。

在采用国际财务报告准则的 54 个"一带一路"沿线国家中，伊朗、哈萨克斯坦、科威特、黑山、卡塔尔是在 2016 年开始要求所有或大多数国内上市公司和金融机构按照 IFRS 编制财务报表。此外，沙特阿拉伯决定从 2017 年起对所有上市公司、2018 年对所有其他公众实体要求按照 IFRS 进行报告。

事实上，会计准则仅仅是影响企业财务报告实施的重要制度因素之一，对企业报告质量和可比性的影响较为有限。学术研究表明，企业报告的应用环境和会计准则的执行力度与财务报表编制所使用的会计准则同样重要，制约着报告质量和可比性。一般来说，企业的报告应用环境受到许多因素的影响，包括：国家的法律机构（例如法治），执行制度的效力（例如审计），资本市场力量（例如，对筹集外部资本的需求），企业的所有权、治理结构及其经营特点，产品市场竞争等。

同时，各国企业的会计准则执行力度制约着报告的质量。即使公司的报告应用环境类似，只要会计准则的执行力度不同，企业报告的普遍可比性就不太可能发生。这适用于任何一套会计标准，不仅仅是国际报告准则。因此调研深入了解"一带一路"沿线各国所采用的会计准则和实际应用环境，旨在帮助专业会计人士了解这些地区的会计政策基本情况、推动会计准则的国际趋同发展、完善和增强财会领域合作机制。

新加坡

新加坡的上市公司必须使用新加坡财务报告准则（SFRS），与 IFRS 实质趋同。根据上市规则，新加坡证券交易所上市的所有外国公司均允许使用 IFRS。

专业机构：新加坡特许会计师协会 http：//isca. org. sg/。

准则制定者：新加坡会计准则委员会 http：//www. asc. gov. sg/。

财务报告准则：新加坡采取直接采用国际财务报告准则的模式。

新加坡现有 3 套经核准的会计准则，分别为：新加坡财务报告准则（SFRS），适用于除采用新加坡中小企业财务报告准则的中小企业之外的企业；与国际财务报告准则完全一致的财务报告准则（IFRS – identical Financial Reporting Standards），适用于新加坡证券交易所上市的当地企业，于 2018 年 1 月 1 日或以后日期开始的年度期间生效；新加坡中小企业财务报告准则（SFRS for SMEs），适用于中小企业。

新加坡当地企业（包括上市及非上市公司），无论是合并财务报表还是单独财务报表，都应当采用与国际财务报告准则几乎相同的新加坡财务报告准则。受访者反馈，新加坡财务报告准则仅对国际财务报告准则做出了少许修订，因此两者很大程度相同，差异主要包括：未采用解释公告第 2 号、对少数准则中某些豁免、过渡性规定或生效日期做出修改，或对某些准则提供额外指引。经新加坡会计和公司监管机构批准后的当地企业，或者在新加坡证券交易所及海外上市且海外证券交易所要求使用国际财务报告准则的当地企业以及在新加坡证券交易所上市的外国企业，可以采用国际财务报告准则。2014 年 5 月 29 日，新加坡会计准则委员会宣布在新加坡证券交易所上市的当地企业将于 2018 年 1 月 1 日或以后日期开始的年度期间采用一套新的与国际财务报告准则完全一致的财务报告框架。非上市的当地企业也可以自愿采用新的财务报告框架。新加坡的中小企业采用新加坡中小企业财务报告准则，该准则直接采用中小企业国际财务报告准则，只是在准则适用范围，即对中小企业的定义方面存在一些差异。受访者认为新加坡会计准则的实际执行效力很好，企业能完全按准则执行。

受访者反馈，新加坡公司必须进行年度审计，除非符合公司法 205B 或 205C 章的审计豁免条款，即公司股东不超过 20 名并且全部为个人股东，公司的年营业额不超过 500 万新加坡元。基于受访者反馈，新加坡审计准则与国际审计准则（即国际会计师联合会颁布的标准）完全一致。

马来西亚

公众公司必须使用马来西亚财务报告准则（MFRS）框架，实质上等同于 IFRS。允许在马来西亚上市的外国公司使用 IFRS。

专业机构：马来西亚会计师公会（IFAC 成员）http：//www. mia. org. my/，马来西亚注册会计师公会（IFAC 成员）http：//www. micpa. com. my/。

准则制定者及主要职责：马来西亚会计准则委员会（MASB）http：//www. masb. org. my。其主要职能包括：发布新会计准则作为经核准的会计准则；审查、修订或采纳经核准的会计准则、现行会计准则；全部或部分修改、替代、暂停、延期、撤回或撤销任何已核准的会计准则；全部或部分发行、批准、审查、修改、替代、暂停、延期、撤回或撤销任何已发布的问题公告、技术公告以及与财务报告有关的任何其他文件；赞助或承担相关会计准则的制定；与其他国家和国际会计准则制定者合作，持续关注其他国家和国际会计准则的发展；参与并促进制定一套全球使用的国际会计准则；监督已核准的会计准则的运作，以评估其持续相关性和有效性；

财务报告准则：马来西亚采取了直接采用国际财务报告准则的模式。

马来西亚现有 3 套经核准的会计准则，分别为：马来西亚财务报告准则（MFRSs），对非公众公司之外的企业适用的财务报告准则；非公众公司财务报告准则（PERSs），适用于非公众公司，于 2016 年 1 月 1 日失效；马来西亚非公众公司财务报告准则（MPERS），适用于非公众公司，于 2016 年 1 月 1 日或以后日期开始的年度期间生效。

在马来西亚，马来西亚会计准则理事会负责认可国际财务报告准则，并不做修改地形成马来西亚财务报告准则（MFRS）。马来西亚的所有公众公司（包括上市公司和金融机构）自 2012 年起，无论是合并财务报表还是单独财务报表，都应当采用国际财务报告准则（当地称为"马来西亚财务报告准则"）；但是，部分过渡性企业（主要是农业企业和房地产企业）可以选择推迟到 2018 年采用，在此之前，仍可采用马来西亚本国会计准则。

就农业企业和房地产企业现行使用的马来西亚本国会计准则，其与国际财务报告准则之间的差异包括：马来西亚本国会计准则未包含国际会计准则第41号、国际财务报告准则第15号及国际财务报告准则解释公告第15号的相关内容；在马来西亚本国会计准则下：农业企业的生物资产按照成本计量；允许房地产企业采用完工百分比法确认房地产开发活动的相关收入和成本。

马来西亚的非公众公司于2016年1月1日或以后日期开始的年度期间使用马来西亚非公众公司财务报告准则，在此之前使用原非公众公司财务报告准则。马来西亚非公众公司报告财务准则直接采用中小企业国际财务报告准则，只是在房产开发活动及一些术语上有所修改。

受访者认为，马来西亚所使用的会计准则，无论是马来西亚财务报告准则（MFRSs）还是马来西亚非公众公司财务报告准则（MPERS）均与国际会计准则非常相似。基于受访者的反馈，马来西亚会计准则的实际执行效力非常强，能够全面按照准则实施。这主要是基于严格的监管环境，对于上市公司来说，除了常规监管机构之外还会受到其他政府机构的监督，即马来西亚股票交易所和证券委员会；对于金融机构和保险公司，还会受到马来西亚中央银行的监管。对于上市公司，马来西亚股票交易所和证监会规定公司需要披露相关的公司治理情况。

根据马来西亚的2016年《公司法》注册成立的所有公司均须接受审计。然而，根据2016年《公司法》，公司注册相关管理部门有权豁免根据这些公司的审计要求。基于受访者的反馈，马来西亚使用的审计准则与国际审计准则（即国际会计师联合会颁布的标准）完全一致。

阿联酋

在纳斯达克迪拜、迪拜金融服务管理局（DFSA）和阿布扎比证券交易所上市的公司均须使用 IFRS。迪拜金融市场（PJSC）上市的公司允许使用 IFRS。在阿联酋上市的外国公司必须使用 IFRS。

专业机构：阿联酋会计师及审计师公会 http：//www. aaa4uae. com/ 。

准则制定者：阿联酋无制定报告准则的机构也无当地准则。直接采用国际财务报告准则。国际财务报告准则由国际会计准则理事会（IASB）制定颁布。

财务报告准则：阿联酋采取了直接采用国际财务报告准则的模式。根据 2015 年 7 月 1 日起执行的《阿联酋商业公司法》的 2 号文，规定要求所有公司需要按照国际财务报告准则编制财务报告（中小企业适用中小企业国际财务报告准则）。

对采用国际财务报告准则的例外情况：对于采用的国际财务报告准则，在某些极个别情况下，阿联酋中央银行会对贷款损失准备金有额外的要求。另外，在实际操作中，IAS–19 员工福利准则中关于辞退福利的部分，由于执行成本或缺乏精算数据的原因而无法适用。对于董事薪酬，当地法律规定须计入权益科目。以上两项都与 IAS–19 的规定不符，但由于其影响较小，在实务操作中也被采纳。经受访者反映，阿联酋公司对国际财务报告准则的实施非常好，都能完全按照准则执行。

受访者指出，除了独资企业以及一些自由区不需要对某些实体进行审计之外，其他所有实体需要根据阿联酋商业公司法的规定进行审计。此外，受访者认为，阿联酋使用的审计准则也与国际审计准则非常相近。

波　兰

所有在受监管市场上从事证券交易的国内企业均须使用 EU IFRS 编制合并财务报表。外国公司必须采用 EU IFRS 编制合并财务报表，但当欧盟认为外国公司所在的本国司法管辖区所采用的财务报告准则等同于 IFRS，则该外国公司可采用其本国财务报告准则。

专业机构：波兰会计师公会 http：//www. skwp. pl/en。

准则制定者：波兰会计准则委员会（KSR）www. mf. gov. pl/。其主要职能为：管理全国会计工作；起草会计法律、行政法规草案；研究提出会计改革和发展的政策建议；拟订并组织实施国家统一的会计准则制度、管理会计标准、内部控制规范、会计信息化标准等；拟订政府会计准则和行政、事业单位会计制度；依法对注册会计师行业进行监督、指导，制定注册会计师行业规章制度和政策措施。

财务报告准则分两种情况。第一，须采用欧盟国际财务报告准则的情况：在 2002 年 6 月，欧盟采纳了国际会计准则的相关规定，要求所有在欧盟资本市场上市的公司，从 2005 年起须采用欧盟国际财务报告准则 IFRS 编制合并财务报告。作为欧盟成员的波兰，其在欧盟（EU）或者欧洲经济区（EEA）上市的公司须采用欧盟国际财务报告准则。对于成员国，欧盟会计准则委员会给予成员国相关选择权，可以要求或允许在编制单体财务报表或非上市公司财务报表时使用欧盟国际财务报告准则。第二，其他情况：对于上述欧盟会计准则委员会给予的选择权，波兰允许上市公司使用欧盟国际财务报告准则编制单体财务报表；要求所有银行使用欧盟国际财务报告准则编制合并财务报表；允许非上市公司在符合特定条件下（其母公司使用欧盟国际财务报告准则编制合并财务报表，或者正在申报上市过程中的公司）使用欧盟国际财务报告准则编制合并及单体财务报表。除此之外，企业应当使用波兰当地的会计准则。

波兰会计准则委员会（KSR）隶属于财政部，负责制定国内的会计准则。无须采用国际财务报告准则 IFRS 的其他企业，可以选择采用波兰会计准则委员会发布的准则。

基于受访者的反馈，波兰当地会计准则与国际会计准则有些相似，但在各项准则上基本都有部分差异，主要差异体现在企业合并、合并财务报表、商誉、收入、金融工具计量与分类等准则及公允价值的运用，具体如下。

1. 企业合并

（1）波兰会计准则中，在原股东未丧失控制权的企业合并中可以使用权益结合法，而国际财务报告准则只允许使用购买法（同一控制企业合并并不在 IFRS 3 范围内）。企业合并的直接相关成本在波兰会计准则下计入收购成本而国际会计准则下计入收购发生当期的损益。

（2）非控股权益的计量，在波兰会计准则下要求按照在被购买方可辨认净资产中所占的比例份额进行计量。而国际准则下，非控制性权益可以选择按上述方法或者按公允价值计量。而对于未丧失控制权下的少数股东股权交易，在波兰会计准则下是作为收购/出售交易，相关影响计入当期损益或商誉。而在国际财务报告准则下，此类交易作为权益交易，相关影响不会计入当期损益或商誉。

（3）控制的定义：波兰会计准则下对于"控制"的定义仍然沿用修订前的国际财务报告准则中的相关描述，即强调对于被投资公司财务及经营决策的控制以达到从其经营活动获得相关利益。

2. 商誉

（1）波兰会计准则下商誉是收购价与被收购资产的净公允价值之间的差额。而国际财务报告准则下商誉为收购对价与被收购方可辨认净资产的公允价值之间的差异。此外，对于或有对价的核算也存在差异，波兰会计准则下只有在导致或有付款的未来事项很有可能发生和支付金额能够可靠确定的情况下，才计入收购对价中。如果实际支付金额与估计数不同，则需要适当调整收购成本和商誉/负商誉。而在国际会计准则下在确定收购对价时均需考虑或有对价，对于或有对价的后续计量则根据其分类为负债或权益而各自按适用准则计量。

（2）波兰会计准则允许对商誉在相关使用年限内进行摊销，如无法可靠确认相关使用年限，准则规定须在不超过 5 年的期间内摊销。相关摊销使用直线法并计入其他经营费用。

（3）商誉减值测试未在波兰相关商誉准则中明确规定，而是在资产减值相关准则中提到须每年进行减值测试。

3. 金融工具

（1）波兰会计准则对金融工具的分类与现行的 IAS 39 大致相同，区别在于，对于银行之外的企业只有交易性金融资产/金融负债才可以按公允价值计量且公允价值变动计入损益，而不允许在初始确认时将金融资产/金融负债指定为以公允价值计量且公允价值变动计入损益；对于银行之外的企业，可供出售金融资产的公允价值变动，可以选择将公允价值变动计入当期财务收入或费用，或者计入重估储备。

（2）波兰会计准则下对金融资产减值的计量没有具体规定。目前，波兰会计准则并未引入 IFRS 9 的相关变化。

4. 合并财务报告的编制

在波兰会计准则下，非公众实体在满足一定条件的情况下可豁免编制合并财务报告，但国际准则中可以豁免的投资性实体在波兰会计准则下无法被豁免。波兰会计准则下，当收购企业仅仅是为了再出售时，可豁免合并该子公司。而国际财务报告准则下则无此项豁免。对于少数股东权益，波兰会计准则将其作为单独的负债及权益类别。国际财务报告准则下作为集团权益来列报。未丧失控制权情况下增加或减少所持有子公司的股权，波兰会计准则下对于子公司权益的变动会确认为财务收入/支出。而国际财务报告准则作为权益交易处理。比例合并法在波兰准则下是被允许的，而在国际财务报告准则下则不被允许。

5. 收入确认

由于波兰会计准则相关收入确认未受到会计法的管辖，在实际操作层面，会与国际财务报告准则 IFRS 15 有大量差异存在。

6. 公允价值的运用

在波兰会计准则下，公允价值的运用范围比较小，比如，不允许使用公允价值模型计量不动产、厂场和设备，除非是法定重估要求；不允许使用公允价值模型计量无形资产。

此外，如果部分会计问题未在 KSR 或者波兰会计法中涉及，企业可以选择参考相关国际财务报告准则的规定。需要指出的是，如果一家企业已经选择采用 KSR 制定的准则，且相关问题在 KSR 或者国内会计准则中有明确规定，企业不得再参考国际财务报告准则的相关规定。受访者认为波兰会计准则的实际执行效力非常强，能够全面按照准则实施，总体来说规模越大的公司实施得更加全面彻底。受访者反馈，波兰很少有公司编制公司治理情况报告。

　　受访者指出在波兰，银行与保险公司、基金、上市公司，及满足以下两个以上条件的企业需要经审计：雇员人数超过 50 人；总资产超过 250 万欧元；销售额超过 500 万欧元。受访者认为波兰使用的审计准则与国际审计准则（即国际会计师联合会颁布的标准）大体一致。

捷　　克

　　所有在受监管市场上从事证券交易的国内企业均须使用 EU IFRS 编制合并财务报表。外国公司必须采用 EU IFRS 编制合并财务报表，但当欧盟认为外国公司所在的本国司法管辖区所采用的财务报告准则等同于 IFRS，则该外国公司可采用其本国财务报告准则。

　　专业机构：捷克会计师公会 https：//www. svaz – ucetnich. cz/。

　　准则制定者：捷克财政部 http：//www. mfcr. cz/。其主要职责包括：管理全国会计工作；起草会计法律、行政法规草案；拟订政府会计准则和行政、事业单位会计制度；其他职能还包括国家预算编制、监督税收、国际收支结算、境外投资监管等职能。

　　财务报告准则包括两种情况。第一，须采用欧盟国际财务报告准则的情况：在 2002 年 6 月，欧盟采纳了国际会计准则的相关规定，要求所有在欧盟资本市场上市的公司，从 2005 年起须采用欧盟国际财务报告准则 IFRS 编制合并财务报告。作为欧盟成员的捷克，其在欧盟（EU）或者欧洲经济区（EEA）上市的公司须采用欧盟国际财务报告准则。对于成员国，欧盟会计准则委员会给予成员国相关选择权，可以要求或允许在编制单体财务报表或非上市公司财务报表时使用欧盟国际财务报告准则。第二，其他情况：对于上述欧盟会计准则委员会给予的选择权，捷克要求上市公司的合并及单体财务报告都需要使用欧盟国际财务报告准则。允许非上市公司在编制合并财务报告时使用欧盟国际财务报告准则。允许非上市公司在编制单体财务报告时在符合特定条件下（其母公司须使用欧盟国际财务报告准则编制合并财务报告）使用欧盟国际财务报告准则。除此之外，企业应当使用捷克当地的会计准则。

　　根据受访者的反馈，在捷克有如下按不同行业划分的会计准则：企业（公告号 500／2002）；银行（公告号 501／2002）；保险公司（公告号 502／2002 和 503／2002）；非营利组织（公告号 504／2002）；市政府和政府机构

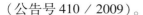

（公告号 410 ／ 2009）。

基于纳税的目的，所有公司都需要按照捷克相关会计准则进行应纳税所得额的计算。经受访者反馈，捷克当地会计准则与国际会计准则有些相似，其在有关收入确认（捷克未采用国际通行的国际贸易术语 INCO-TERMS）、租赁、金融工具等准则方面均有区别之处。具体如下：

1. 总体层面的差别

捷克会计准则下会有法定的科目表及资产负债表/利润表格式而国际会计准则无此规定；部分领域没有相关会计处理的规定，如资产减值等；有时交易形式会重于实质（融资租赁）而非国际财务报告准则下实质重于形式；对于计价模式，捷克会计准则基本以历史成本计价，公允价值模式的使用范围仅适用于证券行业或企业合并等情形下。

2. 股份支付

捷克会计准则对此方面无任何规定。而国际财务报告准则设定有具体条款。

3. 企业合并

捷克会计准则下存在法律形式优先于经济实质的情况，从形式上而不是从实质上定义收购方，因此反向收购在捷克会计准则下不存在；同一控制下的企业合并属于企业合并的范围；某些情况下，公允价值计量也会存在于同一控制下的企业合并。企业合并中公允价值重估导致的增值部分会显示在单体财务报表上，并且此部分会在后续期间进行摊销。相关的交易费用也会资本化。如果公司收购其他公司的股份没有形成业务转型，被收购公司就不会被重估。收购成本与已收购股份账面价值之间的差额为"合并差额"，在合并报表层面按 20 年进行摊销。

4. 合并财务报表

在捷克，如果满足相应条件（总资产/净收入/员工人数）就可以豁免编制合并财务报告，但银行、保险及上市公司无法豁免；捷克会计准则下对子公司与集团的定义也与国际财务报告准则不同，在评估时，由于对术语没有相关指导意见可能会导致不同的结论；对于不丧失控制权的情况下减少对子公司的投资，捷克无此类准则明确规定如何进行会计处理；而国际财务报告准则有明确规定作为权益交易处理；少数股东权益在捷克会计准则下被列在负债部分披露，不同于国际财务报告准则在权益部分披露。

5. 存货

捷克准则下借款利息资本化不能计入存货成本；对于不同制造周期的存货，是否需要分摊期间费用会有不同的要求；而国际财务报告准则允许利息费用资本化金额计入存货，并且期间费用会分摊入存货。在捷克会计准则下，对于如何计算存货减值没有明确的指引。

6. 公允价值计量

捷克无此类准则规定公允价值。除企业合并外，公允价值计量只被用于部分金融工具。

7. 建造合同

捷克没有单独的指引规定建造合同的处理方法，会计处理遵循合同的形式，建造方按照法律规定的期间确认收入和费用。捷克会计准则未采纳完工进度百分比法，合同利润在合同执行过程中无法逐步确认，而仅在开具账单时才予以确认，未结算费用被列为在产品，而国际准则下采用完工百分比法并将未结算费用列为应收款项。

8. 租赁

捷克会计准则下租赁形式重于实质，所以经营租赁和融资租赁的处理方式相同。因此融资租赁的处理方式与国际财务报告准则不同，租赁资产和负债均不在承租人的资产负债表中体现，而是与经营租赁相同，仅在租赁期内按直线法确认租赁费用。

9. 收入确认

捷克会计准则没有明确规定如何进行收入确认。通常是在所有权转移或服务提供后确认，这与国际财务报告准则的规定不同。对于递延支付的收入，捷克会计准则不予折现确认收入，而国际财务报告准则规定要求折现后确认收入。对于有多个组成部分的交易，捷克会计准则没有提供具体指引，而国际会计准则要求对各组成部分单独使用收入确认标准。

10. 金融工具

捷克会计准则在金融工具确认计量方面与国际财务报告准则相似，但是没有那么具体，某些领域并未涉及。对于金融机构而言，金融工具的确认和计量与国际准则非常接近，但是对于非金融机构而言，仍然存在较多的不同，主要差异包括：对非金融机构，不要求确认嵌入衍生工具；没有负债与权益工具的明确定义，依赖于合同形式；可赎回优先股被视为权益工具；不要求区分复合工具的债务和权益部分；金融资产按成本进行初始计量；长期应收/应付不需要折现；没有贷款及应收款的定义，没有规定以摊余成本计量的计量类别；无须使用实际利率法；没有组合套期会计相关指引。

受访者同时也提到捷克会计准则的实际执行效力非常强，能够全面按照准则实施。另外，受访者反馈编制公司经营情况及治理情况报告的捷克公司非常有限。

所有符合捷克会计法定义的公众公司及符合下列条件的公司（股份公司符合其中一项条件，其他企业符合其中两项条件）均须接受审计：资产总额大于4000万克朗；收入总额大于8000万克朗；平均雇员人数大于50人。受访者认为，捷克使用的审计准则与国际审计准则（即国际会计师联合会颁布的标准）完全一致。

卡塔尔

国内公众公司必须使用 IFRS。目前没有外国公司在卡塔尔交易所上市。

专业机构：卡塔尔金融市场管理局（QFMA）http：//www. qfma. org. qa/English/Home. aspx。

卡塔尔金融市场管理局 2012 年 8 号文规定 QFMA 有监督及管理卡塔尔上市公司的权力。上市公司的审计师也需要在 QFMA 登记注册。卡塔尔中央银行会监管所有卡塔尔的银行与保险公司。

准则制定者：在卡塔尔没有专门负责制定准则的机构，而是直接采用国际财务报告准则。

财务报告准则：根据《2002 年卡塔尔商业法》5 号文，该法律明确规定卡塔尔公司在编制合并及单体财务报告时需要采用国际财务报告准则。对采用国际财务报告准则的例外情况：卡塔尔股票交易所允许一些伊斯兰金融机构采用由伊斯兰金融机构会计与审计工会颁布的准则（AAOIFI）。

经受访者反馈，所有在卡塔尔的公司都须经年度审计，且审计师直接采用国际审计标准 IAS 进行审计。卡塔尔税务部门要求全部或部分外资（非海湾合作委员会）企业提交本地注册会计师签署的经审计的财务报表以及税务申报单。此外，2011 年 8 月 7 日的第 4/2011 号通知要求，由卡塔尔或海合会国民全资拥有的公司和常设单位在符合以下条件时，必须提交企业所得税申报表（附有经审计的财务报表）：股本大于等于 200 万卡塔尔里亚尔；或者总收入大于等于 1000 万卡塔尔里亚尔。

匈牙利

　　所有在受监管市场上从事证券交易的国内企业均须使用 EU IFRS 编制合并财务报表。外国公司必须采用 EU IFRS 编制合并财务报表，但当欧盟认为外国公司所在的本国司法管辖区所采用的财务报告准则等同于 IFRS，则该外国公司可采用其本国财务报告准则。

　　专业机构：匈牙利审计师公会（IFAC 成员）http：//www. mkvk. hu/。

　　准则制定者：国家经济部 http：//www. kormany. hu/en/ministry-for-national-economy。该部门的主要职责包括：管理全国会计工作；起草会计法律、行政法规草案；研究提出会计改革和发展的政策建议；拟订并组织实施国家统一的会计准则制度、管理会计标准、内部控制规范、会计信息化标准等；拟订政府会计准则和行政、事业单位会计制度。

　　财务报告准则包括两种情况。第一，须采用欧盟国际财务报告准则的情况：在 2002 年 6 月，欧盟采纳了国际会计准则的相关规定，要求所有在欧盟资本市场上市的公司，从 2005 年起须采用欧盟国际财务报告准则（IF-RS）编制合并财务报告。作为欧盟成员的匈牙利，其在欧盟（EU）或者欧洲经济区（EEA）上市的公司须采用欧盟国际财务报告准则。对于成员国，欧盟会计准则委员会给予成员国相关选择权，可以要求或允许在编制单体财务报表或非上市公司财务报表时使用欧盟国际财务报告准则。第二，其他情况：2015 年 6 月 12 日，匈牙利政府决定扩大国际财务报告准则在匈牙利公司财务报表中的应用。相关规定如下：自 2016 年 1 月 1 日起，在欧洲经济区（EEA）上市的公司或其母公司已使用国际财务报告准则编制合并财务报告并要求其编制国际财务报告准则财务报表的子公司，自愿采用国际财务报告准则。自 2017 年 1 月 1 日起，在欧洲经济区（EEA）上市的公司必须采用国际财务报告准则。自 2017 年 1 月 1 日起，保险公司及财务报表需要强制审计的公司自愿选择采用国际财务报告准则。自 2018 年 1 月 1 日起，所有其他金融机构必须采用国际财务报告准则。其余公司按照匈牙利会计法的规定编制财务报告。

经受访者反馈，匈牙利会计准则与国际财务报告准则非常不同，在对无形资产的确认、收入、费用的确认、财务报表中的一般披露、财务报表的形式方面都与国际财务报告准则存在差异。主要差异介绍如下：

1. 财务报表列示

匈牙利会计准则下，相关资产负债表及利润表的列示在会计法附录中已被规定，而国际财务报告准则给予企业更大的选择权去根据自身的会计政策列示相关财务报告。

2. 其他综合收益

匈牙利会计准则下目前没有其他综合收益表的概念，在国际财务报告准则下计入其他综合收益的交易，在匈牙利会计准则下都直接计入权益或利润表。

3. 固定资产

国际财务报告准则允许企业选择重估模型进行固定资产后续计量，相关重估影响计入其他综合收益，并以重估后的价值作为计提折旧的基础。虽然匈牙利会计准则下也允许重估模式进行固定资产后续计量，但也有不同之处，比如匈牙利会计准则下无其他综合收益表，所以计入权益的重估影响仅在附注中披露。此外，重估模型不会改变折旧的计提基础。

4. 投资性房地产

国际准则下有对投资性房地产的定义及相关计量模式（历史成本模式及公允价值模式）；而匈牙利会计准则下无此概念，通常情况下房地产企业使用成本模式计量投资性房地产，虽然在固定资产准则下企业可以选择以公允价值模式进行后续计量。

5. 无形资产

与固定资产重估模式类似，匈牙利也允许企业对无形资产采用重估模式进行后续计量，重估影响计入权益，但计提摊销的基础仍为历史成本。而国际财务报告准则要求仅当存在活跃市场的情况下，才可以对无形资产采用重估价值，如果使用重估模式，国际财务报告准则要求将重估后价值作为计提摊销的基础。

6. 金融资产

匈牙利会计准则下，每家公司都可以采用公允价值，虽然实务中非常少见。此外，匈牙利会计准则下更加注重法律形式对会计处理的影响，金

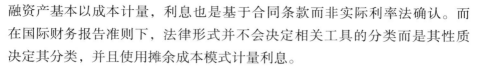

融资产基本以成本计量，利息也是基于合同条款而非实际利率法确认。而在国际财务报告准则下，法律形式并不会决定相关工具的分类而是其性质决定其分类，并且使用摊余成本模式计量利息。

7. 收入确认

匈牙利会计准则下，收入确认更多的是基于法律形式，同时，企业发生的非经常性的业务活动也会作为收入核算。匈牙利没有相关代理人/主要责任人判断的具体规定（全额/净额确认收入）。工程合同及提供服务的相关收入在合同完成时或者重要时点达成时确认。此外，销售折扣基于不同的形式，在匈牙利会计准则下可能会计入收入、其他费用、财务费用或者非经常性费用。对于有多个组成部分的销售合同，也无相关具体指引。收入确认也不会考虑时间价值的因素。以上几点都与国际财务报告准则存在差异。

8. 员工福利

对于设定收益计划，匈牙利会计准则无明确规定。而国际财务报告准则列有非常详细的规定。

9. 股份支付

匈牙利会计准则并没有明确的股份支付的相关规定。而国际财务报告准则对于现金结算或股份结算的股份支付都有明确的规定。

10. 所得税——递延所得税

匈牙利会计准则下，单体报表并无递延所得税的概念，在合并财务报表中，只有少数几类暂时性差异才会导致"因合并财务报表而导致的企业所得税差异"。这与国际财务报告准则非常不同。

11. 企业合并

匈牙利会计准则下，企业可以选择公允价值或者成本模式对被收购对象进行计量，另外，匈牙利对收购方的确定更注重法律意义上的条款。这都与国际财务报告准则不同。

受访者反馈，匈牙利国内对会计准则的实施效力非常强，都能完全按照准则执行。

匈牙利除了部分公司外（公司的前两年收入不超过 3 亿福林，且员工人数不超过 50 人并且符合某些其他条件），都需要接受审计。受访者认为匈牙利使用的审计准则与国际审计准则（即国际会计师联合会颁布的标准）非常相似。

泰　国

国内公众公司必须使用泰国会计准则。泰国会计准则与 IFRS 实质趋同，尽管 IFRS 中的金融工具准则尚未予以采用。泰国会计准则中有些国内的金融工具准则不同于 IFRS。

准则制定者及专业机构：泰国会计职业联合会（IFAC 成员）http：//www.fap.or.th/。其职责主要包括如下方面：管理全国会计工作；起草会计法律、行政法规草案；研究提出会计改革和发展的政策建议；拟订并组织实施国家统一的会计准则制度、管理会计标准、内部控制规范、会计信息化标准等；拟订政府会计准则和行政、事业单位会计制度；负责全国会计人才工作；对注册会计师行业进行监督、指导，制订注册会计师行业规章制度和政策措施。

财务报告准则：泰国正在采取直接采用国际财务报告准则模式的过程之中。泰国现有 2 套经核准的会计准则，以及 1 套将要生效的会计准则，分别为：泰国财务报告准则（TFRSs），公众公司强制使用，非公众公司可以选择使用。泰国非公众公司会计准则（NPAEs），适用于非公众公司，未来将被泰国中小企业财务报告准则（TFRSs）替代。泰国中小企业财务报告准则（TFRSs for SMEs），适用于中小企业，目前正在准备过程中，预计将于 2018 年 1 月 1 日开始生效。

泰国财务报告准则与国际财务报告准则实际趋同，主要差异为与等效的国际财务报告准则生效日期延迟一年，即 2017 年采用 2016 年版本的国际财务报告准则。除此之外，泰国会计职业联合会承诺于 2019 年使用金融工具相关准则，即 IFRS 9、IAS 32 和 IFRS 7，在此之前，泰国会计职业联合会计划于 2017 年发布与 IFRS 9、IAS 32 和 IFRS 7 等同的泰国准则，并鼓励企业提前采用以尽可能减少金融工具方面的准则差异。

泰国的所有上市公司和金融机构，无论是合并财务报表还是单独财务报表，应当采用泰国财务报告准则（TFRSs），但也允许上市公司的财务报告采用一种泰国财务报告准则附加国际财务报告准则的方式，即在使用泰国财务报告准则的基础上，允许上市公司采用尚未被泰国财务报告准则采用的国际财务报告准则。

泰国的非公众公司目前可以选择使用泰国财务报告准则（TFRSs）或者泰国非公众公司会计准则（NPAEs）。泰国会计职业联合会声明泰国非公众公司会计准则非常简短并且使用历史成本为基础。目前，泰国会计职业联合会正在采用泰国中小企业财务报告准则（TFRSs for SMEs）的过程中，预计将于 2018 年 1 月 1 日起生效，该准则将不做修改地直接采用中小企业国际财务报告准则。当前正在研究哪些企业需要适用泰国中小企业财务报告准则。

受访者反馈，由于与国际准则趋同并只有一年的延迟，所以泰国的公司还是很好地实施了相关准则。

受访者指出，在泰国注册的公司都需要审计，其使用的审计准则与国际审计准则 IAS 非常相似。

越　　南

越南未采用 IFRS，必须采用越南会计准则（VAS）。

专业机构：越南注册会计师协会（VACPA）（IFAC 成员）http：//www. vacpa. org. vn/。

准则制定者：财政部 http：//www. mof. gov. vn。

财务报告准则：越南没有采用国际财务报告准则或与之趋同。

越南所有企业，无论是合并财务报表还是单独财务报表，都应当遵循越南财政部颁发的越南会计准则（VAS）。越南财政部在制定越南会计准则时以国际财务报告准则为基础，结合越南经济发展水平以及企业管理水平，选择性地使用国际财务报告准则的原则。至今共颁布了 26 个会计准则（2001 年至 2005 年颁布）以及被称为"通知"（circulars）的附加强制执行指引。

2015 年，越南财政部表示将会考虑朝着国际财务报告准则发展，但目前暂时还没有具体的时间表及趋同路线图。越南会计准则与国际财务报告准则仅为部分相似，两者的差异主要如下：越南会计准则下，投资按照历史成本确认和计量，并针对投资项目的净资产价值下降或作为交易性或可供出售处理的权益证券投资的市场价值下跌计提相应的准备，但不允许就投资标的市场价值上升确认收益或其他综合收益；越南会计准则不要求将权益变动表作为单独的报表列报，此外，越南会计准则有严格的报告格式和科目规定；越南会计准则规定企业合并产生的商誉在收购日起按照不超过 10 年的期限进行摊销；越南会计准则不要求对股份支付、公允价值计量进行相关的会计处理；越南会计准则无资产减值的定义，也没有针对资产减值的具体准则；越南会计准则在摊余成本、套期会计、矿产资源的勘探与评价、农业及职工薪酬方面无相关准则。

受访者提到，对于越南准则（VAS）未做明确规定的事项，企业可以参考相关 IFRS 的规定进行会计处理。受访者认为越南会计准则的实际执行效力很好，企业能完全按准则执行。越南尚未对公司治理方面的披露要求进行规定。

在越南，以下类型企业的年度财务报表需要进行审计：外商投资企业的年度财务报表；根据《信贷机构法》设立和运营的信贷机构的年度财务报表，包括外资银行在越南设立分行的年度财务报表；金融机构、保险企业、再保险企业、保险经纪和非人寿保险企业分支机构的年度财务报表；上市公司、证券发行人和组织的年度财务报表；国有企业的年度财务报表，按照国家保密规定应保密的除外；国家重大项目、政府提供资金的 A 级项目竣工决算报告，按照国家保密规定应保密的除外；国家持股占 20% 以上的公司的年度财务报表；上市机构、发行人、证券业务组织在财政年度末持股 20% 以上的企业的年度财务报表；审计公司及外国审计公司在越南的分支机构的年度财务报表。ODA 资金项目、优惠贷款项目年度财务报告必须由国家审计机构执行审计，或与出资方达成一致，由独立审计师出具审计报告。

受访者认为越南使用的审计准则与国际审计准则比较相似。

俄罗斯

上市公司、金融机构和一些政府所有的公司必须采用 IFRS。在俄罗斯上市的外国上市公司必须采用 IFRS。

专业机构：俄罗斯审计厅（IFAC 成员）http：//www. sroapr. ru/。俄罗斯审计联合会（IFAC 成员）http：//org-rsa. ru/。

准则制定者：俄罗斯联邦财政部 http：//minfin. ru/ru/。其主要职责如下：监管和发展预算、税收和海关政策；监管簿记、会计和报告职能和审计活动；监管国家债务、文件问题；监管和设立国家储备基金和国家福利基金；国际金融关系和国际合作；启动相关改革；金融市场活动；对保险和银行活动、信贷合作、小额金融活动的监管；监管彩票和博彩业公司；"电子预算"制度的建立和发展等。

财务报告准则：俄罗斯目前主要有两种适用的会计准则，分别为俄罗斯会计准则以及国际财务报告准则。第一，须采用俄罗斯财政部签署批准的国际财务报告准则的情况。如下行业的公司须采用国际财务报告准则编制合并财务报表：信贷机构；保险公司（不包括只提供强制医疗保险服务的医疗保险公司）；非政府养老基金；管理投资基金、共同基金、非政府养老基金的公司；清算机构；联邦单位组织，名单经俄罗斯联邦政府批准；联邦政府持有股份的股份公司，名单经俄罗斯联邦政府批准；其他上市公司。俄罗斯有一套审核批准采用国际财务报告准则的流程。所有新准则及修订都要通过国家会计准则专家委员会的批准，国家会计准则专家委员会是俄罗斯财政部下属的机构。第二，须使用俄罗斯当地会计准则（RAS）的情况：所有在俄罗斯注册的法律实体必须采用俄罗斯当地准则 RAS 编制以 12 月 31 日为资产负债表日的财务报告。需要在资产负债表日后的 3 个月报备税务局及相关统计部门。

经受访者反映，RAS 与国际财务报告准则部分相似，受访者提到两者的主要差异描述如下：对于 RAS 报告，严格规定了相关披露要求：报告货币必须是俄罗斯卢布，报告年度为日历年（没有其他选择），并以俄语为报告语言；合并财务报表：在国际财务报告准则中，母公司应编制合并财务报表，只有少数例外存在。在 RAS 中，母公司只有在符合联邦法律规定的要求时，才应根据国际财务报告准则编制合并财务报表，比如保险公司、银行、上市公司及其他规定的企业；公允价值及货币时间价值：根据国际财务报告准则，某些资产和负债应以公允价值计量。而在 RAS 中没有类似公允价值的要求，资产和负债通常按历史成本计量；固定资产减值：根据国际财务报告准则，如果有任何迹象表明资产可能有减值风险，固定资产应进行减值测试。RAS 下没有减值测试要求。国际财务报告准则中在融资租赁情况下，承租人需要在资产负债表中确认租入的固定资产，并将其折旧计入承租人的利润表中。在 RAS 资产中，根据租赁协议的条款确认资产。基于法律形式的不同，将根据租赁协议的条款在承租人或出租人资产负债表中确认固定资产，并据此将其折旧计入承租人或出租人的利润表中。

此外，国际财务报告准则中的某些准则如套期、股份支付、养老金计划等 RAS 都未包含，在这种情况下，公司可以参照国际财务报告准则进行相关会计处理。

对于会计准则的实际实施情况，受访者表示实施情况较好，能做到完全实施。此外，受访者表示，俄罗斯没有相关公司治理方面的非财务报告披露要求。

在俄罗斯，下述企业的财务报表必须执行审计：股份公司；证券交易所有证券交易的公司；银行和其他贷款机构、保险公司、信贷局、养老金和投资基金、证券市场参与者和证券交易所；上一财政年度的年收入超过 4 亿卢布的公司；上一日历年 12 月 31 日的公司总资产价值高于 6000 万卢布的公司；信贷机构；保险公司（不包括只提供强制医疗保险服务的医疗保险公司）；非政府养老基金；管理投资基金、共同基金、非政府养老基金的公司；清算机构；联邦单位组织。名单经俄罗斯联邦政府批准；联邦政府持有股份的股份公司。名单经俄罗斯联邦政府批准；其他上市公司。

受访者反映，根据最近的立法变化，从 2017 年 1 月起，俄罗斯审计部门将按照国际会计师联合会通过并在俄罗斯正式批准的国际审计准则执行。此外，立法规定，审计人员有义务向审计委托人和管理人通报任何腐败和其他违法行为情况以及此类犯罪的潜在风险。如果审计客户代表在 90 天内未采取适当行动，审计人员应通知有关国家当局。

印度尼西亚

印度尼西亚尚未要求国内企业采用 IFRS。印度尼西亚正致力于实现其国家准则与 IFRS 的趋同，但并不打算全面采用 IFRS。所有在公开市场上进行证券交易的外国公司都必须使用印度尼西亚的国家会计准则。

专业机构：印度尼西亚注册会计师协会（IIPCA）（IFAC 成员）http：//iapi. or. id。

准则制定者：印度尼西亚财务会计准则委员会（DSAK IAI 为印度尼西亚会计师协会的组成部分）http：//www. iaiglobal. or. id/。IAI 的主要职责有：举行专业会计师资格考试（印度尼西亚注册会计师考试）；举行持续专业教育以维持专业人员能力；制定和建立职业道德守则、专业标准和会计准则；监督成员纪律；以及在印度尼西亚发展会计职业。

财务报告准则：印度尼西亚采取了与国际财务报告准则趋同的模式。印度尼西亚现有如下 4 套会计准则：第一，财务会计准则，由 DSAK IAI 发布的财务会计准则（PSAK）和会计准则解释（ISAK）组成。这套标准是由国际财务报告准则转换而来。第二，伊斯兰会计准则（SAS）适用于按照伊斯兰教义执行交易的实体。第三，非公共责任实体的财务会计标准（SAK ETAP）旨在由不具有重大公共责任的实体在向外部用户发布通用财务报表时使用。第四，微型、小型和中型实体财务会计准则，适用于没有或者不能满足非公共责任实体财务会计准则（SAK ETAP）的微型、小型和中型实体。

印度尼西亚与国际准则趋同的模式是，保留当地的会计准则（PSAK），逐步将当地准则与国际准则尽可能地趋同。

需要说明的是，当前，印度尼西亚财务会计准则委员会已经完成了第二阶段与国际准则之间趋同的工作，将趋同的国际准则版本从 3 年缩小到 1 年，即实现截至 2015 年 1 月 1 日的印度尼西亚会计准则与 2014 年版的国际财务报告准则实质性相同，但仍会有部分差异。2016 年 5 月国际财务报告

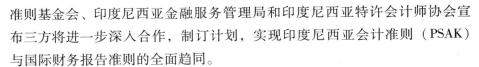

准则基金会、印度尼西亚金融服务管理局和印度尼西亚特许会计师协会宣布三方将进一步深入合作，制订计划，实现印度尼西亚会计准则（PSAK）与国际财务报告准则的全面趋同。

印度尼西亚会计准则（PSAK）与国际财务报告准则的主要差异如下：

1. 合并财务报表

印度尼西亚会计准则在判断是否合并时，不仅考虑是否满足"控制"的定义，同时会加入相关风险报酬的考虑因素。此外，对于控制的定义，印度尼西亚会计准则主要偏重于股权比例的考虑，即当母公司持有一个实体半数以上的投票权时，控制被假定存在，除非在特殊情况下可以清楚地表明这种所有权不构成控制。

2. 对合营企业投资的核算

印度尼西亚会计准则规定，投资方应使用比例合并法，或者作为一种替代方法，使用权益法确认对合营企业的权益。

3. 公允价值

在投资性房地产、无形资产、租赁、收入、金融资产等准则中，印度尼西亚会计准则对于"公允价值"的定义与国际财务报告准则不同。印度尼西亚会计准则中对于公允价值的定义为：在公平交易中，熟悉情况的交易双方自愿进行资产交换或者债务清偿的金额。而在 IFRS 13 中强调公允价值是一种"退出价格"。

受访者反馈，在印度尼西亚会计准则的实际执行效力较强，企业均能完全按准则执行。印度尼西亚目前没有相关就公司治理等非财务报告的披露要求。

受访者指出，根据印度尼西亚对有限责任公司的规定，财务报表须进行审计的实体标准如下：收集和/或管理公共资金的实体（银行、保险等）；向公众发行债务证书（如债券）的实体；上市实体；资产总额高于 500 亿印度尼西亚盾的实体；外国投资实体。

受访者反馈，印度尼西亚使用的审计准则与国际审计准则完全一致。

哈萨克斯坦

所有上市公司、金融机构和大型非上市公司都必须采用 IFRS。允许在哈萨克斯坦上市的外国公司采用 IFRS，或者亦可采用美国通用会计准则。

专业机构：哈萨克斯坦审计师公会 http：//www. audit. kz/。

准则制定者：哈萨克斯坦财政部（MOF）http：//www. minfin. gov. kz/irj/portal/anonymous。其主要职责如下：确保会计和财务报告领域国家政策的形成和实施；确定会计秩序；采纳哈萨克斯坦共和国关于会计和财务报告的规范性法律行为；制定和批准国家标准和准则；制定和批准标准会计科目表；与其他国家机构和专业组织交流会计和财务报告；认可专业组织、认证机构。哈萨克斯坦中央银行（NBK）http：//www. nationalbank. kz/？docid=3321&switch=english。

财务报告准则：对银行业而言，加入哈萨克斯坦存款保险项目的银行都需要按照国际财务报告准则编制财务报表。从 2004 年开始，由于所有银行已加入该存款保险项目，所以银行已全部按照国际财务报告准则编制财务报表。其他所有企业从 2006 年 1 月 1 日开始已全部按照国际财务报告准则 IFRS 编制财务报告。中小企业必须使用基于中小企业国际财务报告准则（IFRS for SMEs）的哈萨克斯坦国家财务报告准则第 2 号（KNFRS#2）。小型企业，根据哈萨克斯坦共和国的税收立法，对农民或农场企业，法人实体农产品生产者实施特殊税收制度，并在简化申报的基础上，使用哈萨克斯坦国家财务报告准则第 1 号（KNFRS#1）。

受访者反映，除了小型企业在准则实施效力方面略微有些不足之外，其他实体在准则的实施过程中的执行力度都非常强，能够完全按准则执行。

经受访者反馈，在哈萨克斯坦需要经审计的主要情况如下：股份公司；在教育和卫生领域设有监事会的国有企业；保险（再保险）组织、保险控股、保险（再保险）组织和保险控股为主要参与者的组织以及保险经纪人；单一累积养老金基金和投资组合经理；银行、银行控股机构以及银行和

（或）银行控股为主要参与者的组织；民航组织，但在哈萨克斯坦共和国政府确定的名单上从事航空工作的航空公司除外；社会保险基金；签署投资合同并提供投资优惠的哈萨克斯坦共和国的法人实体等。

此外，根据 2017 年 3 月 11 日生效的审计法，哈萨克斯坦的有限责任合伙企业，在同时符合以下两项标准时，必须执行强制性的年度审计：第一，他们至少拥有 2 名股东，其中一名股东持有的股份占注册资本比例小于10%；第二，年平均职工人数超过 250 人以及/或者根据月度计算指标年平均收入超过 300 万哈萨克斯坦坚戈。其他实体也可以自愿选择进行审计。受访者反馈，哈萨克斯坦使用的审计准则与国际审计准则一致。

印　度

印度会计准则（Ind AS）是基于并实质趋同于 IFRS。印度尚未要求国内企业采用 IFRS，亦尚未正式承诺采用 IFRS。允许在印度上市的外国公司采用 IFRS。

专业机构：印度特许会计师公会（ICAI）http：//www. icai. org/。

准则制定者：印度国家公司事务部会计准则咨询委员会（NACAS）。

财务报告准则：印度采取与国际财务报告准则趋同的模式。

印度采用印度会计准则，该准则是根据国际会计准则理事会颁布的国际财务报告准则（IFRS）为基础并且与国际财务报告准则（IFRS）实际趋同。印度原计划从 2011 年开始分阶段实施与国际财务报告准则 IFRS 的趋同，但是最终将印度会计准则转换的时间延后至 2015 年。在 2015 年 1 月，印度国家公司事务部会计准则咨询委员会发布了修订后的趋同路径图，其显示出了如下信息：

（1）所有公司，包括未上市的以及在中小企业板上市的公司，在编制自 2015 年 4 月 1 日或以后日期开始的年度财务报表时，可以采用印度会计准则。

（2）下列相关企业在编制自 2016 年 4 月 1 日或以后日期开始的年度财务报表时，必须使用印度会计准则：公司权益或者债券已在印度（不含中小企业板）或者印度以外的资本市场上市或正在上市申报过程中的，且净资产高于 50 亿卢比的公司；其他净资产高于 50 亿卢比的公司；上述公司的控股公司、子公司、合营及联营公司。

（3）下列相关企业在编制自 2017 年 4 月 1 日或以后日期开始的年度财务报表时，必须使用印度会计准则：公司权益或者债券已在印度（不含中小企业板）或印度以外的资本市场上市或正在上市申报过程中的，且净资产低于 50 亿卢比的公司；其他净资产低于 50 亿卢比但高于 25 亿卢比的公司；上述公司的控股公司、子公司、合营及联营公司。

（4）银行，保险公司及其他金融机构。2016 年 1 月 18 日，印度政府宣布商业银行、保险公司及其他非银金融机构，自 2018 年 4 月 1 日起必须按照印度会计准则编制财务报表并附上前期可比数据。

受访者指出印度会计准则适用于单体财务报表以及合并财务报表；海外子公司、联营公司、合资企业和印度公司的其他类似实体可根据特定的管辖要求编制其单体财务报表；一旦印度公司采用了印度会计准则，在随后的年度必须一贯遵循。

受访者反馈，印度会计准则并没有完全与国际财务报告准则趋同，两者的相似程度为部分相同。以下列举了部分主要差异：

1. 租赁

在国际财务报告准则下，租赁付款应在租赁期内以直线方式确认为费用，除非另一种系统的方法更能代表承租人获得利益的模式。而印度会计准则规定，在经营租赁的情况下，租赁费按照租赁协议的约定计入损益表中，除非向出租人支付的款项按照预计的通货膨胀率进行调整，以补偿出租人预期的通货膨胀成本上涨。

2. 企业合并

国际财务报告准则第 3 号要求企业合并产生的廉价购买收益作为一项收入确认在损益表中。而印度会计准则规定廉价购买收入作为资本溢价计入权益。此外，印度会计准则涵盖了同一控制下企业合并的相关规定，而国际准则无此内容。

3. 不动产、厂场和设备

国际财务报告准则允许使用重估价值模式核算不动产、厂场和设备，而印度会计准则禁止使用这一模式。此外，在国际财务报告准则中与资产相关的政府补助可以扣减资产的账面金额，而在印度会计准则下禁止使用这一方法。

4. 投资性房地产

国际财务报告准则允许两种模式计量投资性房地产，即成本模式及公允价值模式，而印度会计准则只允许成本模式计量。

受访者反映会计准则在当地的实际实施情况非常好。

自 1913 第一部公司法通过以来，对公司账户的审计在印度是强制性的。此后，印度特许会计师公会（ICAI），负责管理在印度的注册会计师并维护印度的会计准则。所有的注册会计师都是 ICAI 的成员，必须遵守 ICAI 与审计与鉴证准则委员会规定的标准（AASB）。

印度的审计一般分为法定审计、内部审计及税务审计。法定审计用以向印度政府和股东报告公司财务状况和账目情况。此类审计由合格的审计人员作为外部和独立的第三方执行。法定审计的审计报告以政府机构规定的格式出具。内部审计是按照内部管理的要求进行的，以检查公司的财务健康状况，分析组织的运作效率。内部审计可以由独立的第三方或公司自己的内部人员来执行。税务审计是印度 1961 年《所得税法案》第 44ab 条规定的规定业务营业额超过 1000 万卢比，以及那些行业收入超过 500 万卢比的对象，必须由独立注册会计师进行审计。应当指出，税务审计适用于每个人，无论是个人、合伙企业、公司或任何其他实体。

在印度的审计工作根据印度的审计准则执行，受访者认为其与国际审计准备颇为相似。

巴基斯坦

在公开市场进行证券交易的国内公司和外国公司、金融机构、公共事业和大型公司必须使用巴基斯坦采纳的 IFRS。IFRS 当中的一些重要的准则尚未采纳。

专业机构：巴基斯坦特许会计师公会（ICAP）http：//www. icap. org. pk/。巴基斯坦成本与管理会计师公会（ICMAP）https：//www. icmap. com. pk/。

准则制定者：巴基斯坦特许会计师公会（ICAP）http：//www. icap. org. pk/。巴基斯坦特许会计师公会（ICAP）负责审查和通过巴基斯坦的会计准则。ICAP 也是伊斯兰财务会计准则的制定机构。ICAP 关键职责还包括：就有争议事项提供会计意见和就会计及审计问题发布技术信息；编制财务法案和公司法提案草案；对成员和其他机构的询问作出答复。

财务报告准则：巴基斯坦规定上市公司、银行及其他金融机构及对国家经济有重大影响的企业（ESE）适用国际财务报告准则。中型企业采用中小企业国际财务报告准则。小型企业采用 ICAP 制定的小型企业会计及财务报告准则。要注意的是，巴基斯坦采纳了大部分但并非全部国际财务报告准则。主要差异如下：IFRS 1（首次采用国际财务报告准则）未被巴基斯坦采纳。IFRIC 4（确定一项协议是否包含租赁）以及 IFRIC 12（服务特许权协议）也未被采纳。巴基斯坦正在考虑是否采纳 IFRS 9（金融工具）。IFRS 14（递延管制账户）、IFRS 15（客户合同收入）以及 IFRS 16（租赁）也还未被采纳。此外，IAS 39、IAS 40 以及 IFRS 7 未被受巴基斯坦国家银行（SBP）监管的银行及其他金融机构采纳。SBP 已经为此类金融机构制定了银行及其他金融机构如何确认计量相关金融工具的标准。但是这些准则适用于其他不受 SBP 监管的公司。

受访者反馈，巴基斯坦会计准则的实际执行效力很好，企业都能够完全按准则执行。巴基斯坦证券交易委员会（SECP）提供的非财务披露指引是交易所上市规则的一部分。SECP 根据最佳国际惯例，为上市实体、公共部门公司、非上市实体和保险公司提供了公司治理指南，详细说明了必须披露的强制性披露要求。

在巴基斯坦，所有按《公司条例1984》在 SECP 注册的公司，都被要求在每次年度股东大会上委任审计师（《公司条例》第 233 条和第 252 条）。最近颁布的 2017 年《新公司法》规定，对实收资本少于一百万卢比的公司提供豁免。但在该豁免情况下，公司仍需提交正式认证的财务报表至 SECP 公司注册处。此外，受访者指出，巴基斯坦使用并一贯遵循国际审计准则。

第二部分 "一带一路"沿线国家
税制与税负差异

"一带一路"沿线 65 个国家的经济发展水平各异,既有以新加坡为代表的高收入国家,以罗马尼亚为代表的中高收入国家,也有以印度为代表的中低收入国家,还有以柬埔寨为代表的低收入国家。不同国家在税制方面的共性在于均以公司所得税、个人所得税(个别国家没有,如阿联酋和卡塔尔)和货物与劳务税(大多为增值税)为主,差异在于税制结构因经济发展水平不同而不同。经济发展水平越高,则所得税比重越高,货物与劳务税比重越低。

具体到税种和税负,公司所得税的平均税率为 19.3%,最高为阿联酋的 55%,最低为乌兹别克斯坦的 7.5%;个人所得税的平均税率为 23.4%,最高为以色列和斯洛文尼亚的 50%,最低为黑山的 9%;货物与劳务税的平均税率为 16.7%,最高为匈牙利的 27%,最低为也门的 5%。社会保障税(或缴费)也是企业的重要负担,雇主负担的平均税(费)率为 18.5%,最高为俄罗斯的 47.5%,最低为缅甸的 3%;雇员负担的平均税(费)率为 11.2%,最高为波黑的 31%,最低为白俄罗斯的 1%。

企业"走出去"的过程中不仅关注东道国的税种、税率和税收优惠情况,更加关注税收风险。

企业对外投资的税收风险主要包括五个方面:第一,重复征税的风险。第二,未充分享受税收协定待遇的风险。第三,因转让定价和反避税问题导致的风险,83% 的受访企业将转让定价问题视为防止税基侵蚀和利润转移(BEPS)行动计划中对企业最大的挑战。第四,海外并购标的企业的历史税收问题的风险。第五,税收歧视风险。

我国已与"一带一路"沿线 54 个国家签订了双边税收协定,大多数协定不仅给予我国"走出去"企业在利息、股息和特许权使用费等预提所得税上的优惠税率待遇，而且成为企业"走出去"防范税收风险，保护自身权益的重要保障。

应对税收风险的正确路径是"制度、企业和税务部门"三管齐下，统一发力。

首先，完善国内和国际税收制度，做好顶层设计。一方面，面对"一带一路"倡议下企业大规模"走出去"的现实需要，我国涉外税收制度亟待完善。比如，当前"分国不分项限额抵免"的制度会导致"高税率国家抵免不尽、低税率国家抵免结余但不能调剂"的重复征税问题更加突出。另一方面，陈旧、过时的税收协定需要尽快修订。

其次，企业积极应对，防控税收风险。在顶层设计的保障之下，防控税收风险的关键在于企业主动作为。

最后，发挥税务部门力量，国际协调托底。企业在对外投资中因对制度、政策、协定理解的分歧或税收歧视，几乎不可避免会发生税务争议事件，仅凭企业自身可能难以保障合理的权益，应发挥我国税务部门的力量，通过国际税收协调来解决问题。

新加坡

1. 税种、税负及税收优惠

（1）税种及税负。

新加坡公司所得税的纳税人分为居民纳税人和非居民纳税人，如果一家公司的管理和控制地在新加坡境内，该公司即为新加坡居民企业。新加坡公司所得税税率为17%。居民企业及在新加坡设有常设机构的非居民企业就来源于新加坡的经营所得以及在新加坡收到的来源于新加坡以外的收入纳税。没有常设机构的非居民公司仅就来源于新加坡的所得（如利息、特许权使用费、技术服务费等）纳税。对于股息收入（包括股票红利收入）一般是免税的。与取得所得相关的收益性支出，可以在计算应税所得额时予以扣除。其他可扣除费用包括以前年度结转的资本折让、税务亏损等。亏损可以无限期地向以后年度结转，但须通过股权合规测试。在通过股权测试的情况下，亏损及未抵扣资本折让可以向前结转1年，最高限额为10万新加坡元。

新加坡不征收资本利得税及其他的附件税，无参股免税、控股公司特殊规定的相关法规。

新加坡对提供应税货物和服务以及进口货物征收货物与劳务税，标准税率为7%，对国际服务和出口贸易为零税率。这一货物与劳务税类似于我国的增值税。

新加坡个人所得税的纳税人分居民纳税人和非居民纳税人，新加坡对来源于新加坡的所得征税，而不论个人是否在新加坡居住或款项在哪里取得，来源于新加坡以外的所得通常情况下不征税。以雇佣所得为例，对来源地的判断取决于雇佣劳务在哪里发生，而非哪里支付或雇主是否为新加坡居民。新加坡的个人所得税按累进税率征税，税率为2%～20%。非居民个人的受雇所得以15%的统一税率（未扣除任何个人免税部分）和居民所得税率中较高者纳税。非居民个人来源于新加坡的所有其他收入，包括董事费和顾问费，应按 20% 的统一税率征税。非居民个人（公司董事除外）在新加坡的短期受雇（即受雇时间不超过 60 天），可免于纳税。

新加坡居民企业支付给非居民的相关收入应缴纳预提所得税。一般来说，利息和租金收入的预提所得税税率为 15%，特许权使用费的预提所得税税率为 10%。对于与新加坡签订了双边税收协定的国家，该国居民来源于新加坡的所得有可能享受更低的预提所得税率。

整体而言，新加坡税制简单，企业税负较低。

（2）税收优惠。

新加坡对新兴产业、公司总部活动、金融业、资产证券化、基金经理、国际海事活动、国际贸易、研发活动等提供多种税收优惠激励措施。

2. 税收协定

新加坡与包括我国在内的多个国家签订了双边税收协定。根据中加税收协定，股息预提所得税税率为 5% 或 10%；利息预提所得税税率为 7% 或 10%，非协定国家为 15%；特许权使用费预提所得税税率为 6% 或 10%，非协定国家为 10%。税收协定使我国企业可以享受更低的税负。

3. 税收风险及争议处理

关于税务争议，新加坡税制简单，执法较为规范，发生税务争议事件较少。发生税务争议可依据税收协定进行协商，或通过法律途径解决。受访者表示，整体来看，在新加坡投资经营的企业税负较低，税制透明度、稳定性、法定化程度和执法规范度均较高，企业税收风险较小。税务争议事件较少，且发生后可通过协商或法律途径解决。

新加坡现行主要税种及税率参考　　　　　　　　单位:%

税　　种	税率（比例）
公司所得税	17
个人所得税	2 ~ 20
货物与劳务税	7
雇主负担的社会保险	17
雇员负担的社会保险	20

马来西亚

1. 税种、税负及税收优惠

（1）税种及税负。

公司所得税的纳税人分为居民纳税人和非居民纳税人，管理与控制在马来西亚的企业是马来西亚居民企业。公司需就来源于马来西亚的收入纳税，来源于外国的收入则不需纳税，除非公司从事银行业、保险业、航空运输或船运业务。公司所得税的标准税率为24%。中小型居民企业最初获得的50万林吉特应纳税所得额将按照18%的税率征税，超额部分适用标准税率。亏损可无限期向以后年度结转进行抵扣（休眠公司的所有权发生重大变更的情况除外），亏损不可向以前年度进行追溯调整。

马来西亚居民企业支付给非居民的相关收入应在马来西亚缴纳预提所得税。对支付给非居民的股息不征税。对支付给非居民的利息和特许权使用费分别适用15%与10%的预提税。对向非居民支付的技术服务费征收10%的预提税。对向非居民支付的动产租金、在马来西亚提供的安装服务费及某些一次性收入征收10%的预提税，对于与马来西亚签订了双边税收协定的国家，该国居民来源于马来西亚的所得有可能享受更低的预提所得税率。

整体而言，马来西亚企业的税负水平居中。

（2）税收优惠。

马来西亚对于特定行业比如制造业、信息技术服务业、生物技术业、伊斯兰金融业、节能与环保业，有较多税收优惠政策。优惠政策包括：针对处于行业领先地位的企业给予长达10年的免税期；对资本投资给予60%~100%的免税额，可长达10年；以及加速折旧和摊销、费用加计扣除、再投资免税政策等。具体而言，包括以下方面：

对于获得"新兴工业地位"资格的外商投资企业，从生产之日（指日产达到最高产量的30%当天）起，5年内只对公司30%的营业利润征缴所得税。

对于高科技公司、从事科学研究与开发及在"多媒体超级走廊"内设立电子信息通讯科技企业的，5年内免缴所得税。

对设立机构进行科学技术转让及培训的，10年内免缴所得税。对于向马来西亚国内公司或个人转让先进技术的外商企业，其技术转让费免缴所得税。对涉及国家重大利益和对国家经济发展有重大影响的战略性项目，及对生产优先开发的机械设备及其零部件的，10年内免缴企业所得税。

投资于环保产业领域，5年内公司营业利润的70%免缴所得税，但对于从事植树造林的，10年内免缴企业所得税。

对于投资于财政部核定的粮食生产（包括槿麻、蔬菜、水果、药用植物、香料、水产物及牛羊等牲畜饲养）的企业，10年内免缴企业所得税。对于出口鲜果和干果、鲜花与干花、观赏植物和观赏鱼的，可免缴相当于其营业利润10%的所得税。

对于生产清真食品（HALAL），为取得HALAL食品品质验证和鉴定的支出，可相应从其所得税中扣除。

对于出口型企业，如其出口额增长30%，出口增加额的10%免缴所得税；如其出口额增长50%，出口增加额的15%免缴所得税。

对信息与通讯科技企业，其出口增加额的50%免缴所得税。

对在兰卡威岛从事豪华游艇维修服务及在马来西亚提供豪华游艇出租服务的，5年内免缴所得税。

对在马来西亚设立地区营运总部和采购中心的，5年内免缴所得税，5年期满后，经申请核准后，可再延长5年免缴所得税。

对参与马来西亚工业发展计划的外商投资企业，5年免缴所得税，其用于培训员工、产品开发测试及公产审计方面的支出，可从其所得税中扣除。如作为供应商，其产品在价格、品质和技术含量上能达到世界水平，经核准后，可免缴10年的所得税。

对为出口产品（出口量占其生产量的80%以上）而进口的原材料和零部件免缴进口税。对国内不能生产或虽能生产但质量或标准不符合要求的机械设备，免征进口税和销售税。

对国内能生产且质量和标准符合要求的机械设备，如用于环境保护、废物再利用及有毒有害性物品的储存和处理的，用于研发机构和培训的以及用于种植业的机器设备，经申请，也可免缴进口税和销售税。用于旅馆和旅游服务的进口材料和设备免缴进口税和销售税。

对于经核准的外商投资的教育培训设备（包括实验设备、车间、摄影室和语言实验室等）可免缴进口税、销售税和国产税（注：马来西亚对国内生产的一些特定产品，包括香烟、酒类、纸牌和麻将牌及机动车辆等，征收国产税）。

对直接用于财政部核准的服务业项目的原材料和零部件及其消耗品，如国内无法生产或虽能生产但质量或标准不符合要求的，可免缴进口税和销售税，本地采购的设备和机械免缴销售税和国产税。

对设在"多媒体超级走廊"内的企业所用的有关设备免征进口税。基础建设及工业建筑税减免。为特定目的建造和购买建筑设施（包括经核准的行业用于工业生产、研发和员工生活自用的房屋等），第一年可免缴10%的工业建筑税，以后每年可免缴3%，最长期限为30年。投资在东马来西亚和"东部走廊"的公司，可免缴全部的基础建设费。有关费用豁免。

对为促进马来西亚产品及品牌而发生的广告费用支出，经申请核准后，可相应从其所得税中扣除。

2. 税收协定

马来西亚与包括我国在内的72个国家签订了双边税收协定，税收协定在避免双重征税、降低企业税负方面发挥了重要的作用。当然，随着经济活动的日益频繁，一些新的经济收入尚未被纳入双边税收协定，需在未来修订税收协定时进行完善。

3. 税收风险及争议处理

关于税务争议案件的相关问题，受访企业表示没有明显的税务争议。如果有则通过协商解决，若协商无法达成一致，则通过法律途径解决。受访者表示，整体来看，在马来西亚投资经营的企业税收风险可控。但同时，马来西亚税务机关对于纳税人自觉遵从的要求越来越高，要注意做好与当地税务机关的事前沟通，降低税收风险。

马来西亚现行主要税种及税率参考　　　　　　　　单位:%

税　　种	税率（比例）
公司所得税	24
个人所得税	0～28
货物与劳务税	6
房产盈利税	5～30
进口税	5～35
房产交易印花税	1～3
股票交易印花税	0.3
雇主负担的社会保险	12
雇员负担的社会保险	12

阿联酋

1. 税种、税负及税收优惠

（1）税种及税负。

阿联酋主要税种是公司所得税，且只适用于石油和天然气开采和生产公司、外国银行分支机构和特定政府特许协议下的某些石化公司，对其他公司的所得不予征税。外国银行分支机构根据其运营地所在酋长国的法定税率缴税，目前统一税率为20%。而对石油和天然气开采和生产公司，统一税率为迪拜50%和阿布扎比55%。

阿联酋没有附加税，无股息的征税、资本利得、可替代最低税、境外税收抵免、参股免税方面的规定，不征收预提所得税。同时，阿联酋对个人收入不予征税。阿联酋可能于2018年1月1日征收5%的增值税。

整体来看，企业在阿联酋投资运营税负较低。

（2）税收优惠。

阿联酋在其自由贸易区内，对于进口至自贸区的货物给予50年的税收优惠或豁免（可延期）。

2. 税收协定

阿联酋与包括我国在内的70多个国家签订了双边税收协定，税收协定在避免双重征税、降低企业税负方面发挥了重要的作用。

3. 税收风险及争议处理

关于税务争议案件的相关问题，由于税制相对简单，受访企业表示没有明显的税务争议。

受访者表示，整体来看，在阿联酋投资经营的企业税收负担较低，但在透明度、法定化程度和执法规范性上还有待提升，风险可控，但要做好应对。

阿联酋现行主要税种及税率参考　　　　　单位:%

税　　种	税率（比例）
外国银行分支机构统一税率	20
石油天然气开采和生产公司（迪拜）	50
石油天然气开采和生产公司（阿布扎比）	50

波　兰

1. 税种、税负及税收优惠

（1）税种及税负。

波兰公司所得税的纳税人分为居民纳税人和非居民纳税人，如果公司或者有限股份制合伙企业（有些情况下例外）的注册地或管理地在波兰，则该公司为波兰的居民纳税人。居民纳税人就其全球收入纳税，非居民纳税人仅就来源于波兰的收入纳税。波兰公司所得税的标准税率为19%。

波兰在销售货物、提供劳务、进出口货物以及同一实体间不同分支机构采购销售货物需要缴纳增值税，标准税率为23%。部分货物及劳务适用5%和8%的优惠税率；其他货物与服务（例如，同一实体内销售、出口等）可适用零税率或免税。

波兰个人所得税的纳税人分居民纳税人和非居民纳税人，居民纳税人需要就全球收入在波兰进行纳税，非居民纳税人就其来源于波兰的收入纳税。波兰个人所得税适用18%~32%的累进税率，从事经营活动的个人也可选择适用特别规定，即通常适用19%的税率但同时不予任何减免。

波兰居民企业支付给非居民的相关收入应缴纳预提所得税。一般来说，向非居民纳税人支付的股息应征以19%的预提税，利息收入的预提所得税税率为20%，特许权使用费的预提所得税税率为20%。与波兰签订双边税收协定的国家，其预提所得税税率往往较低。

整体而言，波兰企业的税负水平居中。

（2）税收优惠。

在税收优惠方面，在某些情况下，为获得知识产权所发生的支出可抵减应纳税所得额。小型企业与新办企业也可享受一项不超过50000欧元的一次性折旧扣除。设立于波兰经济特区的企业可享受一定程度的税收优惠。

2. 税收协定

波兰与包括我国在内的多个国家签订了双边税收协定，税收协定在避免双重征税、降低企业税负方面发挥了重要的作用。根据我国与波兰的税收协定，股息预提所得税税率为 10%，利息预提所得税税率为 10%，特许权使用费预提所得税税率为 7% 或 10%。

3. 税收风险及争议处理

关于税务争议案件的相关问题，受访企业表示没有遇到明显的税务争议。受访者表示，整体来看，在波兰投资经营的企业税负适中，但税制透明度、稳定性和法定化程度均不高，税收制度执行规范程度一般，有可能带来较大税收风险。

波兰现行主要税种及税率参考　　　　　　　　单位:%

税　　种	税率（比例）
公司所得税	19
个人所得税	18 ~ 32
增值税	5、8、23
雇主负担的社会保险	20.61

捷　　克

1. 税种、税负及税收优惠

（1）税种及税负。

捷克公司所得税的纳税人分为居民纳税人和非居民纳税人，如果一家公司在捷克成立或实际管理和控制地在捷克，该公司即为捷克的居民纳税人。居民纳税人就其全球收入纳税，非居民纳税人仅就来源于捷克的收入纳税。捷克公司所得税的标准税率为 19%。亏损可向以后年度结转 5 年，不得向以前年度追溯调整。一些反滥用的法律条款限制了税收亏损的利用，即当参与公司股权或控制的组成人员有重大变化时税收亏损不可扣除，除非 80% 的所得是由发生亏损的相同活动所产生的。

捷克就出售货物和提供服务征收增值税。进口货物和国内货物采用相同的税率缴纳增值税，非欧盟国家出口的货物免缴增值税。捷克的标准税率为 21%，减免税率为 15%。

捷克个人所得税的纳税人分居民纳税人和非居民纳税人，居民纳税人需要就全球收入在捷克进行纳税，非居民纳税人就其来源于捷克的收入纳税。个人所得税的法定税率为 15%。如果一个日历年内工资薪金所得超过平均基本工资的 48 倍，税率将增加 7%。个人都应进行独立的纳税申报，不能进行联合申报。个人所得税的应纳税所得有 5 个基本来源：雇佣、实业经营、资本运作、财产租赁和其他。来源于国内的股息和利息所得按一次性代扣代缴，并且分开纳税。资本利得通常按 15% 的税率征税；但是，如果满足某些条件，资本利得可免税。抵押贷款利息、人寿和补充养老金保险以及赠与可以在税前扣除。纳税人可享受其自身、配偶和子女的法定扣除额度。但是，如果纳税人选择了一次性扣除费用或者领取养老金的情况下，扣除与减免将受到限制。

捷克居民企业支付给非居民的相关收入应缴纳预提所得税。一般来说，股息、利息和特许权使用费的预提所得税税率为 15% 或 35%。对于与捷克签订了双边税收协定的国家，该国居民来源于捷克的所得有可能享受更低的预提所得税税率。

整体而言，捷克企业的税负水平居中。

（2）税收优惠。

税收优惠方面，在一定情况下有投资激励，包括为期 10 年的税收减免、创造就业拨款、员工再培训补助和与房地产相关的激励。从事研发活动的企业可享受研发费用加计扣除的优惠政策。

2. 税收协定

捷克与包括我国在内的 70 多个国家签订了双边税收协定，税收协定在避免双重征税、降低企业税负方面发挥了重要的作用。根据我国与捷克的税收协定，股息预提所得税税率为 5% 或 10%，非协定国家为 15% 或 35%；利息预提所得税税率为 7.5%，非协定国家为 15% 或 35%；特许权使用费预提所得税税率为 10%，非协定国家为 15% 或 35%。

3. 税收风险及争议处理

关于税务争议案件的相关问题，受访企业表示在捷克有标准、规范的流程来解决税务争议。受访者表示，整体来看，在捷克投资经营的企业税负适中，且税制透明度较高、稳定性较强，虽然法定化程度一般，但执法较为规范，税收风险可控。但也需注意 "实质重于形式" 的原则，并防范滥用法律条款带来的风险。

捷克现行主要税种及税率参考　　　　　　　　单位:%

税　　种	税率（比例）
公司所得税	19
个人所得税	15、22
增值税	15、21
雇主负担的社会保险	34
雇员负担的社会保险	11

卡塔尔

1. 税种、税负及税收优惠

卡塔尔税收体系和制度较为简单。

（1）主要税种及企业税负。

企业所得税：卡塔尔的企业所得税采用属地原则，在卡塔尔境内活动产生的所得须向卡塔尔缴纳企业所得税。由卡塔尔公民全资拥有和由海合会国家公民拥有的实体，免征公司所得税；合资公司的纳税义务取决于外国投资方在合资利润中所占的份额。基本税率为10%，经营石油天然气适用税率为35%。资本利得并入企业所得税征收，外国公司出售卡塔尔公司股权应就其资本利得缴纳10%的所得税。

个人所得税：无。卡塔尔对工资薪金不征收个人所得税，个人仅须就其源于卡塔尔境内的经营所得缴纳企业所得税。卡塔尔公民及居住于卡塔尔的海合会成员国公民，其收入在卡塔尔免税。其他个人在卡塔尔实施商业活动将按相关的公司所得税法的规定征税，如果被视为非居民，将按在卡塔尔总收入的5%或7%扣缴预提税。

社会保险缴费：雇主需要为在卡塔尔的员工支付社保缴款，费率为10%，但没有义务为其他国籍的员工缴纳社保款。雇员方面，若卡塔尔公民是加入养老金计划的雇员，则每月须缴纳相当于基本工资5%的养老金。

增值税：目前，卡塔尔尚未征收增值税或营业税，但在2016年2月阿拉伯财政论坛（AFF）上，海湾国家已就在2018年开征增值税达成一致，税率将在5%左右。

（2）税收优惠。

卡塔尔金融中心（QFC）税收优惠：拥有卡塔尔金融中心许可证的实体进行的活动，适用卡塔尔金融中心自有税务法规。每个在卡塔尔金融中心注册的实体，来源或产生于卡塔尔本地的应税所得按10%缴纳企业所得税。卡塔尔所有权占90%以上的企业，可享受与卡塔尔国税法中类似的优惠。金融中心公司不需要缴纳预提所得税。

卡塔尔科技园区（QSTP）税收优惠：卡塔尔科技园区是卡塔尔唯一的免税区。注册于卡塔尔科技园区的企业，可由外国投资者全资持股，并且允许在卡塔尔从事直接贸易，而无须当地中介。持有标准执照的科技园区内企业免税，且其进口货物及服务可享受卡塔尔附加税与关税免税。

2. 税收协定

卡塔尔已生效的税收协定有 58 个（截至 2015 年底）。《中华人民共和国政府和卡塔尔国政府关于对所得避免双重征税和防止偷漏税的协定》于 2001 年签署，自 2008 年 10 月 21 日生效，2009 年 1 月 1 日起执行。该税收协定对 17 类跨境所得的征税原则进行了明确。

3. 税收风险及争议处理

卡塔尔设有"税收申诉委员会"，专门处理税务争议案件。第三方税收服务机构可以作为客户的代理人，向委员会提出申诉。一旦出现涉税争议问题，可委托专业机构通过合法程序解决。

卡塔尔现行主要税种及税率参考　　　　　　　　　　单位:%

税　　种	税率（比例）
公司所得税	10、35
雇主负担的社会保险	10
雇员负担的社会保险	5
增值税（2018 年开征）	5

匈牙利

1. 税种、税负及税收优惠

（1）主要税种。

匈牙利现行税制以所得税为主体，辅以其他税种。主要包括企业所得税、增值税、个人所得税、社会保障税、地方营业税等。此外，针对特殊行业和产品，匈牙利还征收消费税、健康税、环保产品税、能源税等。

企业所得税：应税所得为按照税法进行调整后的年度财务报表中的会计利润，适用税率为9%。2010年起对能源、金融、零售、电信等企业征收附加税。征管方面，不允许合并纳税，不同实体之间的盈利与亏损不得相互弥补。

增值税：在匈牙利国内提供商品和服务，以及进口需要缴纳增值税，标准税率为27%，两档优惠税率分别为18%和5%。须注意的是，企业或个人在匈牙利从事经营活动之前均须进行增值税登记，且无登记限额（除远程销售），若未按照规定及时进行登记，可以在事后补登，但可能产生高额罚款。提供金融服务、保险服务、公共邮政服务、教育、财产租赁、证券销售、土地出售或租赁、人类医疗保健、民间工艺等商品和服务，无须缴纳增值税且不可抵扣进项税。

地方营业税：营业税在匈牙利是地方税种，地方政府议会在本辖区内可自行废立或调整该税。税基为企业收入或税前利润，税率为2%。

社会保障税：依据雇佣合同在匈牙利工作的所有个人，无论国籍，均须参加匈牙利社会保险。社会保障税为雇主缴纳的社会保险部分，税率为27%，另须缴纳1.5%的培训基金缴款。

个人所得税：匈牙利实行单一税率个人所得税，不设累进税率，税率为15%，资本利得通常也按此税率征收。

（2）企业税负。

匈牙利的社会保障税构成企业税负的主要部分，据世界银行《企业营商环境调查报告 2017》披露，社会保障税支出约占企业利润的 30.46%，其次为地方营业税 5.89%，企业所得税约占 4%。企业在匈牙利承担的平均税负率（缴税占总利润百分比）为 46.5%。

（3）税收优惠。

发展性税收优惠适用于某些投资项目，期限长达 10 年。享受发展性税收优惠，需满足投资金额、投资地区、投资行业、创造岗位数量、工资支出规模、投资内容等方面的具体规定。比如，公司在自由创业区投资规模达到 1 亿福林（约合 370000 美元），或者向食品卫生、环境保护、影视制作等领域的投资规模达到 1 亿福林，或者中小企业在任意地区的投资，均可以申请发展性税收优惠。这项优惠采取税基减免的方式，最多可减少公司 80% 的应纳税所得额，使有效税率降低至 2%（适用税率 10%）或 3.8%（适用税率 19%）。

研发费用加计扣除。双倍扣除：公司经营活动范围内发生的基础研究、应用研究与开发的直接成本，享受双倍加计扣除。不要求研发活动发生于匈牙利，且包含关联企业或非关联外国企业发生的研发费用。三倍扣除：纳税人和匈牙利国家认可的公共或私人研究中心合作开展的特定研发活动而发生的研发费用，享受三倍加计扣除，但扣除上限为 5000 万匈牙利福林（约合 185000 美元）。

其他优惠。特定类型收入适用优惠税率：特许权使用费所得计税基础扣减 50% 计算。特定行业的税收减免：影视税收、体育税收、文化税收等特定行业税收，满足一定条件可享受相应的税收优惠政策。个人所得税可享受家庭赡养扣除，以及营业扣除（约为 10% 扣减额）。

2. 税收协定

匈牙利签订税收协定的国家范围较广，约与 80 余个国家签订了税收协议（截至 2017 年 5 月）。受访者认可税收协定对境外企业在匈牙利经营发挥的促进作用，并认为，广泛的双边税收协定，以及较为优厚的国内企业所得税优惠制度，使匈牙利吸引了许多境外机构投资建厂。

3. 税收风险及争议处理

受访者表示，税务争议案件可以首先通过税务当局的特定处理程序解决，这一解决途径由两轮协商程序组成。若仍未解决，纳税人可以向法庭提起诉讼，是否决定启动法律程序一般与税收争议额度有关。涉税案件可以上诉至最高法院。

匈牙利现行主要税种及税率参考

单位:%

税　　种	税率（比例）
地方营业税	2
企业所得税	9
社会保障税	22
增值税	27
个人所得税	15
雇主负担的社会保险	28.5

泰   国

1. 税种、税负及税收优惠

（1）主要税种和企业税负。

在泰国经营的企业主要缴纳增值税和企业所得税，雇员还须缴纳个人所得税。据世界银行 doing business 调查数据，泰国企业平均税负率（税收占利润比率）约为 32.6%。整体而言，在泰国经营的企业税收负担适中。

企业所得税：一般的公司和法人股份公司，企业所得税税率为净利润的 20%。课税基数除了净利润外，根据不同情况，还可以为扣除开支前的收入、在泰国内或从泰国获得的收入以及汇往国外的利润。如从事特定业务并在泰国设有办公室的外国公司，即按总收入的 3% 征税。

增值税：增值税的标准税率为 10%，出口商品和劳务适用零税率。目前法令宣布临时减税，将税率从 10% 降至 6.3%，加上地方行政税收 0.7%，合计税率为 7%。任何纳税年度内的增值税应税收入达到 180 万泰铢，纳税人须进行登记；非临时经营业务的非居民供货商亦须登记。

个人所得税：实行 5%、10%、15%、20%、25%、30% 和 35% 的 7 级超额累进税率。泰国居民纳税人和非居民纳税人，均仅就来源于泰国的收入纳税。只有当居民纳税人在取得来源于境外收入的当年即将收入汇回泰国时，才须对该来源于境外的收入纳税，以后年度汇回，则免缴个人所得税。泰国居民纳税人的规定是一个日历（纳税年度）在泰国停留超过 180 天，则将成为居民纳税人。

（2）税收优惠。

据受访者反馈，泰国有诸多税收优惠，面向制造业、服务业、国际贸易等行业，或面向特殊地区或特殊人群。比如，受投资促进委员会（Thailand Board of Investment，BIO）鼓励的业务活动，可享受最高 13 年的所得税税率减免期。又如，地区运营总部及其外籍员工，可分别享受 0 至 10% 的净利润税率和 15% 的固定个人所得税税率的税收优惠。

2. 税收协定

泰国已缔结了 58 个税收协定。受访者认为，泰国税务当局重视并尊重税收协定的效力。然而，与许多国家的税务机关类似，泰国税务机关也往往倾向于从令自身受惠的角度去解读税收协定的有关条款。

3. 税收风险及争议处理

当税务争议出现时，通常情况下税务机关和纳税人可以通过协商达成一致。若经过协商，纳税人仍不同意税务机关的评估结果，此时可以通过法律程序解决。然而，受访者表示近年来泰国最高法院在处理税务争议案件时，常常做出更有利于税务机关的判决。

泰国现行主要税种及税率参考 单位:%

税 种	税率（比例）
企业所得税	20
增值税	7
特别营业税	最高为 3.3
个人所得税	5 ~ 35
雇主负担的社会保险	5.2 ~ 6.2
雇员负担的社会保险	5
财产税	12.5

越　　南

1. 税种、税负及税收优惠

（1）主要税种。

企业在越南经营涉及的主要税种包括增值税、企业所得税、个人所得税、关税、牌照税、外国合同遗留税6种。

增值税：税率为10%，每月20日前申报缴纳上月增值税，采取销项税额减进项税额的方法计算当期应交税金，销项税额大于进项税额，按照差异金额缴纳；销项税额小于进项税额，差异部分累计到下月继续抵扣。越南政府规定的免税项目已支付的增值税进项税额可定期办理退税。

企业所得税：主要有以下两种申报方式。登记按照利润总额的20%（2014年以前为25%，2014~2015年为22%，2016年调整为20%）缴纳企业所得税，法人公司必须使用该方式。采取此申报方法，必须按照越南的会计制度建账并进行各项会计核算，税务局对各类成本的审查较为严格。以此方式申报企业所得税，每季度需申报并预缴一次，在季度终了的次月30日前完成，次年3月30日前需对上年度企业所得税进行汇算清缴。当年实现的利润可在弥补以前年度的亏损后再计算当年应纳税额，最多可弥补前5个年度的亏损额。登记按照包税制缴纳企业所得税，计税基础及计算方法为：（收入－成本）×2%。该申报方式的优势在于计算简便，税务局对成本的关注面较小，以该方式申报企业所得税，每月20日前必须申报并缴纳上月税金，次年3月30日前对上年度企业所得税进行汇算清缴。

个人所得税：外籍员工及当地员工均需负担个人所得税，由公司负责代扣代缴，每月20日前需申报并缴纳上月个人所得税金，次年3月30日前完成上年度汇算清缴工作。越南现行个人所得税税率为7档累进，分别为5%、10%、15%、20%、25%、30%和35%。减免方面，目前主要可税前扣除午餐补助73万越南盾（定期调整），申请其他减税需办理相关证明材料（翻译、公证、认证），外籍员工办理存在难度。

关税：进口各种材料需按照越南海关核定的关税税率缴纳进口关税，并需缴纳10%的增值税，关税税金可计入成本，增值税金可作为进项税额予以抵扣。

牌照税：该税种为定额税，按年度征收，标准如下：注册资本金100亿越南盾以上的公司，300万越南盾/年；注册资本金100亿越南盾以下的公司，200万越南盾/年；分公司、代表处及其他性质机构，100万越南盾/年。

外国合同遗留税：与越南境外公司或者个人签订分包、服务类合同，汇款给境外单位或个人前需先缴纳外国合同遗留税，税金承担方根据合同约定执行，境内公司负责代扣代缴。计税基础为双方结算额，按照5%左右的比例征收外国合同遗留税（不同类型的业务征税比例略有不同，通常为5%），同时按照结算额加外国合同遗留税税额作为计税基础征收5%增值税。外国合同遗留税可计入公司成本，5%的增值税可作为进项税额用于抵扣。

（2）企业税负。

越南企业税负水平适中偏高。某受访公司为建筑类企业，其在越南的实际税负水平占营业收入的比重约为5%。另据世界银行doing business数据库披露，越南企业的实际税负占利润比重，平均约为39.4%。

（3）税收优惠。

越南政府对纳税者从事鼓励投资的项目，或在政府规定的社会经济不发达地区进行投资，分别给予10%优惠税率（持续15年）和20%优惠税率（持续10年）。自获得利润第1年或创收年度第4年中先实现的年度起，4年内免税，9年内减半征收。

受访的两家中国企业表示，目前在越南不享受任何税收优惠。某企业下属的东南亚公司于2007年在越南某省设立的预制场符合工业区税收优惠政策，曾经按照规定申请了分公司"一免两减半"的企业所得税优惠（第1年免企业所得税，第2～3年减半征收企业所得税）。

2. 税收协定

越南政府与中国政府于1995年5月17日签订了《中华人民共和国政府和越南社会主义共和国政府关于对所得避免双重征税和防止偷漏税的协定》，该协定于1996年10月18日生效并于1997年1月1日正式执行。

该协定在避免双重征税和偷漏税方面发挥了重要作用，公司在越南缴纳的所得税和个人在越南缴纳的个人所得税可以在中国进行抵扣，税收协定发挥作用。实际执行中，越南境内公司从境外取得的收入，如果在境外尚未履行纳税义务，需按照越南税法规定补交税金，如已经在境外履行纳税义务，需提供证明文件，实际纳税额低于越南税法规定标准的，需补交差额。

3. 税收风险及争议处理

（1）税务争议案件处理。

实际情况下，越南税务纠纷一般通过行政税收制度来解决。法庭诉讼可行，但是不受欢迎，行政税务申报制度规定了2级申诉，一级在地方或者省级，另一级上级。然而实际上，如果受害人有良好的上诉理由，可以逐案接受进一步上诉。在行政上诉程序的任何时候，纳税人都可以退出行政法庭诉讼程序。虽然没有明确的规定，一旦纳税人起诉法院诉讼，通过行政上诉制度的上诉可能不被税务机关接受。因此，一般纳税人在诉讼之前用尽行政诉讼，目前的行政税务申诉制度没有规定替代性争议解决方案。

越南税法规定的税收异议、申诉制度如下：自收到税务干部、税务机关纳税通知或税务处分决定之日起30天内，申诉人向直接管理税收机关递送申诉书。在等待处理期间，纳税人须按税务机关的通知或决定纳税。

税务机关在收到税务申诉书之日起15天内必须审查处理；案情复杂的，处理期可以延长，但不得超过30天。如不属税务机关权力范围，应向有权机关移送有关卷宗或报告，并在收到申诉书10天内通知申诉人。

受理的税务机关有权要求申诉人提供申诉有关的卷宗和材料。如申诉人无正当理由而拒绝提供卷宗和材料，税务机关有权拒绝审理。

在收到上级税务机关或法定权限机关的决定15天内，税务机关必须向纳税人退还税款和罚金。

税务机关如发现瞒税、偷税或者错收，负责补征自发现之日起前五年内的税款和罚金，或退还前五年内的税款。如开发资源的组织和个人不报税、纳税，补征税款和罚金期限从开发日起算。

上级税务机关首长有责任处理纳税人对下级税务机关的税务申诉。财政部长对税务申诉的处理决定为最终决定。

（2）典型税务风险案例。

中国A建筑施工企业，2014年在越南海防市承建一条高速公路路面10

标，组建工程项目部，2016年12月项目竣工，2017年4月海防市税务部门审计该企业时，提出了下列问题：

A建筑施工企业，在越南岘港有另一路基项目，在2015年，A企业10标项目部曾经向海防项目暂借款600亿越南盾，但因属于同一企业，没有收取任何利息费用。海防税务部门审计后认为海防项目部应当按照越南同期银行贷款利率收取利息，并缴纳营业所得税，并按照每天万分之五的利率缴纳滞纳金和罚款。

A企业海防项目在施工工程中实际使用沥青13000吨，但按照越南施工定额为11000吨，对于超定额的2000吨。海防税务局要求项目部提供超方量的客观原因和证据，如果没有全部按照管理原因导致，不应当从应纳税所得额中扣除，需补缴营业所得税，并缴纳罚款和罚息。

越南现行主要税种及税率参考　　　　　　单位:%

税　　种	税率（比例）
企业所得税	20
增值税	10
个人所得税	5~35
牌照税	100万~300万越南盾/年
外国合同遗留税	5
雇主负担的社会保险	21.5
雇员负担的社会保险	10.5

俄罗斯

1. 税种、税负及税收优惠

（1）主要税种。

企业及相关个人在俄罗斯境内需要缴纳的主要税种有：增值税、利润税（企业所得税）、社会统筹保险、个人所得税等。

增值税：标准税率为 18%，税基为提供商品与劳务的增值额。以建筑类企业为例，缴税时一般按照预付款，或者按照完成工作量为计税依据，两者不重复计算。

利润税（企业所得税）：税率为 20%，与大部分国家相比并不算高。预提所得税方面，支付给俄罗斯公司或个人的股息按 9% 税率缴纳预提税，支付给外国公司或非居民个人的股息则按 15% 缴纳；支付给非居民纳税人的利息和特许权使用费，按 20% 缴纳。

个人所得税：采取 13% 的单一税率，在国际上被公认为是个人所得税平均税率最低的国家之一。

社会统筹保险：俄罗斯企业需要缴纳的社会统筹保险负担较重，而且全部由雇主缴纳。几经升降，目前社会统筹保险的综合税率为 30%，包含养老保险、医疗保险等部分，其中养老保险费率最高。特定情况下，雇佣的外籍员工收入可以享受社会统筹保险优惠政策或免于缴纳养老保险。

（2）企业税负。

企业整体税负较重。据受访企业反馈，该企业（建筑类）在俄罗斯经营的税收负担率，大约为 30% ~ 35%。另据世界银行营商环境调查数据库（doing business），企业税负率为 47.4%（2016 年），在 2010 年曾高达 54%。

从分税种的税负结构看，社会统筹保险及增值税税负较重，而所得税税负相对较轻。某受访企业 2016 年缴纳的增值税额度为 5100 万卢布（约合 510 万元人民币），社会统筹保险为 4700 万卢布（约合 470 万元人民币），因自公司成立以来持续账面亏损，可以抵减利润收入，因此尚未缴纳过企业所得税。由于实行13%单一税率个人所得税，高收入雇员可以节省大笔个税支出。

俄罗斯税负结构有其特殊性。作为转轨制国家，出于吸引投资以及扩大所得税税基等诸多考虑，俄罗斯在多次激进改革后设定了级次扁平、数值较低的所得税税率体系，总体上降低了企业和个人的所得税税负。实际上，俄罗斯的社保缴费也曾"费改税"并改高费率为低税率，然而由于人口老龄化程度高，较低的缴费标准难以覆盖巨大的社保资金缺口，因而不得不由税又改为费，并且提升了费率，大大增加了企业的负担。

（3）税收优惠。

近年来，俄罗斯政府扩大了税收激励的规模以吸引企业来俄经营。篇幅所限，本报告选取主要内容列举如下。

地方税收激励：作为财政分权的联邦制国家，俄罗斯各联邦主体享有较大的调整地方税收制度的空间。各联邦主体往往根据区域性发展目标，拟定一系列税收优惠政策。如俄罗斯利润税采取联邦与地方按税率分成的形式，标准税率为20%意味着联邦政府享有2%、各联邦主体政府享有18%。而地方政府有权将分配给地方的利润税税率由18%降至13.5%，因而在俄经营企业的利润税税率可能低至15.5%。此外，有些联邦主体还可以对特定固定资产提供2.2%的财产税税率，或者为企业提供贷款补贴等。

经济特区税收优惠：特别经济区的法律框架提供了大量税及既其他方面的特权。25个经济特区目前分为四类：制造业，科技创新业，旅游娱乐业，以及港口物流业。特别经济区的税收优惠多种多样，比如利润税税率可以降至2%甚至0，财产税可享受10年免税期，可免关税，研发费用加计扣除以及增值税豁免等。

地区性投资项目税收优惠：自2014年1月1日起，俄罗斯一项联邦法律开始执行，给予远东联邦管区及西伯利亚联邦管区设立地区性利润税税率的权力。这项法案规定，自利润产生起5年，利润税税率不得超过10%，随后5年利润税税率不得低于10%。目前15个符合条件的联邦主体中，已有13个降低了利润税税率。

经济快速发展区税收优惠：2015年引入的经济快速发展区，是俄罗斯政府为提振远东地区经济、改变其经济结构单一局面而部署的战略规划。

至今已经建立 9 个经济快速发展区，2017 年至少还有 5 个以上即将设立。每个快速发展区，可以保持政策 70 年不变，并可享受增值税返还、利润税低税率、矿藏开采税低税率、社会统筹保险低费率等诸多税收优惠政策。

然而，受访中国企业表示，目前没有享受俄罗斯税收优惠，这可能既与受访企业所属行业有关，也与企业未能充分了解俄罗斯税收优惠政策有关。同时，受访企业表示正在享有中俄相关协议约束下的优惠政策。

2. 税收协定

俄罗斯联邦与许多国家及地区签订了双边税收协定。2017 年，与中国香港、新加坡、中国、塞浦路斯、哈萨克斯坦等国和地区的一系列双边税收协定及修正案即将或已经开始执行。中国与俄罗斯签有双边税收协定，同时，中俄两国政府间于 2000 年签订的《关于华人在俄和俄人在华临时劳务工作的协议》，约定了有关税收事项，比如中国来俄工作人员，可以免缴费率为 22% 的养老保险。但是，目前存在宣传不够、执行滞后的情况，使企业未能及时、充分地受惠。

3. 税收风险及争议处理

在多年实践中，俄罗斯已建立了审前及审理税务争议案件的合理机制。据受访者反馈的近期情况，75% 的税收争议事项可以在税务机关的帮助下得以解决。争议最多的问题集中在：实际收益人的定义；资本弱化；"不守信用"的供应商。受访者表示，曾在税务争议案件中胜诉，并表示在俄罗斯，与税务部门接触均能够依法执行。

俄罗斯现行主要税种及税率参考　　　　　　　　　单位:%

税　　　种	税率（比例）
增值税	18
利润税（企业所得税）	20
个人所得税	13
社会统筹保险	30

印度尼西亚

1. 税种、税负及税收优惠

（1）主要税种和税负。

与企业经营有关的税种主要有增值税、企业所得税、社会保障税、个人所得税等。受访者认为在印度尼西亚经营的企业总体税收负担尚可，世界银行 doing business 数据库披露的税负调查结果为 30.6%（该税负率数据为企业承担的税负占利润的平均比重）。

增值税：标准税率为 10%，对提供商品和劳务的纳税人征收。应税商品或应税服务的年销售额超出一定金额的公司，须进行增值税登记。

企业所得税：标准税率为 25%，应税所得为应税收入减除可扣除费用后的净利润额。

社会保障税：企业和个人均需缴纳。企业方面，如果雇主雇佣 10 名或以上雇员或每月发生工资费用为 100 万印度尼西亚盾以上，则雇主须向印度尼西亚社保基金供款。个人方面，在印度尼西亚受雇佣则必须缴纳社保税，其中养老保险税率相当于其月薪的 2%，健康保险为 0.1%。

个人所得税：以家庭为一个单位申报，应税所得包括经营所得、公司所得、资本利得等，实行 5%、15%、25%、30% 四级超额累进税率。

（2）税收优惠。

企业所得税方面，若企业年收入低于 500 亿印度尼西亚盾可适用低税率。对于年收入不超过 48 亿印度尼西亚盾的企业纳税人（常设机构除外）可享受总收入 1% 的优惠税收待遇。对于总收入为 48 亿～500 亿印度尼西亚盾的居民收入企业，其总收入在 48 亿印度尼西亚盾以下部分所对应的应纳税所得额，可享受企业所得税税率减半政策。但是若为常设机构，则仍须按 20% 税率缴纳企业所得税。

2. 税收协定

印度尼西亚已缔结了超过 60 项税收协定。受访者认为，税收协定的地位和作用在法律框架下已予以明确，印度尼西亚当地税务机关能够充分尊重税收协定的内容，严格按照协定规范征税以及处理税收争议问题，不存在对协定的误用或滥用情况。印度尼西亚与中国签有双边税收协定。受益于税收协定，中国企业可按10%缴纳企业所得税。

3. 税收风险及争议处理

在印度尼西亚，纳税人向税务机关提出异议是比较普遍的行为。税收争议问题的处理程序在印度尼西亚税法中有明确规定。纳税人若不同意审计结论，有权提出异议，并可以进一步提请纳税评估，但需要依照有关规定充分准备材料及数据。

印度尼西亚现行主要税种及税率参考 单位:%

税　　种	税率（比例）
利润税（企业所得税）	25
增值税	10
个人所得税	5~30
雇主负担的社会保险	10
雇员负担的社会保险	2.5

哈萨克斯坦

1. 税种、税负及税收优惠

（1）主要税种和企业税负。

据世界银行 doing business 数据库披露，哈萨克斯坦企业的平均税负率（税收负担占净利润的比率）为 29.2%。综合法定税率与调研结果，我们认为在哈萨克斯坦经营的企业税收负担处于适中水平。

（2）税收优惠。

哈萨克斯坦政府提供了多种多样的税收优惠措施，如对中小型企业实行简易征收办法；设立经济特区，为经济特区设置了企业所得税、财产税、土地税等多重税收减免政策；资本性支出的税收优惠政策（加速折旧）；增值税的优惠缴纳政策；特定投资协议可享最长 10 年的企业所得税、财产税和土地税豁免政策等。

2. 税收协定

哈萨克斯坦已签订 51 项双边税收协定。税收协定相对于国内法规具有优势地位，经常被企业应用于跨境交易。

3. 税收风险及争议处理

涉税争议事项可以通过一种庭前程序进行处理。如果未能解决，争议案件可以向法院提出诉讼。据受访者反馈，从以往经验看，"跟税务局打赢官司的可能性非常低"。主要涉税争议点：转移定价问题；企业所得税的税前抵扣问题；地下资源使用的税务事项；进口货物关税分类等。

哈萨克斯坦现行主要税种及税率参考　　　　　　　　　　单位:%

税　　种	税率（比例）
企业所得税	20

税　　种	税率（比例）
增值税	12
个人所得税	10
社会税（社会保障税）	11
财产税	最高为 1.5

印　　度

1. 税种、税负及税收优惠

（1）税种及税负。

印度公司所得税的纳税人分为居民纳税人和非居民纳税人，根据印度法律注册成立或其管理控制完全在印度的公司为印度居民纳税人。居民纳税人就其全球收入纳税，非居民纳税人仅就来源于印度的收入纳税。印度国内公司所得税的税率为30%，外国公司的所得税税率为40%。考虑到附加税费和地方税，国内公司和外国公司的有效税率分别为33.99%和43.26%。在2017～2018财年，对于营业额不足5亿卢比的公司，公司所得税税率适用25%，95%的印度国内公司将会受益于此。

营业亏损与资本亏损可以向以后年度结转8年，短期亏损可抵销长、短期资产的资本利得，而长期亏损则仅可抵销长期资本利得。除未抵扣折旧（可无限期向后结转）外，亏损在按期提交纳税申报表后，方可向以后年度结转。未抵扣折旧可以抵减任何所得，而营业亏损只可以抵扣营业所得。

针对应纳税额低于其账面利润18.5%的企业征收可替代最低税，可替代最低税超出按正常收入计算的应交税款的部分可以抵减应纳所得税额，在10年内向后结转、抵减所得税。

印度销售货物和提供服务的增值税是有限度的增值税，包括中央消费税、销售税、邦级销售税等17种不同形式的货物与劳务税，税率繁多，包括0、5%、12%、18%、28%等。根据印度2017年4月的税收法案，从7月1日起，将建立统一的增值税制度。

印度个人所得税的纳税人分居民纳税人和非居民纳税人，居民纳税人需要就全球收入在印度进行纳税，非居民纳税人就其来源于印度的收入纳税。2017～2018财年，印度个人所得税的税率为5%、20%和30%，其中免征额为25万卢比。年收入高于500万卢比而低于1000万卢比，征收附加税率10%；年收入高于1000万卢比，则征收附加税率15%。

印度居民企业支付给非居民的相关收入应缴纳预提所得税。对支付给非居民企业的股息免征预提所得税，但发放股息的公司需要缴纳16.995%的股息分配税。对于与印度签订了双边税收协定的国家，该国居民来源于印度的所得有可能享受更低的预提所得税率。

整体而言，印度当前税制较为复杂，企业尤其是外国公司的税负水平偏高。

（2）税收优惠。

印度的税收优惠政策较多。如对特定行业发生的研发支出以及向特定科研组织支付的研发支出可以加计扣除，扣除额最高达200%。税收减免优惠同样适用投资于以下的行业或项目：低温运输系统、农产品仓储设施、天然气、原油或石油管道网络、开发的经济适用房和生产肥料等。对于内陆集装箱中转站、集装箱货运站等其他特定设施的建立和运营产生的费用，也有类似的扣除政策。位于经济特区的企业，出口利润免税。根据产业、地区不同，也有相应的税收优惠。

2. 税收协定

印度与包括我国在内的多个国家签订了双边税收协定。根据中印税收协定，股息预提所得税税率为10%，非协定国家为0，但发放股息公司需要缴纳16.995%的股息分配税；利息预提所得税税率为10%，非协定国家为20%；特许权使用费预提所得税税率为10%，非协定国家为25%。税收协定使我国企业可以享受更低的税负，但要注意，如果非居民没有永久性账号（PAN），即税务登记号码，那么需按照适用的协定税率及20%两者间较高的一档税率缴纳预提所得税。

整体上看，印度比较尊重税收协定，相对于国内税法，给予税收协定优先权。

3. 税收风险及争议处理

关于税务争议，印度精细化的税务机构中有专门处理税务争议的部门，这也表明在印度常常发生税务争议。解决税务争议的重要途径是通过法院，但解决争议的时间往往非常漫长。受访者表示，整体来看，在印度投资经营的企业税负偏高，税制较为透明，比较稳定，法定化程度非常高，但执法不够规范，由此导致企业税收风险较大。而且，发生税务争议的频率较高，虽然印度有系统的解决争议的法律途径，但耗时较长，效率较低。

印度现行主要税种及税率参考 单位:%

税　　种	税率（比例）
国内公司所得税	30
外国公司所得税	40
个人所得税	5 ~ 30
有限度增值税	0、5、12、18、28
雇主负担的社会保险	12.5
雇员负担的社会保险	12

巴基斯坦

1. 税种、税负及税收优惠

（1）税种及税负。

巴基斯坦公司所得税的纳税人分为居民纳税人和非居民纳税人，根据巴基斯坦法律注册成立或其管理控制完全在巴基斯坦进行的实体为巴基斯坦居民纳税人。居民纳税人就其全球收入纳税，非居民纳税人仅就来源于巴基斯坦的收入纳税。巴基斯坦公司所得税的标准税率为35%。居民对股息收入按10%的税率纳税。经营亏损（不包括投机业务亏损）可抵减同一税务年度任何类别的应税所得，超过应税所得的亏损可自下一年度起向后结转最多6年。投机业务亏损和资本损失可结转至下一纳税年度抵减该年的投机业务所得和资本利得。处置特定证券（包括上市公司股份和证券）的亏损可抵减同一纳税年度相关的利得，但不可向后结转。经营亏损不可抵减按最终纳税机制课税的经营业务收入。

销售持有1年以上的资本性资产的所得可减少25%的基础来征税。对于2012纳税年度以后处分持有少于6个月的上市公司股份的资本利得所适用的税率为10%，如果持有超过6个月但是少于12个月适用的税率为8%，持有1年及以上的股份不需要征税。

居民公司和其他特定纳税人申报的营业额适用按0.5%的流转税率征税，纳税人亏损或收入产生的税收少于流转额0.5%的情况下适用可替代最低税。

国外公司办事处在巴基斯坦按照合同收入额的7%缴纳公司所得税。

巴基斯坦的增值税分为消费税和销售税两种。联邦政府通常对商品销售征收消费税，标准税率为17%，省级政府会对该省内发生的服务征收销售税，税率为13%~16%，具体税率因省而异。

巴基斯坦个人所得税的纳税人分居民纳税人和非居民纳税人，居民纳税人需要就全球收入在巴基斯坦进行纳税，非居民纳税人就其来源于巴基斯坦的收入纳税。政府不允许联合申报，要求个人必须单独进行纳税申报。应纳税所得超过40万巴基斯坦卢比的工薪阶层和非工薪阶层都要缴纳个人所得税，税额根据不同层级而定。工薪阶层的税率为5%~20%，而经营行为纳税人的税率为10%~25%。

巴基斯坦居民企业支付给非居民的相关收入应缴纳预提所得税。对于与巴基斯坦签订了双边税收协定的国家，该国居民来源于巴基斯坦的所得有可能享受更低的预提所得税税率。

整体而言，巴基斯坦企业的税负水平居中。

（2）税收优惠。

巴基斯坦对工厂、机器和设备在巴基斯坦设立的电力生产项目，农村和不发达地区建立的工业企业、巴基斯坦证券交易所上市的公司等提供相应税收优惠。

巴基斯坦对外商直接投资占比超过50%的企业给予公司所得税20%的优惠税率。对于个别行业或项目会享受特殊税收优惠。比如，在信德省的道路施工免除服务销售税；再如，从2015年7月起对"绿地"项目减免相应进口关税。

2. 税收协定

巴基斯坦与包括我国在内的50多个国家签订了双边税收协定。中巴税收协定于1989年签订，根据协定规定，股息预提所得税税率为10%，非协定国家为12.5%或20%；利息预提所得税税率为5%或10%，非协定国家为20%；特许权使用费预提所得税税率为12.5%，非协定国家为15%。表面上看，税收协定使我国企业享受更低的税负，但实际执行效果并不理想。比如，中巴税收协定规定非居民公司（代表处）是按营业利润征税，但巴基斯坦所得税法近年做了修改，规定了两种计算方法（加了一个按当年会计利润计算），从高征税，对纳税人不利（有时累计亏损还要交税），违反了税收协定的规定。

某种程度上讲，随着时代发展，中巴税收协定的部分内容已经过时了，需要进一步修订完善。

3. 税收风险及争议处理

关于税务争议案件的相关问题，受访企业表示在巴基斯坦每年均有较多的税务争议，收到的税务通知较多，引发税务官司频繁。企业每年均会与税务局打官司，直至高院和最高院。征纳双方均可依法上诉，纳税人的权利基本能够得到保障，但即使胜诉，也很难实现被扣税款返还。

由于巴基斯坦税制经常变化，非常不稳定，给企业投资经营带来较大风险。比如，巴基斯坦于 2015 年第一季度首次征收一次性的"超级税"。多数公司认为这是"一次性"税收而未在未来年度内考虑，但 2016 年和 2017 年又再次征收。

再如 2011 年 2 月 26 日，我国一企业驻巴基斯坦代表处被税务机关下达税单要求补缴 2008 年税款 91120371 卢比，我国企业于 2011 年 3 月 18 日申请复议，主要理由包括：第一，未给申诉方充分的时间和机会辩解；第二，补税决定主观臆断；第三，判罚过重；第四，别有用心。2011 年 6 月 1 日复议结果作出了对我国企业有利的判决，补缴税款大幅减少为 400 多万卢比。但税务机关表示不服，于 2011 年 7 月 26 日向税务法庭上诉，上诉理由是行政复议申请人（中资公司驻巴基斯坦代表处）在听证期间补交给行政复议官的资料并未向应诉人（税务机关）出示，不符合有关程序。2015 年 4 月 14 日，税务法庭做出裁决，维持行政复议结果。

受访者表示，整体来看，在巴基斯坦投资经营的企业税负适中，但税制不透明，非常不稳定，法定化程度一般，且执法不规范，由此导致税收风险较大。企业需做好相应规划，防范税收风险。

巴基斯坦现行主要税种及税率参考　　　　　　　　单位:%

税　　　种	税率（比例）
公司所得税	35；合同额 7
个人所得税	5 ~ 20
消费税	17
销售税	13 ~ 16；因省而异

第三部分　国际化财会人才培养

随着国家"一带一路"倡议的推进，越来越多的中国企业走出国门、走向世界，在中国企业乘风破浪走向全球市场化之际，如何更好地培养具有全球化视野的专业财会人才，这是摆在"一带一路"沿线企业、教育机构、会计行业监管机构和行业组织面前的一个重要课题。

"一带一路"建设能否成功，人才的质量很重要。人才能起到桥梁和纽带的作用，所以人才培养在"一带一路"建设当中发挥着非常重要的作用。如何培养优秀的财务人才以促进"一带一路"建设，我们面临着许多未知。例如，目前"一带一路"沿线国家的企业对财会人员的胜任能力或技能有哪些要求？企业通过怎样的培养方式提高财务人员的胜任能力或技能？不同国家的企业在培养模式上有哪些不同之处？有哪些经验值得互相借鉴？

一、探究沿线国家财会人员的胜任能力

通过对"一带一路"沿线国家相关制度的研究，笔者们发现这些国家对会计人才的职业准入比较注重专业技能（通常称为硬技能），而对会计人员胜任能力的研究比较缺乏。本书通过问卷的形式针对 12 项财会人员胜任能力进行深入调查，包括财务会计的知识及方法（财务报告、财务管理等）、管理会计工具的知识及方法（成本管理、预算管理、绩效管理等）、税务的知识、数据分析的能力、懂得运用科技及相关的软件、风险管理的知识及方法、公司治理的知识及方法、审计和认证业务的知识及方法、熟悉企业的商业模式、对战略选择的评估能力、能把握宏观经济对企业的影响和行业前沿与把握的能力。

二、探索国际化人才培养新模式

我国财务人员胜任能力培养方式方面的文献较少。本书提出的培养方式包括在职提高学历、专业资格培训、参与外部培训及论坛、组织内部培训、轮岗、在职的自我摸索、在职上司指导、对外考察交流、公司内跨部门的讨论、暂调业务部门作深入了解等，本书将针对这些方式的重要性、有效性、普及性做出评价。

随着知识和科技急剧发展、经济结构快速转型，每一个会计专业人士都应该保持终生学习的态度和能力，财会人员需要持续地经历所在行业的变化、专业知识技能的变化的历程。沿线国家的会计行业人才是否具备这样的学习动机和意识？会计监管机构是否有继续教育的要求？是否具备多元化的管道和方式来支持会计行业人才的自我提升？有哪些教育资源？这都是值得关注的。

三、财会人才：推动价值创造的新动力

2016 年 ACCA 的调研指出，财务高管、财务团队与内外部业务合作伙伴之间的有效协作和融合，是推动企业成功创新和增长的关键。但是，仅认识到其必要性和有意愿协作还远远不够。实现业财融合，往往要求企业转变其文化、思维模式、组织模式和行为方式，才能更好地实现企业战略落地、优化资源配置、进行绩效评估，甚至是投资决策、税务筹划以及兼并收购支持等。通过调研，ACCA 旨在了解企业是否已经落实了明确的人才目标、发展计划、绩效管理等，而这些机制是否有效？财会人才是否真正提高了公司绩效、实现了价值创造？

三方联合调研将就以上问题一一给出答案。笔者们希望为"一带一路"沿线财会专业人才培养献计献策，共享沿线企业国际化人才培养的经验，共建"一带一路"财会专业人才智库，努力推进在"一带一路"倡议下国际化人才培养的新模式。

新加坡

专业机构：有各种专业会计机构吸引和发展会计师，包括国家会计机构 ISCA（新加坡特许会计师协会），以及 ACCA 等国际专业会计机构。

财会人才能力研究：SAC（新加坡会计委员会）是指导会计部门和会计人才发展的主要政府机构。相关研究报道包括：Accountancy Sector Survey，2013 会计部门研究（ACCA 管理研究项目）；AE（Accounting Entities）Survey（会计实体调查 2016）；AE Regionalisation Survey AE（区域化调查 2016）（ACCA 是研究伙伴）。

企业财会人才的胜任能力标准/培养计划：SAC（新加坡会计委员会）与专业会计机构（包括 ACCA）合作，各政府机构（WSG－新加坡劳工和 SSG－新加坡技术组织）为会计师制定技能标准的框架。该框架为各级会计人才提供了详细的能力和技能要求。

企业培养财会人才胜任能力的方法及评价。培养方法有：在职提高学历、专业资格培训、参与外部培训及论坛、组织内部培训、轮岗、在职的自我摸索、在职的上司指导、对外考察交流、公司内跨部门的讨论、暂调业务部门作深入了解等。各类公司采用上述培养方法的组合。公司与公司间有很大的不同，但是很多大公司几乎全部投入使用。政府也推出了技能计划（Skills Future programs）。最受欢迎的培养方法为：教育改善、内部和外部培训。

企业财会人才年度绩效考核：大部分新加坡公司会有财会人才的年度绩效考核。

企业财会人才培训时间：有培训时间的要求，时间长短取决于会员类别。

财会人才对公司绩效的重要性：受访者认为财会人才对公司绩效的提高"重要"（4分）。

财会人才胜任能力排序（5 分为最重要）

能力/技能	重要度（分值）
财务会计的知识及方法	4
管理会计的知识及方法	4
税务的知识	4
数据分析的能力	5
懂得运用科技及相关的软件	5
风险管理的知识及方法	4
公司治理的知识及方法	4
审计和认证业务的知识及方法	4
熟悉企业的商业模式	5
对战略选择的评估能力	5
能把握宏观经济对企业的影响	5
行业前沿与把握	5

马来西亚

专业机构：马来西亚会计师公会（IFAC 会员）http：//www. mia. gov. my/v1/；MICPA（马来西亚注册会计师公会）（IFAC 会员）http：//www. micpa. com. my/；ACCA（IFAC 成员和 CAPA 成员）http：//www. accaglobal. com/my/en. html。

财务人才能力研究：马来西亚没有相关的会计人才能力研究报告。

企业财会人才培养计划：上市公司经审计的财务报表必须由马来西亚会计师公会注册会员签字。

一般来说，马来西亚的大型公司对会计师的技能有所要求，不同的企业有不同的具体要求。这些技能可能包括已获得的专业资格和专业会计机构的注册会员。这些企业可能在人力资源部门实施会计人才培训计划，该计划一般定期更新或以需求为基础。

马来西亚培养财会人才胜任能力的方法包括：在职提高学历；专业资格培训；参与外部培训及论坛；组织内部培训；在职的上司指导；对外考察交流；公司内跨部门的讨论；暂调业务部门作深入了解。受访者认为这些方法是有效果的。

财会人才绩效考核：马来西亚存在财会人才年度绩效考核。

财会人才培训时间：一般来说，马来西亚企业每年对会计人员的 CPD 时间没有要求。但是，作为 MIA、MICPA、ACCA 等注册会员的会计人才需要具有一定的最低 CPD 小时数。另外，德勤等专业会计师事务所每年对会计人员的 CPD 时间亦有要求。

财会人才对公司绩效的重要性：受访者认为财会人才对公司绩效的提高"重要"（4 分）。

财会人才胜任能力排序（5分为最重要）

能力/技能	重要度（分值）
财务会计的知识及方法	4
管理会计的知识及方法	4
税务的知识	3
数据分析的能力	4
懂得运用科技及相关的软件	5
风险管理的知识及方法	3
公司治理的知识及方法	3
审计和认证业务的知识及方法	3
熟悉企业的商业模式	3
对战略选择的评估能力	3
能把握宏观经济对企业的影响	4
行业前沿与把握	3

阿联酋

专业机构：会计师和审计师协会 http：//aaa4uae.ae/en/；阿联酋特许会计师公会 https：//www.icaiauh.org/。

财会人才能力研究：没有这类研究及研究报告。

企业财会人才的胜任能力标准/培养计划：能力要求通常围绕着国际财务报告准则、财务计划和报告、增值税、风险管理知识等。

大多数公司没有专门负责财会人才培养的部门；因为大多数公司依靠四大会计师事务所向其组织提供培训，或通过参加国际财务报告准则研讨会进行提升。

企业培养财会人才胜任能力的方法及评价。培养方法有：专业资格培训、组织内部培训、在职的自我摸索、在职的上司指导、对外考察交流、暂调业务部门作深入了解。评价：非常有效。受访者来自于1家四大会计师事务所，所以该公司提供的会计培训水平远远高于行业内公司提供的会计培训。

企业财会人才绩效考核：财会人才的年度绩效考核取决于公司的规模，因公司而异。

企业财会人才培训时间：在没有认证管理机构的情况下，没有培训时间的要求。然而，一些监管机构（如 DFSA）需要保证一定的继续教育时间。

财会人才对公司绩效的重要性：受访者认为财会人才对公司绩效的提高"重要"（4分）。

财会人才胜任能力排序（5分为最重要）

能力/技能	重要度（分值）
财务会计的知识及方法	5
管理会计的知识及方法	3

能力/技能	重要度（分值）
税务的知识	1
数据分析的能力	3
懂得运用科技及相关的软件	4
风险管理的知识及方法	3
公司治理的知识及方法	3
审计和认证业务的知识及方法	2
熟悉企业的商业模式	3
对战略选择的评估能力	3
能把握宏观经济对企业的影响	2
行业前沿与把握	3

波　兰

专业机构：无。只有会计专业组织（如波兰财政部 http：//www.mf.gov.pl/en/news），没有专门的财会人才培养机构。

财会人才能力研究：大多数经济类大学正基于各自的教学培养计划对本国会计人才进行研究，但研究报告都没有正式发表。

企业财会人才的胜任能力标准/培养计划：无统一的能力标准，这取决于企业的实际需要。

企业培养财会人才胜任能力的方法及评价。培养方法：专业资格培训、组织内部培训、在职的自我摸索、暂调业务部门作深入了解。评价：这些培养方法使员工更自信。所有员工都必须接受培训，其中短期的借调在高层次员工中很受欢迎。

企业财会人才绩效考核：企业每年会对财会人员做绩效考核。

企业财会人才培训时间：企业没有规定财会人员每年必须接受的培训时间，波兰注册会计师协会对会员的继续教育时间也没有要求。

财会人才对公司绩效的重要性：受访者认为财会人才对公司绩效的提高介于"重要"（4分）与"非常重要"（5分）之间。

财会人才胜任能力排序（5分为最重要）

能力/技能	重要度（分值）
财务会计的知识及方法	4
管理会计的知识及方法	4
税务的知识	3
数据分析的能力	5
懂得运用科技及相关的软件	4
风险管理的知识及方法	4
公司治理的知识及方法	4

续表

能力/技能	重要度（分值）
审计和认证业务的知识及方法	4
熟悉企业的商业模式	3
对战略选择的评估能力	4
能把握宏观经济对企业的影响	4
行业前沿与把握	3

捷　　克

专业机构：国家会计委员会——为会计人才、会计师职业道德和会计方法提供支持的独立专家机构。会员如下：捷克共和国审计商会 http：//www. kacr. cz/en/，捷克共和国税务顾问商会 https：//www. kdpcr. cz/，会计师工会 http：//www. svaz-ucetnich. eu/index_en. php，经济贸易大学 http：//ffu. vse. cz/english/，ACCA 组织 http：//www. accaglobal. com/crsh/en. html。

财会人才能力研究：没有这类研究及研究报告。

企业财会人才的胜任能力标准/培养计划：没有能力标准与培养计划。

企业培养财会人才胜任能力的方法及评价。培养方法有：在职提高学历、专业资格培训、参与外部培训及论坛、组织内部培训、轮岗、在职的自我摸索、公司内跨部门的讨论、暂调业务部门作深入了解。评价：有效且受欢迎。

企业财会人才绩效考核：没有。

企业财会人才培训时间：取决于企业，通常是在每年 10～20 小时之间，如果是审计人员则超过 20 小时。

财会人才对公司绩效的重要性：受访者认为财会人才对公司绩效的提高"一般"（3 分）。

财会人才胜任能力排序（5 分为最重要）

能力/技能	重要度（分值）
财务会计的知识及方法	5
管理会计的知识及方法	4
税务的知识	4

续表

能力/技能	重要度（分值）
数据分析的能力	4
懂得运用科技及相关的软件	4
风险管理的知识及方法	3
公司治理的知识及方法	2
审计和认证业务的知识及方法	3
熟悉企业的商业模式	3
对战略选择的评估能力	3
能把握宏观经济对企业的影响	2
行业前沿与把握	3

卡塔尔

专业机构：卡塔尔没有设置会计人才培养的专门机构或组织。

财务人才能力研究：卡塔尔没有相关的会计人才能力研究报告。

企业财会人才培养计划：卡塔尔明确会计人才所需的技能包括：第一，至少拥有会计学学士学位；第二，拥有国际认证 CPA ／ ACCA ／ CA 资格。

卡塔尔培养财会人才胜任能力的方法包括在职提高学历、专业资格培训、参与外部培训及论坛、组织内部培训、轮岗、在职的自我摸索、在职的上司指导、对外考察交流、公司内跨部门的讨论、暂调业务部门作深入了解。受访者认为这些方法是有效果的。

财会人才绩效考核：卡塔尔存在财会人才年度绩效考核。

财会人才培训时间：在卡塔尔没有具体的要求。但是德勤内部要求每年有 20 小时的 CPE，并且在 3 年后达到总计 120 小时。卡塔尔的注册会计师协会对会员继续教育没有时间要求。

财会人才对公司绩效的重要性：受访者认为财会人才对公司绩效的提高"非常重要"（5 分）。

财会人才胜任能力排序（5 分为最重要）

能力/技能	重要度（分值）
财务会计的知识及方法	5
管理会计的知识及方法	5
税务的知识	4
数据分析的能力	4
懂得运用科技及相关的软件	4
风险管理的知识及方法	3

续表

能力/技能	重要度（分值）
公司治理的知识及方法	3
审计和认证业务的知识及方法	3
熟悉企业的商业模式	5
对战略选择的评估能力	3
能把握宏观经济对企业的影响	3
行业前沿与把握	5

匈牙利

专业机构：匈牙利审计师商会。

财务人才能力研究：匈牙利没有相关的会计人才能力研究报告。

企业财会人才培养计划：匈牙利没有相关的财会人才培养计划。

匈牙利培养财会人才胜任能力的方法包括在职提高学历、专业资格培训、参与外部培训及论坛、组织内部培训、在职的上司指导、公司内跨部门的讨论、暂调业务部门作深入了解。受访者认为这些方法是非常有效的发展方法。

财会人才绩效考核：匈牙利不存在财会人才年度绩效考核。

财会人才培训时间：审计师和会计师都有具体的培训要求。培训的一般要求是 10～20 小时之间，但可能更多地取决于专业。

财会人才对公司绩效的重要性：匈牙利的财会人才对公司业绩的提高非常重要（5分）。

财会人才胜任能力排序（5分为最重要）

能力/技能	重要度（分值）
财务会计的知识及方法	5
管理会计的知识及方法	4
税务的知识	3
数据分析的能力	4
懂得运用科技及相关的软件	4
风险管理的知识及方法	5
公司治理的知识及方法	3
审计和认证业务的知识及方法	5
熟悉企业的商业模式	3
对战略选择的评估能力	3
能把握宏观经济对企业的影响	3
行业前沿与把握	3

泰　　国

专业机构：会计专业联合会（FAP）http：//en. fap. or. th/。

财务人才能力研究：泰国没有相关的会计人才能力研究报告。

企业财会人才培养计划：泰国企业没有具体的技能要求。然而，获得泰国注册会计师执照后，注册会计师持有者必须每年完成 20 个小时的正式培训和 20 个小时的非正式培训作为继续教育。

泰国培养财会人才胜任能力的方法包括在职提高学历、专业资格培训、参与外部培训及论坛、组织内部培训、在职的自我摸索、在职的上司指导、对外考察交流、公司内跨部门的讨论、暂调业务部门作深入了解。泰国全体员工遵守公司的人才发展政策是强制性的。受访者认为这样的发展是有效的，并且将随着公司的发展而使员工获得更好的技能。

财会人才绩效考核：泰国存在财会人才年度绩效考核。来自德勤的泰国受访者认为公司会进行半年度和年度绩效评估。

财会人才培训时间：泰国会计专业联合会（FAP）要求所有注册会计师持有人必须每年完成 20 小时正式培训和 20 小时非正式培训作为继续教育。

财会人才对公司绩效的重要性：受访者认为财会人才对公司绩效的提高非常重要（5 分）。

财会人才胜任能力排序（5 分为最重要）

能力/技能	重要度（分值）
财务会计的知识及方法	5
管理会计的知识及方法	4
税务的知识	5
数据分析的能力	5
懂得运用科技及相关的软件	5
风险管理的知识及方法	5

续表

能力/技能	重要度（分值）
公司治理的知识及方法	5
审计和认证业务的知识及方法	4
熟悉企业的商业模式	5
对战略选择的评估能力	4
能把握宏观经济对企业的影响	4
行业前沿与把握	5

越　南

专业机构：越南注册会计师和审计师协会（VACPA）。越南人才培养计划暂时未有相关信息，但是 VACPA 为越南提供了大量的专业人才。

财务人才能力研究：未提供相关答案。

企业财会人才培养计划：越南存在相关的会计法规明确规定了相关要求。以下从 2003 年会计法中摘录，第 50 条：会计师的标准、权利与责任。会计师必须满足如下条件：拥有职业道德、诚实、清廉并且遵守法规；必须拥有专业的会计资格证书；会计师拥有在专业会计工作中独立工作的权力；会计师必须按法规要求记账，执行分配给他们的工作并且对所做的工作负责，当会计师离职时，离职会计师必须将相关会计工作和会计档案移交给继任会计师，并对工作期间的会计工作负责。

越南培养财会人才胜任能力的方法包括在职提高学历、专业资格培训、参与外部培训及论坛、组织内部培训、轮岗、在职的自我摸索、公司内跨部门的讨论、暂调业务部门作深入了解。受访者认为以上相关方式对于培养财务人员是很适合的、有效的，在绝大多数会计师事务所，以上方式是比较流行的。

财会人才绩效考核：越南大多数公司存在财会人才年度绩效考核。

财会人才培训时间：越南对于财务人员每年接受培训有明确的时间规定，一般要求培训时间不低于 40 小时。

财会人才对公司绩效的重要性：受访者认为财会人才对公司绩效的提高"重要"（4 分）。

财会人才胜任能力排序（5分为最重要）

能力/技能	重要度（分值）
财务会计的知识及方法	5
管理会计的知识及方法	2
税务的知识	3
数据分析的能力	4
懂得运用科技及相关的软件	2
风险管理的知识及方法	4
公司治理的知识及方法	3
审计和认证业务的知识及方法	5
熟悉企业的商业模式	3
对战略选择的评估能力	2
能把握宏观经济对企业的影响	4
行业前沿与把握	4

俄罗斯

专业机构：没有专门负责会计人才发展的机构。不过可以通过参加专业会计师团体的专业考试获得专业资格，包括：ACCA http：//www. accaglobal. com/gb/en. html，CPA http：//www. cpa. org. ru/about/en/a-bout – EICPA。

财会人才能力研究：没有这类研究及研究报告。

企业财会人才的胜任能力标准/培养计划：政府从 2016 年开始引进专业标准会计师。根据本标准，参与会计职能的员工应该具备一系列的知识和技能（例如，准备主要文件、准备财务报表、了解立法、技术应用）。公司没有专门开设培训计划或负责人才培养的部门。

企业培养财会人才胜任能力的方法及评价。培养方法有：在职提高学历、专业资格培训、参与外部培训及论坛、组织内部培训、轮岗、在职的自我摸索、在职的上司指导、对外考察交流、公司内跨部门的讨论、暂调业务部门作深入了解等。评价：所有上述方法都适用于俄罗斯。它们的有效性和受欢迎程度取决于业务规模和企业经营的行业。

企业财会人才年度绩效考核：没有。

企业财会人才培训时间：政府层面没有强制性的培训时间要求。

财会人才对公司绩效的重要性：受访者认为财会人才对公司绩效的提高"重要"（4 分）。

财会人才胜任能力排序（5 分为最重要）

能力/技能	重要度（分值）
财务会计的知识及方法	5
管理会计的知识及方法	5
税务的知识	5
数据分析的能力	5

续表

能力/技能	重要度（分值）
懂得运用科技及相关的软件	5
风险管理的知识及方法	3
公司治理的知识及方法	3
审计和认证业务的知识及方法	3
熟悉企业的商业模式	4
对战略选择的评估能力	3
能把握宏观经济对企业的影响	4
行业前沿与把握	5

印度尼西亚

专业机构：大学为会计人才发展承担责任，主要由印度尼西亚大学负责网站：http://www.feb.ui.ac.id/akuntansi/。

财会人才能力研究：相关研究请访问印度尼西亚大学网站：http://www.feb.ui.ac.id/akuntansi/。

企业培养财会人才胜任能力的方法及评价。培养方法有：专业资格培训、参与外部培训及论坛、组织内部培训。评价：非常有效。

企业财会人才年度绩效考核：受访者认为印度尼西亚会进行年度绩效考核。

企业财会人才培训时间：受访者认为印度尼西亚必须满足最低40小时的继续教育学时，该要求同样适用于认证会员。

财会人才对公司绩效的重要性：受访者认为财会人才对公司绩效的提高非常重要（5分）。

财会人才胜任能力排序（5分为最重要）

能力/技能	重要度（分值）
财务会计的知识及方法	5
管理会计的知识及方法	3
税务的知识	5
数据分析的能力	5
懂得运用科技及相关的软件	5
风险管理的知识及方法	4
公司治理的知识及方法	3
审计和认证业务的知识及方法	5

续表

能力/技能	重要度（分值）
熟悉企业的商业模式	4
对战略选择的评估能力	3
能把握宏观经济对企业的影响	3
行业前沿与把握	4

哈萨克斯坦

专业机构：哈萨克斯坦没有专门负责会计人才发展的机构。不过，哈萨克斯坦的专业会计机构会提供会计师教育服务。也可以通过专业考试，获得专业资格，包括 ACCA、认证会计从业员（CIP）、认证国际专业会计师（CIPA）和专业会计师等。

财务人才能力研究：哈萨克斯坦没有相关的会计人才能力研究报告。

企业财会人才培养计划：根据哈萨克斯坦共和国"关于会计和财务报告"的规定，截至 2012 年 1 月 1 日，专业会计师可以任命为公共利益组织的总会计师（法律第 9 条）。专业会计师是根据 2007 年 12 月 13 日哈萨克斯坦共和国财政部长第 455 号通过的资格要求，具有专业会计师证书的个人。哈萨克斯坦没有要求在公司开设培训计划或特殊部门。

哈萨克斯坦培养财会人才胜任能力的方法包括在职提高学历、专业资格培训、参与外部培训及论坛、组织内部培训、轮岗、在职的自我摸索、在职的上司指导、对外考察交流、公司内跨部门的讨论、暂调业务部门作深入了解。受访者认为所有上述方法都适用于哈萨克斯坦。它们的有效性和受欢迎程度取决于业务规模和企业经营的行业。

财会人才绩效考核：哈萨克斯坦不存在财会人才年度绩效考核。

财会人才培训时间：哈萨克斯坦在政府一级没有强制要求 CPD 时间。

财会人才对公司绩效的重要性：受访者认为财会人才对公司绩效的提高"重要"（4 分）。

财会人才胜任能力排序（5 分为最重要）

能力/技能	重要度（分值）
财务会计的知识及方法	5
管理会计的知识及方法	5
税务的知识	5

续表

能力/技能	重要度（分值）
数据分析的能力	5
懂得运用科技及相关的软件	5
风险管理的知识及方法	3
公司治理的知识及方法	3
审计和认证业务的知识及方法	3
熟悉企业的商业模式	4
对战略选择的评估能力	3
能把握宏观经济对企业的影响	4
行业前沿与把握	5

印　　度

专业机构：没有具体的机构或组织负责会计人才的发展。

财会人才能力研究：受访者不了解该国是否有这类的研究。

企业财会人才的胜任能力标准/培养计划：没有具体的能力标准。

企业培养财会人才胜任能力的方法及评价。培养方法有：专业资格培训、参与外部培训及论坛、组织内部培训、轮岗、在职的自我摸索、在职的上司指导、暂调业务部门作深入了解。

企业财会人才年度绩效考核：会计人才在评估过程中有年度绩效考核。不过，可能并不是所有公司都如此。

企业财会人才培训时间：CPE（继续教育）小时要求不同类别的会员遵守3年（2017.1.1～2019.12.31）的封锁期限。第一，所有持有执业证书（年龄在60岁以下）的所有成员（居住在国外的成员除外）必须在3年的滚动期内完成至少120个CPE学时，在每个日历年度完成系统化学习的最低20个CPE学时，60个CPE信用时间（每个日历年度最少20个CPE学时）可以通过系统化或非系统化的学习完成（根据每个成员的选择）。第二，所有没有持有执业证书的成员（年龄在60岁以下），以及所有在国外居住的成员（不论是否持有执业证书）都必须在3年的滚动期内，通过系统化或非系统化的学习（根据每个成员的选择）完成至少60个CPE学时，在每个日历年度内，完成系统化或非系统化学习（根据每个成员的选择）的最低15个CPE学时。第三，另对60岁及以上持有执业证书的所有成员以及不受CPE学时要求的成员有具体要求。

财会人才对公司绩效的重要性：受访者认为财会人才对公司绩效的提高非常重要（5分）。

财会人才胜任能力排序（5 分为最重要）

能力/技能	重要度（分值）
财务会计的知识及方法	5
管理会计的知识及方法	5
税务的知识	4
数据分析的能力	5
懂得运用科技及相关的软件	3
风险管理的知识及方法	3
公司治理的知识及方法	3
审计和认证业务的知识及方法	4
熟悉企业的商业模式	4
对战略选择的评估能力	2
能把握宏观经济对企业的影响	1
行业前沿与把握	1

巴基斯坦

专业机构：参与开发会计人才的本地专业团体包括：巴基斯坦特许会计师公会（ICAP）http：//www. icap. org. pk/，巴基斯坦公共财政会计师公会（PIPFA）http：//pipfa. org. pk/，巴基斯坦成本与管理会计师协会（IC-MAP）https：//www. icmap. com. pk/。发展会计人才的外国专业团体包括：ACCA 巴基斯坦 http：//www. accaglobal. com/pk/en. html 等。在本地开展会计人才的最著名的大学有：海洋管理科学大学（LUMS）https：//lums. edu. pk/，工商管理学院（IBA）https：//www. iba. edu. pk/，卡拉奇大学（UoK）http：//uok. edu. pk/。

会计教育提供者：ICAP 批准注册会计教育辅导员（RAET）被授权为 ICAP、MFC 学生举办辅导班。这些 RAET 是本地会计人才发展的组成部分。这些 RAET 的列表可以在链接中找到：https：//goo. gl/WaMcu5。ICAP 要求学生在批准的执业公司和外部培训机构（TOOP）进行培训。这些组织也增进了全国会计人才的发展。该链接列出已批准的雇主：https：//goo. gl/xx-qgNR。

财务人才能力研究：受访者对相关的会计人才能力研究报告并不清楚。

企业财会人才培养计划：巴基斯坦总体上没有指定组织或企业的指导方针，但是存在根据不同的职业描述定义不同的能力或技能。在某些情况下，有相关部门提供的具体指导方针，如巴基斯坦证券交易所的上市条例为上市公司任命内部审计总监和首席财务官提供指导。根据指导，候选人应该是公认的专业机构的成员。组织通常有一个学习和开发部门，负责会计人才的培训计划。例如，学习部门定期修改培训内容，进行促销培训，软件更新培训等。

巴基斯坦培养财会人才胜任能力的方法包括：专业资格培训，组织内部培训，在职的自我摸索，暂调业务部门作深入了解。

受访者认为选定的发展途径非常有效。因为从其他专业人士那里学习，并从所在的组织那里得到培训，能够得到更好的反馈和更好的学习应用。使用培训师模式，将学习传授给群众，并具有涓滴效应。对于内部培训，可聘请外部专业培训师从中受益于特定的专业培训。

财会人才绩效考核：巴基斯坦会计实务或行业工作人员按照组织的政策进行评估。

财会人才培训时间：巴基斯坦企业普遍没有 CPD 小时的具体要求，但不同企业的人力资源政策要求有所不同。专业团体的成员必须遵守专业机构的 CPD 要求。例如，ICAP 根据其指令 8.01 提供 CPD 指导，可从以下网址获得：https：//goo.gl/A7DzJa。

财会人才对公司绩效的重要性：受访者认为财会人才对公司绩效的提高"重要"（4 分）。

财会人才胜任能力排序（5 分为最重要）

能力/技能	重要度（分值）
财务会计的知识及方法	5
管理会计的知识及方法	5
税务的知识	4
数据分析的能力	5
懂得运用科技及相关的软件	5
风险管理的知识及方法	4
公司治理的知识及方法	5
审计和认证业务的知识及方法	4
熟悉企业的商业模式	4
对战略选择的评估能力	4
能把握宏观经济对企业的影响	4
行业前沿与把握	4

后　记

　　习近平主席 2013 年提出"一带一路"倡议后，在国内外引起了巨大反响。许多机构都十分重视研究"一带一路"倡议可能带来的机遇，响应习主席号召，采取切实行动，积极推动"一带一路"建设。会计在一国经济运行和国际经济交往中发挥着重要的基础支撑作用。在"一带一路"倡议推进过程中，在会计及相关的税收、金融等领域，必然会碰到很多新问题、新挑战。加强对这一类问题的研究，加强沿线国家之间在会计及相关问题上的沟通与协调，必然会对"一带一路"建设起到积极的推动作用。2016年 11 月，在访问 ACCA 总部与白容（Hellen Brand）总裁交流的过程中，我们发现双方有共同的关切，迅即达成共识，决定由上海国家会计学院和 AC-CA 依托各自的优势，成立联合课题组，对"一带一路"会计相关问题进行研究，并在研究基础上召开高层研讨会。双方随即组织力量，成立了课题组，而拥有国际专家网络的德勤的加入，使课题组的力量进一步壮大。令人高兴的是，课题组成员克服了各种困难，如期完成了可以说是行业内第一份以"一带一路"会计及相关问题作为调查研究内容的较为系统的研究报告。纵然报告还有很多值得改进之处，但令人欣喜的是，很多方面都对报告的研究思路及其价值给予了高度肯定。

　　2017 年 5 月，"一带一路"国际合作高峰论坛在北京的成功举办使我们备受鼓舞，在财政部领导和会计司领导的大力支持下，中国会计学会加盟作为"会计基础设施助推'一带一路'"高层研讨会的联合主办方及在"一带一路"沿线国家成功开拓业务的浪潮集团等作为协办方加盟，则更进一步增强了我们举办一次成功的高质量论坛的信心。在各方的共同努力下，特别是来自政府部门、学术界、企业界的专家们的大力支持下，2017 年 7月在上海国家会计学院举办的研讨会取得了巨大的成功，这不仅是因为我们首次提出了"会计基础设施"概念并得到了大家的一致认同，还因为许多与会专家的高质量演讲给与会的国内外人士以深刻的启迪。为了让更多的人士从研讨会的成果中受益，我们成立了编辑小组，请所有专家对演讲稿进行了进一步的修改、充实和完善，并翻译了中英文两个文本，便于国内外朋友参考。现在奉献在大家面前的就是研讨会专家和编辑组成员们在过去几个月中共同辛勤劳动的成果。

在这本文集行将付印出版之际，我要特别感谢赵鸣骥部长助理和高一斌司长对我们工作的大力支持。赵助理从百忙之中亲临研讨会发表高屋建瓴的演讲，既表达了财政部对"一带一路"会计相关问题的高度重视，也为我们进一步开展相关工作提供了重要的指导。我也要感谢我的老朋友中国交通集团傅建元副总经理、亚洲开发银行经济研究与区域合作局高级顾问赤松范隆（Noritaka Akamatsu）先生、浪潮集团王兴山执行总裁等所有专家的支持。无论是研究工作的开展还是研讨会的组织，抑或是这本文集的编辑出版，都是精诚合作、协同努力的结果。我要借此机会对担任本书联合主编的财政部会计司王鹏副巡视员、ACCA 白容总裁和德勤中国首席执行官曾顺福先生表示衷心感谢。我还要感谢经济科学出版社的编辑们为本文集出版付出的艰苦努力。最后，我要感谢为本书出版付出巨大努力的幕后英雄们，他们是德勤中国的刘明华女士、任铮女士；ACCA 的梁淑屏女士、钱毓益女士、朱晓云女士；以及上海国家会计学院的葛玉御博士、佟成生博士、刘晓强先生、傅秋莲女士、吕晓雷先生和李昕凝博士等。

"一带一路"倡议自提出以来，已经取得了丰硕的成果，还将取得更加丰硕的成果。"一带一路"在路上，倡议的推进需要会计界作出更加积极的努力。我们期待着与各界朋友一起，精诚合作，共襄盛举，夯实会计基础设施，打造美好未来！

上海国家会计学院院长　李扣庆
二〇一七年十月二十一日

Accounting Infrastructure：
A Booster to the Belt and
Road Initiative

Edited by LI Kouqing   Wang Peng   Helen Brand   Patrick Tsang

中国财经出版传媒集团

经济科学出版社
Economic Science Press

Contents

Preface

Enhancing the Accounting Infrastructure to Promote the Belt and Road Initiative

Zhao Mingji [*]

In 2013, President Xi Jinping put forward the major initiative to build the Silk Road Economic Belt and 21st Century Maritime Silk Road, triggering sensational positive responses at home and abroad. During the past four years, China's enablement and the joint efforts of all countries concerned have proved fruitful in terms of policy coordination, infrastructure connectivity, unimpeded trade, financial integration, and people-to-people bond (a five-pronged approach). In May 2017, the Belt and Road Forum was successfully held in Beijing, which attracted attention of the whole world. At the forum, a positive signal was issued, seeking a concerted effort to promote international cooperation under the Initiative as well as to build a community of shared future for mankind, which is vital to the world and China alike.

In recent years, following the deployment by the Central Government, the Chinese Ministry of Finance has been functioning actively to facilitate the rollout of the Initiative and the five-pronged approach from policy and funding aspects, and achieved satisfactory positive results. Policy coordination is an important guarantee for the well-being of the Initiative, and the MOF leverages the international dialogue mechanism to deepen intergovernmental macro-policy coordination and enable regional economic integration in the principle of seeking common ground while sharing differences. At the same time, the MOF played its part in promoting

---

[*] Assistant Finance Minister, Member of the Party Leadership Group of the Ministry of Finance.

unimpeded trade by focusing on avoidance of double taxation and implementation of the free trade zone strategy. Financial integration is a pillar of the Initiative. The Chinese government has initiated the establishment of Asian Infrastructure Investment Bank (AIIB), Silk Road Fund and other relevant financial organizations, and has deepened cooperation with traditional multilateral development agencies such as the World Bank, striving to create a Belt and Road financing network that takes shape with a clear hierarchy. People-to-people bond is the social basis for the Belt and Road Initiative. In recent years, the central finance has strongly supported various exchanges with the Belt and Road countries, laying a rock solid foundation of public will to deepen bilateral and multilateral cooperation. Last month, Research Center for The Belt and Road Financial and Economic Development had been established by MOF, which responded the initiative arose by President Xi Jinping in the Belt and Road Forum for International Cooperation, for further establishment in think-tank and the platform of cooperation and exchange which is serviced to the development of the Belt and Road Initiative. Finance, as the cornerstone of governance of a state, will further play an active role in keeping the Belt and Road Initiative steady and sustainable.

As an underlying business language for interconnectivity, accounting is an important basis for modern social and economic activities. The quality of internal accounting within an economy is directly related to the efficiency of its macro as well as micro operations, while differences in accounting standards or systems between different economies will directly affect trade and financial integration. It can be argued that accounting is an important infrastructure for international economic ties and progress, while the accounting standards, talents and regulatory systems determine the quality and efficiency of a country's accounting work.

The Belt and Road jurisdictions differ in terms of nation and culture, with over 50 official languages and more than 10 accounting systems in use. In the face of the gap in the accounting system, including disparities in accounting standards, systems and professionals, we have to answer an essential question: how to take effective measures to promote the interoperability of national accounting systems so as to achieve common, inclusive and green development. At the parallel round-table themed "Facilitate Financial Integration", Finance Minister Xiao Jie clearly pinpointed that financial integration is born to guarantee steady and sustainable progress of the Belt and Road Initiative. Efficient and secure financial integration requires the institutions concerned in all Belt and Road countries to strengthen coordination and cooperation in accounting, taxation, finance and other aspects so as to facilitate regional cargo circulation and financial integration. Given the concerted efforts across the community to translate the Initiative into reality, the accounting community also echoes through collective research on the accounting infrastructure to push forward the Initiative. The forum today has a good theme, which fits in well the current stage of implementing the Belt and Road Initiative, and needs to be discussed seriously.

To achieve the magnificent concept of the Belt and Road Initiative, the construction of accounting infrastructure is of great significance, yet also takes long way to go.

First, promote the convergence or coordination of accounting standards and systems on an ongoing basis to reduce the transaction costs of financial integration and unimpeded trade.

It is an inherent need of globalization to promote the international convergence of accounting standards as well as to strengthen the communication and coordination between accounting systems in various countries. The advancement of the Belt and Road Initiative has put forward more urgent requirements in this regard. Since the beginning of reform and opening up in the late 1970s, the Chinese government has attached great importance to the reshaping of China's accounting systems and regarded it as one of the crucial measures to foster the socialist market economy, striving for the convergence of the Chinese accounting standards with the international financial reporting standards (IFRS). There are different approaches to the construction of national accounting standards in the Belt and Road countries. Some adopt the complete IFRS, and some use their own unique standard system. I think that Belt and Road countries should exchange more of their experiences and lessons learned in the construction of the accounting standards system to find out the best way to converge or coordinate the accounting standards that differ most among them, reducing cross-border transaction costs and promoting mutual trade and financial integration.

Second, step up the training of international accountancy professionals as well as the cooperation with Belt and Road countries in accounting personnel training.

Hu Ai, a Chinese philosopher in the Northern Song Dynasty (AD 960 – 1127), has a famous saying: "Good governance is based on talent, while talent on education. " The Belt and Road Initiative draws a blueprint for building a community of shared future for mankind, and the key to realize this vision lies in the ability to nurture sufficient and eligible professionals for the implementation of the Initiative. In the past few years, China and many Belt and Road countries have launched a series of measures for high-end personnel training. The MOF of China launched a national training project for leading accounting personnel in 2005 and achieved remarkable results. The project was delegated to the National Accounting Institutes that have enrolled a total of 1, 587 trainees in 38 classes in more than a decade, of whom 601 trainees graduated successfully, and a total of 27 trainees were recruited under a three-session special support program. In addition, the local financial authorities nationwide have also launched campaigns for accounting leading personnel training in line with their unique features. The head of SNAI (AFDI) told me that the institute celebrated the graduation of its first masters in Accounting in Developing Countries, a proof of the training outcome and a valuable experience in strategic talent pooling for the Belt and Road Initiative.

Although we have done a lot of work in personnel training, there remains a large gap in senior accounting talent supply for international practice when compared to the talent needed for the Initiative as well as for our engagement in global economic governance, and we still need to cultivate more practitioners who are able to adapt well to the Belt and Road Initiative. To this end, I think the Initiative should be incorporated into their respective talent training frameworks, with the corresponding investment doubled and cooperation between countries enhanced in the training of accounting personnel. I also hope that the National Accounting Institutes and other institutions concerned will blaze a new trail and make greater contributions.

Third, strengthen communication across accounting community in Belt and Road countries, including the academia, government departments and the CPA profession.

President Xi has stressed that in the rollout of the Belt and Road Initiative, we should strive to form a cooperation model out of the organic combination of the government, market and community, as well as a government-led architecture featuring corporate participation and civil facilitation. To realize the Belt and Road Initiative, we must develop a cultural landscape of mutual appreciation, mutual understanding and mutual respect among the peoples in Belt and Road countries. To foster such an atmosphere, the accounting profession should make its own contribution with sustained efforts to establish all-inclusive, multi-channel communication mechanisms and platforms for coherent, enhanced understanding and consensus. The forum is a perfect platform, and the keynote speakers include government officials, academic experts, and representatives from international organizations and model enterprises engaged in the Belt and Road Initiative. I look forward to more similar communication platforms in the accounting community, which will respond positively to the Initiative for its practical implementation. In this regard, I have a special suggestion for the academic, intermediary and business circles in Belt and Road countries to strengthen the cooperative research on accounting, taxation, finance and other related issues in the implementation of the Belt and Road Initiative so that we can spot problems in this process, address public concerns, put forward feasible solutions, and contribute new wisdom as well as voice of accounting for better policy coordination.

The Belt and Road Initiative is a major strategic proposition that benefits the whole world. Accounting infrastructure is an important part of the endeavor, which is more demanding in a more developed economy. The well-established accounting infrastructure is a powerful driving factor for accelerating social and economic activities, and will facilitate economic exchanges and trade between countries.

The forum held today is to point out our destination, and I believe it will be a good start. I hope that all parties concerned will continue to study and hone the connotation of accounting infrastructure and jointly promote the Belt and Road Initiative. In doing so, we shall give full play to the role of accounting as a common business language and a new driving force for the great practice of the Initiative.

Forward

Given the significance of accounting infrastructure in driving the cooperation between the countries along the Belt and Road Initiative, Shanghai National Accounting Institute (SNAI), the Association of Chartered Certified Accountants (ACCA) and Deloitte China jointly set up a research team at the end of 2016 to work on the setting of accounting standards, the training of accounting talents and the taxation systems in the Belt and Road Initiative countries. In July 2017, the three parties joined hands with Accounting Society of China (ASC) and Inspur Group in hosting a high-level symposium on "Accounting Infrastructure" Promotes "Belt and Road Initiative". Here are the Chinese and English versions of research reports and meeting papers.

The issues, such as accounting standards collaboration, tax risk regulation and cross-border capital cooperation, identified during the implementation of the Belt and Road Initiative have been demonstrated from different perspectives in research reports and speeches made by experts at the symposium, which will be helpful references for any friends who are committed to studying the relevant issues. The Belt and Road initiative is an impressive, colossal-scale blueprint with far-reaching implications. We sincerely hope that the book will play its due and positive role in pushing forward the researches on accounting issues relating to putting the grand plan to work, thus laying a far more solid accounting infrastructure for the Belt and Road initiative.

Editorial Board

If there is any inconsistency between the English and Chinese version, the Chinese version shall prevail.

What is Accounting Infrastructure? ①

Li Kouqing   Ge Yuyu

I. The concept of accounting infrastructure

Infrastructure, as a key concept in socio-economic field, was first proposed by Paul Rosenstein-Rodan, who was an expert in development economics, in 1943. He divided the total social investment into two categories including social overhead capital and private capital that the former one is also called 'infrastructure'. This categorization is generally accepted and followed by later generations. As social development goes on, the connotation of infrastructure has been enriched. In the *World Development Report 1994* released by the World Bank, infrastructure is divided into 'economic infrastructure' and 'social infrastructure'. The former refers to the construction facilities to be used for a long time and their services for economic activities and household, including: a) public utilities, such as electricity, telecommunications, pipeline, gas, tap water, sewage, garbage collection and treatment; b) public projects, such as dams, hydro-power projects and roads building; and c) transport networks, such as railway, city, traffic, port, watercourse and airport. Hence, economic infrastructure is also called 'hard infrastructure'. In comparison, social infrastructure mainly refers to education, healthcare, legislation, regulation and financial systems, hence is also called 'soft

① Professor, President and CPC Party Secretary, SNAI; Lecturer, Teaching & Research Department, SNAI; My acknowledgements go to Tong Chengsheng, Ye Xiaojie, Song Hang, Zhao Min and Wang Lei, for their great support.

infrastructure'.

Infrastructure is pioneering and foundational that the public services, included in infrastructure, are the precondition and basis of social production and people's livelihood. Therefore, infrastructure is meaningful to a lot for socio-economic development. Theoretically, domestic and foreign literatures prove that infrastructure can improve economic efficiency, lower transaction cost and drive economic growth (Easterly & Rebelo, 1993; Gramlich, 1994; Liu Shenglong & Hu Angang, 2010; Zhang Guangnan & Song Ran, 2013). In practice, economic growth is indeed driven by nation-wide infrastructure investment and construction, especially in the emerging economies. Therefore, both theory and practice have proved infrastructure's significance for economic growth. In 2017 report released by Asian Development Bank ("ADB"), it illustrated that for promoting economic growth, infrastructure investment in Asia needs to reach USD 26 trillion during the period of 2016 – 2030, averagely USD 1.7 trillion per year, which goes far beyond its current lending capacity. As a result, at the initiation of China and with the participation of many nations, the Asian Infrastructure Investment Bank (AIIB) was set up in December 2015, whose key mission is to support infrastructure constructions promote regional cooperation and economic intergration.

Apparently, all countries are committed to infrastructure development, and even have conducted some effective cross-border collaborations driven by economic globalization. However, the effort is focused far more on the 'hard infrastructure' like transport, energy and telecommunications than the supportive 'soft infrastructure' like accounting, taxation, finance and legislation. In fact, hard infrastructure development is largely dependent on the support of soft infrastructure. Furthermore, if soft infrastructure lags behind, the hard infrastructure like transport and energy will play a diminished role in economic development. Huang Yasheng (2005) found out that soft infrastructure will generate long-term driving force, which should be valued to the most. Therefore, accounting as an integral part of the soft infrastructure and also a universal business language is playing an ever increasingly important role in economic growth. It is not only the case for domestic business activities and financing but also true for cross-border trade in goods and services, and capital flows. Therefore, it is quite essential to propose the concept of 'accounting infrastructure' and have a further study into it.

II. Connotation of accounting infrastructure

At the 3rd Plenary Session of the 18th CPC Party Congress, it was officially stated "Finance is the basis and key pillar of state governance". As we know, national finance indeed plays a fundamental role in state governance and economic growth, whereas accounting plays a fundamental role in the national finance or even the whole national economy. At the micro level, the quality of accounting data, namely accuracy, timeliness, sufficiency and relevance, determines the reasonability of price signals in resources allocation, thus influencing investor's investment decisions. At the macro level, the quality of accounting data may have an impact on the accuracy of the macroeconomic data, then further down on the formulation and results of national finance, taxation and monetary policies. From a broader global perspective, due to the discrepancy of accounting standards in different economies as well as in different regulation intensity and staff expertise, accounting data may not be directly communicated to each other. As a result, such business language barriers will definitely increase cross-border trading cost, thus hampering trade and economic cooperation at multiple levels.

In light of the accounting infrastructure definition given above, the paper purports that accounting infrastructure refers to the infrastructure that provides quantitative data support for a country's economic performance and cross-border transactions. Specifically, accounting infrastructure includes three parts: accounting standards, regulation and professionals. First, accounting standards refer to the standardization of accounting and reporting practices when it comes to a certain stage, with a purpose to improve financial data consistency, authenticity and comparability for decision making. Generally speaking, the quality of a country's accounting infrastructure largely depends on the quality of its accounting standards. Without scientific and reasonable accounting standards, the accounting

3

measurement and settlement would lose ground. Second, as financial data is a scarce resource, it is necessary to improve financial regulation to combat information mismatch caused by power division under modern corporate system. Zhang Yikuan (2003) believed that the purpose of regulation is to avoid data distortion and guarantee data validity for decision-making in management and investment. In fact, accounting standards and financial regulation are consistent in nature: accounting standards are the basis of regulation in that high standards lead to better regulation, whereas regulation must be based on reliable financial data, and the effectiveness of regulatory indicators is determined by the quality of standards. Strong regulation makes sure the implementation of the standards to avoid accounting risk. Third, as standards development, improvement, implementation, and financial regulation are all executed by individuals, the quantity, quality and structure of professionals will determine whether the accounting infrastructure can support a nation's economic growth. In a nutshell, standards, regulation and professionals are three key pillars of a sound accounting infrastructure to support economic growth. The relationship of the three can be summed up like this: the accounting standards are the basis, the regulation is the safeguard and the professionals are the key. And more relevant elements will derive from the three key factors, such as finance education and professional training, various accounting services, supervisory regulators, etc.

The past experience in many countries has shown that better accounting infrastructure is an indispensable precondition for economic growth. To a large extent, it can ensure economic sustainability. Since the Reform and Opening-up, the Chinese government has attached great importance to accounting infrastructure development and regarded it as a guarantee for high-speed economic growth. As early as in June 1995 when an on-site meeting was held to discuss the establishment of a CPA training center (the predecessor of the National Accounting Institute), Zhu Rongji, the then Vice Premier of the State Council, said: "This is epoch-making event, the foundation of a socialist market economy and one of the most important things that we must do. " In 2006, China published its corporate accounting standards converging with international financial reporting standards (IFRS), which took effect on 1 January 2007. Thanks to it, the quality of Chinese companies' financial data has improved remarkably, constituting a huge boost for the development of the capital market. So far, China's corporate accounting standards has the same effect as the Hong Kong financial reporting standards and the IFRS adopted by the EU. The competent authorities are still working on to improve the existing standards to adapt to the latest developments so as to keep converging with the IFRS. On the financial regulation front, China has gradually set up a regulatory model featuring governmental regulator dominance complemented with industry self-discipline. It is designed to keep improving regulation mechanism, define regulation approaches, clarify obligation and responsibility of each authority, avoid overlap regulation, and reduce regulatory cost and accounting risk. In terms of professional training, China has taken measures like establishing National Accounting Institutes to build a comprehensive professional training system by mobilizing all the resources. In 2010, the Ministry of Finance released the *Mid-and-Long-term Financial Professionals Development Programme* 2010 – 2020, a guideline for financial professional training, and a systematic and strategic planning for the development of financial professional. Generally speaking, we have made valuable exploration on the construction and improvement of the accounting infrastructure, achieved remarkable results, and provided important support for the sustainable rapid development of socialist market economy.

III. Accounting infrastructure under the Belt and Road Initiative

Since 2013, the Belt and Road Initiative has scored great achievements in terms of "policy coordination, facilities connectivity, trading smooth, financial integration and people-to-people bonds". In particular, "facilities connectivity" is not only the key to the Belt and Road Initiative but also the precondition for "trading smooth" and "financial integration". Accounting infrastructure as an integral part of "facilities connectivity" determines the results of the Initiative.

Frankly speaking, the accounting infrastructure in the Belt and Road countries has two deficiencies. The first one is that financial standards, talents and regulations in some countries lag far behind. Secondly, the infrastructure varies greatly from country to country. The divergent accounting standards and systems hold back connectivity and increase trading cost.

Considering the complexity of the local contexts in the Belt and Road countries with the significance of strengthening accounting infrastructure, we need closer cross-border cooperation in the fields of financial standards, regulations and talents, so that the Belt and Road Initiative can bring about more benefits to the countries. Firstly, conduct in-depth researches. We need to examine the connotation and denotation of accounting infrastructure, and investigate the Belt and Road Initiative-related issues like accounting, taxation and financing. It is also essential to integrate the resources of the Belt and Road countries and relevant international organizations to find out how to promote the accounting infrastructure development and connectivity in the Belt and Road countries. Secondly, jointly start the Belt and Road accountancy professionals training. For instance, some measures, like cross-border training programs, exchange programs, etc. , are necessary for a frog-leaping development of backwater infrastructure in some countries. Thirdly, a multi-channel and multi-level communication mechanism should be established to better coordinate regulatory policies, prevent financial risks, promote standards convergence/equivalence and connectivity, and reduce cross-border trading cost, so as to boost the Belt and Road Initiative.

References

1. Guo Yongqing, "How To Build the Financial Professionals Training System in China". *Accounting Research*, 2008 (10).

2. Huang Yasheng. "Comparison of Hard and Soft Infrastructure in Economic Growth: Should China Learn from India?" . *World Economic and Politics*, 2005 (1).

3. Jin Ge. "Capital Stock Estimate of China's Infrastructure" . *Economic Research Journal*, 2012 (4).

4. Liu Shenglong & Hu Angang. "Test of Infrastructure Externality in China: 1988 –

2007". *Economic Research Journal*, 2010 (3) .

5. Zhang Guangnan & Song Ran. "The Impact of Transport on Factor Input of China Manufacturing". *Economic Research Journal*, 2013 (7) .

6. Zhang Yikuan. "The Financial Regulatory System with Chinese Characteristics". *Journal of Audit & Economics*, 2003 (1) .

7. Easterly, W. and Rebelo, S. "Fiscal Policy and Economic Growth: An Empirical Investigation". *Journal of Monetary Economics*, 1993, 32 (3) .

8. Gramlich, E. "Infrastructure Investment: A Review Essay". *Journal of Economic Literature*, 1994 (32) .

9. World Bank, World Development Report 1994: Infrastructure for Development, Oxford: Oxford University Press, 1994.

Accounting Infrastructure as Support for the Belt and Road Initiative

Helen Brand[*]

In my many years of visiting China, I've had the privilege of seeing the country's accountancy profession go from strength to strength. And I'm proud of the part ACCA members in China have played in building this reputation, for almost three decades and counting.

The esteem the profession enjoys here owes a great deal to the contribution of China national accounting institutes and the great work they do. ACCA has enjoyed a long and fruitful partnership with the Shanghai National Accounting Institute and we are delighted to be partnering with them again on this forum, which also marks the launch of a new report on Belt and Road with SNAI and Deloitte.

In this new piece of research, we explore the vital role that professional accountants will need to play as Belt and Road develops. Such an ambitious international trade route will only be successful if the economies along it collaborate productively. As a passionate support of global standards, we at ACCA have seen that this aids not only the flow of capital across borders but also creates huge opportunity for talent within our profession.

This new "Accounting Infrastructure" report shares our thoughts on how the internationalisation of accountancy policies, the harmonisation of international tax policies and the cultivation of workforces with cross-border skills and understanding will benefit increased trade. We're also delighted to be able to add to our own perspective with representatives from both the EU Parliament and the Pakistan

---

* Chief Executive, ACCA.

China Institute.

To do this, We've taken a very practical approach that captures the insights of accounting and tax experts working in firms across more than 20 countries on the Belt and Road route. This report presents our initial findings from 14 selected countries, with further and wider insights to come in future reports.

At ACCA, we are hugely excited about the opportunity Belt and Road presents for our members and the profession. Our ethos as a professional accountancy has been all about connecting our world and facilitating links that create sustainable growth. As a result, we now have an amazing 198,000 members and 486,000 students across 180 countries, supported by 101 ACCA offices and centres. ACCA has operations in 52 countries around the world and 21 of these countries sit directly on the Belt and Road footprint. In this way, the ACCA world is very much aligned to that of Belt and Road. The diversity of our membership base, their youth, mobility and professional standards of financial management expertise underpinned by strong ethics mean that our members are an ideal human resource in a connected and highly complex commercially-driven environment.

As the glue that binds our members around the world together, ACCA looks forward to playing its part in connecting the communities of professional accountants who can contribute to the success of this new Silk Route together. The report we are launching today is further evidence of our commitment to this exciting initiative and we thank SNAI and Deloitte sincerely for working with us to create it.

As we all continue this exciting journey, we at ACCA look forward to supporting and enabling our members to bring the promise of Belt and Road to life.

Supporting the Belt and Road Initiative by Deloitte China

Patrick Tsang [*]

In the fall of 2013, President Xi Jinping proposed the initiative to build the Silk Road Economic Belt and the 21st Century Maritime Silk Road, getting extensive attention and positive response in the international community. During past three years, our efforts in all aspects have achieved fruitful results. Facts have proved that the Belt and Road initiative conforms to the pursuit of peace and development in this age, complies with the inner desire of all countries to accelerate development, and facilitates economic development along the route and economic prosperity around the globe. According to the data released by the MOFCOM, throughout 2016, China's domestic investors made non-financial outbound direct investment in more than 7,900 overseas enterprises in 164 jurisdictions worldwide, reaching a historical high of USD 170 billion; overseas M&A transactions also rocketed in 2016, when Chinese-funded enterprises launched a total of 729 overseas M&A deals, totaling about USD 330 billion. At the same time, due to the global operation, the number of Chinese companies ranking among the world's top 500 list increased to 110 from 23 in 2006. What is more striking is that we find Chinese companies are changing their way of doing international business, shifting from the original project contract pattern towards the development of large-scale infrastructure, mineral resources and industrial parks through multiple models, such as cross-border M&A, green field investment and PPP, so that enterprises can get higher returns in the high-end of the value

* Deloitte China CEO.

chain. Besides, this can drive the whole industry chain to go globe, from manufacturing, engineering, operation, to technology and standards, namely, enabling enterprises to upgrade from mere contractors to investors and service providers.

It can be seen that the global expansion of Chinese enterprises is an irreversible trend. Confident in their leadership in the new process of globalization, with a mission to assist their engagement in international cooperation and competition, Deloitte has been keeping a close eye on their progress. We earlier conducted a questionnaire survey of senior managers serving 54 SOEs controlled by the central and local governments. When asked about the ability they need to strengthen the most in their global performance or engagement in the Belt and Road Initiative, 60% of the respondents selected the development of international strategy, 54% chose the financing support from the government, financial institutions or social capital, 46% highlighted the ability to assess, prevent and address the political, legal, tax, cultural (religious) and other types of risk in the investment / construction destination, and 33% prioritized the need to reserve international talents who are aware of both the local laws and regulations and culture and the operation and management. The cultivation of international professionals deserves our attention and discussion, and is interwoven with all the topics of today's forum, including the differences between and coordination of accounting systems, the identification and avoidance of tax risks, the integration and development of capital markets.

There is no doubt that accounting information plays a decisive role in operations abroad. Accounting, as a universal business language, is the basis of all kinds of investment planning, decision-making, management, control and evaluation. The more developed an economy gets, the more important accounting will be. The well-established accounting infrastructure will greatly accelerate social and economic activities and facilitate inter-country economic exchanges and trade. We thank SNAI for taking lead in hosting the forum, providing a big platform for mutual exchange and understanding, communication and further cooperation between accountancy professionals and friends from the political, business and academic circles. I hope that, at the forum, you can express freely to share your insights, brainstorm, and explore the successful experiences, opportunities and challenges as well as bottlenecks of the businesses engaged in the Belt and Road Initiative, so as to offer guidance to new comers, provide a basis for the decision-makers, and contribute advice and strategy to the accounting profession for a better-established Belt and Road Initiative. As a world-class professional agency, Deloitte has a wide range of professional services and a global network covering over 150 countries, and will, as always, strive to provide a full range of professional services in support of Chinese companies taking part in the Initiative.

I expect all of you here today to work side by side to spread the voice of and write a new chapter in carrying out the Belt and Road Initiative.

Coordination in the International Accounting System by Chinese Enterprises in the Belt and Road Initiative

Fu Junyuan[*]

As we know, with the rolling out of the Belt and Road Initiative, our 'hard power' is going out, but the 'soft power' still lags behind. How we can make the soft power, especially the soft power of accounting, play its due role in the Belt and Road Initiative is an important issue to be investigated. During theimplementation of Belt and Road Initiative, there are many projects which bear so much significance that they have attracted a close attention from the general public and local governments, including both the ruling and opposition parties. So if accounting is handled improperly, there would be risks and troubles. That's why it should be fully investigated.

I. Differences in Accounting Standards: Six Accounting Systems in the Belt and Road Countries

China Communications Construction Company Limited ("CCCC") is a pioneer practitioner of the Belt and Road Initiative. 66 countries along the belt and road are located in Asia and Africa, and more than 130 countries participated in the Belt and Road Summit this year, meaning the Initiative's coverage has

13

---

* Executive Director of China Communications Construction Company Limited.

expanded extensively across the globe. This perfectly matches CCCC's global footprint since its products and services are sold to and provided for more than 150 countries in the world and it has set up 193 expat agencies in 103 countries across the globe. It is well connected with the accounting systems and businesses of most countries in the world. So today I'm going to talk about the accounting standards in those countries where CCCC operates.

Recently, China's accounting standards are becoming more and more converged with the international standards. Now CCCC is both a H-share company listed on SEHK and an A-share company listed on SSE, which means that it has to disclose information according to both the Chinese and international accounting standards. A decade practice shows that the disparity between these two standards is dwindling, indicating a strong converging trend, with slight differences in measurement, reporting and disclosures. Therefore, today I'm not going to focus on these two standards.

Instead I'm going to focus on the accounting standards in the Belt and Road countries and many other countries in the world. Each country has its own unique accounting standards, but quite a number of countries share some common features, based on which we can categorize the accounting standards. According to the generally accepted categorization, in particular the American Accounting Association's country-based categorization, the accounting standards fall into the following models, namely the British Commonwealth model, the French model, the German model, the American model and the Communist country model. As for CCCC, we, on the basis of the actual situations of countries where we operate, group the accounting models into six language-based categories, namely the French family, the Portuguese family, the Spanish family, the US family, the English family and the Russian family.

This categorization takes full account of the current conditions of over 150 countries where we operate and also the colonial legacy of these countries. For instance, the English family covers the so-called British Commonwealth countries or the former British colonies that have similar accounting regime and shared standards. The Russian family largely refers to the former USSR which later was divided into 15 union republics, plus the former Yugoslav. The US family refers to the pro-US accounting systems. The Portuguese family refers to some countries in South America, such as Brazil. The Spanish family includes the former colonies of Spain, such as Colombia, Venezuela, etc.

The French family includes countries from the central and western Africa, such as the Republic of Congo, Equatorial Guinea and Senegal. These countries share common features in terms of accounting regime, accounting management and supervision, and international convergence. Based on the *Traité relatif à l'Harmonisation du Droit des Affaires en Afrique* signed by financial ministers from 16 central and western African countries at the Port Louis, Mauritius, some laws in relation to unified accounting practice, accounting legislation and accounting standards were all aligned accordingly. There are 17 such countries in total, including 7 in western Africa and 10 in central Africa, whose accounting systems are highly influenced by France. The accounting standards of this family largely mirror the French accounting bill, basically converging with international standards.

II. Coordination in Accounting Standards: Practices and Principles

Accounting coordination and handling need to follow three principles. First, it should satisfy the requirements of tax declaration and check in its own country. Many African countries do not care much about disclosure or public listing but care about corporate tax payment, reasonableness of accounting treatment and compliance with local regulation. Therefore, for high-profile projects in particular, accounting treatment must satisfy the tax declaration rules required by the local government. Second, it needs to satisfy the Chinese government's requirements concerning tax declaration and check and information disclosure by listed companies. Third, it needs to satisfy China's accounting and auditing standards.

In practice, there are two ways of financial handling. First is the "one account" model: putting all economic activities into one financial statement according to the accounting standards either in local or Chinese. But if it follows

15

the local standards, adjustments have to be made in order to follow the Chinese standards as well. As you can see this model has both advantage and disadvantage. On the positive side, it reduces workload, involving just minor revisions because of overlap of key businesses and the fact that more and more local accounting standards are required to converge with the international standards. On the downside, such adjustments cannot be made without a thorough understanding of the difference between the local and Chinese standards. As a result, it is highly likely to miss out something or make mistakes. If serious missing or mistakes are made, the consequences would be dire. We suffered it before.

Second is the "two accounts" model: a local account is established by the local standards to meet the requirement for tax declaration, while a Chinese account is made according to Chinese standards. This model also has pros and cons: on one hand, the two accounts are separate which may minimize the accounting and tax risks and mistakes, but on the other hand this model is costly.

Generally speaking, there are three ways to handle external accounting. First, company's in-house financial professionals who know very well about the local standards can handle it. Second is to hire professional agencies from outside. In some countries where the local conditions are very complex but the business is very simple, it is not a bad idea to hire a well-established local accounting firm to handle the external accounting, for instance we may hire PWC or Deloitte in some African countries to do the work. Third is to hire local accountancy professionals where possible to handle local accounting. This approach is cost-effective because as China's population dividends are disappearing, sending expats is much costly than hiring locals. That's why this model is now widely used. This is also what CCCC is doing overseas and the results are quite encouraging.

III. Summary and Outlook

First, there are still a lot of difference of accounting standards between the Belt and Road countries and China, particularly in some African countries where the local economies are less developed and show little sign of market economy, and other countries in the former Soviet bloc where the planned economy still dominates. While China's accounting standards have converged with international standards, quite a number of countries are still far behind convergence, the French and Russian families in particular.

Second, most of Chinese companies have not prepared complete financial report to satisfy the local requirements. This is quite risky. CCCC started its global journey quite early, so after two to three decades of development, our financial system is becoming mature. In contrast, as the Belt and Road Initiative rolls out, quite a number of Chinese companies are rushing to go global without any experience what may be disastrous caused only a single misstep considering that the Belt and Road countries differ a lot politically and economically.

Third, under current circumstance, it is better to adopt the "two-account" model in accounting work. The 'one-account' model might be quite tricky for us due to our insufficient capability and skills. But for some countries whose accounting standards are very close to ours, the 'one-account' model may apply while keeping an eye on its convergence progress and making adjustment accordingly.

Accounting Regulation and International Convergence in the BRICS Countries

Wang Peng [*]

According to the research on the BRICS accounting regulation and international convergence studied by the MOF Accounting Department and the Accounting Society of China (ASC), I would like to share with you some relevant results of aforementioned research from three major perspectives, i. e. new requirements, new positioning and new starting point. The inherent logic within the three perspectives is that: (1) ASC, as a national accounting academic organization under MOF, must adapt to the new situation and follow the new requirements in its work; (2) Hence, it calls for ASC to determine its new positioning; and (3) with this new positioning, ASC shall make new efforts, which can be regarded as our new starting point.

Ⅰ. New Requirements

First of all, I'd like to make a brief introduction to the new requirements that we are faced with. Since the 18th CPC National Congress, the CPC Central Committee has made the general requirement for comprehensively deepening reforms in China, and the MOF Accounting Department and ASC have also been implementing these new requirements. Considering the theme of Belt and Road

---

 * Deputy Inspector of the Accounting Department, Ministry of Finance, and Secretary General of Accounting Society of China.

Initiative, Chinese President Xi Jinping at the opening ceremony of the Belt and Road Forum for International Cooperation on May 14 2017. In this speech themed on "Work Together to Build the Silk Road Economic Belt and The 21st Century Maritime Silk Road", President Xi emphasized that, "Four years on, over 100 countries and international organizations have supported and got involved in this initiative. Important resolutions passed by the UN General Assembly and Security Council contain reference to it. Thanks to our efforts, the vision of the Belt and Road Initiative is becoming a reality and bearing rich fruit. " These four years have seen deepened policy connectivity, enhanced infrastructure connectivity, increased trade connectivity, expanded financial connectivity, and strengthened people-to-people connectivity. "We welcome efforts made by other countries to grow open economies based on their national conditions, participate in global governance and provide public goods. Together, we can build a broad community of shared interests. " "Think tanks should play a better role and efforts should be made to establish think tank networks and partnerships. " "The Belt and Road Initiative is rooted in the ancient Silk Road. It focuses on the Asian, European and African continents, but is also open to all other countries. "

While researching on the accounting convergence and development strategy under the Belt and Road Initiative, including accounting convergence in the BRICS countries, we may also find that President Xi Jinping has already put forward many new topics in his speech. For instance, he called upon us to participate in global governance and provide public goods, and build a broad community of shared interests together. The Accounting Standards for Business Enterprises (ASBE), in essence, is a kind of public good. Particularly amid the current global economic integration and implementation of the Belt and Road Initiative, ASBE is even more of an international public good. So the international convergence of ASBE is indeed a key part and way of participating in global economic governance. Another example is that President Xi Jinping asked us to give better play to the role of think tanks, and stressed that the Belt and Road Initiative is rooted in the ancient Silk Road. While focusing on the Asian, European and African continents, it is also open to all other countries. Therefore, we must also base our research on an international vision.

II. New Positioning

Second, ASC has proposed a new "trinity" positioning according to the new requirements. It includes three main aspects. First, turn ASC into a high-end think tank of the Finance Ministry, and focus researches on important national strategies and major finance ministerial topics. Second, develop ASC into a national-brand social organization. And third, build ASC into a Chinese accounting academic organization that commands substantial international influence. All these three aspects constitute the new positioning of the development of ASC in the next step. With this new positioning, ASC shall make new efforts to both make a louder voice and build its own characteristic image. The former means that ASC must voice its opinion to the upper, middle and lower level audiences from the accounting perspective, while the latter means that ASC must highlight its own characteristics in terms of its brand value, leadership, guiding role and cohesive nature. It is important to develop the think tanks no matter in the new positioning or in the new efforts to be made. In this regard, we shall give full play to the role of ASC in service and networking; set up a platform to link the roles of government, society, market and higher education institutions; and build a bridge to smooth both top-down and bottom-up communications, so as to jointly play our due role in implementing major national strategies.

Around the topic of today's symposium— "Accounting Infrastructure" Promotes "Belt and Road Initiative", we have also done some preliminary research on accounting convergence. As accounting convergence and strategy under the Belt and Road Initiative is an extremely huge topic, we have therefore adopted a strategy of doing the research in multiple steps. We started our research by centering on the BRICS countries, and proposed a work scheme featuring "synchronous competition, full coverage, and combination of theory and practice".

To realize "synchronous competition", ASC has built five teams to research on accounting convergence in the BRICS countries. "Full coverage" means that the research should cover every aspect concerning the BRICS countries and their accounting practice, such as the ASBE developers, issuers and regulators, as well as the ASBE legal system. The "combination of theory and practice" means that the accounting theorists and practitioners must work on the same issue to ensure our high research quality. Based on such a consideration, ASC has built a "4 + 1" team consisting of Shanghai University (SHU), Southwestern University of Finance and Economics (SWUFE), Chongqing University (CQU), Zhejiang University of Finance and Economics (ZUFE, as well as ZET which is also present at today's workshop. The "4 + 1" team includes four theorist groups and one practitioner group, ultimately generating a "1 + 5" work result. The five groups developed five independent research reports and submitted them to the Accounting Department of the Ministry of Finance which then integrated the five documents into one single general report. This is what we call a form of work result that features "one general report plus five independent reports".

III. New Starting Point

New Starting Point includes the following five modules:

1. An overview of the development, issuance, approval and regulation of ASBE in the BRICS countries.

2. The legal system of ASBE in the BRICS countries.

3. The implementation of ASBE in the BRICS countries.

4. Accounting convergence of ASBE in the BRICS countries.

5. The latest developments and my personal observations of ASBE convergence in the BRICS countries.

(I) The overview of ASBE in the BRICS countries

We will take a look at the development, issuance and regulation of ASBE in the four BRICS countries, i. e. Brazil, India, Russia and South Africa, respectively.

1. Brazil

The developer of ASBE in Brazil is called CPC, a non-profit organization that is not affiliated to the government. Apart from developing ASBE in Brazil, it is also responsible for approving the adoption of the International Financial Reporting Standards (IFRS) in Brazil. So it is not only the developer of ASBE, but also the approver. As for the implementation and regulation of ASBE in Brazil, three major parties are involved: Securities and Exchange Commission of Brazil (CVM), Central Bank of Brazil, and Insurance Regulatory Agency, which are in charge of the implementation and regulation of ASBE in the country.

2. India

The Institute of Chartered Accountants of India (ICAI) is responsible for developing the accounting standards in India, and the Accounting Standards Board (ASB) established under ICAI is responsible for the drafting work. ICAI is a statutory body founded in 1949 in accordance with the Chartered Accountants Act. The approver of ASBE in India is the National Advisory Committee on Accounting Standards (NACAS) established by the Indian Ministry of Corporate Affairs (MCA). The committee is responsible for reviewing ASBE, which will then take effect with the approval and issuance of MCA. Such arrangements are stipulated by India's Companies Act, which requires that ASBE developed by ICAI shall be approved and announced by the central government. In India, the regulators of ASBE mainly include MCA, Reserve Bank of India (RBI) and other finance and insurance regulatory authorities. Meanwhile, the Securities and Exchange Board of India (SEBI) shall supervise the implementation of ASBE in the public companies.

3. Russia

The developers of ASBE in Russia are more complicated. The Ministry of Finance of the Russian Federation (MFRF) is responsible for developing and issuing ASBE in Russia, and the Central Bank of Russia (CBR) for developing accounting standards applicable to the central bank and other financial institutions. Other government departments are allowed to set ASBE for specific industries based on the industry characteristics. At the same time, MFRF is also responsible for developing and issuing accounting standards for Russian companies. If Russia needs to adopt the IFRS, it requires the National Organization of Financial Accountants (NOFA)—an independent organization designated by MFRF—to conduct the technical assessment first. Those which have passed such assessment will then be enacted after the joint issuance by MFRF, CBR and MJRF (Ministry of Justice of the Russian Federation) . As for the regulators, MFRF, CBR and FCSM (Federal Commission of Securities Market) are all responsible for regulating the implementation of ASBE.

4. South Africa

The developer of ASBE in South Africa is the Financial Reporting Standards Commission (FRSC), an independent agency established by the Department of Trade and Industry (DTI) in 2006 based on the newly revised Companies Act and financially supported by the state funding. South Africa Accounting Standards Board (SAASB), a functional department under FRSC, is responsible for drafting the announcements and interpretations of ASBE. Meanwhile, DTI and Johannesburg Securities Exchange (JSE) are both responsible for regulating the implementation of ASBE.

(II) The legal system of ASBE in the BRICS countries

The four countries have their distinctive characteristics in terms of the legal system of ASBE. In Brazil, India and South Africa, the developers of ASBE are all non-profit organizations not directly attached to the government bodies. The companies act in these countries have also stipulated on the business financial reporting to various degrees. However, Russia has developed systematic laws and regulations concerning thedevelopment of ASBE and governing of the accounting industry. The three major laws are: (1) Accounting Act of the Russian Federation, which is similar to China's Accounting Law; (2) Consolidated Financial Statement Act, which stipulates the main bodies and basic requirements for companies to prepare their consolidated financial statements; and (3) Procedure Act for Russia to adopt the IFRS, which stipulates the assessment process and auditing procedure of the IFRS.

(Ⅲ) The implementation of ASBE in the BRICS countries

In this part, I will present a brief summary of how the four countries implement their ASBE. They not only share some similarities in doing so, but also have their own features.

1. Brazil

At present, the public companies and most financial institutions in Brazil choose to adopt the IFRS in their consolidated financial statements and the Brazilian ASBE in the individual financial statements. The latter is converging with the former. However, there are still individual differences between the two, such as in the assets revaluation and the presentation of profit statements.

2. India

The public companies and large enterprises in India all use the new Indian ASBE in their consolidated and individual financial statements, as the Indian ASBE is converging with the IFRS. Yet small companies are still using the ASBE for India's indigenous companies. Despite the convergence between the new Indian ASBE and the IFRS, there still remain certain differences, such as convertible bond denominated in foreign currency, business combination, investment property, and statement of comprehensive income.

3. Russia

The public companies and financial institutions in Russia now adopt the IFRS in their consolidated financial statements. But all companies should apply the Russian ASBE in their individual financial statements. The Russian ASBE now still contains the accounting standards for individual industries, and mainly serves to the purpose of taxation.

Moreover, there are many differences between the Russian ASBE and the IFRS. For instance, the former has not introduced the concept of "fair value", in addition to quite many other differences in the accounting standards on leasing and inventory. Besides, the Russian ASBE has no stipulation concerning assets impairment, derivative financial instruments, hedge accounting, and investment property.

4. South Africa

The public companies and financial institutions in South Africa are now alladopting the IFRS to both consolidated and individual financial statements, while the small-and—medium-sized enterprises directly adopt the IFRS for SMEs. The major responsibility of FRSC is to simply issue interpretations on individual operations.

(Ⅳ) Accounting convergence of ASBE in the BRICS countries

Among the four countries, South Africa has fully adopted the IFRS due to the historical and language reasons, while the other three countries have their own characteristics in terms of the scope and extent of ASBE convergence under the influence of different legal, cultural and language factors. In Brazil and Russia, only the public companies and certain financial institutions should adopt the IFRS in the consolidated financial statements, while their own national ASBE is more or less different from the IFRS. However, India has opted for the convergence mode. The difference remains huge despite that India has claimed to realize the convergence between its own ASBE and the IFRS.

(Ⅴ) The latest developments and outlook of ASBE convergence in the BRICS countries

According to the Xinhua news report on June 19, the 2nd BRICS Finance Ministers and Central Bank Governors Meeting were successfully held in Shanghai on the same day. The five BRICS countries reached a consensus on the fiscal and financial cooperation outcome document, and agreed to strengthen cooperation in nine major areas, which prepared the fiscal and financial policies and outcomes for the BRICS summit later to be held in Xiamen. Amid the nine areas, the BRCIS countries agreed to conduct cooperation on the accounting standards convergence and audit supervision equivalence so as to provide an institutional guarantee for the connectivity of the BRICS bond markets. Hence, the BRICS countries have indeed yielded some results in the convergence of ASBE.

First of all, the four countries, in addition to China, have all proposed to establish one single set of high-quality ASBE applicable to the entire world. It is a goal that was first put forward at the G20 Summit. The five countries, all as the G20 member states, are supportive of this move.

Second, the BRICS countries are all emerging economies. Therefore, they have the need to enhance the right to speak on the IFRS in order to safeguard the interests of the emerging economies.

Third, in terms of current actual needs, realizing the connectivity of the BRICS bond markets has already been placed on the agenda. So, the international convergence of ASBE should provide an institutional guarantee for this attempt.

Fourth, the relationship between the Belt and Road Initiative and ASBE international convergence has posted a new topic under the new situation. The international convergence strategy for China's ASBE was actually presented as early as in 2006. So far, China's ASBE, which has achieved material convergence with the IFRS, has been adopted in the country for a decade. Yet the historical background, against which the ASBE international convergence took place in 2006, is not entirely the same as the new situation in which the Belt and Road Initiative is implemented today. Out of this reason, we should consider how to further improve the strategy and method of ASBE international convergence in China in the new situation.

Fifth one is the relationship between the ASBE international convergence and the audit supervision equivalence. The international convergence of ASBE is actually the uniformity of ASBE worldwide, which is the "connectivity of accounting languages". And then what comes to the next problem is inevitably the implementation of these standards and the regulation of the implementation. At the government level, a major problem lies in audit supervision equivalence. So we may say the international convergence of ASBE and the audit supervision equivalence are "the two sides of a coin" which need to be deployed, coordinated and promoted synchronically.

Sixthly, it is the relationship between the multiple levels of ASBE and its categorized implementation. Through the earlier analysis, we may already notice this clearly. For instance, different ASBEs are adopted between domestic and foreign companies, public and non-public companies, individual and consolidated financial statements, as well as medium-and large-sized enterprises and small ones. The Ministry of Finance has already listed the revision of the Accounting Law into its working priorities in 2017. So I suggest that we reflect on this revision work by taking into consideration the new accounting practice in China as well as the new background of implementing the Belt and Road Initiative.

ZTE's Experience in the Global Financial Management for Chinese Enterprises Going Global

Chen Hu [*]

I. Internationalization Brings Challenges to Corporate Financial Management

ZTE Corporation was founded in 1985, and went abroad from 1995 when only one staff was sent to the Geneva Telecom Expo to exhibit our products. Now nearly 50% of our sales revenue comes from off-shore markets. ZTE branches are present in 107 countries, and ZTE products are sold to more than 160 countries and regions across the globe. In fact, ZTE footprint covers all countries with a population over a million. Moreover, we have permanent offices in 53 of 60 plus Belt and Road Initiative countries.

Globalization brings significant challenges to corporate finance. There is a well-known quote from Benjamin Franklin that "In this world nothing can be said to be certain, except death and taxes." I want to say for an enterprise nothing can be said to be certain, except finance and legal matters, since they never break away with a company from the start to the end.

Doing business in mainland china is a bit like boating in an inside river, while going global like sailing in an ocean, where you face a lot of challenges. From a financial perspective, It has five challenges: First, operating cost may

* Vice President of ZTE Corporation.

increase significantly that making top-down supervision by head office even harder due to time difference and physical distance between different companies located various regions. Second one is compliance control that may bring global supervision and overseas talents turnover. Third, lack of uniform accounting standards may result in uncertain accounting policies, arbitrary chart of account settings, chaotic bookkeeping and incompatible data systems. Fourthly, financial security is not guaranteed, and there will be more risks arising from foreign exchange controls, interest rate losses and foreign exchange fluctuations. Fifthly, there have different tax regimes and policies may have a big impact on compliance, daily operations and TP and PE-related risks. And last, differences in language and culture, laws and regulations, war situation, environment, employee security, time lag, Internet networks, etc. may exert great influence on an organization's financial management and daily operations. And these challenges are exactly what we have met as only one enterprise.

I used to show a PPT slide to my staff, and said that an accounting and financial employee in overseas should act as a CFO although he/she only acts as an accountant in China. He/she is supposed not only to understand about the local accounting system, that know how to deliver management report, but also know about business, taxation, capital, foreign exchange, inventory, performance, operation analysis, payment, budget, project, financial investment, language and human resource management. How long can such a CFO be able to be trained by enterprises? Generally speaking, a fresh MA postgraduate from a Chinese well-known university would have to work in the country for at least 5 years before such an intellectual acquisition is completed in him. But if he leaves and goes back to China after having worked in a country, such as Nigeria, South Africa, Brazil, etc. , enterprises would have to train another person all over again. So what do you do if there are so many risks involved, so many things to do and so hard to train a CFO? One global financial management system has been established through ZTE Group's exploration.

II. Establishment of Global Financial Management System in ZTE

Such a forementioned system in global financial management must fully support business operating, guarantee compliance and timely feedback. So it consists of four parts. First, establishing a global financial network and training globalized financial professionals. Second, developing a complete set of business solutions ranging from ATT (accounting, treasure and tax) and risks, through the extended functions for support of business strategy, operation, project management and risk control, to a complete IT solution. It is estimated that there are a total of 50 – 60 IT systems used by our branches in 107 countries. Therefore, an integrative IT platform is necessary to establish through the establishment of a global financial sharing network in advance.

1. The Structure of Global Finance Shared Service

Aforementioned global financial sharing network suggests a globalized financial organizational structure based on a 'three-triangular' principle. In the first triangular, the global structure is centered on head office's overall financial strategy acting as a brain for decision-making; All the executive branches across the globe acting as sensors and executing agencies to converge all fundamental businesses through the establishment of cloud-based financial data sharing center. The second triangular is a local one. The first piece is the CFO-led team from China, responsible for supporting local business operation, making administrative decisions and facilitating decision-making process. At the same time, the local financial team is also responsible for promoting financial localization, because without it a business could not become a local corporate citizen, or a real globalized organization. The local financial team is better at dealing with banking business, local customers, local firms, taxation agencies and regulatory authorities. As conclusion, it is the remote control system, or a cloud-based platform, which is a smart system. Overall, the key issue is that we need to establish such a global tripartite system to support a local team.

2. The Training of Global Professionals

Regarding the training of global professionals, Chinese talents should be trained as global professionals firstly that we would like to see more financial professionals trained by Chinese universities. Five years ago we began to call on to cultivate accountancy professionals with a global vision, since at that time professionals were trained by just following the MOF's standards. On the other hand, we need to develop a localized financial team consisting of foreign professionals that these foreign professionals are familiar with Chinese culture can promote Chinese companies to do businesses in overseas. Therefore, I hope in the future Chinese universities will not only cultivate Chinese professionals with a global perspective but also train overseas professionals. Additionally, the universities also need to encourage more foreign students to work in China in the future.

3. The Establishment of Accounting System

From the business perspective, capital management, taxation and risk management are very important in establishing a sound financial accounting system. Therefore, we have made "five integrations", "two accounting dimensions", and "integrative approach". "Five integrations" include uniform accounting policies, uniform accounting chart of accounts, uniform accounting procedures, uniform IT systems and uniform data standards. Based upon "five integrations", "two accounting dimensions" refer to local book-keeping and the group book-keeping with the requirement of management accounting report. With the "integrative approach", it suggests one set of accounting rules can satisfy the requirements from aforementioned three accounting dimensions. We usually require the financial department to guarantee the data source and combine management and settlement. That is to say, the data should come from the original source and be verifiable either according to the requirement of disclosure or the financial reporting. In addition, combine management and settlement means that settlement and management are combined that settlement is operated for management.

4. Global Tax Management

Global tax management not only involves the declaration, but also involves tax planning, global taxation policies research, overseas permanent establishment, inter-group's transfer pricing policy, local business model, global tax compliance, specifically local tax risk control, etc. All of these issues should be started even before going global. In other words, relevant arrangements of tax management must be considered before business started. Second, a tax accounting regime should be established. ZTE has many overseas branches and has no plan to go public in other jurisdictions except in Hong Kong and mainland of China. So the first priority issue is tax compliance in line with local tax regulations what includes tax declaration with other relevant requirements. At the same time, response plans for tax audit requested by local tax authorities also should be established.

An integrative approach is essential for group's tax, local tax and global tax accounting platform, in order to manage the global tax risks well. Global capital management calls for unified management of bank accounts across the globe. Now our global sharing center is managing thousands of accounts in 110 countries and regions across the globe, through which every cash flow is made. Sub-capital pools are built up just like regional hubs of an airliner, acting as an intersection hub of key flight routes. An integrative global foreign exchange regime should be set up to guarantee capital backflows and minimize the impact on financial statement and capital risks.

Global risk management is a big challenge to finance. We have to take into account the risks arising from going global, jurisdiction, operation, compliance and finance, which will finally be reflected in the operating results. Well then, how to set up a complete risk prevention mechanism? Actually taking all these factors into account can help to develop a global financial management system, which will support Chinese businesses' global operations.

III. The "Knowledge Database" of ZTE's Global Operation

Finance is a company's key information and management supporting system. In China, the financial data system is adendritical structure whereas global operation depends on a neural network structure where all issues include accounting, taxation, capital, trading, risks, etc. , need to be developed as nerve cell. ZTE has established a complete knowledge database to support global operations, including global financial knowledge and country-specific guidelines. The global accounting support system is broken down into corporate management level and country level. The tax-related knowledge system is broken down into GAER, reduction of international double taxation, tax avoidance and anti-avoidance, tax treaty and global taxation trend. It is further broken down into tax life cycle, tax credits, international tax disputes, tax planning, cross-border taxation risks, global tax policy database, and global tax management trends. Countries may vary in terms of tax avoidance, taxation and accounting policies. If a global financial knowledge system and a country-specific trading knowledge system are established, it will be a big leg-up for a company's global operations.

Regarding the country-specific guidelines, four BRICs country-specific guidelines has been completed with colorful contents that 100 − 200 pages for each BRICs countries. Currently, we are now working for all the countries along the Belt and Road routes listed in the catalogue. It is a tough road for going-global journey. But only by going global, can China and the Chinese nation become great again.

Tax Management in Multinational Corporations

Katherine Wu [*]

Unilever has four major business units globally including cleaning supplies, personal care products, food, and ice cream and beverage. In China, the most popular products include Lux shampoo and shower gel, OMO washing powder, Clear shampoo and Wall's ice cream.

Globally, Unilever has 170,000 employees, and the business turnover is about 50 billion euros, about 60% of which is from developing countries. Unilever's operations have a strong presence in about 190 countries and regions, and we have built financial share service centers at multiple locations.

One of the major missions for Unilever is long-term and sustainable growth, which looks to ease the burden on environment while ensuring continuous business development. We are committed to procuring all agricultural products in a 100% sustainable way to protect the local environment. Unilever has also been working with local governments and social organizations, as well as with local farmers and commercials to gain a sustainable development while improving productivity.

In all our global plants and warehouses, we are also committed to operating in line with safety, environmental protection and sanitation requirements. Through our brands and products such as Blueair air purifier units and Qinyuan water purifier units, we look to improve the livelihood, safety, sanitation and health for local people.

This point has been emphasized because in the process of globalization,

[*] Vice Present of Finance in North Asia, Unilever.

enterprises keep entering into new markets, and local consumers and governments care for something more than just economic growth, products development and employment: in this hugely globalized world which features a wide use of the Internet and information, many consumers, governments and organizations focus on the value a company can create for the local livelihood and environmental protection. Therefore, we believe it is indispensable for a company's globalization strategy whether its development is sustainable and whether its business is helpful to the local environment.

As a company has a long history, Unilever was established about a hundred years ago in the Netherlands and the United Kingdom. In the course of the hundred years, Unilever has gone through the process of going out and expanding into various countries around the world. We find 4 aspects to be very useful and practical in operating globally: first, understanding the country and local culture; second, cultivating the right people for local demands; third, devising strategies for long-term purposes; and fourth, operating under international standards. Two points are worth emphasizing here:

Firstly, it is cultivating the right people for local demands. The operation of business requires people to have not only profound knowledge about the company or its business modules, but also keen insight into the local environment, culture, communication methods and cooperation models with business partners. This insight may only be found in local staff. It is therefore very important for global companies to strike a balance between delegates and local staff from the start to a mature stage, and devise specific and systematic projects to train local talent to become future leaders and general managers of their departments.

Second one is operating under international standards. Some countries haven't set up sophisticated national standards, or the requirements of the national standards are relatively low. Therefore, if a global company adopts local standards, it has an obvious cost advantage in the short term. But if it focuses on long-term development, consumers will have various channels to understand what are better standards and better products. So Unilever takes the highest standards we know or capable of in all countries we operate, which may in the short term uplift costs, but it benefits the long-term development, establishment of the brand, and the building up of consumer confidence.

Now, it would like to share Unilever's experience in tax management as a global company from four aspects as below.

The first is an understanding of the local environment, regulations and management systems. The second is the establishment of a professional tax team. In the third part I will elaborate on the building of a compliance system. The last part is about building the capacity for adaptability.

I. Understanding of local environment, regulations and management systems

It is necessary to gain a profound and thorough understanding of the local tax environment, tax culture, tax system and tax regulations when enter into a country. There is sufficient information about the market, but it is more about grasping dynamics of the market and the economic environment and conducting compliance efforts in such dynamics than merely understanding the text. Especially in many developing countries, the text of tax laws is quite general, without specific provisions in implementation. It is challenge to company's tax department that include how to operate in real-world tax practice, in what aspects companies need tax authorities' engagement in devising a solution, etc. It is beneficial for companies to build their own tax compliance systems to understand the changes in the general environment and get to know the implementation of various local cases through cooperating with local enterprises, chambers of commerce and tax authorities.

II. Establishment of a professional tax team

Unilever operates in 190 countries, so the tax environment is very complex. In Unilever, the tax division is divided to regional tax team and professional tax team. These regional tax teams not only take charge of routine tax filing and statements, but also are engaged in local tax planning, risk management, communication with local tax authorities, understanding the development trends of tax policies and updates of laws and regulations. On the other hand, professional tax team mainly takes charge of complex tax issues arose from cross-border transactions, such as related party transactions, international mergers and acquisitions. The knowledge required in these areas is very specific, and the laws involved are more complex. For these tax issues, it requires to employ regional or global tax specialists.

III. Establishment of a compliance system for related party transactions

Two challenges will be posed to global companies. The first of which is to maintain tax compliance in every region, and the second of which is to the avoidance of double taxation. In 2015, almost 60 countries participated in BEPS Action Plan that requires multinational companies to conduct a very clear value chain analysis, and ensure that tax levy should be in consistence with the place of the origin of value. BEPS also has very specific requirements, including the value chain analysis, and three tier documentation framework for transfer pricing (i. e. Local File, Master File and Special Issue File), so as to enhance transparency and certainty in the international tax collection and management. As a leader of the G20, China has played a leading role in implementing BEPS.

Generally, multinational companies have a long value chain and the origin places of profits are across the globe. The problem, how avoids double taxation, is necessary to mention here. To apply for advance pricing arrangement ("APA") is one of the more effective solutions, because the company can join hands with tax bureaus to make unilateral and bilateral pricing strategies for the future, which could bring in a clear pan. The advantage is that it will avoid double taxation, and there is a certainty for the future to strengthen cooperation between the tax authorities and companies, but it requires a lot of manpower and other resources. As a whole, it will still be very helpful for the transparency and compliance in the entire tax system.

IV. Enhancing the adaptability of changes

Recently, some countries are undergoing a tax reform, such as India, which just initiated the GST Reform on 1st July 2017. The GST Reform not only re-defines the tax burden for companies, but also influences the upstream and downstream section of a business. For example, it may influence the profits of the enterprise, the price for consumers, or stocks of the clients, all of which are a challenge for the businesses; it may also change the valuation of the stock, IT systems and practice under accounting standards, all of which is a significant challenge to company's accounting and financial team. In this regard, the tax team should lead all related departments in a company to deal with these changes.

Tax Risk of Chinese Enterprises Going Global in the Belt and Road Initiative

Zhu Qing[*]

That is different between going out and engagement in operation or investment in China what refers to multiple countries. Investment in China is at most inter-provincial, while going out at least involves two countries where China as the home country and the target country is called the host country. In most cases, this owes much to the fact that companies often go out through countries or regions, such as Hong Kong, Singapore, etc., which will also involve tax issues in the intermediary jurisdiction. Thus, three issues regarding tax risk a business going out may encounter.

I. Tax issues in EPC projects

EPC ("Engineering Procurement Construction") project is one business model, which packaged engineering, procurement and construction together, that usually adopted by many construction enterprises. For example, one project, which is worth 1 billion totally, included 200 million for engineering, 600 million for procurement of Chinese equipment, and 200 million for construction and installation. Which part of the three expenses in the project, which is worth 1 billion totally, shall be taxable in the host country? Many companies reflect that in an EPC project, the major controversy, or say dispute, lies in the 600 million parts. Should the 600 million expenses of domestic equipment procurement be

---

* Expert in International Taxation, Professor of Renmin University of China.

taxed in the host country? This is a complex issue of international taxation. Let us assume that there is no Parts E ("engineering") and C ("construction"), but there is only Part P ("procurement"), namely equipment procurement. When the equipment is sold to the host country from China, shall the host country levy any tax on the deal? In accordance with the provisions of international taxation, especially the requirements of the International Tax Convention, if the Chinese enterprise selling the equipment does not have a PE ("permanent establishment") in the host country to complete the deal, the host country will not levy any tax on it. But the complexity lies in the part of construction, which may constitute a PE. Under the international tax convention and the international taxation rule, whether the part of construction shall constitute a PE depends on the duration of equipment installation and commissioning.

In the tax treaties signed between China and other jurisdictions, the routine duration for any construction or installation to be recognized as a PE used to be 183 days or six months basically, but in many newly signed agreements, the duration has been extended to 9 or 12 months (even 18 months in the agreements signed with Russia and some former USSR and East European countries). In this case, any equipment installed within six months (or one year accordingly) shall not constitute a PE. Then what's the trouble? The installation of general large-scale equipment, such as hydropower stations or power generation facilities, may take more than half a year. As a result, many Chinese enterprises engaged in global business find that the part of construction constitutes a PE. The seller may be taxed on the profits, which is derived from the equipment payment of 600 million, in the host country. Many companies had disputes with the host countries because of aforementioned issues. Some won the case, and others lost. So, this can represent crucial tax risk for businesses going global, and it is necessary to identify the relevant issues in the contract signing process. Thus, it is necessary that the EPC contract shall clearly define the functions and responsibilities of each section to prevent the host country from taking the contract as a compound consisting of two or more parties (i. e. recognizing Parts E, P and C as a community), which will make the contract more prone to be taxed. As responses, some companies try to split the contract for preventing the taxation levied from the part of procurement.

II. Tax issues in transfer pricing

The tax burden varies dramatically across Belt and Road countries, as the rate can be put to extremes. For instance, in former USSR and East European countries, the tax rates are very low, only 8% in Turkmenistan and 9% in Kazakhstan, while in African countries, the tax rates stand considerably high, such as 35% in Zambia. Thus, both scenarios with high and/or low tax rate can cause troubles for Chinese enterprises engaged in global operation. In low-tax countries, the problem occurs when an enterprise remits the profits to the Chinese parent company after local tax payment in the host country, and the parent company shall then declare tax filing in China. China's corporate income tax rate is 25%, in other words, the parent company has to make up for the gap of 16% or 17% in addition to the 8% or 9% already paid overseas, so that the companies going out felt that they did not get benefits from operation in low-tax countries.

The key issue involved here is whether China should tax domestic enterprises on their overseas profits. I published an article in Vol. 4 of the *International Taxation in China* periodical, calling on a tax exemption method instead of a tax credit method in China. Foreign profits are taxed in only three countries among major economies, respectively the United States, China and Ireland, while taxpayers in European countries are exempt from overseas income tax, especially Japan, the UK and Canada following suit in 2009. Trump's tax reform claims a cut in corporate tax from 35% to 15%, and there is another important move, though not spotlighted, that he proposes to exempt offshore profits from taxation, namely to replace tax credits by tax exemptions. China's competent authorities have also taken action for considering how to response Trump's tax reform mainly from two aspects: first, whether the current corporate income tax rate (25%) should be reduced; second, whether overseas profits should be tax-free. For the high-tax countries, such as those in Africa, where you cannot change the tax rate, companies pursuing a lighter tax burden tend to shift their profits out of high-tax countries through transfer pricing, which will constitute a tax avoidance conduct, and tax avoidance is what the host country is against in the current BEPS environment that all countries have strengthened tax management regarding transfer pricing. Now in a lot of countries that transfer pricing and profit shifting are subject to not only tax payment in arrears but also overdue tax payment or even punishment. For example, in India, the maximum penalty can amount to 3 times, while in Vietnam the overdue payment rate stands at 35%. In some countries, transfer pricing abuse is deemed and fined as a tax evasion conduct. However, China only charges an overdue on tax evasion and an interest on tax avoidance. China has not imposed heavy penalties on foreign-invested enterprises using transfer pricing for tax avoidance purposes. Academics have advised the National People's Congress and the Ministry of Finance to punish such conducts. Unfortunately, it is difficult to come true in the short term, because China needs to attract foreign investment. However, Chinese enterprises as global players must pay attention to this to avoid being fined.

III. Tax issues arose from unreasonable group structure

Going global often needs appropriate group structure that an intermediate holding company in a third country is necessary to use. For example, if a Chinese company intends to invest in Rwanda, since Rwanda and China have not yet signed a tax treaty, the company has to pay a corporate income tax of 30% and a withholding tax of 15%. Thus establishment of intermediate holding company, as group structure, is usually necessary during the process of outbounding. For example, investment in Rwanda through Belgium is more economical that the dividends paid to Belgian residents by Rwandan residents shall be exempt from withholding tax under the agreement signed between the two countries. Furthermore, since China and Belgium have also agreed that the withholding tax levied in Belgium can be reduced to 5%. Unfortunately, this behavior belongs to constitute tax treaty abuse for tax avoidance actually. Until June 7 2017, more than 70 countries worldwide had signed a *Multilateral Convention to Implement Tax Treaty Related Measures to Prevent Base Erosion and Profit Shifting*, a package of more than 1,000 revised bilateral tax treaties. China now has a total of 105 tax treaties in effect, including 102 signed with foreign jurisdictions and 3 signed with Hong Kong, Macao and Taiwan. Under the *Convention*, the anti-tax avoidance provisions in OECD's 15 action plans on BEPS added to the tax treaties, including Action 6 on preventing treaty abuse. Action 6 sets out two kinds of anti-abuse measures, respectively PPT ("principals purpose test") to judge whether a treaty is signed or a transaction is done for tax avoidance purposes, and LOB ("limitation on benefits") to prevent eligible third-country residents from obtaining any tax benefits provided by tax treaties. To illustrate, under the tax treaty signed between Rwanda and Belgium what has been mentioned above, a Chinese enterprise will constitute a third-country enterprise and cannot enjoy the benefits agreed in the treaty. Thus, a lot of Chinese companies going out are employing the group structure, but when the *Convention* comes into effect, they will find many practices no longer available, and they will face considerable risks if they choose to do so.

Tax Management in Overseas M&A by Chinese Companies Going Global

Song Ning [*]

2014 was the heyday of its overseas M&A. I spent two and a half years in almost all of the Group's overseas M&A projects, including the purchases of Legendary Pictures, the WTC (World Triathlon Corporation), and the $10 billion investment in industrial city in India.

Actually, Wanda had another story compared to ZTE that all Wanda's overseas investments were focused on M&A, and the Group took a direct approach to many projects without any preparedness due to the tight schedule. What's more, in many cases, we took over a project with a fait accompli investment structure or an overseas entity, thus exposed to more and more pressure and challenges. For instance, Wanda is very proud of its first movie theater chain project, which the Group invested in the United States in 2012 and began to make profit immediately. Then a lot of tax problems surged accordingly. We have to accept this fait accompli investment structure. When considering the investment, few took into account the tax structure. This happened not only to China's private enterprises in overseas investment, but also to many SOEs in overseas investment and M&A. They had no intention to seek advice from the tax team. So far there are still many SOEs that do not have a dedicated tax director. As Chinese enterprises plan to go global or are already operating along the Belt and Road route, they have to deal seriously with

---

[*] Executive Chairman of China Chamber of International Commerce Taxation Committee, Former Tax Director of Wanda Group.

the tax work. This is a challenging job.

Here are 18 words to share: enter a market successfully, keep steadily, grow quickly, develop largely, get returns, and obtain more. In this way, I divide overseas investment into three stages: M&A, operation, and investment recovery.

Ⅰ. Enter a market successfully and keep steadily

1. Enter a market successfully

What does it mean referred to enter a market successfully? It means acquaintance with China's policy orientation for overseas investment to guarantee that a project's overseas investment can be approved. Since the Chinese government often adjusts the overseas investment policy, Chinese businesses often encounter problems when applying for M&A approval despite of a number of strategic terms fulfilled in the early stage. If an M&A case has reached a certain stage, especially when the contract and agreement have been signed, a failure in going out is likely to end up in huge indemnity. In fact, Wanda also paid a lot of "break-up fees" in this regard, and we should try to avoid the awkward situation in going out. At this stage, companies shall consider from the tax perspective if government approval can be obtained for M&A or green field investment, and how to transform their sunk costs into tax deductible expenses when uncertainties occur to the investment.

2. Keep steadily

The second problem is about a steady cycle. It is common for Chinese enterprisesto meet their Waterloo in the international debut, private enterprises and SOEs alike, which reveals the lack of tax due diligence or tax planning. Tax due diligence must become an integral part of overseas investment. In 2014, there are two all overseas investment to be detailed. The first one is environmental due diligence for overseas business environment. Take Wanda's investment in the

Indian industrial city as an example to illustrate the importance of overseas due diligence. Before the final decision making to invest in India, the chairman had selected ten Belt and Road countries in Southeast Asia for comprehensive due diligence, with four agencies selected to take this comprehensive due diligence what covered the infrastructure, the economic and financial environment, and finance and taxation. Based on the due diligence report, we developed our investment recovery models and decisions so that we were much less exposed to investment risk. What comes next is tax due diligence of the target company. In overseas M&A, many Chinese enterprises pay much more attention to legal and financial risks than to tax risk. For example, a Chinese SOE acquired a Nordic oil company, but in the following year of the acquisition, the company had its one-billion-dollar tax loophole exposed. It was China's SAT that had to help shooting the problem through bilateral consultations finally. As ordinary private enterprises, we find it is really difficult to respond such tax risk. So, it's better to do a good job in due diligence before the risk is coming.

II. Grow quickly and develop largely

How to make our overseas companies growing bigger and faster? Tax compliance is a key point. Many of the Fortune 500 companies set examples for us. Wanda analyzed many foreign-funded enterprises, such as IBM, Schneider, etc. , to study their features in global tax management and control. Moreover, Wanda also visited outbounded domestic private enterprises to analyze see their characteristics in global tax management and control. Then, Wanda overseas tax management and control model was established through combining findings of aforementioned researches.

On the basis of overseas tax management and control, we used in-house business arrangements of our Group for tax planning according to our business features. It is necessary to leverage preferential treatments from treaties actively when suffer from a relatively high overseas tax burden or some variances in tax treaties. During the process of leveraging preferential treatments from treaties, it should pursuit to reduce the tax burden while eliminate tax risk. Thus, tax management is critical, for it is based on three conditions: a reasonable business purpose, an authentic business substance, and a real business beneficiary. For example, When Wanda acquired the US-based WTC, it also acquired Swiss firm Infront Sports & Media at the same time. Since the tax treaties between the United States, Switzerland and China were different, a minimum tax burden was feasible via authentic transaction and business arrangements. It is the only way for a business to achieve its local development goal of growing to pay back its shareholders.

III. Get returns and obtain more

The third part is about recovery. There includes two things: dividends and withdrawal of equity capital. Many Chinese companies going out only strive to win the bid rather than consider the follow-up arrangements for the target project. Thus, Tax architecture must be flexible, namely adaptive. For example, if the boss says we plan to hold a certain company, you must begin to consider the dividend distribution; If the boss intends to carry out a domestic IPO, you have to take into account the corresponding arrangements for domestic tax architecture; The boss may also prefer Hong Kong to mainland for its IPO venue, and may aim to issue overseas bonds or overseas financing, etc. , we need to develop plans in advance in response to all the uncertainties. Therefore, tax planning calls to consider investment recovery even as early as in the investment-planning stage of "going out" .

Overview of Indian Tax System

Rohan Solapurkar[*]

India is a very complex large country, and to talk about the Indian tax system, its special merits and a number of challenges could take significant time. This speech is about important issues and opportunities available in India, and also gives inputs on oversight of investment in India and how it presents—for companies are now expanding on this Belt and Road Initiative—and some of the issues you'll face when you invest in India.

I. Main Tax Types

India is run by a central government which is based in Delhi. There are 29 states in India. These are like provinces in China. So each state has its state government which also collected the state's other taxes, for example, property tax or stamp duty, VAT and now GST. The Indian tax system is basically split into two parts: one is run by the central government, which is income tax, and one which is run by the state government. The state government collects the VAT and GST. The VAT is now subsumed into GST and GST is now all across India. India also has customs duty and they have other indirect taxes. Customs duty is also run by the central government. They have stamp duty, and other taxes which are collected by state governments. That's all for the snapshot of taxes in India.

* Tax Partner, Deloitte Singapore.

II. Corporate Income Tax

1. General Information

As for corporate taxes, Indian companies get taxed on global income. For Indian companies which have a presence overseas and have foreign subsidiaries', dividends remitted by these foreign subsidiaries to the Indian parents are also taxed. Foreign companies which have a "permanent establishment", or a project office are taxed in India on the profit or income which is attributable to the Project office or the permanent establishment. Foreign companies get taxed at different rates. India has a dividend distribution tax. Indian incorporated companies (i. e. companies which are legally set up in India), irrespective of the fact that there are foreign shareholders, would have to pay a dividend distribution tax in India before declaring any dividends to its shareholders. This dividend distribution tax has to be paid by the Indian company. There is no withholding tax at the time of distributing the dividend to the shareholders.

2. Deduction and Exemption

Generally, internal reorganizations and mergers are exempt from taxation, provided certain conditions are satisfied. If you have a loss in business operation in India, you can carry forward that loss for eight years. If you have a loss as the result of depreciation, that loss can be carried forward infinitely. In February, 2017, a new provision was introduced which restricted the interest deduction to 30% of EBITDA in respect of interest paid on debt taken from non-resident related parties. This is similar to having thin capitalisation rules in India.

3. Effective Tax Rates and Tax Burden

The basic situation of India's corporate income tax burden is as follows. (1) If the turnover of the company is less than approximately US $8. 5 million in Financial Year 2015 – 2016 and the taxable income is less than approximately US $160,000, the effective tax rate is 25.75%. If the income is greater than approximately US $ 160,000 but lower than US $ 1.6 million, the effective tax rate is 27.55%. If the taxable income is greater than US $ 1.6million, the effective tax rate is 28.84%.

(2) If the turnover of the company is greater than approximately US $ 8.5million in Financial Year 2015 – 16 and the taxable income is less than approximately US $ 160,000, the effective tax rate is 30.90%. If the income is greater than approximately US $ 160,000 but lower than US $ 1.6 million, the effective tax rate is 33.06%. If the taxable income is greater than US $ 1.6million, the effective tax rate is 34.61%.

(3) For smaller companies, if the turnover of the company is less than approximately US $ 800,000 in Financial Year 2014 – 15 and the taxable income is less than approximately US $ 160,000, the effective tax rate is 29.87%. If the income is greater than approximately US $ 160,000 but lower than US $ 1.6 million, the effective tax rate is 31.96%. If the taxable income is greater than US $ 1.6million, the effective tax rate is 33.45%.

Over time, the objective of the Indian Government is to drop the tax rate down to 25%. With the depreciation claims and the tax deductions, it is likely that the effective tax rate would be around 21% ~22%.

4. Other Rules

There's also a tax we said earlier—Dividend Distribution Tax. Companies which distribute dividends to their shareholders must pay a dividend distribution tax. The effective tax rate is 20.36%. Since this is a tax payable by the Indian companies, it is unlikely that the foreign companies can claim any credit for the Dividend Distribution Tax paid by the Indian companies. Hence it becomes a cost. For foreign companies, whether it is a branch or a permanent establishment, the effective tax rate is 41.2%. So there is a slight distinction when it comes to the tax rate results of an Indian company and the tax rates of a foreign branch or permanent establishment.

India also has what is called the "Minimum Alternative Tax" applicable to domestic companies. It is not applicable to foreign companies that do not have a PE in India. MAT is applicable when the tax liability computed under the normal income tax provisions is not more than 18.5% of the adjusted book profits. The MAT rates range from 19.05% to 21.34% depending on the income of the company. This is similar to the process in the United States, where they call it the "Alternative Minimum Tax". The MAT which is paid over and above the normal tax liability is a credit and can be carried forward and set off against the normal tax liability in the future years.

The withholding tax is levied on interest on eligible foreign debt and long-term infrastructure bonds. So it's not very different from all the other countries.

III. International Taxation and Transfer Price

India also has a large treaty network with almost all in Europe, Africa, Asia and the United States.

Transfer pricing—The tax authorities have always been aggressive in the context of Transfer Pricing in India. A significant amount of litigation in India has been in Transfer Pricing. However, there are some good rulings which have come out in the context of Transfer Pricing in India which are also eagerly awaited by the tax regulators of other jurisdictions. In addition, India is aligned with the BEPS reports on most issues. Some of the issues which the Indian tax authorities look at very closely and have been the point of litigation in India are Advertising, Cross border services, Cost recharges, Royalties, and Location savings.

IV. Goods and Services Tax Reform

GST—GST has been introduced from July 1, 2017 and it's a significant change in India. India would now be one jurisdiction for the purpose of computing GST. Earlier, each state had its own VAT. From east to west, you need to pay various taxes. Now those taxes were replaced with a unified GST. There are a range of GST rates available: 5%, 12%, 18% and 28%. 5% is for essential goods and 28% is for luxury goods.

There are some key areas for which we must watch out after GST has been implemented: First, the ERP system needs to be changed to minimise disruptions. Secondly, there could be situations where there could be an increase in working capital requirements and this would need to consider. Thirdly in the case of contracts—these may have to be re-negotiated since this is a change in law and hence there could be some re-negotiation required. I can say that this has been one of the biggest changes in the Indian tax system since India's independence in 1947. It will have far-reaching influences on the economy of India. We also believe that India will see an economic growth of 8% ~ 8. 5% in the future because of the GST.

V. Other Tax Issues

Now, a quick snapshot of the forms of business presence in India. If you set up unincorporated companies, incorporated companies or partnerships, then you can start your business. You can set up a representative office, a liaison office, or a branch office. You can set up a project office. As for incorporated companies, you can set up a subsidiary, a joint venture, or now a limited liability venture. So you can set up many sorts of business presence in India.

What other regulations does India have apart from the above taxes? We also have exchange control regulations which controls the inflow and outflow of foreign exchange. This does not mean that payments in foreign exchange cannot be made. It can be made easily, but appropriate documentation needs to be submitted to the Bank. In addition, we also have the Corporate Laws which provide regulations relating to working of companies. Furthermore there are industrial and other laws, such as environmental laws which need to be followed. For example, if you set up a hotel by the seaside, you need to consider whether you would violate the environmental protection law? What impact does it have on the environment? Listed companies or companies which are planning to be listed are covered by the SEBI regulations, which provide regulations relating to listed companies and investor protection. There are also employment related laws which provide regulations relating to minimum wages etc.

Now the Indian government focuses on "Make in India", and expects to attract investors to come and invest in the manufacturing industry, so as to revive India's manufacturing industry, and increase the share of the manufacturing sector in India's GDP from 16% to 25%. There are some key sectors, such as defense equipment, textiles and garments, where they want to attract more foreign investments. And preferential treatment is available for the National Investment Manufacturing Zones. Especially for the related sectors, the Indian government offers more investment supports.

In addition there are also some tax incentives for the above-mentioned infrastructure and manufacturing companies. There are also incentives provided for scientific research or for hiring new employees. At the same time, there are tax holidays for setting up SEZs like the one set up in China.

Next, I'll quickly give you a description of the Dispute Resolution Process. India, as you know, has a large amount of cases of litigation. But fairly speaking, the Indian tax system is very robust, and taxpayers and the related tax authorities have the ability to appeal to the higher authorities' right up to the Supreme Court for any issues. In fact many of the rulings issued by the Indian courts have been appreciated internationally, and although the Indian judicial system may be a bit slow in giving rulings, are very fair.

Capital Market: Integration and Development

Noritaka Akamatsu [*]

I would like to talk about the integration and development of capital market under the Belt and Road Initiative, with a focus on the Asian Bond Market Initiative as a way to support the financing of Belt and Road Initiative.

I. Financial Integration

Financial integration is as one of the five goals of Belt and Road Initiative, and the other goals include policy coordination; facilities connectivity; unimpeded trade; and people-to-people bonds. Developing financial market in each individual country has been a challenge, the cooperation and integration of capital market therefore is even more challenging. Financial integration under Belt and Road Initiative aims to promote financial regulatory cooperation and coordination among countries along the route, to develop RMB bond market for governments and bluechip companies and to establish credit information systems for banking and debt markets.

The current financing arrangement of Belt and Road Initiative is consisted of Asian Infrastructure Investment Bank, New Development Bank, Shanghai Cooperation Organization (SCO) financing institution, Silk Road Fund as well as Asian Development Bank. Among these, Asia as a whole region has accumulated rich experience in regional integration, particularly financial integration. Mr.

* Senior Advisor, Financial Cooperation & Integration, Asian Development Bank.

Akamatsu specifically elaborated the Asian Bond Market Initiative (ABMI) under ASEAN + 3 financial cooperation process. ABMI was first initiated in 2002 to address the root cause of Asian Financial Crisis, i. e. , double mismatch problem. ASEAN + 3 developed roadmaps of ABMI, and four Task Forces have been established since then to implement them, including the TF1 with a focus on supply of local currency (LCY) bonds, TF2 with a focus on demand for LCY bonds, TF3 with an aim to enhance and harmonize regulatory frameworks, and TF4 on regional settlement infrastructure.

II. Development of Capital Market

With the Asian Bond Market Initiative, the ASEAN + 3 LCY bond market has grew steadily recent years. However, the development is imbalanced within the region. Due to the massive differences in the level of economic and financial development, some ASEAN countries are faced with barriers and challenges than others in developing LCY bond market, especially in cross border bond issuance, investment and trading. To address these issues, ASEAN + 3 Multicurrency Bond Issuance Framework (AMBIF) was developed create mutually recognized common standards for issuance by focusing on the professional market segments in the region. Meanwhile, CSD-RTGS Linkage was chosen as a model to implement regional settlement infrastructure in ASEAN + 3. It should enable Delivery versus Payment (DVP) settlement of LCY bond trades with central bank money, which ensures safety of settlement and is compliant with the international standards while being cost-efficient.

Other challenges in financing Belt and Road Initiative, such as financing land route infrastructure in areas of modest population density, safety and security along the networks, and debt management capacity of the governments of participating countries including contingent liabilities management. Last but not least, unimpeded trade and investment is also crucial to financial integration under Belt and Road Initiative.

Relationship between China and European Union in the Belt and Road Initiative

Anna Saarela [*]

Capital mobility is an important issue, not only for China's Belt and Road Initiative, but also generally for Europe. Foreign direct investments are very important in this context. Currently, national authorities' coordination regarding, notably, regulatory frameworks in various areas such as accounting, accounting standards, taxation as well as financial policies are critical elements to make capital flows easier. This is not only to "invest" across the countries along the Belt and Road, but also across Europe as well as connecting the whole world, as the era of globalization is coming.

I will first introduce a number of elements about the European Union (EU)-China relations. Bilaterally, China and EU are close allies and we have very mature relations. Furthermore, I would like to link the Belt and Road Initiative with the European initiatives in this area, as well as beyond.

I. The connection between EU and China

Interconnectivity is very important that not only roads, but also communication and people-to-people exchanges. We celebrated the European Union's 60th anniversary in 2017. It was a long way to go, and a step-by-step process from

* Administrator, Trading Division under Policy Department of the European Parliament.

customs union towards a single market (free movement of capital, goods, services and people). With the opportunity of recent G20 Summit in Hamburg, Germany, it is necessary to highlight the importance of multilateral cooperation, where the EU and China showed their commitment towards the common multilateral goals at the global level again.

1. The EU-China relations

EU-China relations have come a long way and we have learned a lot from each other. Under the strategic partnership, the EU and China are cooperating very closely in various trade and economic areas. Under the umbrella of the political level annual summits—the 19th EU-China Summit, entitled "Delivering Stronger Partnership", took place on 2 June 2017 in Brussels—bilateral cooperation has expanded over the years, and there are nowadays around 60 various sectoral dialogues in different substantive areas. Additionally, the 12th EU-China Business Summit, organised annually, took place in the margins of the EU-China Summit. It gives business representatives a direct channel of communication to the political leaders from both sides to exchange views on the challenges and other issues on the bilateral economic relationship.

The 7th EU-China Strategic Dialogue, a part of the preparatory process of the summit, was held in China in April 2017. The 6th annual EU-China High-level Economic and Trade Dialogue took place last year, in October 2016, and the next annual Dialogue is expected to take place later this autumn. A Joint Committee on Trade and Investment at the technical level is preparing the groundwork. All these different layers of interactions, and in different areas of cooperation and coordination, amongst others, help to strengthen bilateral relations between the EU and China.

The cornerstone of the EU-China relations is the jointly agreed EU-China 2020 Strategic Agenda for Cooperation, which is the highest-level joint document in EU-China relations and provides strategic guidance on the various areas of cooperation that feed into the annual summit. It was jointly adopted in 2013, and in the same year as the overall Belt and Road Initiative was launched by the Chinese side. Both the EU and China have changed considerably since then. In response, the EU has upgraded its strategy *vis-a-vis* China last year, under the EU Joint Communication on the "Elements for a new EU strategy on China" .

As we are discussing investment here, and we share the views on the importance of capital mobility, we should encourage investors by creating a climate of confidence, such as whether it be through mutually recognised accounting standards, or whether it be done through protection of investors and investments. The EU and China are together currently negotiating a comprehensive and modern EU-China Investment Agreement. The 13th round of negotiations took place in May, 2017, and a speedy progress towards conclusion of these negotiations is a priority. This bilateral agreement would encourage investment flows between two partners for the further development of the Belt and Road Initiative.

2. China remains the major driver of global growth

Even though China's economic growth is slowing down and spill-over effects are estimated to follow. China is still estimated to be the biggest contributor to the global economic growth in 2017. This is based on the projection of 2017 data from the IMF and our study in the European Parliament. But together we both count: if the European Union and China are taken together, their contribution to the global economy is huge at over 37% of world total GDP in 2016. The transformation of China, it's rebalancing from investment to consumption, and from manufacturing to services, according to the OECD Economic Outlook of 2017, is estimated to slow China's growth to 6. 6% in 2017 and 6. 4% in 2018. This being said, in comparison the euro area is projected to have a steady growth at 1. 8% in 2017 and 2018; and the US's growth is projected to be 2. 1% this in 2017, reaching 2. 4% in 2018. Indeed, China has played and will continue to play a major role in the global economy.

II. The Belt and Road Initiative and the EU Investment Plan for Europe

Already in 2015 when the EU Investment Plan for Europe (The EU

Investment Plan) was set up, the EU and China agreed to continue exploring mutually beneficial synergies between the EU Investment Plan and the Belt and Road Initiative. In fact, China also agreed to contribute to the EU Investment Plan. The European Fund for Strategic Investment (EFSI) is one of cornerstones of the EU Investment Plan as this year a Memorandum of Understanding was signed on the margins of the EU-China Summit.

Today, the EU is China's biggest trading partner, while China is the EU's second largest trading partner after the United States. Therefore, fostering transport connections between the EU and China is important. Infrastructure links should, however, not be designed in isolation, but the 'Belt and Road' Initiative also needs to complement the networks already in place: such as the European Union initiative called the Trans-European Transport Networks. In fact, a part of the Trans-European Transport Network projects is coordinated within the framework of the Expert Group on Investment and Financing of the EU-China Connectivity Platform. This demonstrates close collaboration and connectivity between and within China and Europe, whether it is over sea, a land road or the 'Silk Road'.

1. European Fund for Strategic Investment

As noted already, the European Fund for Strategic Investment (EFSI) is the cornerstone and heart of the EU Investment Plan. The EFSI is operating under the European Investment Bank Group (EIB). The ESFI finances infrastructure, education, research, innovative renewable energy and energy efficiency, in fact, covering the same kind of areas than those of the Belt and Road Initiative.

Following the commitment made by China in 2015 to explore opportunities to contribute to the EU Investment Plan-on the margin of the EU-China Summit-a Memorandum of Understanding was signed between the European Investment Fund (EIF), part of the European Investment Bank Group, and China's Belt and Road Fund. It aims at jointly investing in private equity and venture capital funds that will in turn invest in small and medium-sized enterprises (SMEs) located primarily in the EU. The total expected commitment amounts to about EUR 500 million, which is equally shared between the two parties. Further, the establishment of the China-EU Co-Investment Fund would generate further synergies between the China's Belt and Road Initiative and the EU Investment Plan.

The cooperation between the EU and China on connectivity, in and with Asia and Europe, goes well beyond roads, railways and airports, including also energy cooperation (through the EU-China High Level Energy Dialogue). It also covers cooperation in the field of the ICT. ZTE Corporation, as example, has succeeded through a step-by-step approach in the ICT development field. The EU and China have also recognised the importance of cooperation on information technology for the digital economy: a joint declaration on cooperation in the area of the fifth generation of mobile communication networks was concluded in 2015. The EU and China have deepened cooperation on the ICT with the aim of achieving better synergies between the European digital agenda and China's Internet Plus (+) strategy, which is estimated to benefit around 1. 1 billion internet users in both China and EU.

2. Regional Integration

From what has been mentioned before, the EU has its 60th anniversary in 2017, and ASEAN celebrates its 50th anniversary. Moving towards regional integration takes time and is a step-by-step process. China's Belt and Road Initiative is a "kind" of regional integration project, which will take time. In order for this initiative to succeed, it needs to be mutually beneficial for all parties, including third countries, it requires, what is the most important, an equal engagement from everybody, and last but not least it requires jointly agreed the "rules of the game" . In our globalised world, trade and investment, as well as people, are very interconnected and interlinked. Currently, it has already learned about the global value chains today, as well as about "roads" towards deeper regional integration. Both enhance productivity, efficiency and resource management, for the benefit of all, and the wellbeing of our people, as they are also important elements for poverty reduction. We also need to engage actively in global governance, and to tackle together regional and global challenges. Climate change was mentioned in the context of the G20 Summit. One of the examples is indeed the Paris Climate Agreement, where the leaders from Europe, such as the host Germany, as well as China and energy producers such as Saudi Arabia joined forces within the framework of G20 and agreed to go forward, because of the future, not only for our future, but also for our next generation.

3. Multilateralism

In 2016, G20 Hangzhou Summit was held successfully, the one upon which the Hamburg Summit was building in 2017. The United Nations' framework is also important, not only in the context of climate change, but also on the Sustainable Development Goals of 2030 as well as on security, where we also work together with China and other partners.

The World Trade Organisation (WTO) is the cornerstone of the rules-based international trading system. It is a forum where further cooperation could enhance transparent implementation and effective and timely enforcement of multilateral rules, amongst all WTO member countries. I need to emphasize the Base Erosion and Profit Shifting action plan (BEPS) specially here that on the side-lines of the recent OECD Forum in June 2017, 76 countries and regions signed, or formally expressed their intention to sign, the new Multilateral Convention to Implement Tax Treaty Related Measures to Prevent Base Erosion and Profit Shifting. This project shows that together we can go forward in multinational fora.

I would like to emphasize that the Belt and Road Initiative can succeed absolutely, but only if is mutually beneficial not only for China and for Europe, but also to the third countries involved. Furthermore, its success depends on jointly agreed "rules of game" and a level-playing field. To close, a level playing field, transparency and predictability are essential for EU businesses and investors. In this context, it should be noted that the EU is China's most important destination for outward investment, which reached around EUR 40 billion in 2016, whilst unfortunately the EU investments in China dropped to around EUR 8 billion, a reduction of 23% in comparison to the 2015 level. Therefore, a solid common ground is needed in order to explore and unlock trade and investment potential, not only through the Belt and Road Initiative, but also in various areas and sectorial interests, where the EU and China already have joint and mutually agreed dialogues to build upon. And indeed, together we can!

The Basics of Chinese Enterprises Investment In The Belt and Road Countries

Wang Yunfan[*]

I . Information Infrastructure for Cross-Border Investment

Morning Whistle Group is mainly engaged in international mergers and acquisitions (M&A) . Today, one of the key words is "infrastructure" here. In fact, very few entities except government and Internet companies are interested in infrastructure development for three reasons: A. largeinitial investment; B. long-term input-output and payback period; and C. limited direct Economic spillover effect. However, on a positive note, it has an industry-pull effect.

Why are Internet companies interested in it? First, Internet companies are able to attract venture capital (VC) to pay for the initial investment that results a special financial method. Second, Internet companies, particularly platform-based companies, are themselves a kind of long-term investment. And thirdly, Internet company has its own special business model-indirect financial returns, i. e., the benefit comes from the price someone else has paid (as we call it, "wools grow on pigs, and dogs pay for them") , so direct return from the initial investment is not the first priority of this model. That also explains why there are so many Internet companies involved in infrastructure construction.

---

[*] Founder & CEO of Morning Whistle Group.

This is also true for Morning Whistle, but our focus is on IT industry infrastructure, namely the market information infrastructure for Chinese companies' cross-border equity investment.

Morning Whistle is a well-known Internet platform in cross-border mergers and acquisitions. It focuses on the market information infrastructure for Chinese companies' cross-border equity investment. The main line of business is matchmaking of cross-border equity investment deals. Therefore, its business positioning is a deal match-maker and service provider in the primary market.

II. The Morning Whistle Group's Database and Services

In this segment market, we have been mainly focusing on four things in the past three years. Here I just want to mention two in particular. First is database building. Every day we keep a close eye on 2, 000 ~ 3, 000 sources of information on the globe in order to grab global M&A information, translate and publish it in realtime, and analyze the major deals on the market. Up till now, we have established a large, complete database, covering more than 9, 000 M&A cases made by Chinese companies since 1978.

Second is the China Merger platform, an innovative equity transaction matching system, likened to be a global online equity exchange. The system consists of two databases. One is the global project database, the largest one of this kind in the world, including more than 13, 000 active projects online, mainly from global elite investment banks (800), law firms (200), PEs (100), as well as investment promotion agencies of various countries. The other is the database of more than 5, 000 potential Chinese buyers, including over 2, 500 Chinese institutes, such as 365 listed companies and over 1, 000 industrial companies and PEs. The buyers publish their cross-border merger needs on the China Merger in the format provided by us.

China Merger is a platform connting the release of global projects (the supply side) and the release of demands of Chinese domestic buyers (the demand side).

Every month, around 60 – 80 non-disclosure agreements will be signed through China Merger between true buyers and sellers on true equity assets, most of which are worth tens of millions to billions US dollars. This is our infrastructure work and this is what we do.

Morning Whistle has done a lot of work in connection with the Belt and Road Initiative. First, on our China Merger platfom, we have dedicated a Belt and Road database to include all projects from the Belt and Road countries. Second, we undertook two Belt and Road research projects launched by Shanghai DRC, namely, the "Promoting the Belt and Road Initiative with the Shanghai free trade zone as the carrier" last year and the "Promoting the Belt and Road Initiative with the Shanghai free trade zone (FTZ) as the bridgehead" this year. We visited and surveyed Shanghai FTZ Belt and Road projects to investigate how to build the Shanghai FTZ into a bridgehead for Chinese companies' going global. Besides, we also won the bid for the Belt and Road part nership training program launched by Shanghai Municipal Commision of Commerce to provide systematic training for Chinese companies to go global. And also, we organize investment promoting salons and roadshows offline every month, including a dedicated Belt and Road theme. This June, Morning Whistle released a *Progress Report on Investment in Mergers & Acquisitions Made by Chinese Companies in the Belt and Road Countries 2014 – 2017*, which attracted huge market attention.

Ⅲ. Data of China's Foreign Investment to Belt and Road Countries

China Belt and Road Initiative consists of three stages: State 1, the proposal of the Initiative in 2013, Stage 2, the formulation of vision and action plan in 2015, and Stage 3, the implementation of the Initiative in 2017. There are two hallmark events, namely, the opening of the high level Belt and Road Summit in May and the Vision for Maritime Cooperation under the Belt and Road Initiative jointly proposed by NDRC and SOA on 20 June, signifying that the Belt and Road Initiative coming into practice.

General speaking, there are two lines of investment as the Belt and Road Initiative rolls out: one is investment in the six economic corridors along the Silk Road, while the other is investment in the three maritime economic belts. According to the MOFCOM data, our ODI can be categorized into three types: the largest category is commodity export, the second is off-shore construction, and the third is direct non-financial investments, including Greenfield investment and equity investment. Furthermore, direct equity investment can be sub-categorized into three types: Type I refers to governmental development aid, which is conventionally decided by the government. Type III is private investment which has been quite active in these years. Type II is a category in-between, relatively new but growing very fast, which is also called development-oriented financial investment. This type also reflects national strategy but adopts a market approach. Nowadays Type II is growing bigger and bigger and attracting more and more private investors. For instance, the CEE Fund launched by the former ICBC chairman Jiang Jianqing years ago has attracted Chinese private company Fosun and many other foreign investors as its LPs. This is a big change.

1. Overseas Equity Investment

For overseas equity investment, Morning Whistle's researches share different scopes: MOFCOM surveys cross-border investments made by companies registered in China, while we examine ODIs made by actual holding companies regardless of registration. For instance, Fosun invests more than USD 10 billion through its overseas platforms every year, which is covered by Morning Whistle, but not by MOFCOM. And also, we usually follow up an investment in five processes from rumours to delivery. That's why our database is much larger than MOFCOM's.

According to statistics, the Belt and Road investment and value accounts for one fifth of the total ODI in the past three years, at about 18% ~ 19% from 2015 to 2017. We found there are 303 deals in total, of which 199 have disclosed transaction value at 102.2 billion yuan, while the value of non-disclosed deals is relatively smaller.

2. Top Investment Targets and Investment Destinations

The hot investment recipient industries in the Belt and Road countriesare very similar to those in the global investment pattern. The six hot industries include TMT, energy & mining, infrastructure utilities, manufacturing, healthcare and financials. On China Merger, there are more than 2,000 Belt and Road projects, accounting for about 20% of the total 13,000 projects on the platform.

The top two investment recipient countries are Singapore and Isreal. Specifically, there are 46 investments in Singapore, 44 in Isreal, 39 in India, 24 in Russia, 19 in Malaysia, and 10 in Indonesia.

3. Features and Requirements of Chinese Acquiers

Generally Speaking, Chinese acquiers' features and needs. In terms of investors by geography, there are eight investor regions. Beijing plus SOEs rank the first, followed by Shanghai, a bridgehead of Belt and Road oveseas investment, particularly the free trade zone where more than 65% of overseas investment occurred. According to the nature of Chinese buyers, it can be found that private companies accounts for 67% of the total but the value takes up only 11%, and the unit investment amount by SOEs is greater than by private companies on average.

According to data statistics, public companies constitute the majority of the Belt and Road investors. Of the 303 cases followed by us, 209 involve publicly listed companies. However, averagely speaking, the non-listed companies invest more than the listed ones, which might be explained by the fact that many investments are made by the parent company of the group corporation.

When it comes to the approach of investment, 65% companies opt for equity investment, 31% for joint venture. There is a small number for Greenfield investment with approximate 30% for mature holding acquisitions. In the 50 Shanghai companies, they intend to invest USD 50 million account for 8.8%, USD 10 – 50 million for 26%, USD 5 – 10 million for 29%, USD 1 – 5 million for 26%, and less than USD 1 million for 8.3%. This is a typical olive-shaped pattern, small at both ends and large in the middle. In fact, this pattern is consistent with what we have observed in the market, i. e. , the mid-cap investments costitute the majority, taking up about 70% of market transactions.

How to Use Hong Kong Capital Market as a Financing Platform

Chen Yongren [*]

Generally speaking, Hong Kong (' HK ') capital market is an internationalized liberal market. As the Belt and Road Initiative rolls out, Chinese companies are desperate to go global by acquiring businesses in other countries. Actually, ultimately all companies will go for securitization strategy either to raise fund on the market or to go public after acquisition. This happens all the time. For instance, after Chinalco acquired a copper mine in Peru, we assisted it to go public in HK 3 years ago. For another instance, after acquiring a copper mine in Zambia, CNMC also got listed in HK, because its structure did not allow it to be listed on the domestic market but went public in HK through spin-off. Furthermore, there are many companies from the Belt and Road countries that have signed public-listing contracts with HK for going public. For instance, we assisted Kazakhstan Copper, as one of the two crown jewel companies in Kazakhstan which has super organization size in Kazakhstan, to make secondary listing in HK. We also helped RUSAL to be listed in HK. Additionally, when many Chinese companies planned to acquire companies from the Belt and Road countries, they usually came to HK to raise fund. Therefore, I would like to brief you on the latest development of the HK capital market, including trends about financing, bond issuing and equity.

[*] Managing Director of Banking Department in China International Capital Corporation Limited.

I. The Introduction of Capital Market in Hong Kong

I would like to say that Chinese companies have taken up half of the HK Exchange market that 50. 2% to be exact in numbers and 64% of the total market value. Some companies are well known by general public, such as Tencent, and HSBC which was started in Shanghai.

SEHK has a main board and a second board (i. e. Growth Enterprise Market-GEM). Unfortunately, GEM did not develop very well. So far SEHK hosts more than 2, 000 listed companies which is very similar to Shanghai Stock Exchange and Shenzhen Stock Exchange in scale. But the difference from them is that the main players on SEHK are institutional investors and there are many value stocks. Some these leading companies, including some well-known Shanghai companies like H-shares of Fosun Pharma, have higher valuation premium. Generally speaking, the performance of these SEHK-listed leading companies is spectacular.

HK ranks the global first in terms of IPO scale on a yearly basis, except the year when Alibaba turned to be listed in the U. S. , which pushed SEHK to start reforms. The years from 2010 to 2015 are bullish years, with IPO reaching more than \$50 billion and \$30 billion respectively. It shows that HK's competitiveness is highly strong, even though A-share financing was not bad either in these two years. Largely speaking, every year Chinese companies are the largest IPO players, including IPO made by the Postal Savings Bank of China last year. They usually come to HK for IPO, but there are also many companies that choose dual-listing, they get listed first in HK, and then go back to China for listing. There is another trend worth noticing here that HK and China stock markets are getting more and more connected. After the start of Shanghai-HK Stock Connect and Shenzhen-HK Stock Connect, every day more than 10 billion RMB flows into SEHK and the same amount of capital flow into China A-share market.

II. The Expectation of Hong Kong Capital Markel in the Belt and Road Initiative

Despite the fact that many Chinese companies are desperate to go global, capital outflow is extremely difficult due to current stringent exchange controls. As a result, a lot of companies, especially some listed in China stock market, usually select SEHK as a base in the Chinese territory before going out to acquire a company in other countries. I assisted Shanghai DaZhong Public Utilities (Group) in 2016, a well-established Shanghai company, to be listed on SEHK. In fact, this company went public in China quite earlier, then it got listed in HK because of less stringent capital controls there in terms of sell-off and refinancing. Considering HK financial market is much freer, so more and more companies are listed on HK market, which include Shanghai Wangsu Technology as instance. Especially, it needs capital to facilitate its global expansion, but unfortunately the money could not flow cross-border due to capital control, so it went to HK for the convenience of capital outflow. Since HK is part of China, if a company wants to expand its business into any of the Belt and Road countries, it usually goes through HK either by getting listed there or by establishing a HK holding platform.

Largely speaking, listing rules in HK are very similar to those in Mainland China. But it has much elasticity, particularly those in relation to market valuation, ie., even non-profitable companies can get listed in HK. For instance, Meitu, a well-known company, got listed in HK even though it was valued at tens of billions but suffered losses of billions. Additionally, many loss making mining companies all choose to be listed on SEHK.

To mining companies, the reason is that many of the Belt and Road countries and regions are under developed, and SEHK makes special provisions to accommodate their public listing. For instance, it provides that the companies have exclusive project license regarding roads, bridges, railways, etc., they can opt for profit immunity and other special financial treatment. But these companies have to prove that their top management has the necessary experience in the first place. If so, SEHK can accept only two-year financial statements instead of three which are basically required by both HK and Mainland China. This could be used as a reference for Belt and Road projects.

Five or six years ago, SEHK wanted to develop a sound mining capital market just like Australia and Canada, so it produced Article 18 of the listing rules, providing that any company that has an internationally accepted reserve report and can verify the cash flow, meet 12 – month demands and prove its management's experience can be listed on SEHK with no profit requirement. Unfortunately such mining companies had a mediocre performance in HK without any surprise because due diligence is difficult to carry out. Investors couldn't see aforementioned mining companies accurately, and if the reserves were proven wrong, the financial expectation would fail.

After consulting the expertise recently, SEHK is considering launching an innovation main board and innovation primary board. Inspired by the "new three board" of the Mainland market, the innovation primary board is designed to attract some non-profitable startup companies. The innovation main board is placed for those up to the requirements, but now it becomes more tolerable particularly to those companies that cannot completely meet the requirements in some areas, such as the equity structure in the Alibaba case or the startups that have only one year performance instead of three years required by SEHK. In fact, this practice is very similar to the "strategic emerging industries board" which is expected to launch in Shanghai. The truth is, SEHK is being reformed drastically and they want to attract emerging businesses, like Meitu, to list. As we know, since its inception in 2009, China's second board has developed so well that many companies have grown into business leaders. On the contrary, the development of HK's second board is under expected, thus it's desperate to attract the emerging companies to be listed there.

Ⅲ. issuing of off-shore corporate debts

Finally, I will analyze HK's another function as an off-shore corporate debt-issuing center for Chinese companies. Generally speaking, Chinese companies make investment in Belt and Road countries in the form of ODI which is highly regulated now. However, it is much difficult for a Chinese company to buy a football team or a theater or even properties overseas. Acquiring a foreign company involves a lot of red tapes, so many companies use HK to issue USD-dominated corporate debts for fundraising, taking just about 3 or 4 months. In HK, there is no requirement of 40% net assets, while the Mainland has. What's more, both NDRC (National Development and Reform Commission) and SAFE (State Administration of Foreign Exchange) encourage the backflow of capital. HK financing structure is quite flexible in that Chinese companies can directly issue corporate debt there, or the parent company can guarantee for its overseas subsidiaries. The latter is a ring fencing structure, ie., the parent company will never give up overseas valuation: if there is any financial problem, it is ready to repay the debts. So you can see the structure is highly flexible and totally depends on whether a company has overseas subsidiaries or whether it needs a guarantee mechanism.

Guarantee is a very simple approach, but it will incur tax issues and the on-shore investor has to pay the withholding income tax. So many companies choose the alternative: setting up an off-shore platform to guarantee the on-shore investor that issues corporate debt directly. This is the most popular approach.

According to statistics, it can be found that Chinese investors issued debts valued at over $150 billion in 2014 and 2015 respectively. The figure dropped slightly in 2016 because many Chinese companies chose to be listed on the domestic market, but 2017 witnessed an upward trend again, approximating $200 billion according to estimation. Currently, many companies expand their businesses into Europe and Africa that they may first borrow money from banks in dollar bonds to acquire foreign business, and then repay the banks by issuing

USD-dominated debts.

Thus, as an off-shore financial hub, HK has flexible regulations. If Chinese companies want to acquire foreign businesses in the Belt and Road countries, the facilitative capital market in HK can be a great booster for Chinese companies' global ambitions.

Forging "Business Community": Chinese Companies Are Integrating with the Globle Market

Qian Yuyi[*]

Since 2013 that President Xi Jinping proposed the Belt and Road Initiative, the program has still been focusing on the "five aspects" of the initiative to grow extensively and intensively. The five aspects are policy coordination, facilities connectivity, unimpeded trade, financial integration and people-to-people bonds. Therefore, more Chinese companies start doing business in the Belt and Road countries to cooperate with local companies, by means of EPC, investment and financing project, supply chain integration, technology transfer, etc., for exploiting the particular advantages of each other. Initially, companies in some industries, like infrastructure, financial services, professional services, telecoms, manufacturing, logistics, etc., seized the development opportunities immediately to go global as frontrunners. Furthermore, with the development of the Belt and Road Initiative, companies in other industries, like E-commerce, energy, life science, healthcare, etc., are also expecting to expand their presence beyond borders, and they will become a new force of Chinese globalization.

In ACCA Professional Insights report entitled *The Belt and Road Initiative: Reshaping the Global Value Chain*, ACCA pointed out that translation of the Initiative into practice may also be challenged by such factors as geopolitical tensions, economic uncertainties, unsophisticated financial markets, risks arisen

* Head of Policy, China, ACCA.

from foreign exchange fluctuation and foreign currency payment, insufficient knowledge of local laws and regulation policies, as well as immature labor markets.

In order to help Chinese companies learn from successful experiences and best practices, guest speakers, from the Pakistan-China Institute, Deloitte China, CRBC and Inspur Group, all contributed valuable opinions. Three Chinese experts shared with us three main points including industry-specific experience when going global from Chinese companies' perspectives, how a professional service-provider helps hundreds of MNCs develop their "global strategies", and about digitization helps with the Initiative implementation. Actually, they have one thing in common that China business expansion is not simply about sale of products or services, but more about export of corporate governance, brand and influence. Generally speaking, any company that wants to have an edge on the global market must learn to cooperate with people of different cultures, faiths or customs. The Pakistani guest has a strong belief in it, saying that only by respecting the local culture and conventions, having awareness of environment protection, committing to green development and paying due attention to public relations and public image can assist Chinese companies to win the heart of the local people.

Part One: The Introduction of China-Pakistan Economic Corridor

Mustafa Hyder Sayed[*]

The Pakistan-China Institute is playing a very important and frontline role in the Belt and Road Initiative, particularly in the context of the China-Pakistan Economic Corridor. The China-Pakistan Economic Corridor, which is one of six corridors of the Belt and Road Initiative, is a flagship project thus far of the Belt and Road Initiative. The China-Pakistan Economic Corridor was initiated about 3 years ago, through a series of MOU, worth 46 billion USD which were signed under the former prime minister of Pakistan Muhammad Nawaz Sharif and president Xi Jinping. Recently, the worth of MOU's has increased from 46 billion USD to 62 billion USD, which comprises of energy, railway, infrastructure, and Gwadar Port projects.

I. Strategic position of Gwadar Port

Why is Gwadar Port so important strategically and economically? Why it is different from other ports in Asia and Middle East. Gwadar is actually the converging point of the Silk Road Economic Belt and the Maritime Silk Road. It means the maritime trade route by sea and the land route converge in Gwadar, providing Gwadar a privilege-a trade privilege, a strategic privilege, a political privilege. And Gwadar gives a very exceptional access to the Persian Gulf and it also provides access to Europe, Africa and Middle East.

---

[*] Executive Director of Pakistan-China Institute.

When it comes to the land route for explaining how the goods from China can cut across Gwadar through the land routes. The Xinjiang Uygur Autonomous Region borders with the Gilgit Baltistan province of Pakistan. And from there, actually the person who is from the China Road and Bridge Corporation expressed that they have built the key project of the Karakoram Highway, which starts from Xinjiang into Pakistan and goes up that route, goes up to Gwadar, making the trade from China to Pakistan easier and efficient.

From the sea route perspective, Guangzhou and Shanghai Ports conduct all their sea trading through the straits of Malacca route which is about 11,000 to 12,000 kilometers. If Gwadar was used, the total distance is 3,000 to 4,000 KMs. So right now, the goods are coming from China's ports like Guangdong and Shanghai that cross South China Sea and must go all around countries. If the Gwadar port is to be used, this will be the route which connects the land route and the maritime route, so this is a context of the strategic location of Gwadar Port. This is a port that's being developed by the China Overseas Port Holding Company, which is again a subsidiary of the China Communication Construction Company. Thus, Gwadar is the flagship project of the Belt and Road Initiative.

II. Cooperation in China-Pakistan Economic Corridor

The most important thing about the China-Pakistan Economic Corridor is that it has become a regional framework mechanism of cooperation not only between China and Pakistan, but also around neighboring countries like Iran, Afghanistan, Turkey, Kazakhstan, etc. All these countries have expressed interest to participate in the China-Pakistan Economic Corridor and become beneficiaries of the China-Pakistan Economic Corridor. And they will automatically become beneficiaries of this project of this magnitude because as the chairman of PCI who is also the chairman of the Parliamentary Committee on the China-Pakistan Economic Corridor says that the Belt and Road is not only about energy infrastructure, but it is also about cultural connectivity as well. So this connectivity is happening naturally with the China-Pakistan Economic Corridor in South Asia. And it's actually giving rise to a thoughtful greater South Asia, or the pan-regionalism, in which, the whole region is emerging with a lot of excellent growth indicators, because there is a lot of job creation happening. Thousands of local people in developing countries like Pakistan are going to be given jobs due to the projects emerging from CPEC.

Around five thousand megawatts have already been added to the national grid in Pakistan. And this is very important for a country like Pakistan because Pakistan had a very big power crisis with a shortfall of energy. Out of a total of 46 billion USD more than 70% of the amount will be invested on build, operate and transfer (BOT) model for energy projects. The guaranteed return of 17% is being given to Chinese companies. Thus, Chinese companies are generating the power and selling it to the government at a regionally negotiated tax. So the government is making money. Pakistan is benefiting as energy is being produced while the Chinese companies are benefiting as they are making money, so this is what call a win-win partnership in which most of the countries are benefiting.

And there is a cooperation mechanism in a framework to which it has been slowly expanded. It started from energy, and in 2016, the power generation has increased incredibly compared to what was in 2013 in this slide. These are some of energy projects which are being done in the China-Pakistan Economic Corridor, and now because it has progressed to another stage of development, which is SEZ, special economic zones.

Special economic zones ("SEZs"), which are very important to the development of the Belt and Road Initiative in the long-term, are areas planned which have been given special tax holidays, free land and other incentives by the Government of Pakistan. SEZ's will be developed by Chinese companies in collaboration with the local government as well as local and International companies. And these SEZs will boost manufacturing units which will not only cater to the markets in Pakistan and China but to the markets in the regional countries, in the neighboring countries. So the whole central Asia is there, Kazakhstan, Kyrgyzstan, Uzbekistan, Iran, Afghanistan, India, etc. Furthermore, all of these countries will benefit from the special economic zones which have been set up now in this part of the China-Pakistan Economic Corridor.

There are two special economic zones in every province in Pakistan, and the first economic zone had been set up in Gwadar Port because Gwadar is the epicenter of CPEC. Shenzhen would be illustrated as example to demonstrate the value of aforementioned SEZ in Pakistan. What Shenzhen was 30 years ago, a city where there were subsistence fishermen who were not very affluent. And now Gwadar is undertaking the development that Shenzhen took about 25, 30 years ago, so it's very similar to that. And along with the fishery project, there's a power project being set up and there's also a very unique industrial complex being set up to have manufacturing units. So what is important for companies since talking about accounting and tax in other professional organizations previously, is to understand that how the "Belt and Road" project will be on the ground. If companies want to benefit from Belt and Road project, companies want to benefit and have a business which will generate revenue, and companies want to align their policies, companies' vision with the Belt and Road. It is urgent to bring those stakeholders under one roof while it is also important to understand the model of China-Pakistan Economic Corridor because this is a model that should be duplicated to other relevant projects in other Belt and Road countries. This successfully standard mechanism, which has been coordinated by the NDRC of China, will also be applicable in other Belt and Road countries. Therefore, the estimation of ports is crucial to the Belt and Road Initiative, exploitation of energy, and interconnection of roads, railways and tubes.

As assistant minister of the finance mentioned, all the Belt and Road countries should work in harmony to develop Belt and Road project. The SOEs, POEs and other professional organizations, like ACCA, Deloitte, etc. , have worked in harmony in order to maximize the benefits and dividends of the Belt and Road projects.

Coordination mechanism mentioned above is very important so that the left side should know what the right side is doing, and the right side should know what the left side is doing. I think that is imperative. Companies like China Communication Construction Company etc. can also share the details of what the projects that they have matured in Pakistan and other Belt and Road countries to show what are the time frames, how they are executed, what are the accounting companies and auditing firms which are used.

In other ways, one issue arose, when China-Pakistan Economic Corridor is mentioned, as a national issue which is security. Regarding the issues of security of investments and sustainability of investments, Pakistani Government and the military have taken a very unique step and set up the Special Security Division which is a specialized and designated security force of the military to protect the China-Pakistan Economic Corridor projects, to protect the Chinese companies and their workers in Pakistan and also to make sure that the projects are fully secured, and are not exposed to any mishaps and any unprecedented issues of security. Due to a better security position, Pakistan has hit a 5.2% GDP growth rate. Jack Ma, as the chairman of Alibaba, selected to Pakistan for future investment which is a big achievement for Pakistan. And other investors are also coming to Pakistan to reap the benefits from China-Pakistan Economic Corridor under the open policies of Pakistani Government. For example, in the cement and steel industry, people are putting up more and more steel and cement plants which cater to the needs for the China-Pakistan Economic Corridor projects.

Moreover, there is expansion in financial area in Pakistan that it's easier to get financing for investment projects in Pakistan. According to the MCIA index, Pakistan has been categorized as an emerging market, as opposed to a frontier market which was the status in 2016. It suggests Pakistan is now an emerging market with the likes of Russia, Brazil and India. PCI would like to invite all the interested parties present in this conference to come to Pakistan and join in PCI's conferences, which will help in better understanding of China-Pakistan Economic Corridor and its policies.

Part Two: Cloud and the Belt and Road Initiative

Wang Xingshan[*]

As a service provider of cloud computing and big data, Inspur is a participant in the Belt and Road Initiative and a partner of the Chinese enterprises going global. In the past few years, Inspur has vigorously developed international projects, through which Inspur can share with the world Chinese practices in informatization and Internet economic development, promoting data interconnectivity between China and Belt and Road countries for a win-win scenario built and shared by all.

Internationalization is one of Inspur's four major development strategies. So far, Inspur has expanded its business to 108 jurisdictions around the world, with its major projects covering half of Belt and Road countries. Inspur's practices include a cloud computing center signed with a Russian enterprise, assistance in the construction of smart cities in Indonesia, Thailand and Saudi Arabia, education cloud, date palm gene research and so on.

In addition to Cloud Computing and big data services, Inspur has also been keen on "concept export", that is to provide IT-based personnel training and promoting mature "China programs" to all the Belt and Road countries. Inspur has hosted and sponsored more than 500 technical training and preaching sessions overseas, trained more than 10,000 technical experts and officials as well as over 1,000 foreign tax officers in total for Belt and Road countries. "Tax risk" is chosen as an example here. China implements the "invoice-based taxation", a philosophy of controlling tax by invoices. Inspur has shared this philosophy to more

* CEO of Inspur Group Co., Ltd.

than 20 Belt and Road countries through Inspur's IT-based tax service programs. In Jun Wang's business trip to an offshore informatization program of Inspur in 2015, Jun Wang, as Administrator of the State Administration of Taxation, praised Inspur for choosing the right path, and encouraged the promotion of China's advanced practices in tax handling and tax informatization in more jurisdictions. Following the Belt and Road Forum in May 2017, government heads of Curacao, Ethiopia and some other countries visited Inspur, expressing their affirmation of Inspur's engagement in building the digital Silk Road.

As look back at Inspur's global expansion in recent years, it found that information playing a key supporting role. In a context of multi-language, multi-currency, multi-time zones and multi-accounting standards, a business needs to internalize uniform standards, a common language and other relevant factors into its IT system, as well as to employ cloud and the sharing model for rapid deployment and simple application. Therefore, "cloud and the Belt and Road Initiative", as one topic, would be shared in the following aspects:

I . Interconnection is supported by information exchange

Since the world has ushered in an era of digital economy, the role of interconnected information infrastructure outperforms any other infrastructure (e. g. utilities), as you cannot live without information wherever you are. Informatization has become a must for businesses. For Inspur, a better information system calls for intensified learning and studying in the accounting infrastructure. For example, it is necessary to provide a comprehensive and systematic training on the theme of "Accounting Infrastructure Promotes the Belt and Road Initiative".

As the carrier of the accounting infrastructure going global, cloud is a pillar of the initiative landing of the Belt and Road initiative. Take finance as an example, more and more enterprises are providing services for overseas projects through the financial cloud sharing model, treating management and control and service on an equal footing. Drawing on the success of its shared service center in

China, CCCC is preparing to set up a shared financial service center in Southeast Asia. Additionally, SHEC and THEC under the CCCC have co-completed the construction of the shared center in Malaysia, which serves Malaysia, Vietnam, Thailand, Brunei, the Philippines and some other countries.

Ⅱ. Supporting the Belt and Road Initiative by prioritising the cloud strategy

To push forward the Belt and Road initiative, a business should follow a cloud priority strategy to speed up the adoption of cloud, shifting to the fast lane on the information express by integrating cloud in infrastructure, operation and management and seeking entry into the digital Silk Road. A new generation of information technology is flourishing, represented by cloud computing, big data, the Internet of things and artificial intelligence. Cloud computing is the first to appear in the public sight. If there were no cloud, there would never be any big data, not to mention artificial intelligence. In the emerging technology package, cloud is the underlying factor that cloud priority strategy must be insisted. Currently, Cloud application has been inaugurated across businesses. On 12 April 2017, the provincial government of Zhejiang Province issued an action plan for cloud application in 100,000 enterprises, followed by similar government decrees in Jiangsu Province and Jinan City. To illustrate, Xiaoshan District of Hangzhou got its assigned share of 4,200 enterprises yesterday, which will then be distributed hierarchically to a variety of enterprises in townships, a microcosm of the popularity of cloud application across Chinese businesses.

In order to support cloud application across businesses, Inspur officially released Inspur Corporate Cloud on May 26, providing all-round cloud services for large-, medium-, small-and micro-sized enterprises, including field cloud and industry cloud. Driven by the philosophy of " connectivity, share and intelligence", Inspur is committed to helping businesses build an intelligent brain in support of digital transformation. In the financial domain, Inspur cooperate closely with SNAI, Deloitte and ACCA, etc. , and constantly improve product and service capabilities, expecting Inspur Shared Finance Cloud to enjoy a global outreach rather than act in China alone. Additionally, construction cloud, as one of the industry clouds, is also vital to Inspur, since large construction enterprises can be deemed as pioneers of the Belt and Road initiative. Therefore, Inspur are going to reinforce cooperation with CCCC, CREC and other strategic partners, providing IT support for more companies seeking global performance.

The newly launched Inspur Corporate Cloud has five features respectively that: 1) cloud structure, 2) integrated business, finance and taxation, 3) intelligence, 4) security and reliability, and 5) brand-new user experience. The Cloud structure supports a variety of cloud deployment models and payment models to meet different ways of cloud application across businesses. As for the integration of business, finance and taxation, the interoperability between taxation and business and finance, which is an important orientation for future management software and corporate cloud. Inspur will step up to promote the integration of the new generation information technology and management accounting, striving for integrated business, finance and taxation as well as for industrial chain synergy through end-to-end processes. In addition, Inspur Corporate Cloud also supports seamless connection with JD. com and Ctrip, enabling the unimpeded data flow and offering all-round cloud services covering personnel, talent, things and clients to help businesses build the corporate cloud ecology.

As a practitioner of the Belt and Road initiative, Inspur has provided IT-based services for the pioneers of the initiative, including CCCC, CGN, PowerChina and so on. Inspur will continue to strengthen collaboration with Inspur's strategic clients for innovation, enhance industry-university-institute cooperation, and expand overseas R&D investment, striving to make contribution to the Belt and Road initiative.

Part Three: The Basics of Companies' Involvement in the Belt and Road Initiative

One: The Basics of Deloitte's Involvement in the Belt and Road Initiative

Jiang Ying *

Deloitte had provided Chinese companies going global with integrated professional services. Deloitte has been involved in Chinese companies going global for ten years even before the Belt and Road Initiative. Especially, some Chinese construction companies started off to go global with EPC ("Engineering, procurement construction") projects through consulting services provided by Deloitte. Deloitte positioned its professional services as "Chinese enterprises go global-Deloitte is by your side". Deloitte is dedicated to helping Chinese companies go global and become truly global enterprises as the Belt and Road Initiative rolled out which is also the vision of Deloitte. To this end, Deloitte set up a Deloitte China Service Team in 2003 to attract foreign investments. In the past 8 or 9 years, Deloitte's focus has shifted to how to help Chinese companies go global. So far this team has 600 professionals who perfectly speak Chinese and

* Vice CEO of Deloitte China

understand China, and have rich local experiences across 150 countries in the world to help Chinese companies go global. With the help of the team, Chinese companies can achieve their global ambition.

Meanwhile, Deloitte also assisted many government bodies, including SASAC and MOFCOM, to jointly issue reports on the risks of going global for Chinese companies. Deloitte made insightfulindustry analyses of six or seven hot sectors, such as rail transit, agriculture, ecology, environmental protection, etc. Generally speaking, Deloitte as the global largest professional service-provider is capable of and responsible for helping Chinese companies go global and participate in the Belt and Road Initiative that assist companies to grow bigger and stronger, go out, go in and go up.

Two: The Basics of CRBC's Involvement in the Belt and Road Initiative

Dong Futang *

CRBC began its global journey in 1958 when four companies were chosen by the Chinese government to offer economic aid to other countries. With the inception of Reform and Opening-up, CRBC was corporatized. Until now, CRBC has established subsidiaries in 63 countries and regions across the globe, becoming one of China's key off-shore construction companies in the world.

So far, CRBC has expanded its business into many Belt and Road countries by tracking and promoting more than 300 projects and constructing some demonstrative projects of connectivity. To name just a few: a) South East Asia: Surabaya-Madura Strait-crossing Bridge and Solo Road in Indonesia, Highway 57B

---

* Chief Accountant of China Road and Bridge Corporation, Chinese Leading Accounting Reserve Talent

in Cambodia, The Pakbeng Mekong River Bridge in Laos, and Cao Lanh Cable-Stayed Bridge Project in Vietnam; b) South Asia: Pakistan Karakoram Highway Up-gradation Project, and karannapli Tunnel in Bangladesh; c) Central Asia: Tajikistan-Ukraine Road, China-Kirgizstan-Ukraine Road, Tajikistan-China Road, and Shahristan Tunnel, with a total mileage of over 2000 km; d) East Africa: Mombasa-Nairobi Standard Gauge Railway in Kenya, and Nairobi-Malaba Railway in Kenya, with a total mileage of over 1000 km at contract value of over 10 billion USD. The operating performance is quite satisfactory, which shows that CRBC has forged a full business chain ranging from construction to operating. Meanwhile, the Nairobi-Malaba Railway under construction goes through the Port of Mombasa connecting the networks of 6 Eastern African countries. e) Central and East Europe: Zemen-Borca Bridge in Serbia, E763 in Serbia, Hungry-Serbian Railway, South-North Expressway Project in Montenegro, and M5 Extension Project in Belarus. These projects have broken down the bottlenecks of development in host countries, upgraded the accessibility of roads, and improved the transportation networks along the Belt and Road countries and regions. Besides, CRBC also participated in multiple projects of some major Belt and Road countries like Afghanistan, Iran, Egypt, Turkey, etc. In addition to conventional business, CRBC also develop capacity partnership with other countries to build up special economic zones, free trade areas, and industrial parks, such as the Mombasa Economic Zone, the Serbia Industrial Park, the Mauritania Industrial Park, the Madagascar Industrial Park, the Indonesia Bitung Port Park, and two industrial parks in KPG Province of Pakistan, etc.

Part Four: Problems in the implementation of Belt and Road Intiative

One: The importance of the cultural exchange in the Belt and Road Initiative

Mustafa Hyder Sayed *

During the process of cooperation between Pakistan-China Institute ("PCI") and its business partners, cultural exchange is still an integral part. Cultural exchange is the basis of economic exchange, with each of them being one side of a coin. It's quite essential for companies to learn about the local culture, language, custom, etc. That's why PCI provides Chinese course for Pakistani engineers, professors, businessmen and intellectuals to enhance contacts and exchanges with PCI's partners. This has increased the cultural exchanges. Meanwhile, PCI also send delegations to China to visit Chinese companies and administrative institutions. Due to the differences of culture, society and way of governance, it is ever necessary to know more of each other for further cooperation. It is better that make friends with the Chinese people before doing business. Essentially, this is a cultural exchange, and also a key component of "connectivity" proposed by the Belt and Road Initiative. CRBC is chosen as one salient example to illustrate that cultural exchange plays a significant role in the cooperation.

---

* Executive Director of Pakistan-China Institute

Two: The importance of the public relationship building in the Belt and Road Initiative

Jiang Ying*

Cultural exchange for mutual understanding is crucial, and mutual understanding, integration and win-win cooperation are all very important. Deloitte used to focus on going out, but what's even more important is "going in and going up", fitting into the local culture and environment. Deloitte needs to think how to guarantee a sustainable growth and bring some value and a win-win partnership with the local companies which is the long-term development path followed by companies. But unfortunately sometimes Deloitte do not give due attention to PR work or how to project the image and strength. In a foreign country, business operation and compliance is not enough, Deloitte also need to improve cultural integration and PR building.

Three: The importance of the local environmental protection in the Belt and Road Initiative

Dong Futang**

There are three principles are quite essential for overseas operation and

* Vice CEO of Deloitte China
** Chief Accountant of China Road and Bridge Corporation, Chinese Leading Accounting Reserve Talent

partnership.

First is values proposition. Being guided by President Xi's idea "to build a community of shared future", it needs to practice high moral standards and altruism policies so as to create unique off-shore corporate culture. Due attention should be paid to cultural exchanges alongside with economic cooperation so as to advocate Chinese traditions and promote cultural integration. It also needs to think to bring higher GDP, better livelihood, higher income, more job opportunities, etc. through mutual complementarity and co-development during the process of pushing forward the Belt and Road Initiative. If they grow, Chinese companies' businesses will grow too and insist the development model of win-win cooperation.

Second is green growth. China is going to build a "Green Silk Road", so it is necessary to comply with the local environment laws and try to make environmental protection cross-cut the design, construction and management processes. For instance, when building up the Mombasa-Nairobi Railway, CRBC set up a dedicated passage for some wild animals to make them cross safely according to their migration habits and routes. CRBC also organize and participate in EP activities and animal relief, like rescuing wild elephants trapped in mud and organizing garbage cleaning in national parks. In Serbia, CRBC strictly follow European standards during the process of work, and try to avoid secondary pollution to the environment. China's business mode and philosophy is so well appreciated in South East Asia and Africa that many colleges are studying questions in class, such as why has it developed so well in the past 3 decades since the Reform and Opening-up? So CRBC needs to copy the success into other countries with particular attention in overseas sustainable development for arriving at the environmental protection compliance especially.

Third is cultural integration. As overseas operation is often challenged by cultural difference, that means Chinese companies need to adapt to the local culture and respect their customs. To some extent, a trivial thing in Chinese mind may mean a lot locally. For instance, Chinese people eat dog meat but it is forbidden in Madagascar that a little disrespect may cause a lot of trouble. At present, the companies under CBRC hire 10 local staff for every one Chinese staff, so cultural shock is unavoidable. That's why two-way adaptation is very important for cultural integration. For companies operating overseas, this may be trivial things, but if take them seriously, the cooperation and partnership will become better and better, not only conducive to business development but also to the proposition of values.

Four: The importance of the local technical training and public value in the Belt and Road Initiative

Mustafa Hyder Sayed[*]

Two important points are worth supplementing here. One is technical training. Provision of technical training to local labor force is very important, especially in developing world so that they can get a better job and better participate in the Belt and Road Initiative. It can boost sustainable development of the enterprises, as professional training and education can cultivate more skilled labors so that it help a nation to grow better and improve labor force of the enterprises.

The other one is public relations. What an enterprise should do is to give the right message to the people in other countries and regions. How to tell the story, or how to do PR work, is a demanding job. Many Chinese companies have done a lot of work in different countries including in Pakistan, but they don't know how to tell their story and what to tell. PR is not bluffing. Instead, it is to tell people what you do is for the benefit of the local people and the host country. In practice, Chinese companies have done a lot of good things, and they also need to learn how to tell the story well.

* Executive Director of Pakistan-China Institute

Part Five: Opportunities for Chinese companies in the Belt and Road Initiative

One: Business opportunities from the infrastructure development

Jiang Ying [*]

As one Chinese folk adage that *If you want to be rich, you must first build roads*. Thus, in the Belt and Road Initiative, infrastructure development always goes first in terms of project category and size. Infrastructure means a lot for the national economic growth. In the past, Chinese companies went global on their own in infrastructure development. But now it is an integrative process ranging from overall designing to construction. Take a large LNG project for instance: it is not only a company but a whole group or several groups including relevant industries that go global operating from the beginning right to the end of the project. These projects cannot be processed by a single group, but require the cooperation among a lot of groups. It can be found further that telecommunications and EP projects (e. g. waste water treatment, garbage disposal and new energy) will see more opportunities. It should be believed that there will be large market in the countries along the Belt and Road at the result of overall economic

---

* Vice CEO of Deloitte China

development. Along with construction and telecommunications companies going global, equipment manufacturing companies will also follow suit. In fact, all these industries are highly related. Soon afterwards, the financial industry also has many opportunities, such as global financing and off-shore presence of Chinese banks. So the Belt and Road Initiative involves the full production chain, which may result in business clustering and integrated strategic development.

To sum up, there are four going-global methods to companies, include: 1) M&A, acquiring local projects, 2) EPC, 3) Greenfield investment, and 4) Trading. In terms of investment scale, M&A and EPC-based infrastructure development are the two biggest.

Two: Business opportunities arose from the Belt and Road Initiative

Dong Futang[*]

Firstly, there are enormous business opportunities in Africa. Since the Reform and Opening-up, CRBC has more than 30 years of work experience in Africa that feels the business opportunities are enormous there. But the key is how to grasp them, and we need to show out complementary strengths, which is very important. As a matter of fact, China's infrastructure capacity is extraordinary as there are no roads, bridges or ports that cannot build. Additionally, the Belt and Road Initiative has increased the demand for infrastructure development, which also explains why China needs to set up the AIIB, the China-Africa Development Fund, the Silk Road Fund, as well as many other industrial funds. So far many of the Belt and Road countries are plagued by huge debts, even exceeding the

* Chief Accountant of China Road and Bridge Corporation, Chinese Leading Accounting Reserve Talent

financing cap defined by IMF, so they desperately need a China solution to this problem. This is what we need to consider in designing the financing model.

Second, off-shore financial industry is quite promising. So far Chinese banks have only limited number of branches in Africa, but Chinese companies' business is huge there, especially trade financing, RMB exchange, and financial investment including local banks' significant needs for intermediary products what suggest there is great potential there.

Third, telecom and Internet businesses have great opportunities. Now ZTE and Huawei have wide presence overseas with quite reliable services in telecom and Internet what is much better than the local telecom service. Wherever there is ZTE or Huawei, the FSC sharing would be implemented successfully. Thus, Internet service is so important to the financial infrastructure.

Forth, industry cooperation is quite important. Developing off-shore industrial park is a very brilliant idea. By this it can avoid the mistakes made in the past in China, such as fragmented lay-out, which cannot be exported to other countries. The reason, that China needs to develop industrial parks overseas, is an integrative design may help these countries grow faster, just like what is being done in China that putting the fragmented industrial parks together. In fact, the industrial parks which have developed with the rolling-out of the Belt and Road Initiative are well received overseas. Serbia as a salient example, the local government officials who asked to help them develop food processing business as the local milk and honey are fine. Therefore, Chinese competitive industries like light industry, home appliances, electronic appliances, electronics, etc. , should go global and build off-shore industrial parks there to meet the local demand. China needs to build a high ground overseas and it can be believed in the future African and South East Asia have great potential.

Three: Challenges and opportunities under the globalization of IT industry

Wang Xingshan [*]

The philosophy of win-win cooperation proposed by the Belt and Road Initiative is agreed. Chinese companies go global not just for unfavorable capacity export, regardless of local resources and environment. For example, building Gwadar Port through the Belt and Road Initiative to help local grow economically and give local people a better livelihood, which is a substantial contribution to China and the whole world.

The Belt and Road initiative suggests opportunity for China, but challenge cannot be ignored either. Take smart grain storage for instance. Nearly all such storages in China are built by Inspur. But in Africa, grain storages are surely not in large cities, instead, they are most in remote areas just like in China, so there will be a lot of hardships, including human resources. So localization of human resources is a daunting challenge.

Absolutely, there are also some challenges bringing about opportunities that pushing China's IT industry to be globalized, not only support the going global of Chinese companies, but also go global itself with the Chinese companies. Currently China imports a lot of products, management software in particular which deprives independence. Why China's IT industry was very hard to be globalized, the management in particular, mainly because it involved cultural issue, managers' thinking and habit, as well as standards issue. Now as the Belt and Road Initiative rolls out, the software needs to take into consideration of taxation, accounting standards, etc., to absorb local culture, management

---

* CEO of Inspur Group Co., Ltd.

concept, management model, which pushes back our companies to improve globalization. The establishment of CCCC off-shore finance share service centre is a salient sample.

Part Six: Major Risks in Participating in the Belt and Road Initiative

One: Due diligence in the globalization of companies

Mustafa Hyder Sayed [*]

When a company goes global for the first time, it needs to find a good local partner to make up for the lack of experience. The local partner should have rich experience and strong local connections, because companies might be caught up with many problems when in a different country, which may lead to financial losses or legal issues like litigation, land disputes, etc. For mitigating aforementioned risks, prudent investigation before investment is necessary rather than rush in immediately. Thus, it requires to take due diligence properly and seriously.

When the investigation is done, companies still need to be cautious. To some extent, local engineers are quite important because they can give companies some good advice or help companies to find the right channels. A local partner will be usually good for companies since industry reality and culture vary from country to country. Companies need to adapt to the local culture and customs in different countries. The Belt and Road Initiative may involve companies from different cities

* Executive Director of Pakistan-China Institute

or provinces of China like Guangzhou, Shandong, etc. , so their customs may differ from each other. That's why local partners usually give practical suggestions on how to enter a new local market.

For Chinese companies from different provinces, there usually have different strategies. Companies from rich provinces are financially strong and have rich off-shore investment experience. But sadly many of them have little or no information about the China-Pakistan Economic Corridor. Of course, not all companies have off-shore investment experience. Thus, make friends with Chinese companies and that is what PCI should do. PCI wants to inform Chinese companies of the potential investment opportunities.

Furthermore, companies need to choose an appropriate target country, one that has a good relationship with China and is supported by the Chinese government; then, find a suitable local partner. Sometimes companies may feel frustrated to find that the local administration is not very efficient, lower than companies expected, or there is no useful information provided during the process of overseas investment. In that case, companies need to take some investigations, or to make friends before doing business. China is a large country and provinces are greatly different, the economic scale of some is even bigger than that of some countries. That's why President Xi proposes inclusion, understanding, reciprocity and cooperation as the guiding principles for the Belt and Road Initiative.

Two: A long road ahead for the globalization of Chinese companies

Jiang Ying[*]

A long way for the globalization of chinese companies, there are two points

---

* Vice CEO of Deloitte China

worth illustrating here. Firstly, as a global profession service-provider, Deloitte must promote itself continuously to understand and serve Chinese companies better. Take Pakistan project for example. As Deloitte has deeply involved in the China-Pakistan Economic Corridor program, the business there fares very well in the past five to six years, providing professional service for Chinese companies, meeting their demands and getting to know their corporate culture. As a result, business of Deloitte there becomes solid and Deloitte service team grows larger with more work to do. Deloitte's commitment to business cooperation strongly supports the operation of China construction companies overseas. But of course this globalization journey involves running-in and gradual mutual understanding, as serving Chinese companies is different from serving American, European or African companies due to different corporate cultures and features. Deloitte needs a running-in period to accommodate each other, make friends before doing business.

Secondly, there is still a long way for Chinese companies to go global. Deloitte surveyed more than 100 enterprises in Beijing, 2016 with state-owned enterprises accounting for 90% of total sample, to find that over half of their off-shore revenue takes up less than 10% of the total from the first statistics. This indicates that most of their businesses are still in China while their overseas operations are far from satisfactory.

The second statistics is regarding the companies with huge off-shore business, it is curious about how these global companies manage their overseas business: Is there a centralized or distributed organization to handle off-shore projects? The survey shows that 90% of companies have such organization while only 10% have no dedicated department, improvising one according to the nature of the project. But when asked about the infrastructure construction in the organizational structure such as organizational governance and management model, the 90% companies said they are still scrambling. Therefore, for Chinese companies, they need to do more to develop a sound management model and related capabilities.

From the perspective of a professional service-provider, Chinese companies need to develop four capabilities in their infrastructure development. First is long-term strategic planning. Many companies go global without a clear vision. They just take the opportunity and go out. But with their business rolling out, they need to think strategically, such as which area to focus or what kind of business chain to build, so on and so forth. Second is financial capability. It's a quite complex issue, far more than just getting money. The company needs to develop a program or a plan to work with multiple financial institutions and the local financial team, because global projects like power plant and natural gas projects always involve a lot of risks, including repayment scheme, which is highly related with the reserves and output. Third one is risk management. Global companies involve a lot of risks in relation to the production chain, such as financing, accounting and finance, legal affairs, etc. It is worth to consider that companies keep safe with a reliable risk management system. Fourth is regarding internationalized professionals. This is the trickiest issue as HR training takes time from in-house training to continuous strengthening. If the above mentioned four capabilities are developed and consolidated, going global in such a way will be more stable.

Three: Various risks for Chinese companies in the globalization

Dong Futang [*]

Chinese companies are faced with the followoing risks when they go abroad First, keep an eye on the local politics and security. Other countries are different from China. For instance, countries in Africa and South East Asia are usually plagued with political uncertainties, which must be considered seriously before companies' investment.

---

* Chief Accountant of China Road and Bridge Corporation, Chinese Leading Accounting Reserve Talent

Second, check on the investment environment, in particular whether a bilateral investment treaty is available, since many countries haven't yet signed such treaty with China. For instance, whether set up a shareholding structure in a third country to obtain preferential policies at the back of a bilateral investment treaty.

Third, watch out for the financing and foreign exchange-related risks. Especially when the local currency depreciates quite fast, it is necessary to consider that how companies manage the foreign exchange risk, and whether arbitrage or forwarding should be used. In some cases where the investment mode has changed, for instance in a PPP project where companies will be paid in local currency at the end of the project, there will be some foreign exchange-related risks during the construction period. It is also very important to companies to consider whether companies need to build up a financial model from the outset to lock in the risks or guarantee exchange compensation in order to safeguard corporate revenue.

Fourth, pay attention to BEPS-related risks. So far nearly 70 countries in the world have joined the BEPS program which provides that companies shall submit country report to the competent international organization. Such information exchange requires the off-shore financial management should be up to the international level. In a foreign country, companies must abide by the local laws and taxation policies, setting a good example of compliance.

Fifth, Chinese companies need to look for win-win cooperation. Overseas competition between Chinese companies in past years left others a bad impression. Chinese companies need to learn from the Japanese counterparts that are very united, no in-fighting off-shore. This is something Chinese companies should pay attention to when going global.

Accounting Infrastructure: A Booster to the Belt and Road Initiative

Executive Summary

"Accounting, as an international business language, has become a basis for planning, decision making, control and evaluation in international economic exchanges and other aspects. "

During his visit to Central and Southeast Asian countries in 2013, President Xi Jinping proposed a major initiative of building the Silk Road Economic Belt and the 21st Century Maritime Silk Road, which was enthusiastically received at home and abroad. The Initiative not only opens up a vast space for China and the Belt & Road countries to reach a mutually beneficial win-win scenario through complementary advantages, but also provides a historical opportunity to the leap forward of China's economy and engaged deeply in global economic governance. Nearly four years have passed ever since, and the Initiative has proved fruitful in terms of policy coordination, facilities connectivity, unimpeded trade, financial integration and people-to-people bonds. How is accountancy, as an international business language playing its infrastructural role during the process of development of this initiative? To find the answer, experts from SNAI, ACCA and Deloitte China got together in the task force on the Belt & Road Initiative and the Accounting Infrastructure to study how the accounting infrastructure can boost the national Belt & Road initiative.

Infrastructure refers to the engineering facilities that provide public services for social production and residential life. It is a public service system used to ensure the normal social and economic activities of a jurisdiction, being the general material conditions supporting the survival and development of the community. The infrastructure includes the utilities and public service facilities, involving transport, post and telecommunications, water and power supply, commercial services, scientific research and technical services, landscaping, environmental protection, culture and education, public health and so on. They constitute the foundation of the national economy. According to our definition of the accounting infrastructure, in international economic exchanges, we should give full play to the role of accounting as an international business language, serving as a basis for planning, decision-making, control and evaluation in financial cooperation, cross-border investment and financing, economic and trade exchanges and other aspects. Given the collected data on the accounting statements, the government can take effective macro-control and determine the allocation of resources and interests to ensure healthy and orderly development of the national economy, while investors can understand the financial situation of the state and its enterprises and ascertain whether they can obtain the desired return on investment. In modern society, the more developed an economy gets, the higher requirements it will set for the accounting infrastructure. The well-established accounting infrastructure plays a vital role in accelerating social and economic activities and facilitating economic and trade exchanges between countries.

Accounting infrastructure is a grand topic. Given that the Belt & Road countries vary in accounting development, the notion and scope of accounting infrastructure remain to be studied. Initially, the task force involved in the research reported have studied the disparities between accounting standards, tax risk and accounting personnel training across representative Belt & Road countries. First of all, accounting occupies a pivotal position in the capital market. By collecting, processing and summarizing data, accounting constructs an effective information system of economic decision-making and management. Therefore, it is essential to understand the accounting standards of the representative countries. Secondly, along with more and more active outbound investment activities, enterprises are increasingly exposed to taxation-related risks, mainly including dual taxation, incomplete execution of tax treaty benefits, transfer pricing and anti-tax avoidance challenges, legacy tax problems of target enterprises in overseas M&As and tax discrimination, etc. Enterprises going global have to learn how to avoid and deal with these tax risks. Finally, in the pursuit of a more coordinated, better established system of accounting standards and in response to tax risk, the research shows that the training personnel is a prerequisite for international-level financial accounting performance. The countries and businesses concerned are keeping a close eye on how to better cultivate accountancy professionals with a global vision, whether there are specialized institutions or organizations responsible for accounting personnel training in Belt & Road countries, what capabilities are necessary for the accounting team, what measures can be taken to enhance the competence of accounting personnel, how different countries vary in the training model, and what experience is worth learning from each other, and so on and so forth.

In selecting representative countries, the task force drew on the research results of ACCA, the Shanghai Stock Exchange and the national information center on the Belt & Road Initiative and calculated the scores of ' One Belt One Road ' (OBOR) countries ranked by the country cooperation index, where 14 countries were picked up as the first research targets, namely Singapore, Malaysia, the United Arab Emirates, Poland, Czechoslovakia, Qatar, Hungary, Thailand, Vietnam, Russia, Indonesia, Kazakhstan, India and Pakistan. From April to June 2017, the task force conducted a questionnaire survey on corporate executives from these 14 countries (including local enterprises and the branches of Chinese-funded enterprises in these countries), followed by an analysis. The analysis on those selected countries was mainly based on the interviews with Deloitte partners and senior directors, ACCA members and SNAI alumni who have profound knowledge and working experience in the respective country (' Respondents ')

Part One   Coordination and Harmonization of the Accounting Policy between Countries

Coordination of the accounting policy between countries is one of the core mechanisms for information communication across economies. According to the survey, differences in the accounting standards are seen as obstacles to cross-border investment. Therefore, international convergence of the accounting standards will help companies produce high quality, more comparable and more transparent financial reports alleviate the negative impact of country differences in the comparability and transparency of accounting information. Meanwhile, it will facilitate cross-border investment and capital market integration, improving market liquidity. Moreover, it can expand the scope of business investors, reducing international transaction costs through risk sharing for better capital allocation.

The development trend tells that Chinese capital is accelerating entry into overseas markets. According to the 2015 Statistical Bulletin of China's Outward Foreign Direct Investment, China's outbound investment flows ranked second in the world in 2015, with a record high at $145. 57 billion, an increase of 18. 3% year on year. More than 80% (83. 9%) of China's outbound investment stock was distributed in developing economies, while 14% in developed economies and 2. 1% in economies in transition.

According to a report by the Ministry of Commerce, People's Republic of China (MOFCOM) Investment and Cooperation in the Belt & Road Countries 2016, throughout 2016, China directly invested $14. 53 billion in 53 Belt & Road countries, with Singapore, Indonesia, India, Thailand and Malaysia being the major destinations. Led by engineering contracts and supported by financial services, China is constructing a number of cooperative parks and free trade areas alongside the route, striving for a sustainable return on investment, which will become a beacon for its overseas investment.

Overview of the Accounting Standards Adopted by the Belt and Road Countries

The accounting standards adopted by the Belt & Road countries vary. According to the Pocket Guide to IFRS Standards: the Global Financial Reporting Language (Guidance) issued by the IFRS Foundation in March 2017, IFRS is embracing further enhanced quality and increasingly extensive application worldwide. The Guide contains the statistics on the IFRS application in 150 jurisdictions worldwide, including the information on the relevant standards and standard-setting bodies. It indicates that as of the date of release, 126 of the 150 jurisdictions (84%) studied had requested all or the majority of domestic listed companies institutions to prepare financial reports in accordance with the IFRS. Based on the Guide, we tallied the accounting standards of the Belt & Road countries and found the following facts: Among the 65 Belt & Road countries, 54 (83%) have requested all or the majority of domestic listed companies institutions to prepare financial reports in accordance with the IFRS, 3 (Vietnam, Laos and Egypt) are using their own accounting standards, 2 (India and Indonesia) are converging with the IFRS on an ongoing basis, Thailand is directly applying the IFRS, Uzbekistan only requires domestic banks to report in accordance with the IFRS, and the rest 4 (Turkmenistan, Kyrgyzstan, Tajikistan and Lebanon) are not included in the range of the Guide.

Among the 54 Belt & Road countries adopting the IFRS, Iran, Kazakhstan, Kuwait, Montenegro and Qatar began to require all or the majority of the domestic listed companies institutions to prepare financial statements in accordance with the IFRS in 2016. In addition, Saudi Arabia decided to require all publicly traded companies and all other public entities to report in accordance with the IFRS from 2017 and 2018 respectively.

Other Key Factors Decisive to the Quality and Comparability of Reporting

In fact, accounting standards are only one of the important institutional factors that affect the implementation of financial reporting of an enterprise, with a limited impact on the quality and comparability of corporate reporting. Academic research shows that the application environment for corporate report and the enforcement of accounting standards are as important as the accounting standards used in the preparation of financial statements, which determines the quality and comparability of reporting to some extent. In general, the report application environment of an enterprise is affected by many factors, including:

- Legal institutions of the State (e. g. rule of law);
- Effectiveness of the enforcement system (e. g. audit);
- Role of the capital market (e. g. the demand for external capital);
- Ownership, governance and operational characteristics of an enterprise;
- Product market competition.

At the same time, the enforcement of accounting standards across businesses constrains the reporting quality. Even if the report application environment is similar, as long as the enforcement differs, the general comparability of corporate reporting is unlikely to occur. This applies to any set of accounting standards, not just the IFRS. The survey gets in-depth into the accounting standards adopted by the Belt & Road countries and the practical application environment, with a mission to get readers informed of the basic facts of the accounting policy in these areas, promote the integration and international convergence of national accounting standards, and improve and enhance cooperation mechanisms in the accounting domain.

Singapore

Listed companies in Singapore are required to use Singapore Financial Reporting Standards (SFRS), which are substantially converged with IFRS Standards. All foreign companies listed on the Singapore Exchange are permitted to apply IFRS Standards under the Listing Rules.

Professional institution:

Institute of Singapore Chartered Accountants (ISCA) http://isca.org.sg/

Standard-setter:

Singapore Accounting Standards Council (ASC) http://www.asc.gov.sg/

Financial reporting standards:

The model adopted in Singapore is directly applying IFRS Standards.

Singapore has three sets of approved accounting standards now, namely:

- Singapore Financial Reporting Standards (SFRS)—for all companies other than SMEs that apply the SFRS for Small Entities;

- IFRS—identical Financial Reporting Standards-for Singapore incorporated companies listed on the SGX, which will be effective for annual periods beginning on or after 1 January 2018;

- And SFRS for Small Entities-for SMEs.

Singapore—incorporated companies (both listed and non-listed) are required to use the SFRS that is substantially aligned with IFRS Standards for both consolidated and separate financial statements.

According to respondents' feedback, the SFRS only makes a slight revision to IFRS Standards. Therefore, the SFRS and IFRS Standards are largely the same except for the following differences: in the SFRS, the IFRIC 2 has not yet been adopted, several modifications have been made to certain exemptions, transition provisions or effective dates of a few IFRS Standards, and some additional guidance has been provided for certain IFRS Standards.

Singapore—incorporated companies are permitted to use IFRS Standards if approval for the use of IFRS is granted to such companies by the Accounting and Corporate Regulatory Authority of Singapore (ACRA). A Singapore-incorporated company that is listed on both a securities exchange in Singapore and a securities exchange outside Singapore is permitted to use IFRS Standards if the securities exchange outside Singapore on which the company is listed requires the use of IFRS Standards. And all foreign companies listed on SGX are permitted to apply IFRS Standards.

On 29 May 2014, the ASC announced that Singapore incorporated companies listed on SGX will apply a new financial reporting framework identical to IFRS Standards for annual periods beginning on or after 1 January 2018. Non-listed Singapore incorporated companies may also voluntarily apply the new framework at the same time.

All Singapore SMEs are required to use the SFRS for Small Entities, which are completely based on the IFRS for SMEs Standard, except for some differences in the description of the scope and applicability of the SFRS for Small Entities, i. e. the definition of SMEs.

In the respondents' view, the Singapore accounting standards are robust in practical implementation with all companies being generally able to follow the generally accepted standards.

Audit:

According to respondents' feedback, a Singapore incorporated company is required to conduct annual audits, unless it meets the audit exemption criteria prescribed in Section 205B or 205C of the Companies Act, i. e. the company has no more than 20 shareholders and all of which shall be individual shareholders, and its revenue in a financial year does not exceed S $ 5 million. Also, according to respondents' feedback, the Singapore Standards on Auditing are identical to the International Standards on Auditing, a set of standards issued by the IFAC.

Malaysia

Public companies are required to use the MFRS Framework, which is substantively equivalent to IFRS Standards. IFRS Standards are permitted for listings by foreign companies.

Professional institution:

● Malaysian Institute of Accountants (MIA, member of the IFAC) http: // www. mia. org. my/

● Malaysian Institute of Certified Public Accountants (MICPA, member of the IFAC) http: //www. micpa. com. my/

Standard-setter and key responsibilities:

Malaysian Accounting Standards Board (MASB) http: //www. masb. org. my.

The key responsibilities of the MASB are:

● Issuance of any new accounting standards as approved accounting standards;

● Review, revision or adoption of any approved or existing accounting standards;

● Amendment, replacement, suspension, deferral, withdrawal or cancellation of any approved accounting standards in whole or in part;

● Issuance, approval, review, amendment, replacement, suspension, deferral, withdrawal or cancellation of any published Announcement on Issues, or Technical Bulletin and any other documents in relation to financial reporting in whole or in part;

● Sponsoring or undertaking development of accounting standards;

● Collaboration with other national and international accounting standard-setters and continuously monitoring any developments of other national and international accounting standards;

● Participating in and contributing to the development of a single set of accounting standards for international use; and

● Monitoring the operation of approved accounting standards to assess their continuing relevance and effectiveness.

Financial reporting standards:

The model adopted in Malaysia is directly applying IFRS Standards.

Malaysia has three sets of approved accounting standards now, namely:

● Malaysian Financial Reporting Standards (MFRSs)—for entities other than private entities;

● Private Entity Reporting Standards (PERSs)—for private entities, to be withdrawn with effect from 1 January 2016;

● And Malaysian Private Entities Reporting Standard (MPERS)—for private entities, effective for annual reporting periods beginning on or after 1 January 2016.

In Malaysia, the MASB is responsible for the endorsement of IFRS Standards so as to establish the MFRSs, which aims to be identical to IFRS Standards without modification. Malaysian non-private entities (including listed companies institutions) were required to apply IFRS Standards (locally known as the MFRSs) from 2012 for both consolidated and separate financial statements. However, some Transitioning Entities (TEs), primarily agriculture and real estate companies, may elect to defer the adoption of the MFRSs to 2018. Until then, these companies are still permitted to use Malaysia's national accounting standards.

As compared to IFRS Standards, there are some differences in Malaysia's accounting standards currently used by Malaysian agriculture and real estate companies, for example, IAS 41, IFRS 15 and IFRIC 15 are not yet included. And under Malaysia's accounting standards, biological assets in an agriculture company are recognized at cost, and real estate companies are permitted to recognize revenue and cost arising from property development activities using the percentage of completion method.

Malaysian private entities were required to apply the MPERS for annual periods beginning on or after 1 January 2016. Until then, the PERSs were used.

The MPERS is word-for-word the IFRS for SMEs Standard except for the requirements for property development activities, plus some terminology changes.

In the respondents' view, the accounting standards used in Malaysia, including the MFRSs and the MPERS, are very similar to the IFRS. According to respondents' feedback, the Malaysian accounting standards are robust in practical implementation with all companies being generally able to follow the generally accepted standards. This is mainly due to a strict regulatory environment: Listed companies are subject to supervision of other government agencies, such as Bursa Malaysia and the Securities Commission Malaysia, in addition to the routine regulators. Financial institutions and insurance companies are also subject to supervision of Central Bank of Malaysia. Besides, listed companies are required by Bursa Malaysia and the Securities Commission Malaysia to disclose their corporate governance information.

Audit:

All companies that are incorporated under the Companies Act 2016 are required to be audited. However, under the Companies Act 2016, the Registrar has the power to exempt a company incorporated under the Companies Act 2016 from the requirements to have an audit. According to respondents' feedback, the Standards on Auditing used in Malaysia are identical to the International Standards on Auditing, a set of standards issued by the IFAC.

UAE

Compliance with IFRS Standards is required for companies listed on NASDAQ Dubai, Dubai Financial Services Authority (DFSA), and Abu Dhabi Securities Exchange. Compliance with IFRS Standards is permitted for companies listed on Dubai Financial Market PJSC. Compliance with IFRS Standards is required for listings by foreign companies.

Professional institution:

Accountants & Auditors Association http://www.aaa4uae.com/Standard-setter: The UAE has no financial reporting standard setter or national financial reporting standards, and IFRS Standards, which were set and issued by IFRS Standards Board (IASB), are directly used in the UAE.

Financial reporting standards:

The model adopted in the UAE is directly applying IFRS Standards. The UAE Commercial Companies Law No 2 of 2015, which came into force on 1 July 2015, requires all companies to apply IFRS Standards when preparing their financial statements (for SMEs, the IFRS for SMEs Standard applies).

Exceptions to the adoption of IFRS Standards: In some rare cases, the central bank imposes additional loan loss provision requirements. In addition, in practice, IAS 19 Employee Benefits is not applied to certain end-of-service benefit because of the costs and lack of actuarial data. And the law requires directors' fees to be recognised in equity. While these two practices are not consistent with IAS 19, the treatment is accepted in practice because the effect is not material.

According to respondents' feedback, IFRS Standards are robust in practical implementation by the UAE's companies, which are usually being able to follow the generally accepted standards.

Audit:

The respondents noted that all entities are required to be audited under the UAE Commercial Companies Law except for sole proprietorship and some free zones which do not require an audit for some of their entities. Also, in the respondents' view, the Standards on Auditing used in the UAE are very similar to the International Standards on Auditing, a set of standards issued by the IFAC.

Poland

All domestic companies whose securities trade in a regulated market are required to use IFRS Standards as adopted by the EU in their consolidated financial statements. IFRS Standards as adopted by the EU are required in their consolidated financial statements except that a foreign company whose home jurisdiction's standards are deemed by the EU to be equivalent to IFRS Standards may use its home standards.

Professional institution:

Accountants Association in Poland (AAP) http: //www. skwp. pl/en

Standard-setter:

Polish Accounting Standards Committee www. mf. gov. pl/The key responsibilities of the KSR are:

- Management of the national accounting work;
- Drafting the accounting law and administrative regulations;
- Doing research and putting forward proposed policies in relation to accounting reforms and developments;
- Drafting and organizing the implementation of consistent national accounting standards system, management accounting standards, internal control regulations, and accounting informatization standards, etc. ;
- Drafting the government accounting standards and the accounting systems for administrative and public institutions; and
- Supervising and directing the CPA profession according to law, and developing rules and regulations, policies and measures for the CPA profession.

Financial reporting standards:

1. Circumstances where application of IFRS Standards as adopted by the EU is required:

In June 2002, the European Union adopted an IAS Regulation requiring all companies listed in an EU capital market to prepare their consolidated financial statements in accordance with IFRS Standards as adopted by the EU since 2005. Poland is an EU Member State. Consequently, Polish companies listed in an EU/EEA (the European Economic Area) securities market are required to follow IFRS Standards as adopted by the EU.

The EU IAS Regulation gives member states the option to require or permit IFRS Standards as adopted by the EU in separate company financial statements or in the financial statements of companies whose securities do not trade on a regulated securities market.

2. Other circumstances:

For the above-mentioned option, Poland permits IFRS Standards as adopted by the EU in the separate financial statements of a company whose securities trade in a regulated market, requires IFRS Standards as adopted by the EU for the consolidated financial statements of all banks, and permits IFRS Standards as adopted by the EU for both the consolidated and separate financial statements of the following categories of companies whose securities do not trade in a regulated market: i. e. a subsidiary of a company that prepares consolidated financial statements in conformity with IFRS Standards as adopted by the EU, or a company that has filed for admission for public trading. Apart from the above, a company is required to use the Polish national accounting standards.

The Polish Accounting Standards Committee (KSR) within the Polish Ministry of Finance sets domestic accounting standards. Companies that don't have to apply IFRSs in drawing up their financial statements can voluntarily apply the standards issued by the KSR.

According to respondents' feedback, the Polish national accounting standards are somewhat similar to IFRS Standards with certain differences in most of the Standards. Major differences are in Business Combinations, Consolidated Financial Statements, Goodwill, Revenue, and Measurement and Classification of Financial Instruments, as well as in the application of fair value. For example:

1. Business combinations:

a. Under the Polish Accounting Standard, the pooling of interests method is allowed for business combinations where the existing shareholders do not lose control over the entities. While under the IFRS Standard, only the purchase method is allowed in such cases (a business combination involving enterprises under common control is not covered by IFRS 3). Under the Polish Accounting Standard, costs incurred in direct relation to the business combination shall increase the acquisition cost rather than being recognized in profit or loss when incurred as required under the IFRS Standard.

b. Measurement of non-controlling interests: the Polish Accounting Standard requires measuring at the interest's proportionate share of the acquired entity's identifiable net assets, while the IFRS Standard gives the option to measure non-controlling interests either in this way or at fair value. Minority shareholders' equity transactions not resulting in loss of control are accounted for as acquisition/sale with the effects being included in profit/loss or goodwill of the period under the Polish Accounting Standard. While under the IFRS Standard, these transactions are accounted for as equity transactions without including the effects in profit/loss or goodwill of the period.

c. The definition of control: The description of "control" under the previous IFRS Standard was carried forward to the Polish Accounting Standard to define the meaning of control, i. e. stressing managing financial and operational policies of the investee in order to derive benefits from its business activity.

2. Goodwill:

a. Under the Polish Accounting Standard, goodwill is the difference between the acquisition price and the net fair value of the acquired assets, while under the IFRS Standard goodwill is the difference between the consideration and the fair value of the acquired entity's identifiable net assets. Besides, there are also differences in accounting for the contingent consideration: Under the Polish Accounting Standard, contingent payments are included in the acquisition consideration only if occurrence of future events resulting in contingent payments is probable and the payment amount can be reliably determined. If the actual payment amount differs from the estimate, appropriate adjustment of the acquisition cost and goodwill (negative goodwill) is necessary. While under the IFRS Standard, contingent payments are always included in determining the contingent consideration and the applicable standards shall be used respectively for subsequent recognition of contingent payments depending on their classification as liabilities or equity.

b. The Polish Accounting Standard allows goodwill to be amortized over its useful life. Where the useful life may not be determined reliably, goodwill may not be amortized longer than 5 years. Amortization is applied using the straight-line method and charged to other operating expenses.

3. Financial instruments:

a. The classification of financial instruments under the Polish Accounting Standard is very similar as that under the existing IAS 39 except that for entities other than banks, only the financial assets or liabilities held for trading can be measured at fair value and changes in fair value shall be included in profit or loss (disallowed financial assets or liabilities to be designated as measured at fair value through profit or loss on initial recognition). In addition, an entity other than a bank can choose to recognize changes in the fair value of financial assets available for sale in financial revenue or expenses of the period or in revaluation reserve.

b. The Polish Accounting Standard does not provide detailed principles for financial asset impairment measurement.

The corresponding changes in IFRS 9 have not been introduced into the Polish Accounting Standard yet.

4. Preparation of consolidated financial statements:

a. Under the Polish Accounting Standard, relief from the obligation to prepare consolidated financial statements is allowed for non-public entities under specific conditions. But the exemption from consolidation for investment entities under the IFRS Standard is not allowed under the Polish Accounting Standard.

b. Under the Polish Accounting Standard, a subsidiary may be excluded from consolidation when it is acquired solely for resale, but there is no such an exemption under the IFRS Standard.

c. Minority interests are presented as a separate liability and equity category under the Polish Accounting Standard, while as a portion of the group equity under the IFRS Standard.

d. Under the Polish Accounting Standard, in the event of increases or decreases in the parent's interest not resulting in loss of control, changes in the percentage interests in a subsidiary are recognized as financial revenue/expenses. While under the IFRS Standard, such changes are treated as equity transactions.

e. The proportional consolidation method is allowed under the Polish Accounting Standard, but not allowed under the IFRS Standard.

5. Revenue recognition:

Since the Polish Accounting Standard in relation to revenue recognition is unregulated by the Accounting Act, it may be substantially different from IFRS 15 in practice.

6. The application of fair value:

Under the Polish Accounting Standard, the application of fair value is limited. For example, measurement of property, plant and equipment using the fair value model is not allowed, unless it is the requirement of statutory revaluation, and measurement of intangible assets using the fair value model is not allowed, either.

In addition, if a specific accounting matter is not regulated in the KSR standards or in the Polish Accounting Act, companies have the option to use guidance from IFRSs. However, if a company decides to follow KSR standards, applying IFRS guidance is prohibited when a specific accounting matter is regulated under the KSR standards or the domestic accounting standards. In the respondents' view, the Polish Accounting Standards are robust in practical implementation with all companies being generally able to follow the generally accepted standards. In general, the larger a company is, the more thoroughly it will follow the Accounting Standards. According to respondents' feedback, reports on corporate governance are rarely prepared by Polish companies.

Audit:

The respondents noted that in Poland, all banks and insurance companies, funds, listed companies, and entities meeting two or more of the following conditions are required to be audited:

- The number of employees is greater than 50
- The total assets exceed €2.5 million
- The sales value exceeds €5 million.

The respondents considered that the Standards on Auditing used in Poland are generally consistent with the International Standards on Auditing, a set of standards issued by the IFAC.

Czech Republic

All domestic companies whose securities trade in a regulated market are required to use IFRS Standards as adopted by the EU in their consolidated financial statements. IFRS Standards as adopted by the EU are required in their consolidated financial statements except that a foreign company whose home jurisdiction's standards are deemed by the EU to be equivalent to IFRS Standards may use its home standards.

Professional institution:

Union of Accountants of the Czech Republic https: //www. svaz-ucetnich. cz/

Standard-setter:

Ministry of Finance of the Czech Republic https: //www. mfcr. cz/

Its key responsibilities are:

● Management of the national accounting work;

● Drafting the accounting law and administrative regulations;

● Drafting the government accounting standards and the accounting systems for administrative and public institutions; and

● Other responsibilities, including national budgeting, tax supervision, international payment settlement, and foreign investment regulation.

Financial reporting standards:

1. Circumstances where application of IFRS Standards as adopted by the EU is required:

In June 2002, the European Union adopted an IAS Regulation requiring application of IFRS Standards as adopted by the EU for the consolidated financial statements of all companies whose securities trade in an EU capital market starting in 2005. Czech Republic is an EU Member State. Consequently, Czech companies listed in an EU/EEA securities market are required to follow IFRS

Standards as adopted by the EU.

The EU IAS Regulation gives member states the option to require or permit IFRS Standards as adopted by the EU in separate company financial statements or in the financial statements of companies whose securities do not trade on a regulated securities market.

2. Other circumstances:

For the above-mentioned option, the Czech Republic requires IFRS Standards as adopted by the EU in both the consolidated financial statements and separate financial statements of all companies whose securities trade in a public market, permits IFRS Standards as adopted by the EU in the consolidated financial statements of companies whose securities do not trade in a regulated market, and permits IFRS Standards as adopted by the EU in the separate financial statements of a company whose securities do not trade in a regulated market under specific conditions, i. e. if it is a subsidiary of a parent company that uses IFRS Standards as adopted by the EU for preparation of its consolidated financial statements. Apart from the above, a company is required to use the Czech accounting standards.

According to respondents' feedback, the Czech accounting standards are applied to different industries according to specific announcements, as follows:

- For enterprises (Announcement No. 500/2002)
- For banks (Announcement No. 501/2002)
- For insurance companies (Announcement No. 502/2002 and 503/2002)
- For non-profit organizations (Announcement No. 504/2002)
- For municipal governments and government agencies (Announcement No. 410/2009)

For taxation purposes, all companies are required to calculate their taxable profit in accordance with the Czech accounting standards. According to respondents' feedback, the Czech accounting standards are somewhat similar to IFRS Standards with certain differences in a number of standards, such as revenue recognition (the Czech Republic does not apply the Incoterms used by its international peers), leases, and financial instruments. For example:

1. General differences:

Under Czech accounting legislation, 1) there are the mandatory chart of accounts, and the mandatory formats of the balance sheet and the income statement, all of which Czech accounting legislation are unavailable under IFRS Standards; 2) accounting treatments in certain areas are unavailable, e. g. impairment of assets; 3) sometimes the form of a transaction prevails over its substance (e. g. finance leases) versus the substance-over-form principle of IFRS Standards; 4) when it comes to the valuation basis, historical cost prevails and fair value is only used in limited circumstances (it's applicable to securities or business combinations).

2. Share-based payment: Czech accounting legislation does not provide any guidance in this area.

3. Business combinations:

a. Under Czech accounting legislation, there are cases where legal form takes precedence over substance, and the acquirer is defined formally rather than from the point of view of "substance". Therefore, reverse acquisition does not exist.

b. Transactions under common control are considered business combinations. In certain cases, fair value measurement also exists in transactions under common control.

c. The increases arising from the fair value revaluation in business combinations are reported in the separate financial statements, and this portion is amortized over subsequent periods, with the transaction costs being capitalized; and

d. If companies acquire shares in other companies without any business transformation occurring, the acquired company is not revalued. The difference between the acquisition cost and the carrying amount of the acquired shares is the "consolidation difference", which is amortised as part of the consolidated financial statements over 20 years.

4. Consolidated financial statements:

a. In the Czech Republic, the consolidation requirement may be exempted if certain criteria are met (total assets / net sales / headcount), but the relief from the consolidation requirement does not apply to banks, insurance companies and securities issuers;

b. There is a difference in the definition of a subsidiary or a group under Czech accounting legislation as compared to IFRS Standards. The non-existence of guidance on such terms may lead to different conclusions for the purposes of IFRS and Czech accounting legislation when assessing the existence of control;

c. No explicit accounting guidance is provided under Czech accounting legislation for the decrease in an investment in a subsidiary which does not result in loss of control. While this is clearly addressed and recognised as an equity transaction under IFRS Standards;

d. Non-controlling interests (NCI) are disclosed within liabilities under Czech accounting legislation. While under IFRS Standards, NCI are disclosed in equity instead.

5. Inventories: Under Czech accounting legislation, borrowing cost is never capitalised in the cost of inventories, and inventories with different production cycles are subject to different requirements regarding accounting of overheads. While under IFRS Standards, borrowing costs can be capitalised for inventories, and overheads are included in inventories. Besides, there is no precise guideline on calculation of inventory impairment under Czech accounting legislation.

6. Fair value measurement: Such rules are not available under Czech accounting legislation. Apart from business combinations, fair value is only used for valuation of some financial instruments.

7. Construction contracts: Czech accounting legislation provides no separate guidance for construction contracts. Accounting follows the formal contract arrangement. Suppliers account for revenue and expenses in the period to which they relate in compliance with law. The stage of completion method is not included in Czech accounting legislation. Profit from a contract cannot be recognised gradually in the course of the contract, it is only recognised as and when billed. And unbilled expenses are recognised as works in progress. While under IFRS Standards, the stage of completion method is used and unbilled expenses are reported as a receivable from a customer.

8. Leases: When it comes to leases, form takes precedence over substance under Czech accounting legislation. Therefore, finance leases are accounted for in a manner different from IFRS Standards, i. e. leased assets and liabilities are not reflected on the lessee's balance sheet but recognized only in expenses, only over the lease term on a straight-line basis, the same as operating leases.

9. Revenue recognition: No specific guidance on revenue recognition exists under Czech accounting legislation. Usually, revenue is recognised as of the date on which the ownership title to the asset is passed or a service is provided, which is different from the provisions under IFRS Standards. In the case of deferred payment, revenues are not discounted on recognition under Czech accounting legislation, while discounting to the present value is required for recognition of deferred payments under IFRS Standards. For multi-component transactions, Czech accounting legislation provides no guidance on revenue recognition, while under IFRS Standards, the recognition criteria are applied to the separate components separately.

10. Financial instruments: In this respect, Czech accounting legislation is similar to IFRS Standards but is less detailed and some areas are not addressed. For financial institutions, the rules for recognition and measurement of financial instruments are very close to IFRS Standards. However, when it comes to business entities, Czech accounting legislation is very different from IFRS Standards. For example: Businesses are not required to account for embedded derivatives; there is no clear definition of liabilities or equity instruments, and their accounting policies depend on the legal form; redeemable priority shares are considered as equity instruments; no obligation to distinguish between the debt and equity components of compound instruments; financial assets are initially measured at cost; long-term receivables and payables are not discounted; no specification of "loans and receivables"; the measurement category of "carried at amortised cost" is not specified; the use of an effective interest rate is not required; and there is no guidance for accounting for group hedging.

The respondents also noted that the Czech accounting standards are robust in practical implementation with all companies being generally able to follow the generally accepted standards.

In addition, according to respondents' feedback, only a limited number of Czech companies prepare business operation and corporate governance reports.

Audit:

All public interest entities as defined in the Act on Accounting, and companies meeting the criteria set below (join stock companies fulfilling 1 of the criteria and other entities fulfilling 2 of the criteria) are required to be audited:

- Total assets exceed CZK 40 million
- Turnover exceeds CZK 80 million
- Average number of employees is greater than 50

According to the respondents, the Standards on Auditing used in the Czech Republic are identical to the International Standards on Auditing, a set of standards issued by the IFAC.

Qatar

IFRS Standards are required for domestic public companies. Foreign companies are not listed on the Qatar Exchange.

Professional institution:

Qatar Financial Markets Authority (QFMA) http://www.qfma.org.qa/English/Home.aspx

The Law No. 8 of 2012 Qatar Financial Markets Authority gives the QFMA the authority to supervise and regulate the listed companies in Qatar. Auditors of the public companies are required to be registered with the QFMA as auditors. Qatar Central Bank oversees all the banks and insurance companies in Qatar.

Standard-setter:

Qatar has no dedicated standard-setter and has directly adopted IFRS Standards.

Financial reporting standards:

According to Qatar's Commercial Law No. 5 of 2002, all Qatari companies are required to prepare consolidated and separate company financial statements in accordance with IFRS Standards.

Exceptions to the adoption of IFRS Standards:

The Qatar Exchange has permitted some Islamic financial institutions to use accounting standards issued by the Accounting and Auditing Organization for Islamic Financial Institutions (AAOIFI).

Audit:

According to respondents' feedback, all companies in Qatar are required to be audited on an annual basis by auditors following the International Standards on Auditing.

The Tax department of Qatar requires all business entities that are wholly or partially foreign (non-GCC) owned to submit audited financial statements signed by a locally registered auditor together with the tax declaration. Further, Circular No. 4/2011 dated 7 August 2011 requires that companies and permanent establishments wholly owned by Qatari or GCC nationals are required to file corporate income tax returns (accompanied by audited financial statements) if:

- Their share capital is greater than or equal to QAR 2 million; or
- Their gross revenue is greater than or equal to QAR 10 million.

Hungary

All domestic companies whose securities trade in a regulated market are required to use IFRS Standards as adopted by the EU in their consolidated financial statements. IFRS Standards as adopted by the EU are required in their consolidated financial statements except that a foreign company whose home jurisdiction's standards are deemed by the EU to be equivalent to IFRS Standards may use its home standards.

Professional institution:

Chamber of Hungarian Auditors (member of the IFAC) http: //www. mkvk. hu/

Standard-setter:

Ministry for National Economy http: //www. kormany. hu/ en/ministry-for-national-economy

Its key responsibilities are:

- Management of the national accounting work;

- Drafting the accounting law and administrative regulations;

- Doing research and putting forward proposed policies in relation to accounting reforms and developments;

- Drafting and organizing the implementation of consistent national accounting standards system, management accounting standards, internal control regulations, and accounting informatization standards, etc. ; and

- Drafting the government accounting standards and the accounting systems for administrative and public institutions.

Financial reporting standards:

1. Circumstances where application of IFRS Standards as adopted by the EU is required:

In June 2002, the European Union adopted an IAS Regulation requiring all companies listed in an EU capital market to prepare their consolidated financial statements in accordance with IFRS Standards as adopted by the EU starting in 2005. Hungary is an EU Member State. Consequently, Hungarian companies listed in an EU/EEA securities market are required to follow IFRS Standards as adopted by the EU.

The EU IAS Regulation gives member states the option to require or permit IFRS Standards as adopted by the EU in separate company financial statements or in the financial statements of companies whose securities do not trade on a regulated securities market.

2. Other circumstances: in which application of the IFRS, as adopted by the EU, is required or permitted are as follow.

On 12 June 2015, the Hungarian Government decided to extend the use of IFRSs to the individual accounts of Hungarian companies as follows:

a. Voluntary application of IFRSs from 1 January 2016 for companies whose securities are traded in the European Economic Area (EEA) or whose parent company prepares its consolidated financial statements under IFRSs and requires its subsidiaries to prepare IFRS financial statements;

b. Mandatory application of IFRSs from 1 January 2017 for companies whose securities are traded in the EEA;

c. Voluntary application of IFRSs from 1 January 2017 for insurance companies and companies with obligatory audit of their financial statements;

d. Mandatory application of IFRSs from 1 January 2018 for the remaining financial institutions.

The remaining companies prepare their financial statements in accordance with the Hungarian Accounting Law.

According to respondents' feedback, the Hungarian Accounting Regulation ("HAR") is very different from IFRS Standards in terms of recognition of intangibles, recognition of revenue and expenses, general disclosure in the financial statements, and the format of financial statements. The main differences are as follows:

1. Presentation of financial statements: Under HAR, pre-determined balance sheet and income statement templates are provided in the appendix of the Accounting Law that should be applied. While under IFRS, companies have significant freedom in determining the structure and the format of the primary statements based on their accounting policies.

2. Other comprehensive income (OCI): Under HAR, the concept of other comprehensive income statement does not exist. Transactions that are recorded in the OCI under IFRS are recorded in the income statement or directly in equity under HAR.

3. Property, Plant and Equipment (PPE): Under IFRS it is an accounting policy choice to apply the revaluation model for subsequent measurement of property, plant and equipment. When applied, the revaluation of the asset is accounted for in the OCI. The revalued amount becomes the basis of accounting for depreciation. Under HAR similar accounting policy can also be applied, but there are several differences in the details. For instance, the increase in the value recorded against equity is disclosed only in the notes because there is no primary statement of comprehensive income. Besides, the revaluation does not change the basis for depreciation.

4. Investment property: Under IFRS, there is a specific definition of investment property in addition with the models for measurement (i.e. the historical cost model and the fair valuation model). While under HAR, there is no specific definition of investment property. Real estate companies usually carry their investment properties at cost, although companies may decide to apply the fair valuation model for PPE.

5. Intangible assets: Similarly to PPE, under HAR it is also an accounting policy choice to apply the revaluation model for subsequent measurement of intangible assets. The revaluation is accounted for against equity, but the basis of amortization is the initial cost of the asset. However, under IFRS intangible assets can be measured with the revaluation model only if there is an active market for the intangible assets. If the revaluation model is applied, the basis of amortization is the revalued amount.

6. Financial assets: Under HAR every company can apply fair valuation, although this rarely happens in practice. Besides, under HAR the legal form of the asset/liability determines the accounting treatment. Financial assets are generally carried at cost, and interest is recognized based on the contractual terms and not based on the effective interest rate. While under IFRS, the legal form does not drive classification of debt instruments; rather, the nature of the instrument is considered. Additional differences involve financial assets that are carried at amortized cost.

7. Revenue recognition: HAR generally follows the legal form of the transaction when accounting for revenue. Extraordinary activities of the company could also form part of the revenue. There is no specific guidance on agent/ principal consideration that enables the companies to decide whether the transaction should be recorded on gross or net basis. Construction contracts and provision of services are generally accounted for in accordance with the completed contract/milestone method. Under HAR the form of sales discount determines the treatment and it might affect revenue, other expense, financial expense or extraordinary expense. HAR neither provides any guidance on how to account for multiple element arrangements nor takes into account the time value of money for the purpose of revenue recognition. All the above is different from IFRS.

8. Employee benefits: Under HAR there is no specific guidance on accounting for defined benefit plans.

9. Share-based payments: HAR does not contain specific guidance on share-based payment transactions.

10. Income taxes-deferred taxes: HAR does not have the concept of deferred taxation in the separate financial statements. In the consolidated financial statements limited types of temporary differences give rise to " corporate tax difference due to consolidation". This is a significant difference from IFRS.

11. Business combinations: Under HAR entities have an accounting policy choice on whether to account for the acquisition at cost or at the fair value of the assets acquired. The acquirer is determined based on the legal form of the transaction. All the above is different from IFRS. According to respondents'

feedback, in Hungary, the accounting standards are robust in practical implementation with all companies being able to follow the generally accepted standards.

Audit:

All Hungarian companies are required to be audited except for those companies whose annual net sales is less than 300 million forints on the average of the two preceding financial years, and whose average number of employees for the two preceding financial years is less than 50 and in line with certain other conditions. According to the respondents, the Standards on Auditing used in Hungary are very similar to the International Standards on Auditing, a set of standards issued by the IFAC.

Thailand

Thai Accounting Standards are required for domestic public companies. Thai Accounting Standards are substantially converged with IFRS Standards, though the financial instruments Standards that are part of IFRS Standards have not yet been adopted. Thai Accounting Standards include several national financial instruments standards that differ from IFRS Standards.

Standard-setter & Professional institution:

Federation of Accounting Professions (FAP, member of the IFAC) http: // www. fap. or. th/

Its key responsibilities are:

- Management of the national accounting work;

- Drafting the accounting law and administrative regulations;

- Doing research and putting forward proposed policies in relation to accounting reforms and developments;

- Drafting and organizing the implementation of consistent national accounting standards system, management accounting standards, internal control regulations, and accounting informatization standards, etc. ;

- Drafting the government accounting standards and the accounting systems for administrative and public institutions;

- National accounting talents development; and

- Supervising and directing the CPA profession according to law, and developing rules and regulations, policies and measures for the CPA profession.

Financial reporting standards:

Thailand is in the process of fully adopting IFRS Standards.

Thailand has two sets of approved accounting standards and one set of would-be-effective accounting standards, namely:

● Thai Financial Reporting Standards (TFRS)-Mandatory application for listed companies in Thailand, and optional application for non-listed companies;

● Thai Financial Reporting Standards for Non-Publicly Accountable Entities (TFRS for NPAEs)—Applicable to non-listed companies and will be replaced by the Thai Financial Reporting Standard for Small and Medium Enterprises (TFRS for SMEs); and

● Thai Financial Reporting Standard for Small and Medium Enterprises (TFRS for SMEs)—Applicable to small and medium sized enterprises, currently under preparation and expected to be effective on 1 January 2018.

The TFRSs are substantially converged with IFRS Standards, with a one-year delay from the equivalent IFRS Standard's effective date. For example, IFRS Bound Volume 2016 became effective in 2017. Besides, the FAP has committed to adopt IFRS standards relating to financial instruments in 2019, i. e. IFRS 9, IAS 32 and IFRS 7. Between now and 2019, the FAP plans to issue Thai equivalents of IFRS 9, IAS 32 and IFRS 7 in 2017, and to encourage early adoption so as to minimize the differences between various financial instrument standards.

Thai public interest entities institutions are required to prepare both consolidated and separate financial statements in conformity with TFRSs. But listed companies are also permitted to apply "Thai Accounting Standards Plus IFRS Standards" in their financial statements-that is, to use those IFRS Standards that have not yet been adopted as Thai Accounting Standards in addition to those that have been adopted.

Currently SMEs in Thailand can use either Thai Financial Reporting Standards (TFRS) or the Thai Accounting Standard for Non-Publicly Accountable Entities (NPAEs). The FAP states that Thai GAAP for NPAEs is "short and simple and uses a historical cost measurement basis". Thailand is in the process of adopting the IFRS for SMEs Standard in full without modification, to be known as the Thai Financial Reporting Standard for SMEs (TFRS for SMEs), with an expected effective date of 1 January 2018. A study is currently in progress as to which type of entity will be required to adopt the TFRS for SMEs.

According to respondents' feedback, in Thailand, the accounting standards are robust in practical implementation with all companies being able to follow the generally accepted standards.

Audit:

The respondents noted that all companies legally registered in Thailand must be audited, and the Standards on Auditing used in Thailand are very similar to the International Standards on Auditing, a set of standards issued by the IFAC.

Vietnam

Vietnam has not adopted IFRS Standards. National standards are required.

Professional institution:

Vietnam Association of Certified Public Accountants (VACPA, member of the IFAC) http://www.vacpa.org.vn/

Standard-setter:

Ministry of Finance http://www.mof.gov.vn

Financial reporting standards:

Vietnam has neither adopted nor converged with IFRS Standards.

All Vietnamese companies are required to use the Vietnamese Accounting Standards (VASs) issued by the Vietnamese Ministry of Finance to prepare their consolidated and separate financial statements. The Ministry of Finance takes IFRS Standards into account in developing VAS, though some modifications were made to reflect local accounting regulations and environment. To date the Ministry of Finance has issued 26 VASs (these were issued from 2001 to 2005), plus additional mandatory implementation guidance known as "circulars".

In 2015, the Vietnamese Ministry of Finance expressed their intent to move towards IFRS Standards, but no specific timetable or convergence roadmap is available for the time being.

In the respondents' view, VASs are partially similar to IFRS Standards, and the major differences between them are as follows:

1. Under VAS, investments are recognized and measured at historical cost, and a provision shall be made for decline in value of the net assets of the investment item or for decline in market value of the investment of equity securities that are treated as held for-trading or available-for-sale financial assets. But the increase in market value of the investment item shall not be recognized as income

or other comprehensive income (OCI).

2. VAS does not require the statement of changes in owners' equity to be reported as a separate statement. Besides, VAS has strict requirements for the reporting format and accounts.

3. Under VAS, the goodwill arising from a business combination shall be amortized over a period not exceeding 10 years from the date of acquisition.

4. VAS does not require accounting for share-based payments or fair value measurement;

5. VAS does not provide the definition of or any specific guidance on impairment of assets;

6. VAS does not provide any specific guidance on amortized cost, hedge accounting, exploration for and evaluation of mineral resources, agriculture, or employee benefits.

According to the respondents, if a specific accounting matter is not regulated under VAS, a company has the option to use guidance from IFRSs. According to the respondents, VAS is robust in practical implementation with all companies being able to follow the generally accepted standards. Vietnam has no requirements for disclosure of corporate governance.

Audit:

In Vietnam, the annual financial statements of certain types of companies are audited, namely:

- The annual financial statements of foreign-invested enterprises;

- The annual financial statements of credit institutions established and operating under the Law on Credit Institutions, including the annual financial statements of any branches of a foreign bank in Vietnam;

- The annual financial statements of financial institutions, insurance companies, reinsurance companies, insurance brokers, and branches of non-life insurance companies;

- The annual financial statements of listed companies, and securities issuers and organizations;

- The annual financial statements of state-owned enterprises (SOEs) except for those subject to the state's confidentiality provisions;

 ● The final reports on the completion of major national projects and government-funded Grade-A projects, except for those subject to the state's confidentiality provisions;

 ● The annual financial statements of the companies with more than 20% of equity owned by the state;

 ● The annual financial statements of the companies with more than 20% of equity held by listed companies, issuers, and securities institutions by the end of a financial year;

 ● The annual financial statements of audit firms and any branches of a foreign audit firm in Vietnam; and

 ● The annual financial reports of ODA-funded projects and preferential loan projects that must be audited by a government auditor or by an independent auditor upon agreement with investors.

In the respondents' view, the Standards on Auditing used in Vietnam are similar to the International Standards on Auditing, a set of standards issued by the IFAC.

Russia

IFRS Standards are required for listed companies, financial institutions and some government-owned companies. IFRS Standards are required for listings by foreign companies.

Professional institution:

Audit Chamber of Russia (member of the IFAC) http: //www. sroapr. ru/ Russian Union of Auditors (member of the IFAC) http: //org-rsa. ru/

Standard-setter:

Ministry of Finance of the Russian Federation (MoF) http: //minfin. ru/ru/

According to respondents' feedback, its key responsibilities are:

● Control and development of the budgetary, tax and customs policies;

● Control of the bookkeeping, accounting and reporting functions and audit activities;

● Control of state debt and bonds issuance;

● Control and establishment of the National Reserve Fund and the National Welfare Fund;

● Handling international financial relationships and international cooperation;

● Initiating reforms;

● Regulating financial market activities;

● Regulating insurance and banking activities, credit cooperation, and micro finance activities;

● Control of lottery agents; and

● Creation and development of the "Electronic Budgeting System".

Financial reporting standards:

Currently, Russia has two sets of applicable accounting standards, i. e.

Russian Accounting Standards (RAS) and IFRS Standards.

1. Circumstances where application of IFRS Standards endorsed by the MoF is required:

According to respondents' feedback, the following companies are required to use IFRS Standards for consolidated financial statements:

- Credit institutions;
- Insurance companies (excluding medical insurance companies that are committed to compulsory medical insurance services);
- Non-government pension funds;
- Companies managing investment funds, mutual funds and nongovernment pension funds;
- Clearing organizations;
- Federal unitary organizations (as decided by the Russian Government);
- Stock companies that have their shares in federal government's possession (as decided by the Russian Government); and
- Other listed organization.

Russia has a formal process for endorsement of new or amended IFRSs. Newly-issued standards go through a technical assessment made by the National Accounting Standards Board (NSFO), an independent organization designated by the Ministry of Finance.

2. Circumstances where application of RAS is required:

Each legal entity registered in Russia must prepare standalone statutory (RAS) financial statements for each fiscal (calendar) year ending 31 December. RAS financial statements must be filed with the tax authorities and the state statistical register within three months after the end of the calendar year.

According to respondents' feedback, RAS is somewhat similar to IFRS Standards, with the major differences as follows:

- For RAS reporting the requirements are strictly established: RUB currency, calendar year adopted as reporting year (no option for shifting), and reporting in Russian language.
- Consolidation: Under IFRS an entity that is a parent shall present

consolidated financial statements. Generally, this requirement applies to all entities, and only several exceptions exist. While under RAS an entity that is a parent shall present consolidated financial statements in line with IFRS requirements only if the entity meets the criteria of Federal Law (for example, it is mandatory for insurance companies, banks, listed companies and others).

- Fair value and time value of money: According to IFRS some assets and liabilities should be measured at fair value. While no such requirements exist in RAS where assets and liabilities are usually measured at their historical cost.

- Impairment of fixed assets: According to IFRS fixed assets should be tested on impairment if there is any indication that they may be impaired, while RAS has no such impairment requirements.

- Finance leases: Under IFRS, fixed assets received under a finance lease are accounted for in the lessee's balance sheet and their depreciation is recorded in the lessee's profit and loss account. While under RAS, assets are recognized in the balance sheet in accordance with the terms of the lease agreement. Fixed assets received under a finance lease may be accounted for either in the lessee's balance sheet or in the lessor's balance sheet depending on the terms of the lease agreement, and their depreciation is included in the profit and loss account of the lessee or the lessor accordingly.

Besides, certain IFRS topics such as Hedging, Share-Based Payments, and Pension Plans, etc. are not covered in RAS. In absence of RAS guidance, entities may choose to apply relevant IFRSs.

As for the actual performance of the accounting standards, respondents noted that RAS is robust in practical implementation with all companies being able to follow the generally accepted standards. In addition, according to respondents' feedback, Russia does not require non-financial reporting disclosures in respect of corporate governance.

Audit:

In Russia, an annual audit of financial statements is mandatory for:

- Joint stock companies;
- Entities with securities listed on stock exchanges;

- Banks and other lending agencies, insurance companies, credit bureaus, pension and investment funds, securities market participants and stock exchanges;

- Other entities with annual revenue for the preceding financial year exceeding RUB 400 million;

- Other entities with total assets as at the preceding 31 December exceeding RUB 60 million;

- Credit institutions;

- Insurance companies (excluding those with activities limited to obligatory medical insurance);

- Non-government pension funds;

- Management companies of investment funds, investment unit trusts and non-state pension funds;

- Clearing organizations;

- Federal unitary organizations (as decided by the Russian Government);

- Stock companies that have their shares in federal government's possession (as decided by the Russian Government); and

- Other listed organization.

According to respondents' feedback, as a result of recent changes in the legislation, starting from 1 January 2017, audits in Russia are to be performed in accordance with the International Standards on Auditing as adopted by the International Federation of Accountants (IFAC) and officially adopted in Russia. Furthermore, the legislation stipulates an obligation for auditors to inform the owners and management of an audit client about any revealed instances of corruption and other legal offenses as well as potential indicators of risks of such offenses. If the representatives of the audit client do not take any appropriate actions for such instances within 90 days, the auditor is to inform the relevant state authorities.

Indonesia

Indonesia has not adopted IFRS Standards for reporting by domestic companies. Indonesia has been converging its national standards toward IFRS Standards, but without a plan for full adoption of IFRS Standards. All foreign companies whose securities trade in a public market are required to use Indonesian national accounting standards.

Professional institution:

Indonesian Institute of Certified Public Accountants (IICPA, member of the IFAC) http: //iapi. or. id

Standard-setter:

Indonesian Financial Accounting Standards Board (Dewan Standar Akuntansi Keuangan-DSAK IAI, as part of the Indonesian Institute of Accountants (Ikatan Akuntan Indonesia-IAI) http: //www. iaiglobal. or. id/IAI's key responsibilities are:

- Holding professional accountant certification exams (Chartered Accountant-CA Indonesia exams);

- Maintaining competence through continuous professional education;

- Developing and establishing ethical codes, professional standards and accounting standards;

- Enforcing member discipline; and

- Developing the accounting profession in Indonesia.

Financial reporting standards:

Indonesia has adopted the IFRS Standards convergence model. There are four sets of accounting standards in Indonesia:

1. Financial Accounting Standards-Financial Accounting Standards consists of Statements of Financial Accounting Standards (PSAK) and Interpretations of Financial Accounting Standards (ISAK) issued by the DSAK IAI. This set of

standards is a conversion of IFRS.

2. Sharia Accounting Standard (SAS)-Sharia Accounting Standard (SAS) is intended for entities that perform Islamic transactions.

3. Financial Accounting Standards for Non-Public Accountable Entities (SAK ETAP)-Financial Accounting Standards for Non-Public Accountable Entities (SAK ETAP) are intended to be used by an Entity without Public Accountability (ETAP) and to publish general purpose financial statements for external users.

4. Financial Accounting Standards for Micro, Small, and Medium Entities-for Micro, Small, and Medium Entities which are not or have not been able to meet the accounting requirements set forth in SAK ETAP.

Indonesia's approach to IFRS adoption is to maintain its national GAAP (PSAK) and converge it gradually with IFRSs as much as possible.

It is noted that the DSAK IAI is currently completed the second phase of the IFRS convergence process, further minimise the gap between SAK and IFRS Standards, from three years to one year. This takes SAK as at 1 January 2015 to be substantially in line with IFRS Standards as at 1 January 2014, again with some exceptions. In May 2016, the Trustees of the IFRS Foundation, the Indonesia Financial Services Authority (OJK) and the Institute of Indonesia Chartered Accountants (IAI) announced their intention to deepen cooperation as Indonesia develops its plans to achieve full convergence with IFRS Standards.

The significant differences between PSAK and IFRS Standards are as follows:

1. Consolidated financial statements: When making decisions on consolidation, PSAK not only considers satisfaction of the definition of "control" but also includes the element of "risks and rewards". Furthermore, when it comes to the definition of "control", PSAK's considerations are more focused on the property of equity, i. e. control is presumed to exist when the parent owns more than half of the voting power of an entity unless, in exceptional circumstances, it can be clearly demonstrated that such ownership does not constitute control.

2. Accounting for investment in joint ventures: Under PSAK, investors shall recognize their interests in a joint venture using the proportionate consolidation method or, as an alternative, the equity method.

3. Fair value: The definition of fair value under PSAK topics on investment property, intangible assets, leases, revenue, and assets is different from IFRS Standards. That is, under PSAK, fair value is defined as "the amount for which an asset could be exchanged, or a liability settled, between knowledgeable, willing parties in an arm's length transaction. " While under IFRS 13, it is emphasized that fair value is an "exit price".

According to respondents' feedback, in Indonesia, accounting standards are robust in practical implementation with all companies being able to follow the generally accepted standards. Indonesia does not require non-financial reporting disclosures in respect of corporate governance.

Audit:

The respondents noted that based on the Indonesia's regulation for limited companies, the criteria for entities whose financial statements should be audited are as follows:

- Entities that collect and/or manage public funds (banking, and insurance, etc.);
- Entities that issue debt certificates (e. g. bonds) to the public;
- Listed entities;
- Entities with the minimum total assets of Rp 50 billion; and
- Foreign-invested entities.

According to respondents' feedback, the Standards on Auditing used in Indonesia are identical to the International Standards on Auditing, a set of standards issued by the IFAC.

Kazakhstan

IFRS Standards are required for all listed companies, financial institutions and large unlisted companies. IFRS Standards are permitted for listings by foreign companies. Alternatively, foreign companies may use US GAAP.

Professional institution:

Chamber of Auditors of the Republic of Kazakhstan http: //www. audit. kz/

Standard-setter:

Ministry of Finance of the Republic of Kazakhstan http: //www. minfin. gov. kz/irj/portal/anonymous

Its key responsibilities are:

• Ensuring the formation and implementation of the state policy in the field of accounting reporting;

• Determining the order of accounting;

• Adopting the normative legal acts of the Republic of Kazakhstan on accounting reporting;

• Developing and approving national standards and guidelines for them;

• Developing and approving a standard chart of accounts;

• Interacting on accounting reporting with other state bodies and professional organizations; and

• Accreditation of professional organizations and certification organizations.

National Bank of Kazakhstan (NBK) http: //www. nationalbank. kz/? docid = 3321&switch = english

Financial reporting standards:

Kazakhstan has adopted full IFRS Standards.

1. Banks

Banks in Kazakhstan that participate in deposit insurance fund have been required to prepare financial statements using IFRSs. Starting in 2004, all banks are required to participate in the deposit insurance programme. Therefore, all Kazakh banks began preparing IFRS financial statements for 2004.

2. Other enterprises

Starting 1 January 2006, IFRSs are required for other companies.

Small and medium-sized entities (SMEs) are required to use Kazakhstan National Financial Reporting Standards #2 (KNFRS #2), which are based on IFRS for SMEs Standard.

Small business enterprises, that in according to the tax legislation of the Republic of Kazakhstan, are under special tax regimes for peasant or farm enterprises, legal entities of producing agricultural products, and also on the basis of a simplified declaration, use Kazakhstan National Financial Reporting Standards #1 (KNFRS #1).

According to respondents' feedback, despite that the implementation of accounting standards in small business enterprises appears to be a bit unsatisfactory, such accounting standards are nevertheless robust in practical implementation by other entities, which being able to follow the generally accepted standards.

Audit:

According to respondents' feedback, in Kazakhstan, entities subject to mandatory audits are as mainly:

- Joint-stock companies;
- State enterprises with the supervisory board in the spheres of education and health;
- Insurance (reinsurance) organizations, insurance holdings, and organizations in which the insurance (reinsurance) organization and/or the insurance holding are/is the major participant (s), and insurance brokers;
- A single accumulative pension fund and investment portfolio managers;
- Banks, bank holdings, and organizations in which the bank and/or the bank holding are/is the major participant (s);
- Civil aviation organizations, with the exception of those airlines performing

aviation work on a list determined by the Government of the Republic of Kazakhstan;

- Social insurance fund; and
- Legal entities of the Republic of Kazakhstan that conclude a contract for investment, in which investment preferences are provided.

Also, in accordance with the Law on Auditing effective from 11 March 2017, limited liability partnerships in Kazakhstan are subject to obligatory annual audits, provided that two criteria are met simultaneously:

1. They are owned by at least two shareholders, and one shareholder owns less than 10% of shares in the charter capital; and

2. Their annual average number of employees exceeds 250 and/or their annual average income exceeds 3 million based on monthly computation indexes.

Voluntary audits are always an option for all KZ entities. According to respondents' feedback, the Standards on Auditing used in Kazakhstan are consistent with the International Standards on Auditing, a set of standards issued by the IFAC.

India

Indian Accounting Standards (Ind AS) are based on and substantially converged with IFRS Standards as issued by the IFRS Foundation board. India has not adopted IFRS Standards for reporting by domestic companies and has not yet formally committed to adopting IFRS Standards. IFRS Standards are permitted for listings by foreign companies.

Professional institution:

Institute of Chartered Accountants of India (ICAI) http: //www. icai. org/

Standard-setter:

National Advisory Committee on Accounting Standards (NACAS)

Financial reporting standards:

India has adopted the IFRS Standards convergence model.

India has adopted Indian Accounting Standards (Ind AS) that are based on and substantially converged with IFRS Standards as issued by the IASB. India originally intended to converge with IFRSs in a phased approach beginning in 2011, but transition to Ind AS was postponed to 2015.

In January 2015, the Indian Ministry of Corporate Affairs (MCA) released a revised roadmap, setting out the following schedule.

(1) All companies, including those whose securities do not trade in a public market and those whose securities trade on the SME Exchange, are permitted to use Ind AS for accounting periods beginning on or after 1 April 2015.

(2) The following companies are required to use Ind AS starting with accounting periods beginning on or after 1 April 2016:

● Companies whose equity or debt securities are listed or are in the process of being listed on any stock exchange in India (other than the SME Exchange) or outside India and having net worth of INR 5, 000, 000, 000.

● Companies other than those above having net worth of INR 5,000,000,000 or more.

● Holdings, subsidiaries, joint ventures or associate companies of those above.

(3) The following companies are required to use Ind AS starting with accounting periods beginning on or after 1 April 2017:

● Companies whose equity or debt securities are listed or are in the process of being listed on any stock exchange in India (other than the SME Exchange) or outside India and having net worth of less than INR 5,000,000,000.

● Companies other than those above having net worth of INR 2,500,000,000 or more but less than INR 5,000,000,000.

● Holdings, subsidiaries, joint ventures or associate companies of those above.

(4) Banking companies, insurance companies, and non-banking finance companies:

On 18 January 2016, the Government of India announced that commercial banks, insurance companies, and non-bank finance companies will be required to prepare their financial statements using Indian Accounting Standards (Ind AS) starting on 1 April 2018, with comparative financial statements for the prior year.

The respondents noted that 1) Ind AS will be applied to both standalone financial statements and consolidated financial statements; 2) Overseas subsidiaries, associates, joint ventures and other similar entities of Indian companies may prepare their standalone financials statements in accordance with the requirements of their specific jurisdiction; and 3) Once any Indian company applies Ind AS, then it must follow them consistently for future years.

According to respondents' feedback, Ind AS has not fully converged with but is somewhat similar to IFRS Standards. Some significant differences between them are as follows:

1. Leases: Under IFRS, lease payments under an operating lease shall be recognised as an expense on a straight-line basis over the lease term, unless another systematic basis is more representative of the time pattern of the user's

benefit. While under Ind AS, lease rentals for operating leases shall be recognised in income statement as agreed in the lease agreement, unless the payments to the lessor are structured to increase in line with expected general inflation to compensate for the lessor's expected inflationary cost increases.

2. Business combinations: IFRS 3 requires bargain purchase gain arising on business combination to be recognised in profit or loss as income. While Ind AS requires the bargain purchase gain to be recognised in equity as capital reserve. Besides, Ind AS includes business combinations of entities under common control into its scope, while IFRS gives no guidance in this regard.

3. Property, plant and equipment: IFRS permits an entity to account for property, plant and equity using the revaluation model, whereas under Ind AS, the revaluation model is not permitted. Besides, IFRS permits the option of reducing the carrying amount of an item of property, plant and equipment by the amount of government grant received in respect of such an item, whereas this is not permitted under Ind AS.

4. Investment property: IFRS permits both the cost model and the fair value model for measurement of investment properties, whereas Ind AS permits only the cost model.

According to respondents' feedback, Ind AS is robust in practical implementation with all companies being able to follow the generally accepted standards.

Audit:

Audits of company accounts have been compulsory in India since the passing of the first Companies Act in 1913. Since then, the Institute of Chartered Accountants of India (ICAI) has regulated the profession of Chartered Accountants in India and ensured the maintenance of India's accounting standards. All chartered accountants are members of the ICAI, and must comply with the standards stipulated by the ICAI and the Audit and Assurance Standards Board (AASB).

The respondents noted that audits in India are generally classified into the following types: statutory audit, internal audit and tax audit.

Statutory audits are conducted to report the current state of a company's finances and accounts to the Indian Government and shareholders. Such audits are performed by qualified auditors working as external and independent parties. The audit report of a statutory audit is made in the form prescribed by the Government agency. Internal audits are conducted at the behest of internal management in order to check the health of a company's finances, and analyze the organization's operational efficiency.

Internal audits may be performed by an independent party or by the company's own internal staff.

Tax audits are required under Section 44 AB of India's Income Tax Act 1961. This section mandates that those whose business turnover exceeds INR 10 million and those working in a profession with gross receipts exceeding INR 5 million must have their accounts audited by an independent Chartered Accountant. It should be noted that the provisions of tax audits are applicable to everyone, be it an individual, a partnership firm, a company, or any other entity.

Audits in India are performed in accordance with India's standards on auditing, which in the respondents' view are quite similar to the International Standards on Auditing, a set of standards issued by the IFAC.

Pakistan

Domestic companies whose securities trade in a public market, financial institutions, public utilities, and large-sized companies are required to use IFRS Standards as adopted in Pakistan. Nonetheless, some important Standards have not been adopted for companies asserting compliance with IFRS Standards as adopted in Pakistan. And Pakistan has not applied IFRS 1 First-time Adoption of IFRS. Foreign companies whose securities trade in a public market in Pakistan are required to use IFRS Standards as adopted in Pakistan.

Professional institution:

Institute of Chartered Accountants of Pakistan (ICAP) http: //www. icap. org. pk/

Institute of Cost and Management Accountants of Pakistan (ICMA Pakistan) https: //www. icmap. com. pk/

Standard-setter:

Institute of Chartered Accountants of Pakistan (ICAP) http: // www. icap. org. pk/

The ICAP is the body responsible for reviewing and adopting accounting standards. It is also the standard setting body for Islamic Financial Accounting Standards.

ICAP's key responsibilities also include: providing accounting opinions on contentious matters and technical releases related to accounting and auditing; preparation of draft proposals for Finance Bill and Corporate Laws; and responses to the queries of ICAP members and other agencies.

Financial reporting standards:

Pakistan has adopted International Financial Reporting Standards (IFRSs) for mandatory application by listed companies, banks and other financial institutions and Economically Significant Entities (ESE).

Medium-sized entities are required to use the IFRS for SMEs Standard.

Small-sized entities are required to use the Accounting Reporting Standards for Small-sized Entities (AFRS for SSEs) as issued by the ICAP.

It should be noted that Pakistan has adopted most but not all IFRS Standards. According to the respondents, some differences are worth noting:

- IFRS 1 First-time Adoption of IFRS has not been adopted in Pakistan.

- IFRIC 4 Determining Whether an Arrangement Contains a Lease and IFRIC 12 Service Concession Arrangements have not been adopted in Pakistan, either.

- Adoption of IFRS 9 Financial Instruments is currently under consideration by Pakistan.

- IFRS 14 Regulatory Deferral Accounts, IFRS 15 Revenue from Contracts with Customers and IFRS 16 Leases have not yet been adopted.

- In addition, IAS 39, IAS 40 and IFRS 7 have not been adopted for banks and other financial institutions regulated by the State Bank of Pakistan (SBP). The SBP has prescribed its own criteria for recognition and measurement of financial instruments for such financial entities. However, those Standards do apply to other companies not regulated by the SBP.

According to respondents' feedback, Pakistan's accounting standards are robust in practical implementation with all companies being able to follow the generally accepted standards. The Securities and Exchange Commission of Pakistan (SECP) provides guidelines on non-financial disclosure which are part of the listing regulations of the Stock Exchange. The SECP has provided guidelines on corporate governance following best international practices for listed entities, public sector companies, non-listed entities and insurance companies, which detail the mandatory disclosures that are required to be made.

Audit:

All companies registered with SECP under the companies' ordinance 1984 are required to appoint auditors at each annual general meeting. (Section 233 and

252 of the Companies Ordinance, 1984). The new Companies Act 2017 recently

promulgated provides exemption to companies with paid up capital of less than one million rupees from the requirements of audit. In case such exemption is used, the company is still required to submit the duly authenticated financial statements to the registrar of companies in the SECP. In addition, the respondents noted that Pakistan has adopted and always followed the International Standards on Auditing, a set of standards issued by the IFAC.

Part Two   Differences in tax systems and tax rate between the Belt and Road countries

The 65 countries along the Belt & Road route differ in economic development, with high-income countries represented by Singapore and upper middle income countries by Romania, as well as lower middle income countries represented by India and low-income countries by Cambodia. Different countries have something in common in the tax system, where corporate income tax and individual income tax (not available in a few countries such as the UAE and Qatar) and goods and services tax (mostly value-added tax) take the dominant share. Differences often lie in the tax structures, which vary owing to the disparities in economic development: the higher the level of economic development, the higher the proportion of the tax take that is derived from income tax, income tax, and the lower the proportion derived from goods and services taxes.

Across the 65 countries, the average tax rate for corporate income tax is 19.3%, with a peak of 55% in the UAE and a nadir of 7.5% in Uzbekistan. The average tax rate for individual income tax is 23.4%, with a high of 50% in Israel and Slovenia and a low of 9% in Montenegro. The average tax rate for goods and services is 16.7%, ranging from 5% in Yemen to 27% in Hungary. The social security tax (or contribution) is also an important burden for businesses, with an average tax and fee rate of 18.5% for the employer, with a maximum of 47.5% in Russia (accumulated marginal tax rate) and a minimum of 3% in Myanmar. The average social security tax rate for the employee is 11.2%, with Bosnia and Herzegovina at the top by 31% and Belarus at the bottom by 1%.

Tax Risk for Enterprises Going Global and Measures to Prevent and Control Such Risk

In the pursuit of global operation, a business shall not only pay attention to the host country's tax types, rates and incentives, but also keep a close eye on the tax risk, which mainly includes five aspects as the business invests offshore: a) dual taxation; b) inadequate accessibility of concessions granted by tax treaties; c) any risk arising from transfer pricing and anti-tax avoidance, as 83% of the businesses surveyed deem the transfer pricing issue as the biggest challenge to the action plan for the prevention and control of base erosion and profit shifting (BEPS); d) legacy taxation problems of target enterprises in overseas M & A; and e) tax discrimination.

China has signed bilateral tax treaties with 54 Belt & Road countries. Most of the treaties not only carry preferential withholding income tax rate for the Chinese global players on interests, dividends and royalties, but also provide a vital guarantee for these enterprises to prevent tax risk and protect their own rights and interests.

Recommended Approach in Response to Tax Risk

The correct way to deal with tax risk is a three-pronged approach combining the efforts of the system, businesses and tax administrations. First, the domestic as well as international tax system shall be improved, with a well-planned top-down design. On the one hand, in the face of the practical need of massive businesses to go global under the Belt & Road initiative, China's tax system concerning foreign parties needs urgent perfection. For example, the current system of overall credit on a per-country basis will lead to an even more pronounced dual taxation problem that cannot coordinate the tax credit between high tax rate countries and low tax rate countries. On the other hand, obsolete and outdated tax treaties need to be revised as soon as possible.

Next, businesses should actively respond to avoid and control tax risk. Under the top-down design, the key to fulfill the target lies in the initiative of the businesses.

Finally, tax administrations should contribute all powers to participate into international coordination. In outbound investment, due to the disparity in the interpretation of the system, policy or agreement, or plagued with tax discrimination, a business will be almost inevitably involved in tax disputes, where the business may find it difficult to safeguard its appropriate rights and interests. In such cases, the power of Chinese tax authorities should be released so as to solve the problem through international tax coordination.

Singapore

1. Tax types, rates and incentives

a. Tax types and rates

In Singapore, taxpayers of the corporate income tax are divided into resident and nonresident taxpayers, while the enterprises subject to management and control in Singapore are deemed as Singaporean resident enterprises. The tax rate for corporate income tax is 17% across Singaporean companies. Resident companies as well as nonresident companies with permanent establishments in Singapore pay tax levied on income derived from operations in Singapore and income received within Singapore yet derived from beyond Singapore. Nonresident companies without permanent establishments shall be taxed only on income derived from Singapore (e. g. interests, royalties and technical service fees, etc.) Dividend income (including stock dividend income) is generally tax-free. Income gains related to income derived can be deducted when calculating the taxable income. Other deductible expenses include the capital discount, tax losses and so on carried forward in the previous year. Losses can be carried forward indefinitely for subsequent years, while losses and non-deductible capital discount can be carried forward for one year (with the maximum amount of S $ 100, 000), both under the prerequisite of approval through the equity compliance testing.

Singapore does not impose capital gains tax and other surtaxes, and does not have the relevant regulations on shareholding tax exemptions and special provisions for the holding company.

Singapore levies goods and services tax on the provision of taxable goods and services and imported goods at a standard rate of 7%, compared to a zero rate for international services and export trade. This goods and services tax is similar to China's VAT.

In Singapore, taxpayers of Singapore's individual income tax are divided into resident and nonresident taxpayers, both taxed on income derived from Singapore, regardless of whether an individual is living in Singapore or where the money is obtained. In general cases, they will not be taxed on any income derived from outside of Singapore. Take employment income as an example, the judgment of the place of origin depends on where the employment service occurs, rather than where the money is physically paid or whether the employer/employee is a Singaporean resident. Singapore's Individual income tax is taxed at progressive rates of 2% to 20%. Nonresident personal employment income is taxed at either a uniform rate of 15% (including any individual tax exemptions) or the income tax rate for the resident, where the higher of the two shall prevail. All other income from Singapore of nonresident individuals, including director fees and consultancy fees, shall be taxed at a uniform rate of 20%. Nonresident individuals (except company directors) can be exempt from tax payment for short-term employment (ie. no more than 60 days) in Singapore.

A Singaporean resident enterprise shall pay the withholding tax on the relevant income paid to nonresidents. In general, the withholding tax rate for interest and rental income is 15% and that for royalties is 10%. The residents of countries that have entered into bilateral tax treaties with Singapore can possibly enjoy a lower withholding tax rate regarding their income from Singapore.

Overall, Singapore has a simple tax system and a relatively low corporate tax burden.

b. Tax incentives

Singapore offers a variety of tax incentives for emerging industries, activities at corporate headquarters, finance, asset securitization, fund managers, international maritime activities, international trade and R & D, etc.

1. Tax treaties

Singapore has entered into bilateral tax treaties with a number of countries, including China. According to the Taxation Agreement between China and Singapore, the withholding tax rate shall be 5% or 10% on dividends, 7% or 10% on interests (15% in case of a non-signatory which has not signed the bilateral tax treaty with Singapore), and 6% or 10% on royalties (10% in case of a non-signatory). The taxation agreement enables Chinese enterprises to enjoy lower taxes.

2. Tax risk and dispute handling

Since the Singaporean tax system is simple and the enforcement is standardized, tax dispute is not a frequent occurrence in Singapore. Tax disputes can be negotiated on the basis of tax treaties or resolved through legal means.

Respondents say that in general the tax burden on enterprises investing and operating in Singapore are relatively low, the transparency, stability, the completeness of legalization and enforcement standards of the tax system are relatively high, and corporate tax risk is relatively small; tax disputes are infrequent and can be resolved through negotiation or legal means.

Reference for the major tax types and rates in effect in Singapore   unit: %

Tax types	Tax rate (Proportion)
Corporate income tax	17
individual income tax	2 ~ 20
Goods and services tax	7
Employer social insurance contributions	17
Employee social insurance contributions	20

Malaysia

1. Tax types, rates and incentives

a. Tax types and rates

In Malaysia, taxpayers of the corporate income tax are divided into resident and nonresident taxpayers, while the enterprises subject to management and control in Malaysia are deemed as Malaysian resident enterprises. A company is levied on income from Malaysia, while any income from a foreign source is not taxable unless the company is engaged in banking, insurance, air freight or shipping. The standard tax rate for corporate income tax is 24%. Small and medium-sized resident enterprises will be taxed at the rate of 18% on the initially gained MYR 500,000, and the standard tax rate will be applicable to the excess part onwards. Losses can be carried forward indefinitely for subsequent years (except for material changes in the ownership of dormant companies), but cannot be subject to retroactive adjustment to years before the loss was incurred.

A Malaysian resident enterprise shall pay the withholding tax in Malaysia on the relevant income paid to nonresidents. There is no tax on dividends paid to nonresidents, with a withholding tax of 15%, 10% and 10% respectively on the interests, royalties and technical service fees paid to nonresidents. The rental of movable property paid to nonresidents, the charge on installation service provided in Malaysia and certain one-time income shall be levied, with a withholding tax of 10%. The residents of countries that have entered into bilateral tax treaties with Malaysia can possibly enjoy a lower withholding tax rate regarding their income from Malaysia.

Overall, Malaysia has moderate corporate tax rates.

b. Tax incentives

Malaysia has many tax incentives for specific industries such as manufacturing, information technology services, biotechnology, Islamic finance, energy conservation and environmental protection, including a 10-year tax holiday for industry-leading companies, a tax deduction of 60% to 100% for capital investment for up to 10 years, and tax policies for accelerated depreciation and amortization, weighted deduction and tax-free reinvestment, etc. Specifically, the following aspects are covered:

• For foreign-invested enterprises that are eligible for "emerging industrial status", income tax is levied only on 30% of the Company's operating profits, which will last 5 years from the date of production (the date on which the daily output reaches 30% of the maximum output).

• High-tech companies as well as information and communication technology (ICT) companies engaged in scientific research and development and located in the Multimedia Super Corridor (MSC) shall be exempt from income tax for 5 years.

• Any institution established for science and technology transfer and training purposes shall be exempted from income tax for 10 years. For foreign enterprises that transfer advanced technology to local Malaysian companies or individuals, the technology transfer fees will be exempt from income tax. The enterprises involved in significant interests of the State and strategic projects that have a significant impact on the country's economic development, as well as the manufacturers of machinery and equipment and their spare parts on the priority development list, shall be exempt from corporate income tax for 10 years.

• Any company investing in the environmental protection domain shall benefit from a 70% tax exemption of the operating income for 5 years, while an enterprise engaged in afforestation shall be exempted from income tax for 10 years.

• Any enterprise investing in food production approved by the Ministry of Finance (including kenaf, vegetables, fruits, medicinal plants, spices, aquatic products and breeding of cattle and other livestock) shall be exempted from corporate income tax for 10 years. An exporter of fresh and dried fruit, fresh and dried flowers or ornamental plants and fishes can be partially exempted from income tax, equivalent to 10% of its operating profits.

● Companies investing in halal food production and have already obtained halal certification from the Department of Islamic Development Malaysia (JAKIM) are eligible for the Investment Tax Allowance (ITA) of 100% of qualifying capital expenditure incurred.

● For export-oriented enterprises, an export growth of 30% means 10% of the increase in export exempt from income tax, and a growth of 50% will bring the corresponding exempt proportion to 15%.

● Tax is levied on only half of the increase in the export amount made by an ICT company.

● Companies engaged in luxury yacht maintenance services in Langkawi and luxury yacht rental services in Malaysia shall be exempt from income tax for 5 years.

● Any company that established a regional operating headquarters and a procurement center in Malaysia shall be exempt from income tax for 5 years, with an additional 5 years upon approval at the expiration of the first five-year period.

● Any foreign-invested enterprise participating in the Malaysian Industrial Development Program shall be exempt from income tax for 5 years, or 10 years upon review and approval if it is a supplier of world-class products in terms of price, quality and technical content; Such enterprises can have their expenses in employee training, product development and testing and public domain audit deducted from income tax.

● Imports of raw materials and spare parts required for export products (where the export volume accounts for over 80% of the production) shall be exempt from import duty. Where machinery and equipment are imported because domestic manufacturers fail to produce or only provide lower-quality or non-standard products, the imports are exempt from import duty and sales tax.

● Machinery and equipment that domestic manufacturers can provide with appropriate product quality and standard, such as those used for environmental protection, waste recycling, and the storage and disposal of toxic and hazardous substances, or used by R & D institutions and training purposes, as well as plantation can be exempt from import duty and sales tax upon approval of the

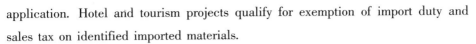
application. Hotel and tourism projects qualify for exemption of import duty and sales tax on identified imported materials.

- Approved foreign-invested education and training equipment (laboratory equipment, workshop, photography room and language laboratory, etc.) can be exempt from import duty, sales tax and excise tax (Note: excise tax is levied on selected products manufactured in Malaysia, namely cigarettes, alcoholic drinks, playing cards, mahjong tiles and motor vehicles.) .

- Raw materials and spare parts and the corresponding consumables directly used for the services projects approved by the Ministry of Finance shall be exempt from import duty and sales tax if domestic manufacturers fail to produce or only provide lower-quality or non-standard counterparts. Locally purchased equipment and machinery shall be exempt from sales tax and excise tax.

- The relevant equipment used by enterprises located in the Multimedia Super Corridor (MSC) shall be exempt from import duty. Additionally, tax relief also can be applied when aforementioned equipment is used for infrastructure and industrial construction. Construction and purchase of construction facilities for specific purposes (including approved industries for industrial production, R & D and employee residence, etc.) shall be exempt from 10% of industrial construction tax for the first year and 3% for each subsequent year, with the maximum duration of 30 years. Companies investing in East Malaysia and the Eastern Corridor can in certain circumstances be exempt from all infrastructure fees and have the related expenses waived.

- Any expenditure on advertising in promoting the Malaysian products and brands can be deducted from the income tax accordingly upon approval of the application.

2. Tax treaties

Malaysia has entered into bilateral tax treaties with 72 countries, including China, and the treaties have played an important role in avoiding dual taxation and reducing corporate tax burdens. Of course, with ever-growing economic activities, some new economic income has not yet been included in the bilateral tax treaties, requiring refinements in the future modification of the tax treaties.

3. Tax risk and dispute handling

When asked about cases involving tax disputes, respondents say there is no obvious tax dispute. If a tax dispute does occur, it should be resolved through consultation or through legal means if the consultation fails to reach a consensus.

Respondents say that, in general, tax risk is controllable across enterprises investing in Malaysia. Meanwhile, as the Malaysian tax authorities become increasingly demanding on taxpayers to consciously follow the requirements, businesses must sufficiently communicate in advance with the local tax authorities to reduce tax risk.

Reference for the major tax types and rates in effect in Malaysia   unit: %

Tax types	Tax rate (Proportion)
Corporate income tax	24
Individual income tax	0 ~ 28
Goods and services tax	6
Property profit tax	5 ~ 30
Import duty	5 ~ 35
Property trading stamp duty	1 ~ 3
Stock trading stamp duty	0.3
Employer social insurance contributions	12
Employee social insurance contributions	12

UAE

1. Tax types, rates and incentives

a. Tax types and rates

The main tax type in the UAE is corporate income tax, which is applicable only to oil and gas explorers and producers, foreign bank branches and certain petrochemical companies under specific government licensing agreements. Other companies shall not be taxed on corporate income. Foreign bank branches shall pay tax according to the statutory tax rate of the emirate where they operate, which is unified currently at 20%. Oil and gas explorers and producers are subject to a uniform tax rate of 50% in Dubai and 55% in Abu Dhabi.

The UAE does not have surtaxes or relevant regulations on dividend tax, capital gains tax, alternative minimum tax (AMT), foreign tax credit and shareholding tax exemptions, and taxpayers are not subject to any withholding tax. In addition, the UAE does not levy an individual income tax, but may impose a VAT of 5% from January 1, 2018 onwards.

Overall, the tax burden for enterprises investing and operating in the UAE is relatively low.

b. Tax incentives

In its free trade area, the UAE has tax concessions or exemptions of 50 years (deferrable) for goods imported into the FTA.

2. Tax treaties

The UAE has entered into bilateral tax treaties with over 70 countries, including China, and the treaties have played an important role in avoiding dual taxation and reducing corporate tax burdens.

3. Tax risk and dispute handling

Respondents say that, in general, enterprises investing and operating in the

UAE have a relatively low tax burden, though there is still room for improvement in terms of transparency, the completeness of legalization and standard enforcement; the relevant risk is under control, but businesses must be well-prepared.

Reference for the major tax types and rates in effect in UAE   unit:%

Tax types	Tax rate (Proportion)
Uniform tax rate for branches of foreign banks	20
Oil and gas explorers and producers (Dubai)	50
Oil and gas explorers and producers (Abu Dhabi)	55

Poland

1. Tax types, rates and incentives

a. Tax types and rates

Taxpayers of the corporate income tax are divided into resident and nonresident taxpayers. If a company or a limited joint-stock partnership (with some exceptions) is registered or managed in Poland, the company shall constitute a Polish resident taxpayer. Resident taxpayers shall pay taxes on their global income, while nonresident taxpayers shall pay taxes only on their income from Poland. The standard tax rate for Polish corporate income tax is 19%.

The standard VAT rate in Poland is 23%, applicable to the sales of goods, the provision of services, the import and export of goods and the purchases and sales of goods between different branches of the same entity. Some goods and services enjoy a preferential VAT rate of 5% or 8%, and some other goods and services (e. g. sales and exports within the same entity) enjoy a zero tax rate or tax exemption.

Taxpayers of Individual income tax are divided into resident and nonresident taxpayers, where resident taxpayers shall pay taxes in Poland on their global income, while nonresident taxpayers shall pay taxes on their income from Poland. Poland's individual income tax is subject to a progressive tax rate of 18% to 32%. Individuals engaged in business activities may also choose to apply special provisions, normally a tax rate of 19% without any relief or exemption.

A Polish resident enterprise shall pay the withholding tax on the relevant income paid to nonresidents. In general, the withholding tax rate for dividends paid to nonresident taxpayers is 19%, while that for interest income and royalties is 20%. The residents of countries that have entered into bilateral tax treaties with Poland often enjoy a lower withholding tax rate.

Overall, Polish enterprises have an average corporate tax burden.

b. Tax incentives

In respect of tax incentives, in some cases, the expenditure incurred in obtaining intellectual property rights can be offset by taxable income in proportion. Small businesses and startups can also enjoy a one-time depreciation deduction of no more than € 50,000. Companies located in the Polish Special Economic Zones can enjoy a certain degree of tax benefits.

2. Tax treaties

Poland has entered into bilateral tax treaties with multiple countries, including China, and the treaties have played an important role in avoiding dual taxation and reducing corporate tax burdens. Under the tax treaty signed between China and Poland, the withholding tax rate is 10% for dividends and interests, and 7% or 10% for royalties.

3. Tax risk and dispute handling

When asked about cases involving tax disputes, respondents say there is no obvious tax dispute given a relatively simple tax system.

Respondents say that, in general, enterprises investing and operating in Poland have a moderate tax burden. However, given the relatively low level of transparency, stability and the completeness of legalization and the average level of enforcement of standard enforcement, there may be considerable tax risk.

Reference for the major tax types and rates in effect in Poland   unit: %

Tax types	Tax rate (Proportion)
Corporate income tax	19
individual income tax	18 ~ 32
VAT	5、8、23
Employer social insurance contributions	20.61

Czech Republic

1. Tax types, rates and incentives

a. Tax types and rates

Taxpayers of the corporate income tax are divided into resident and nonresident taxpayers. If a company is registered or de facto managed and controlled in the Czech Republic, the company shall constitute a Czech resident taxpayer. Resident taxpayers shall pay taxes on their global income, while nonresident taxpayers shall pay taxes only on their income from the Czech Republic. The standard tax rate for Czech corporate income tax is 19%. Losses can be carried forward for 5 years, but shall not be subject to retroactive adjustment. Some anti-abuse legal provisions curtail the use of tax losses, where tax losses cannot be deducted upon a material change in the composition of the company's shareholders or controllers, unless 80% of the income is generated by the same conduct that caused the losses.

The Czech Republic levies VAT on the sales of goods and the provision of services. Imported and domestic goods shall be subject to the same VAT rate, with the goods exported from non-EU countries exempt from VAT. The standard tax rate is 21%, coupled with a preferential tax rate of 15%.

Taxpayers of individual income tax are divided into resident and nonresident taxpayers, where resident taxpayers shall pay taxes in the Czech Republic on their global income while nonresident taxpayers on their income derived from the Czech Republic. The statutory rate for individual income tax is 15%. If a salary is paid above 48 times the average base salary within a calendar year, the tax rate will increase by 7%. Each Individual should make an independent tax declaration, and joint declaration is prohibited. There are five basic sources of taxable income for individual income tax, respectively employment, business, capital operation, property leasing and others. Each domestic dividends and/or interest income is required to one-off withholding tax payment with separate individual income tax payment. Capital gains are usually taxed at a rate of 15%. However, capital gains can be tax-exempt if certain conditions are met. Mortgage interest, life and supplementary pension insurance and donations can be deducted pre-tax. Taxpayers can enjoy the statutory deductions for themselves, spouses and children, while a taxpayer choosing a one-time deduction or pension withdrawal will be subject to limited deduction and concession.

A Czech resident enterprise shall pay the withholding tax on the relevant income paid to nonresidents. In general, the withholding tax rate for dividends, interests and royalties shall be 15% or 35%. The residents of countries that have entered into bilateral tax treaties with the Czech Republic may enjoy a much lower withholding tax rate.

Overall, Czech enterprises have an average corporate tax burden.

b. Tax incentives

In respect of tax incentives, there are incentives for investment, including a 10-year tax concession, job creation allowance, employee retraining subsidy, and real estate-related incentives. Enterprises engaged in R & D activities can enjoy preferential policies for weighted deduction of the R & D expenses.

2. Tax treaties

The Czech Republic has entered into bilateral tax treaties with over 70 countries, including China, and the treaties have played an important role in avoiding dual taxation and reducing corporate tax burdens. Under the tax treaty signed between China and the Czech Republic, the withholding tax rate shall be 5% or 10% for dividends, 7.5% for interests and 10% for royalties (the rates, in the above three scenarios, would be 15% or 35% in cases where there is no tax treaty).

3. Tax risk and dispute handling

When asked about cases involving tax disputes, respondents say there are standard, normative processes for tax dispute settlement in the Czech Republic.

Respondents say that in general enterprises investing and operating in the

Czech Republic have a moderate tax burden, and the transparency and stability of the tax system with relatively standard enforcement, ensures controllable tax risk despite there only have an average-level of completeness of legalization. Meanwhile, it is also necessary to pay attention to the principle of "substance over form" as well as to guard against the risk of abuse of legal provisions.

Reference for the major tax types and rates

in effect in Czech Republic   unit: %

Tax types	Tax rate (Proportion)
Corporate income tax	19
individual income tax	15、22
VAT	15、21
Employer social insurance contributions	34
Employee social insurance contributions	11

Qatar

1. Tax types, rates and incentives

a. Major tax types and corporate tax rates

• Corporate income tax: Qatar's corporate income tax is attributable to the territorial principle according to Qatar's laws, where the proceeds from the activities in Qatar shall be subject to corporate income tax. Entities wholly owned by Qatari or GCC nationals are exempt from corporate income tax; the tax liability of a joint venture depends on the share of the foreign investor in the joint venture profit, with a base rate of 10%, and there is a 35% tax rate applying to oil and gas operations. Capital gains are included in corporate income in taxation, while foreign companies selling equity of Qatari companies shall pay 10% of its capital gains as income tax.

• individual income tax: none. Qatar does not impose any individual income tax on wages and salaries. Individuals are only required to pay corporate income tax on their operating income derived from Qatar. Qatari citizens and GCC nationals living in Qatar are exempt from income tax in Qatar. Other individuals engaged in business activities in Qatar will be taxed in accordance with the relevant corporate income tax laws and, if considered nonresidents, they will be subject to a withholding tax at 5% or 7% of their total income in Qatar.

• Social insurance contributions: Employers are required to pay social security contributions for employees at a rate of 10%, but are not obliged to pay that for employees of other nationalities. On the other hand, if a Qatari citizen is an employee joining the pension plan, he/she is required to pay a pension equal to 5% of the basic wage each month.

• VAT: Qatar has not yet levied a value-added tax or business tax, while at the Arab Financial Forum (AFF) held in February 2016, the Gulf countries agreed on a VAT of about 5% from 2018 onwards.

b. Tax incentives

• Qatar Financial Centre (QFC) offers tax incentives: QFC's proprietary tax laws and regulations shall be applicable to the activities carried out by QFC-licensed entities. For each entity registered with the QFC, taxable income derived or generated from Qatar shall be taxed at 10% as corporate income tax. Enterprises with a Qatari ownership of more than 90% enjoy similar tax incentives in the Qatar tax law. QFC-located companies do not need to pay any withholding tax.

• Qatar Science and Technology Park (QSTP) tax incentives: The QSTP is the only tax-free zone in Qatar. Companies registered in the QSTP can be wholly owned by foreign investors and are allowed to engage in direct trade in Qatar without the presence of local intermediaries. QSTP enterprises holding a standard license are tax-free, and enjoy exemptions from Qatar's surtaxes and tariffs on their imported goods and services.

2. Tax treaties

Qatar had 58 tax treaties in effect as of the end of 2015. The Agreement. between the Government of the People's Republic of China and the government of the State of Qatar for the Avoidance of Double Taxation and the Prevention of Fiscal Evasion of with respect to Taxes on Income was signed in 2001, took effect on 21 October, 2008, and enforced on 1 January, 2009. The Agreement defines the taxation principles for cross-border income in 17 categories.

3. Tax risk and dispute handling

Qatar has a "Tax Appeal Committee" dedicated to tax dispute handling. A third party tax service may act as a proxy for the client and file a complaint with the Committee. Once a tax-related dispute emerges, it can be resolved through legal procedures by a commissioned professional body.

Reference for the major tax types and rates in effect in Qatar   unit: %

Tax types	Tax rate (Proportion)
Corporate income tax	10、35
Employer social insurance contributions	10
Employee social insurance contributions	5
VAT (levied from 2018 onwards)	5

Hungary

1. Tax types, rates and incentives

a. Major tax types

The Hungarian tax system centres on income tax, including corporate income tax and individual income tax supplemented by other taxes, such as VAT, social security tax, local business tax and so on. In addition, Hungary also levies consumption tax, health tax, green product tax, energy tax and so on for special industries and products.

- Corporate income tax: Taxable income shall be the accounting profit in the annual financial statement adjusted according to the tax law. The applicable tax rate is 9%. Surtaxes have been levied on enterprises engaged in energy sources, finance, retail and telecommunications from 2010 onwards. As for the collection and management, consolidated taxpaying is prohibited, while the profits and losses cannot be shared for each other between different entities.

- VAT: Hungary imposes VAT on the provision of goods and services and importation at a standard rate of 27%, coupled with preferential tax rates of 18% and 5%. It should be noted that enterprises or individuals are required to register VAT prior to the entry into business activities in Hungary, and there is no registration ceiling amount (except for remote sales). If not registered in time in accordance with the regulations, a firm can be registered afterwards, but may be subject to a considerable fine. The output VAT regarding specific services provision, i. e financial services, insurance services, public postal services, education, property leasing, securities sales, land sales or leasing, human health care, folk arts, etc. , is exempted, and related input VAT cannot be deductible.

- Local business tax: Business tax is a local tax in Hungary, where the local government council is entitled to establish, abolish or adjust the tax within its jurisdiction. The tax base is corporate income or pretax profits, with a rate of 2%.

- Social security tax: Any individual working in Hungary under an employment contract, regardless of nationality, shall be required to join the Hungarian social insurance scheme. The social security tax is the portion of social insurance paid by the employer at a rate of 27%, coupled with an additional 1.5% as the training fund contribution.

- Individual income tax: Hungary imposes a single (rather than progressive) tax rate of 15% on personal income, while capital gains are also usually levied at the same rate.

b. Corporate tax rates

The social security tax constitutes a major part of the corporate tax burden in Hungary. According to the World Bank survey Doing Business 2017: Equal Opportunity for All, social security tax expenditure accounts for about 30.46% of corporate profits, followed by local business tax at 5.89% and corporate income tax at 4%. The average tax rate (percentage of taxes in the total profits) assumed by enterprises in Hungary is 46.5%.

c. Tax incentives

Developmental tax incentives:

- Development tax incentives apply to some investment programs for a term of up to ten years.

- To enjoy development tax incentives, a business must meet the specific requirements for the investment amount, location and industry, the number of jobs created, the size of wage expenditure and the investment content. For example, a company investing HUF 100 million (about $ 370,000) in the Free Entrepreneurship Zone or in sectors such as food hygiene, environmental protection and film and television production, or an SME investing in any region, are eligible to apply for development tax incentives.

- This concession takes a tax credit approach, with a reduction of up to 80% of the company's taxable income, bringing the effective tax rate down to 2% (with an applicable tax rate of 10%) or 3.8% (with an applicable tax rate of 19%).

Weighted deduction of the R & D expenses:

● Double deduction: Applicable to the direct costs of basic research, applied research and development within the company's scope of business, where the R & D activities are not necessarily located in Hungary, and the R & D expenses incurred by affiliated enterprises or non-affiliated foreign companies are included.

● Triple deduction: Applicable to the R & D expenses incurred by specific R & D activities jointly carried out by the taxpayer and a Hungarian government-recognized public or private research center, with a deduction ceiling of HUF50 million (about $185,000).

Other incentives are available:

● Preferential tax rate applicable to specific types of income: Tax base for income from royalties is reduced to 50%.

● Tax concessions for specific industries: eligible players in specific industries such as film and television production, sports and culture enjoy the corresponding tax preferential policies.

● Individual income tax enjoys household support deductions and business deductions (approximately a deduction of 10%).

2. Tax treaties

● Hungary has signed tax treaties with a wide range of countries (more than 80 as of May 2017).

● Respondents acknowledge the role of the tax treaties in promoting the operation of foreign companies in Hungary and believe that broad-based bilateral tax treaties and favorable domestic corporate income tax incentives enable Hungary to attract many foreign institutions to invest and build factories in its territory.

3. Tax risk and dispute handling

Respondents indicate that tax dispute cases can be resolved first through the specific procedures of the tax authorities, which consist of two rounds of negotiations. If a dispute remains pending after this consultation, the relevant taxpayer may bring a lawsuit to the court, and the decision about starting legal proceedings is generally related to the amount of tax in dispute. Tax-related cases can be appealed to the Supreme Court.

Reference for the major tax types and rates in effect in Hungary   unit: %

Tax types	Tax rate (Proportion)
Local business tax	2
Corporate income tax	9
Social security tax	22
VAT	27
individual income tax	15
Employer social insurance contributions	28. 5

Thailand

1. Tax types, rates and incentives

a. Major tax types and rates

Companies operating in Thailand shall mainly pay VAT and corporate income tax, and employees are required to pay individual income tax. According to the WB survey data (Doing Business 2017), the average tax imposed on Thai enterprises (tax-net profit ratio) is about 32.6%. On the whole, the tax burden on enterprises operating in Thailand is moderate.

● Corporate income tax: The corporate income tax rate in Thailand stands at 20% of net profit across general companies and legal person stock companies. The way net pnofit is calculated, before levying tax, varies according to circumstances, it can be income before expenses, income gained in or derived from Thailand, or outward remittances of profits. Foreign companies engaged in particular operations with an office in Thailand are taxed at 3% of their total income.

● VAT: The standard rate of VAT is 10%, with a zero tax rate applicable to exports of goods and services. The current law has announced a transitory tax cut to 6.3% from 10%, plus a local administrative tax of 0.7%, making a total tax rate of 7%. A taxpayer shall be required to register any taxable income equivalent to and above THB 1.8 million throughout a taxable year. Non-resident permanent operators are also required to register these.

● Individual income tax: a progressive tax rate in excess of a specific amount, ranging through seven levels from 5% to 35%, i.e. 5%, 10%, 15%, 20%, 25%, 30% and 35%. Resident and nonresident taxpayers in Thailand are taxed only on income derived from Thailand. A resident taxpayer shall only be taxed on income derived from overseas when such income is remitted to Thailand within the same year upon its acquisition, and any overseas income remitted back in a subsequent year shall be exempt from individual income tax. Anyone staying in Thailand for more than 180 days in a calendar tax year will become a resident taxpayer.

b. Tax incentives

According to the respondents, Thailand has many tax incentives for manufacturing, services, international trade and other industries, as well as for special regions or groups. For example, business activities encouraged by the Thailand Board of Investment (BIO) enjoy an income tax exemption period up to 13 years. In addition, the regional operations headquarters and the expatriates can enjoy a concession of 0-10% of net profit tax rate and 15% of fixed individual income tax rate.

2. Tax treaties

Thailand has signed 58 tax treaties. Respondents think that the Thai taxation authorities attach importance to and respect the effectiveness of the tax treaties. However, like tax authorities in many other countries, they also tend to interpret the relevant provisions of the tax treaties for their own benefit.

3. Tax risk and dispute handling

In case a tax dispute arises, the tax authorities and taxpayers usually reach a consensus through consultation. If a taxpayer still disagrees to the assessment results of the tax authorities after the consultation, the dispute can be resolved through legal procedures. However, respondents say that in recent years the Thai Supreme Court often favors the tax authorities in dealing with cases involving tax disputes.

Reference for the major tax types and rates in effect in Thailand   unit: %

Tax types	Tax rate (Proportion)
Corporate income tax	20
VAT	7
Specific Business Tax (SBT – an alternative to VAT for certain business)	Up to 3. 3
individual income tax	5 ~ 35
Employer social insurance contributions	5. 2 ~ 6. 2
Employee social insurance contributions	5
Property tax	12. 5

Vietnam

1. Tax types, rates and incentives

a. Major tax types

The taxes involved in the operation of enterprises in Vietnam mainly include VAT, corporate income tax, individual income tax, tariff, license tax, foreign contract legacy tax and social insurance contributions, etc.

- VAT: the rate is 10%, the VAT of the previous month shall be declared and paid before the 20th day of each month. Tax payable is equivalent to output VAT minus input VAT, paid according to the difference amount when the output is greater than the input, or offset cumulatively in the coming month when the input is greater than the output. Paid input VAT on tax-exempt items stipulated by the Vietnamese government can be subject to tax rebates on a regular basis.

- Corporate income tax is usually declared in one of two ways.

A legal person company is required to declare corporate income tax by 20% of its total profits (25% before 2014, 22% in 2014-2015 and adjusted to 20% in 2016). To take this declaration method, a taxpayer must establish accounts and conduct accounting in line with the Vietnamese accounting system, and the various costs are subject to stringent review by the tax bureau. Corporate income tax declared in this way shall be declared and prepaid once on a quarterly basis, and completed before the 30th day of the month following the end of the quarter. The final settlement of corporate income tax shall be made before March 30 of the following year. Profits realized in the current year can make up for the losses of the previous years (with a maximum of five years) before the calculation of tax payable for the current year.

For a taxpayer registering corporate income tax under the tax package system, the tax base and calculation method shall be: (income-costs) * 2%. The advantage of this declaration method lies in the simple calculation and the limited attention paid to costs by the tax bureau. For any corporate income tax declared in this way, that of the previous month must be declared and paid prior to the 20th day of each month, and the final settlement shall be made before March 30 of the following year.

• Individual income tax: both foreign and local employees are required to pay individual income tax, which is withheld by the employers they serve. Individual income tax of the previous month must be declared and paid prior to the 20th day of each month, and the final settlement shall be made before March 30 of the following year. Individual income tax is subject to a progressive tax rate in excess of specific amount of 5%, 10%, 15%, 20%, 25%, 30% and 35%. There are tax concessions, the lunch subsidy of VND 730, 000 per month can be deducted from individual income tax currently (adjusted regularly), other tax reductions must be applied for by submitting the corresponding reference materials (translated, notarized and certified), difficult to handle for foreign employees.

• Tariff: Imports of all kinds of material shall be subject to import duties approved by the Vietnamese customs, coupled with a 10% VAT. Tariffs can be included in costs, and VAT can be deducted as input VAT.

• License tax: This is a fixed tax and is levied on an annual basis as follows:

a) VND 3 million / year for companies with a registered capital of over VND 10 billion;

b) VND 2 million / year for companies with a registered capital below VND 10 billion; and

c) VND 1 million / year for branches, representative offices and agencies of other natures.

• Foreign contract legacy tax: the signers of subcontracts and service contracts with or the remitters to companies or individuals outside the Vietnamese territory shall pay foreign contract legacy tax, where the party taxed shall pay the agreed tax under the contract, which is withheld by the domestic company. The tax base shall be the amount of settlement of the two parties, and the tax is levied at a rate of about 5% (in general cases, varying across different types of business), coupled with a 5% VAT based on the amount of settlement plus the amount of foreign contract legacy tax. Foreign contract legacy tax can be included in corporate costs, and the 5% VAT can be deducted as input VAT.

b. Corporate tax rates

The Vietnamese corporate tax burden is upper moderate. A construction company surveyed reports its actual tax burden in Vietnam is about 5% of its operating income. In addition, the World Bank 2017 survey database discloses the actual tax burden for Vietnamese enterprises is about 39.4% of their profits on average.

c. Tax incentives

• The government of Vietnam stipulates a preferential tax concession of 10% (duration: 15 years) for taxpayers engaged in encouraged investment projects and 20% (duration: 10 years) for taxpayers investing in socially and economically underdeveloped regions, which shall begin from the first year when profits are gained or the fourth year when income is achieved, with four years being duty-free and nine years being half-levied.

• The two Chinese companies interviewed say they do not enjoy any tax benefits in Vietnam for the time being. One of the two companies has a subordinate in Southeast Asia, which set up the ＊＊ prefabricated plant in a Vietnamese province in 2007 eligible for the preferential tax policy for industrial areas and applied for the corporate income tax concession (exempt from corporate income tax for the first year while from half of corporate income tax for the subsequent two years).

2. Tax treaties

The Agreement between the Government of the People's Republic of China and the Government of the socialist republic of Vietnam for the Avoidance of Double Taxation and the Prevention of Fiscal Evasion of with respect to Taxes on Income was signed on 17 May, 1995, took effect on 18 October, 1996, and was enforced on 1 January, 1997.

The Agreement has played a vital role in the avoidance of double taxation and the prevention of fiscal evasion, where a company's income tax paid in Vietnam and an individual's individual income tax paid in Vietnam can be deducted in China under the Agreement. In practice, for any income of a company in Vietnam obtained from abroad, if the corresponding offshore tax obligation has not yet been fulfilled, the company shall pay the tax in arrears according to the provisions of the Vietnamese tax law; where the offshore tax obligation has been fulfilled, the company needs to provide supporting documents concerned and pay the balance in arrears if the actual tax paid is lower than the amount stipulated in the Vietnamese tax law.

3. Tax risk and dispute handling

a. Tax dispute handling

• In practice, Vietnam's tax disputes are generally resolved through the administrative tax system. Court proceedings are feasible, though unpopular, while the administrative tax declaration system stipulates a 2 – grade appeal process, one at the local or provincial level and the other at a higher level. In fact, however, a dispute can be subject to further appeal on a case-by-case basis if the victim has a good reason. A taxpayer may withdraw from the administrative court proceedings at any time during the administrative appeal process. Although there is no clear provision, once a taxpayer has filed a court action, his or her administrative appeal may no longer be accepted by the tax authorities. Therefore, a general taxpayer tends to make the most of administrative litigation before resorting to legal action, and the current administrative tax appeal system does not provide alternative dispute resolutions.

• The Vietnamese tax law provides for tax dissent and appeal system as follows: an appellant shall deliver the letter of appeal to the direct taxation administration within 30 days from the date of receipt of the notice on tax due or tax discipline issued by a tax officer or the tax authority. During the waiting period, the taxpayer shall pay taxes in accordance with the notice or decision of the tax authority.

• The tax authority must examine and deal with the letter of appeal within 15 days from the date of receipt. The treatment period can be extended for complex cases, but shall not exceed 30 days. If a case goes beyond the jurisdiction of the tax authority, the files or reports concerned should be transferred to the relevant authority, with the appellant notified within 10 days of receipt of the letter.

- The competent tax authority shall have the right to request the appellant to provide the relevant files and materials, as well as to refuse to hear the case if the request is rejected by the appellant.

- The tax authority must refund the paid tax and fine to the taxpayer within 15 days from the receipt of the decision of the superior tax authority or the statutory authority, if the decision favours the taxpayer.

- On spotting any tax fraud, tax evasion or wrong taxation, the tax authority shall be responsible for the collection in arrears of the taxes and fines within five years from the date of discovery, or the refunding of the tax levied during the preceding five years. For resources developers (either organizations or individuals) failing to declare or pay the due taxes, the duration for paying the taxes and fines in arrears shall begin from the date of such development.

- The head of a superior tax authority is obliged to deal with taxpayers' tax appeals on subordinate tax authorities. The decision of the Minister of Finance on the handling of the tax appeal shall be final.

b. Typical tax risk cases

A Chinese construction enterprise (Enterprise A) entered a contract to build an expressway surface (Bid 10) in Haiphong, Vietnam in 2014, and set up a project division dedicated to Bid 10. The project was completed in December 2016. When auditing Enterprise A in April 2017, the Haiphong in taxation authority raised the following questions:

- Enterprise A has another roadbed project in Da Nang, Vietnam. In 2015, Bid 10 project division temporarily borrowed VND 60 billion from the Haiphongin project without paying any interest charged since the two projects belonged to the same enterprise. The Haiphong in taxation authority said that the Haiphong project division should collect interest on the bank loan interest rate in the same period in Vietnam and pay the operating income tax as well as an overdue payment and a fine at the rate of 0.05% per day.

● The actual asphalt used in the Haiphong project accounted for 13, 000 tons, exceeding the quota in the Vietnamese construction provisions of 11, 000 tons. The Haiphong taxation authority requires the project division to provide objective reasons and evidence for the excessive consumption of 2, 000 tons, which, if proved to be a management failure, should not be deducted from the taxable income, with Enterprise A required to pay the operating income tax in arrears as well as a fine and a penalty interest.

Reference for the major tax types and rates in effect in Vietnam   unit: %

Tax types	Tax rate (Proportion)
Corporate income tax	20
VAT	10
individual income tax	5 ~ 35
License tax	VND 1 - 3 million per year
Foreign contact legacy tax	5
Employer social insurance contributions	21. 5
Employee social insurance contributions	10. 5

Russia

1. Tax types, rates and incentives

a. Major tax types

Enterprises and individuals concerned in Russia need to pay the following main taxes: VAT, profits tax (corporate income tax), social coordination insurance and individual income tax, etc.

- VAT: the standard rate is 18%, with the incremental value of goods and services being the basis of the charge. Take construction enterprises as an example, VAT is generally levied in the form of pre-payment or calculated on the workload completed, without double counting.

- Profits tax (corporate income tax): the tax rate is 20%, no higher than that of most countries. The withholding tax rate is 9% for dividends paid to Russian companies or individuals and 15% for that paid to foreign or nonresident individuals, and 20% for interests and loyalties paid to nonresident taxpayers.

- Individual income tax: A single tax rate of 13%, recognized internationally as one of the countries with the lowest average individual income tax rate.

- Social coordination insurance: Russian companies bear a considerable social security burden, all paid by the employer. After several adjustments, the current comprehensive tax rate is 30% for social coordination insurance, including pension insurance, medical insurance and other components, among which pension insurance represents the highest rate. Under certain circumstances, a foreign employee shall enjoy the benefits of social coordination insurance policy or be exempt from pension insurance contributions.

b. Corporate tax rates

- The overall tax burden for businesses is heavy. According to the feedback of a respondent from the construction sector, operation in Russia is subject to a tax burden of about 30% to 35%. According to the World Bank report Doing Business 2017, Russia has a corporate tax rate of 47. 4% in 2016, which was as high as 54% in 2010.

- Social coordination insurance and VAT constitute the heaviest tax burden, and the income tax burden is relatively light. The amount of VAT and social coordination insurance paid by a surveyed company throughout 2016 is RUB 51 million (about RMB 5. 1 million) and RUB 47 million (about RMB 4. 7 million) respectively, which can be offset by continuous book loss arose by the company since its inception, so the company has not yet paid any corporate income tax. As a result of the 13% single rate of individual income tax, high-income employees are taxed for less than in other jurisdiction.

- Russia's tax burden structure has its idiosyncrasies. As a country of transition, in order to attract investment and expand the income tax base, Russia has established a flat and lower-amount income tax rate system after repeated radical reforms. In general, Russia has reduced the income tax burden on enterprises and individuals. In fact, Russia once made a "tax-for-fee" trial in social security contributions, one could pay a fee to reduce one' s tax rate. Owing to the ageing population, the low contribution standards failed to cover the huge social security funding gap, the government was later forced to abolish the trial and raise the contribution standards, putting much more pressure on the businesses.

c. Tax incentives

In recent years, the Russian government has expanded the scale of tax incentives to attract foreign businesses. In this report, the selected content is listed below.

- Local tax incentives: As a federal government of fiscal decentralization, the Russian federal authorities are entitled to make substantial adjustments to the local tax system. The federal counterparts often develop a series of tax incentives based on their regional development goals. For example, the corporate profit taxes are split into federal and regional shares, with a standard rate of 20% , of which

2% goes to the federal government, and 18% goes to the regional governments. Since the latter has the right to cut the allocated profits tax rate to 13.5%, a business operating in Russia may enjoy a profit tax rate as low as 15.5%. In addition, some federal subjects provide a property tax rate of 2.2% for specific fixed assets, or loans to subsidize enterprises.

- Special Economic Zones (SEZ) tax incentives: The legal framework for Special Economic Zones provides massive privileges in taxation and other aspects. Russia's 25 SEZs are divided into four categories: manufacturing, technology innovation, tourism and entertainment, and port logistics. SEZs enjoy a variety of tax incentives, such as a reduction in the profits tax rate to 2% or even 0%, a 10 – year exemption from property tax, customs tariff exemption R & D expenses super deduction VAT exemption, etc.

- Tax incentives for regional investment projects: A federal law has been implemented in Russia as of 1 January, 2014, giving the Far Eastern Federal District and the Siberian Federal District the right to establish a regional profit tax rate. The bill provides that the profit tax rate shall not exceed 10% in the first five years since a profit is generated, and shall not be less than 10% in the following five years. 13 out of the current 15 eligible federal entities have reduced their profit tax rates.

- Tax incentives for advanced development territories (ADTs): The ADT introduced in 2015 is a strategic plan deployed by the Russian government to boost the economy of the Far East and restructure its economy. Nine ADTs have been set up, with at least five on the way in 2017. Each of them can expect an unchanged policy environment for 70 years while enjoying VAT refunds, low profits tax and mineral extraction tax rates, low social coordination insurance contributions and many other tax incentives.

Nonetheless, the Chinese companies surveyed say they do not currently benefit from Russian tax incentives currently, which may be owing to the sectors in which they operate, but may also have something to do with their lack of awareness of the Russian tax incentives. At the same time, the respondents say they are benefiting from the preferential policies under the relevant agreements between China and Russia.

2. Tax treaties

a. Bilateral tax treaties: The Russian Federation has signed bilateral tax treaties with many countries. In 2017, it signed a series of bilateral tax treaties and amendments with Hong Kong, Singapore, China, Cyprus, Kazakhstan and other countries, which have already been or will be implemented.

b. Other agreements with China: Before the recent tax treaty between Russia and China, in 2000 the two governments signed the Agreement on Temporary Labor Services regarding Chinese in Russia and Russians in China, agreeing on the tax matters concerned, such as the exemption from pension insurance contributions (at the rate of 22%) for Chinese working in Russia. Owing to the insufficient publicity and delays in execution, Chinese enterprises have failed to timely and fully benefit from the preferential policies.

3. Tax risk and dispute handling

Through years of practice, a reasonable mechanism has been established in Russia for pre-trial and case hearing of tax disputes. According to the recent feedback from respondents, 75% of the tax disputes can be resolved with the assistance of the tax authorities. The most controversial issues include:

- Definition of the de facto beneficiary
- Thin capitalization
- "Bad faith" suppliers

Respondents say they have won cases involving tax disputes, and all contacts with the Russian tax authorities are made in compliance with the law.

Reference for the major tax types and rates in effect in Russia   unit: %

Tax types	Tax rate (Proportion)
VAT	18
Profits tax (Corporate income tax)	20
Individual income tax	13
Social coordination insurance (paid by employers only)	30

Indonesia

1. Tax types, rates and incentives

a. Major tax types and rates

Taxes related to business operations mainly include VAT, corporate income tax, social security tax, individual income tax and property tax, etc. Respondents deem the overall tax burden on enterprises operating in Indonesia as acceptable. The Word Bank publication Doing Business 2017 discloses the corporate tax rate survey results of Indonesia at an average of 30.6% of profit.

- VAT: with the standard tax rate of 10%, levied on taxpayers providing goods and services. Any company whose annual sales of taxable goods or services exceed a certain amount must register for VAT.

- Corporate income tax: with the standard tax rate of 25%, tax payable calculated against the net profit after deductible taxable income.

- Social security tax: levied on both businesses and individuals. In the case of an enterprise, an employer is required to contribute to the Indonesian Social Insurance Fund if it has 10 or more employees or pays a monthly wage of more than IDR 1 million. As for individuals, an employee in Indonesia shall be subject to social security tax, with an old-age insurance tax and a health insurance tax equivalent to 2% and 0.1% respectively of the employee's monthly salary.

- Individual income tax: a progressive tax rate is charged on incomes in excess of specific amount of 5%, 15%, 25% and 30% is applicable. Taxable income shall be declared on a household basis, covering income from business, income from company, capital gains and so on.

b. Tax incentives

In respect of corporate income tax, Enterprises with an annual income of less than IDR 50 billion shall apply a low corporate tax rate. Taxpayers (excluding permanent establishments) with an annual income of not more than IDR 4. 8 billion enjoy a 1% discount on total income tax. Resident taxpayers with a total income of between IDR 4. 8 billion and 50 billion enjoy a halved corporate income tax rate for part of their taxable income (the portion below IDR 4. 8 billion). However, any permanent establishment shall still be subject to a rate of 20%.

2. Tax treaties

Indonesia has entered into more than 60 tax treaties. Respondents think that the status and role of the tax treaties have been clarified in the legal framework, while the local Indonesian tax authorities fully respect the contents of the tax treaties, and collect tax and settle tax disputes in strict accordance with the agreed standards. There is no misuse or abuse of the treaties. Indonesia has signed a bilateral tax agreement with China, where Chinese enterprises as beneficiaries can pay corporate income tax at a preferential rate of 10%.

3. Tax risk and dispute handling

In Indonesia, it is very common for taxpayers to raise objections to tax authorities. Tax dispute handling procedures are clearly defined in the Indonesian tax law. Any taxpayer disagreeing with the audit conclusion from tax authorities shall have the right to raise an objection and apply for the tax assessment, but shall be required to prepare sufficient evidence and data in accordance with the relevant legal provisions.

Reference for the major tax types and rates in effect in Indonesia　unit:%

Tax types	Tax rate (Proportion)
Profits tax (Corporate income tax)	25
VAT	10
Individual income tax	5 ~ 30
Employer social insurance contributions	10
Employee social insurance contributions	2. 5

Kazakhstan

1. Tax types, rates and incentives

a. Major tax types and rates

Kazakhstan's major taxes include corporate income tax, VAT, individual income tax, social tax and property tax. According to the World Bank publication Doing Business 2017, the average tax imposed on Kazakhstan's enterprises (tax-net profit ratio) is about 29.2%. Based on the statutory tax rates and research results, we believe that the tax burden on enterprises operating in Kazakhstan is at a moderate level.

b. Tax incentives

The government of Kazakhstan offers a wide range of tax incentives, such as:

- Simple collection measures for SMEs;

- Special economic zones subject to multiple tax concessions, covering corporate tax, property tax, land tax and other taxes;

- Tax incentives for capital expenditures (accelerated depreciation);

- VAT payment incentives; and

- Tax exemption policy for up to 10 years for specific investment agreement, covering corporate income tax, property tax and land tax, etc.

2. Tax treaties

a. Bilateral treaties: Kazakhstan has entered into 51 bilateral tax treaties.

b. Value of tax treaties: The tax treaties take precedence over domestic regulations and are often used by enterprises in cross-border transactions.

3. Tax risk and dispute handling

a. Disputed case handling Tax-related disputes can be handled through a pre-court procedure. If not resolved, the disputed case can be brought to court. According to the respondents, the past practices reveal "a very low possibility of winning a case against the tax bureau. "

b. Major tax-related controversies, these have involved:

- Transfer pricing issues;

- Pre-tax deduction of corporate income tax;

- Ax affairs involving the use of underground resources; and

- Tariff classification regarding import goods, etc.

Reference for the major tax types and rates
in effect in Kazakhstan   unit: %

Tax types	Tax rate (Proportion)
Corporate income tax	20
VAT	12
individual income tax	10
Employer social security contributions	11
Property tax	Up to 1.5

India

1. Tax types, rates and incentives

a. Tax types and rates

Indian corporate income taxpayers are divided into resident and nonresident taxpayers, where companies incorporated under the laws of India or whose management and control lies entirely in India shall constitute resident taxpayers. Resident taxpayers shall pay taxes on their global income, while nonresident taxpayers only pay taxes on their income from India. The corporate income tax rate is 30% for domestic companies and 40% for foreign companies. With surtaxes and local taxes taken into account, the effective rates for domestic and foreign companies are 33.99% and 43.26% respectively. In the fiscal year 2017 – 2018, the corporate income tax rate shall be 25% for companies with a turnover of less than IDR 500 million, benefiting 95% of domestic companies.

Business losses and capital losses can be carried forward for 8 subsequent years. Short-term losses can offset the capital gains of long-and short-term capital gains, while long-term losses can only offset long-term capital gains. Losses shall be carried forward to the subsequent years only after the timely submission of tax returns, excluding non-deductible depreciation (which can be carried back indefinitely). Non-deductible depreciation can be deducted from any income, while business losses can only be deducted from operating income.

For a business whose tax payable amount is below 18.5% of its book profits, alternative minimum tax shall be applicable, and the surplus of alternative minimum tax over the normal income tax payable can be deducted from the tax payable, carried back and deducted from income tax within 10 years.

In India, VAT levied on the sales of goods and the provision of services is limited, including 17 different forms of goods and services tax, such as central consumption tax, sales tax and state sales tax, and there are multiple tax rates applicable, including 0% , 5% , 18% , 28% and so on. According to the Indian tax bill issued in April 2017, a uniform VAT system will be set up from 1 July onwards.

Taxpayers of individual income tax are divided into resident and nonresident taxpayers, where resident taxpayers shall pay taxes in India on their global income while nonresident taxpayers on their income derived from India. The statutory rate for individual income tax is 15% . In the fiscal year 2017 – 2018, India's individual income tax rate stands at 5% , 20% and 30% , including a zero bracket amount of IDR 250,000, with an additional 10% for any annual income of more than IDR 5 million and less than IDR 10 million, and 15% for income over IDR 10 million.

An Indian resident enterprise shall pay the withholding tax on the relevant income paid to nonresidents. The withholding income tax rate for dividends paid to nonresident enterprises shall be zero, while companies issuing the dividends shall pay a dividend distribution tax at a rate of 16. 995% . The residents of countries that have entered into bilateral tax treaties with India may enjoy a preferential withholding tax rate.

Overall, the current India tax system is complicated, and enterprises, foreign companies in particular, have a relatively high corporate tax burden.

b. Tax incentives

India provides many tax incentives. For example, up to 200% of R & D expenditures incurred in specific industries and paid to specific research organizations is tax deductible. Tax concessions also apply to investment in the following industries/projects: low-temperature transport systems, agricultural warehousing facilities, natural gas, crude oil or oil pipeline network, the development of affordable housing and production of fertilizers. There are similar deduction policies for the costs incurred in the establishment and operation of inland container transit stations, container freight stations and other designated facilities. Enterprises located in the special economic zones shall be tax-exempt from export profits. There are also industry-and region-specific tax incentives accordingly.

2. Tax treaties

India has entered into bilateral tax treaties with a number of countries, including China. According to the Taxation Agreement between China and India, the withholding tax rate shall be 10% for dividends (0% in case of a non-signatory, but companies issuing the dividends shall pay a dividend distribution tax at a rate of 16. 995%), 10% for interests (20% in case of a non-signatory), and 10% for royalties (25% in case of a non-signatory). The taxation agreement enables Chinese enterprises to enjoy lower taxes. However, it should be noted that if a nonresident does not have a permanent account number (PAN), ie., the tax registration number, the withholding tax shall be paid at rate of the applicable rate agreed or 20%, whichever is higher.

On the whole, India respects the tax treaties and they take precedence over domestic tax laws.

3. Tax risk and dispute handling

When asked about tax disputes, respondents say the specific Indian tax authorities have a special division to deal with tax disputes, which also suggests the high frequency of tax disputes across India. An important way to resolve tax disputes is the court hearing, which, though, often takes a very long time.

Respondents say that, in general, enterprises investing and operating in the India have a relatively high tax burden; the tax system is relatively transparent and stable, high completeness of legalization but not sufficiently standardized regarding the enforcement, which leads to greater corporate tax risk. Moreover, tax disputes occur frequently, and although India has a systematic way to resolve disputes through legal means, it proves time-consuming and ineffective.

Reference for the major tax types and rates in effect in India   unit: %

Tax types	Tax rate (Proportion)
Corporate income tax for domestic companies	30
Corporate income tax for foreign companies	40
individual income tax	5 ~ 30
Limited VAT	0、5、12、18 and 28
Employer social insurance contributions	12. 5
Employee social insurance contributions	12

Pakistan

1. Tax types, rates and incentives

a. Tax types and rates

Pakistani corporate income taxpayers are divided into resident and nonresident taxpayers, where companies incorporated under the laws of Pakistan or whose management and control lies entirely in Pakistan shall constitute resident taxpayers. Resident taxpayers shall pay taxes on their global income, while nonresident taxpayers only pay taxes on their income from Pakistan. The corporate income tax rate is 35% for domestic companies, and residents are taxed on their dividends at a rate of 10%. Operating losses (excluding speculative business losses) can be deducted from taxable income of any category for the same tax year, and losses exceeding taxable income can be carried forward from the subsequent year for up to six years. Speculative business losses and capital losses can be carried forward to the following tax year to offset the year's speculative business income and capital gains. Losses from the disposal of specific securities (including shares and securities of listed companies) can be deducted from the relevant gains of the same tax year, but cannot be carried forward. Operating losses shall not be deducted from taxable operating business income under the final taxation mechanism.

Income from the sales of capital assets held for more than one year can be taxed on a basis of 75%. The tax rate applicable to the disposal of capital gains from the shares of a listing company after tax year 2012 shall be 10% for the shares held for less than 6 months, 8% for that held for more than 6 months but less than 12 months, and 0% for that held for over one year.

The commodity turnover amount declared by resident companies and other specific taxpayers shall be taxed for commodity turnover at a rate of 0. 5%. Unless an alternative minimum tax shall apply to circumstances where tax derived from a taxpayer's gains or losses or income is less than 0.5% of the turnover amount.

Foreign corporate offices in Pakistan shall pay corporate income tax at 7% of the contract revenue.

Pakistan's VAT is divided into consumption tax and sales tax. The federal government usually levies a consumption tax on merchandise sales at a standard rate of 17%. The provincial government will impose a sales tax on services incurred within the province at a rate of 13% ~ 16%, which varies from province to province.

Taxpayers of individual income tax are divided into resident and nonresident taxpayers, whereby resident taxpayers shall pay taxes in Pakistan on their global income while nonresident taxpayers pay income tax only on their income derived from Pakistan. Each Individual is required to make an independent tax declaration, and joint declaration is prohibited by the government. Wage earners and nonwage earners with a taxable income of more than PKR 400,000 are required to pay individual income tax, though at different rates based on the income level: 5% ~ 20% for wage earners as employees, while 10% ~ 25% for taxpayers engaged in operations.

A Pakistani resident enterprise shall pay the withholding tax on the relevant income paid to nonresidents. The residents of countries that have entered into bilateral tax treaties with Pakistan may enjoy a reduced withholding tax rate.

Overall, Pakistani enterprises have an average corporate tax burden.

b. Tax incentives

Pakistan offers tax incentives for plants, machinery and equipment, electricity production projects established in Pakistan, industrial enterprises established in rural and underdeveloped areas, and companies listed on the Pakistan Stock Exchange.

Pakistan has reduced corporate income tax to 20% for enterprises in which foreign direct investment (FDI) accounts for more than 50% of their share capital. Certain industries and projects will enjoy special tax incentives, including road construction in Sindh shall be exempt from service sales tax, and the concessions for import tariffs on "Greenfield" projects from July 2015.

2. Tax treaties

Pakistan has entered into bilateral tax treaties with a number of countries, including China. According to the Taxation Agreement between China and Pakistan signed in 1989, the withholding tax rate shall be 10% for dividends (12.5% or 20% in case of a no signatory), 5% or 10% for interests (20% in case of a non-signatory), and 12.5% for royalties (15% in case of a non-signatory). The taxation agreement enables Chinese enterprises to enjoy lower taxes on paper, while in practice the effect is not ideal. For example, the Agreement stipulates that a nonresident company (representative office) shall be taxed on its operating profits, but the Pakistani income tax law modified in recent years spells out two calculation methods (with a newly added accounting profit calculation for the current year), with the higher rate of the two prevailing, which is detrimental to taxpayers (sometimes taxed on accumulated losses) by violating the provisions of the Agreement. To some extent, the Agreement has become partially obsolete and needs further revision for perfection.

3. Tax risk and dispute handling

When asked about issues involving tax disputes, respondents reported that there are many tax disputes in Pakistan each year, with many tax notices received, which may trigger frequent tax lawsuits. Enterprises will go to court with the tax bureau each year, and a case hearing can go all the way to the Supreme Court. Both parties (tax collectors and taxpayers) shall be entitled to appeal according to law, and the rights of taxpayers can be guaranteed, but it is difficult to get a refund of the tax collected.

As the Pakistani tax system often is highly unstable due to its frequent changes, it imposes greater risk on the investment and operation of businesses. For example, in the first quarter of 2015, Pakistan levied a "super tax", which most companies regarded as a one-time tax and did not consider in the following years, but the super tax was also collected again in 2016 and 2017.

Another case goes as follows: on 26 February, 2011, a Chinese business office in Pakistan received a tax bill issued by the tax authority, requiring it to pay the tax of 2008 in arrears (PKR 91,120,371). On 18 March, 2011, the business applied for reconsideration based on four arguments: a) the appellant was not given enough time and opportunity to justify itself; b) the tax recovery notice was based on subjective assumptions; c) excessive penalties for overdue; and d) the tax authority had ulterior motives. On 1 June, 2011, the reconsideration results proved favorable for the Chinese enterprises, with the tax payable significantly reduced to over PKR 4 million. But the tax authority expressed dissatisfaction, and appealed to the tax court on the 26 July, 2011, arguing that the administrative reconsideration applicant (office of the Chinese company in Pakistan) failed to meet the relevant procedures during the hearing, since the supplementary evidence submitted to the administrative reconsideration officer was not showed to the respondent (tax authority). On 14 April, 2015, the tax court affirmed the original judgment of the administrative reconsideration.

Reference for the major tax types and rates in effect in Pakistan   unit: %

Tax types	Tax rate (Proportion)
Corporate income tax	35; 7 of the contract amount
individual income tax	5 ~ 20
Consumption tax	17
Sales tax	13 ~ 16, differing across provinces

Part Three The development of international accountancy professionals

As the Belt and Road Initiative evolves, more and more Chinese enterprises are starting to operate outside China. At this historic moment, developing accountany professionals with a global vision has become a major issue for enterprises operating along the routes of Belt and Road countries, related educational institutions, accountancy industry regulators and accountancy industry organizations.

High-caliber talents are essential for the success of the Belt and Road Initiative, who will act as bridges and ties between China and other countries along the routes of Belt and Road. Therefore, it is vital to train talents for this purpose. However, there are numerous uncertainties regarding how excellent accountancy professionals should be trained for promoting the development of the Belt and Road Initiative. For example, what are current requirements regarding the competency or skills of accountancy staffs asked by enterprises operating along the routes of Belt and Road countries? Which approaches are adopted by enterprises to promote their accountancy staffs' competency and skills? What are the differences between enterprises in different countries in the training models? What experience is worth drawing on from each other?

Understanding the Competence of Accountancy Professionals in Countries along the Routes of Belt and Road Initiative

Through the study of relevant systems in countries along the routes of Belt and Road Initiative, we find that these countries pay more attention to professional skills (often referred to as hard skills) of accountants in their career, and there is lacking in the relevant research to accountants' competence. Therefore, we have conducted an in-depth investigation to study, through one questionnaire, 12 major competencies of accountancy professionals, which include the knowledge and approaches to financial accounting (e. g. financial reporting, financial management, etc.), the knowledge and approaches to management accounting (e. g. cost management, budget management, performance management, etc.), the knowledge of taxation, capabilities of data analysis, understanding in application of emerging technologies and related software, the knowledge and approaches to risk management, the knowledge and approaches to corporate governance, the knowledge and approaches to audit and assurance, the understanding of organizations' business models, the capability of evaluating different strategic options, the capability of grasping the macroeconomic impact to organizations, and the ability of keeping abreast of the industry frontier.

Exploring the New Training Model for International Talents

There is only limited literature in China regarding how to enhance the competence of the accountancy professionals. We will evaluate the importance, effectiveness and popularity of training methods that we recommended include on-the-job education upgrading, professional qualification training, participation in external training and forums, internal training, job rotation, on-the-job self-exploration, on-the-job guidance by supervisor, external communication and studying, cross-departmental discussion, shuffling to business departments for in-depth understanding, etc.

With the rapid development of knowledge and technologies and the drastic economic restructuring, each accountancy professional should maintain an attitude and ability of lifelong learning considering that accountancy professionals must to experience the change and evolution in industry and professional knowledge and skills on an ongoing basis. Do the accountancy professionals in countries along the routes of Belt and Road Initiative have such motives and awareness? Do the accounting regulators have Continuing Professional Development (CPD) requirement? Do there have any diversified channels and approaches to support the self-improvement of accountancy professionals? What educational resources are available? All aforementioned issues are worth paying more attention here.

Accountancy Professionals: New Impetus to Promote Value Creation

According to one ACCA survey carried out in 2016, it points out that the crucial issue to driving the successful innovation and growth of organization is effective collaboration and integration between finance executives, finance team and internal and external business partners. However, it is far from enough to only realize its necessity and willingness to collaborate. It usually requires organization to change its culture, mindset, organization structure and business behaviors for realizing the integration of business and finance while bringing the better implementation of corporate strategy, optimization of resources, performance appraisal, and even investment decision making, tax planning and M&A support, etc. Through the survey mentioned above, we aim at finding out that whether an enterprise has clear talents objectives, development plans and performance management in place, whether these mechanisms are effective, and whether accountancy professionals can substantially improve the performance of the company and realize the value creation.

This tripartite joint research will answer all aforementioned questions. We hope to provide suggestions regarding the cultivation of accountancy professionals along the routes of Belt and Road Initiative share the cultivation experience of international talents in enterprises in the countries involved. build a think tank of accountancy professionals, and strive to promote the new training model of international talents under the Belt and Road Initiative.

Singapore

Professional Institutions:

There are a variety of professional accountancy institutions to attract and develop accountants, including the national accountancy institution (ISCA— Institute of Singapore Chartered Accountants) as well as the Association of Chartered Certified Accountants ("ACCA") and other international accountancy institutions.

Research on the Competence of Accountancy Professionals:

SAC (Singapore Accountancy Commission), as the main government agency, is engaged in guiding the development of accountancy sectors and relevant talents. The related research reports include:

- Accountancy Sector Survey 2013 (ACCA Project for Management Research)

- Accounting Entities (AE) Survey 2016

- AE Regionalisation Survey 2016 (ACCA as research partner)

Competence Standards / Training Plans for Accountancy Professionals in Organizations:

SAC collaborates with professional accountancy institutions (e. g. ACCA, etc.) and certain government agencies (e. g. Workforce Singapore (WSG), Skills Future Singapore (SSG), etc.) to set a standard framework for accountants' skills and aims at providing detailed requirements of competence and skills to accountancy professionals at all levels.

Approaches of Competence Training to Accountancy Professionals in Enterprises with Relevant Comments.

The main approaches to training used in Singapore are:

- on-the-job educational upgrading

- professional qualification training
- participation in external training and forums
- internal training
- job rotation
- on-the-job self-exploration
- on-the-job guidance by supervisor
- external communication and studying
- cross-departmental discussion
- moving between business departments to acquire in-depth understanding.

The portfolio of aforementioned training approaches would be adopted by a variety of companies. Although there are significant differences between different companies' portfolios, almost all training approaches would be adopted by a lot of large companies. Additionally, the government has also introduced the Skills Future Programs.

Comments: The most popular training approaches are education improvement and internal and external training.

Annual Performance Appraisal to Accountancy Professionals in Enterprises:

Yes, the majority of Singaporean companies conduct annual performance appraisal for their accountancy employees.

CPD of Accountancy Professionals in Enterprises:

Accountancy bodies have various requirements for the CPD for different categories of membership.

The Importance of Accountancy Professionals to Corporate Performance:

The respondents considered that the accountancy professionals as "important" (scoring 4 points out of five) to a company's performance improvement.

The Importance of Competencies of Accountancy Professionals
(importance up to 5 points)

Capabilities / Skills	Importance (1 – 5 points)
Knowledge and Approaches to Financial Accounting	4
Knowledge and Approaches to Management Accounting	4

Capabilities / Skills	Importance (1 – 5 points)
Knowledge of taxation	4
Capabilities of Data Analysis	5
Understanding in Application of Emerging Technologies and Related Software	5
Knowledge and Approaches to Risk Management	4
Knowledge and Approaches to Corporate Governance	4
Knowledge and Approaches to Audit and Assurance	4
Understanding of Organizations' Business Models	5
Capability of Evaluating Different Strategic Options	5
Capability of Grasping the Macroeconomic Impact to Organizations	5
Ability of Keeping Abreast of The latest development in accountancy	5

Malaysia

Professional Institutions:

- Malaysian Institute of Accountants (MIA, member of the IFAC)
http: //www. mia. org. my/
- Malaysian Institute of Certified Public Accountants (MICPA, member of the IFAC) http: //www. micpa. com. my/
- ACCA (member of the IFAC and CAPA) http: //www. accaglobal. com/my/en. html

Research on the Competence of Accountancy Professionals:

There is no relevant research report on the competence of accountancy professionals in Malaysia.

Training Plans for Accountancy Professionals in Organizations:

The audited financial statements of a listed company must be signed by admitted members of MIA.

In general, large Malaysian companies have skill requirements for their accountancy employees, but different companies have different specific requirements. These skills should be mastered by all accountancy professionals who might obtain professional qualifications and/or admit as one member of professional accountancy institutions already. These enterprises may implement training plans, which are generally updated periodically or on demand, to accountancy professionals in HR department.

Approaches of Competence Training to Accountancy Professionals in Malaysia. The main approaches to training used in Malaysia are:

1. On-the-job Educational Upgrading

2. Professional Qualification Training

3. Participation in External Trainings and Forums

4. Internal Training

5. On-the-job Guidance by Supervisor

6. External Communication and Studying

7. Cross-departmental discussion

8. Moving between Business Departments to acquire In-depth Understanding

The respondents considered that aforementioned approaches are effective.

Annual Performance Appraisal to Accountancy Professionals:

There is annual performance appraisal to accountancy professionals in Malaysia.

CPD of Accountancy Professionals:

In general, companies registered in Malaysia do not require annual CPD hours to accountants mandatorily. However, accountancy professionals, as admitted members of MIA, MICPA, ACCA and other professional accountancy institutions, are required to complete a minimum hours of CPD annually.

Additionally, professional accountancy agencies (e. g. Deloitte, etc.) also have the requirements of CPD hours to accountancy professionals per year.

The Importance of accountancy Professionals to Corporate Performance:

The respondents considered that the accountancy professionals as "important" (four points out of five) to a company's performance improvement.

The Importance of Competencies of Accountancy Professionals

(importance up to 5 points)

Capabilities / Skills	Importance (1 – 5 points)
Knowledge and Approaches to Financial Accounting	4
Knowledge and Approaches to Management Accounting	4
Knowledge of taxation	3
Capabilities of Data Analysis	4
Understanding in Application of Emerging Technologies and Related Software	5
Knowledge and Approaches to Risk Management	3
Knowledge and Approaches to Corporate Governance	3
Knowledge and Approaches to Audit and Assurance	3
Understanding of Organizations' Business Models	3
Capability of Evaluating Different Strategic Options	3
Capability of Grasping the Macroeconomic Impact to Organizations	4
Ability of Keeping Abreast of The latest development in accountancy	3

UAE

Professional Institutions:

Accountants and Auditors Association http: //aaa4uae. ae/en/

Institute of Chartered Accountants of UAE https: //www. icaiauh. org/

Research on the Competence of Accountancy Professionals:

There is no relevant study and research report on the competence of accountancy professionals in UAE.

Competence Standards / Training Plans for Accountancy Professionals in Organizations:

Requirements of competence to accountancy professionals are generally centered on the knowledge of IFRS, financial planning and reporting, VAT and risk management, etc.

Most of companies do not have a department that takes charge of training of accountancy professionals. Companies in UAE generally enhance accountancy professionals skills rely on the training offered by professional accounting agencies (e. g. Big Four, etc.) or by sending their accountancy employees to attending IFRS seminars.

Approaches of Competence Training to Accountancy Professionals in UAE.

The main approaches to training used in UAE are:

- professional qualification training
- internal training
- on-the-job self-exploration
- on-the-job guidance by supervisor
- external communication and studying
- moving between business departments to acquire in-depth understanding.

Comments: Highly effective. The respondent comes from one of Big Four, so that the training provided by the firm has far outperformed other accounting trainings provided by other companies.

Annual Performance Appraisal to Accountancy Professionals in Enterprises:

The annual performance appraisal to accountancy professionals varies with different companies that depend on the sizes of companies.

CPD of Accountancy Professionals in Enterprises:

There have limited certificated administrative authorities with limited requirement for CPD. On the other hand, some regulators (e. g. Dubai Financial Services Authority (DFSA), etc.) do have CPD requirements.

The Importance of Accountancy Professionals to Corporate Performance:

The respondents considered that the accountancy professionals as "important" (scoring four points out of five points) to a company's performance improvement.

The Importance of Competencies of Accountancy Professionals
(importance up to 5 points)

Capabilities / Skills	Importance (1 – 5 points)
Knowledge and Approaches to Financial Accounting	5
Knowledge and Approaches to Management Accounting	3
Knowledge of taxation	1
Capabilities of Data Analysis	3
Understanding in Application of Emerging Technologies and Related Software	4
Knowledge and Approaches to Risk Management	3
Knowledge and Approaches to Corporate Governance	3
Knowledge and Approaches to Audit and Assurance	2
Understanding of Organizations' Business Models	3
Capability of Evaluating Different Strategic Options	3
Capability of Grasping the Macroeconomic Impact to Organizations	2
Ability of Keeping Abreast of The latest developments in accountancy	3

Poland

Professional Institutions:

None. There is no training institution to accountancy professionals, but professional accountancy organizations (such as the Polish Ministry of Finance http: //www. mf. gov. pl/en/news) .

Research on the Competence of Accountancy Professionals:

Most of economic universities start relevant researches regarding domestic accountancy professionals based on their own teaching and training programmes separately, but no report has been officially published.

Competence Standards / Training Plans for Accountancy Professionals in Organizations:

There is no uniform competence standard what totally depend on the actual demand of enterprises.

Approaches of Competence Training to Accountancy Professionals in Enterprises.

The main approaches to training used in Poland are:

- professional qualification training
- internal training
- on-the-job self-exploration
- moving between business departments to acquire in-depth understanding.

Comments: These training approaches promote the self-confidence to employees. All employees must be trained, and short-term secondment is very popular among high-level employees.

Annual Performance Appraisal to Accountancy Professionals in Enterprises:

Organizations impose annual performance appraisal to accountancy employees on an annual basis.

CPD to Accountancy Professionals in Enterprises:

Enterprises do not impose a requirement on accountancy employees to take training sessions, and the Accountants Association in Poland also does not arise any requirement regarding CPD hours to its admitted members.

The Importance of Accountancy Professionals to Corporate Performance:

The respondents considered that accountancy professionals as between "important" (four points out of five) and "very important" (five points) to a company's performance improvement.

The Importance of Competencies of Accountancy Professionals
(importance up to 5 points)

Capabilities / Skills	Importance (1 − 5 points)
Knowledge and Approaches to Financial Accounting	4
Knowledge and Approaches to Management Accounting	4
Knowledge of taxation	3
Capabilities of Data Analysis	5
Understanding in Application of Emerging Technologies and Related Software	4
Knowledge and Approaches to Risk Management	4
Knowledge and Approaches to Corporate Governance	4
Knowledge and Approaches to Audit and Assurance	4
Understanding of Organizations' Business Models	3
Capability of Evaluating Different Strategic Options	4
Capability of Grasping the Macroeconomic Impact to Organizations	4
Ability of Keeping Abreast of The latest developments in accountancy	3

Czech Republic

Professional Institutions:

National Accounting Committee-a body of independent expert's body provides support to accountancy professionals, accountant professional ethics and accounting methods. The members include:

- Chamber of Auditors of the Czech Republic http: //www. kacr. cz/en/
- The Chamber of Tax Advisers of the Czech Republic https: //www. kdpcr. cz/
- Union of Accountants of the Czech Republic http: //www. svazucetnich. eu
- University of Economics, Prague http: //ffu. vse. cz/english/
- ACCA http: //www. accaglobal. com/crsh/en. html

Research on the Competence of Accountancy Professionals:

There is no relevant study and research report on the competence of accountancy professionals in Czech.

Competence Standards/Training Plans for accountancy Professionals in Organizations:

There is no mandatory competence standard or training plan to accountancy professionals.

Approaches of Competence Training to Accountancy Professionals in Enterprises with Relevant Comments:

The approaches to accountants' development include on-the-job educational upgrading, professional qualification training, participation in external training and forums, internal training, job rotation, on-the-job self-exploration, on-the-job guidance by supervisor, outbound communication and studying, cross-departmental discussion, moving between business departments for in-depth understanding, etc.

Comments: effective and popular.

Annual Performance Appraisal to Accountancy Professionals in Enterprises: None.

CPD of Accountancy Professionals in Enterprises:

The CPD totally depends on the individual enterprise but is usually between 10 and 20 hours per year to general accounting employees, while more than 20 hours for auditors specifically.

The Importance of Accountancy Professionals to Corporate Performance:

The respondents considered that the accountancy professionals as "averagely important" (three out of five points) to a company's performance improvement.

The Importance of Competencies of Accountancy Professionals
(importance up to 5 points)

Capabilities / Skills	Importance (1 – 5 points)
Knowledge and Approaches to Financial Accounting	5
Knowledge and Approaches to Management Accounting	4
Knowledge of taxation	4
Capabilities of Data Analysis	4
Understanding in Application of Emerging Technologies and Related Software	4
Knowledge and Approaches to Risk Management	3
Knowledge and Approaches to Corporate Governance	2
Knowledge and Approaches to Audit and Assurance	3
Understanding of Organizations' Business Models	3
Capability of Evaluating Different Strategic Options	3
Capability of Grasping the Macroeconomic Impact to Organizations	2
Ability of Keeping Abreast of The latest developments in accountancy	3

Qatar

Professional Institutions:

There is no specialized agency or organization for training to accountancy professionals in Qatar.

Research on the Competence of Accountancy Professionals:

There is no relevant research report on the competence of accountancy professionals in Qatar.

Competence standards/Training Plans for Accountancy Professionals in Organizations:

The skills are clearly required by accountancy professionals in Qatar include:

1. A minimum educational level of a bachelor degree in accounting

2. International certification or qualification of CPA/ACCA/CA

Approaches to competence training of accountancy professionals in enterprises

The main approaches to training used in Qatar are:

- on-the-job education upgrading
- professional qualification training
- participation in external training and forums
- internal training
- job rotation
- on-the-job self – exploration
- on-the-job guidance by supervisor
- external communication and studying
- cross-departmental discussion
- moving between business departments to acquire in-depth understanding.

Annual Performance Appraisal to Accountancy Professionals:

Accountancy professionals shall be subject to annual performance appraisal in

Qatar.

CPE of Accountancy Professionals:

There is no specific requirement of CPE in Qatar. But Deloitte requires minimal 20 hours of CPE per year, and accumulate to 120 hours at least after three years.

Qatar's Institute of Certified Public Accountants has no requirement of CPE to its admitted members.

The Importance of Accountancy Professionals to Corporate Performance:

The respondents considered that the accountancy professionals as " very important" (maximum five points) to a company's performance improvement.

The Importance of Competencies of Accountancy Professionals
(importance up to 5 points)

Capabilities / Skills	Importance (1-5 points)
Knowledge and Approaches to Financial Accounting	5
Knowledge and Approaches to Management Accounting	5
Knowledge of taxation	4
Capabilities of Data Analysis	4
Understanding in Application of Emerging Technologies and Related Software	4
Knowledge and Approaches to Risk Management	3
Knowledge and Approaches to Corporate Governance	3
Knowledge and Approaches to Audit and Assurance	3
Understanding of Organizations' Business Models	5
Capability of Evaluating Different Strategic Options	3
Capability of Grasping the Macroeconomic Impact to Organizations	3
Ability of Keeping Abreast of The latest development in accountancy	5

Hungary

Professional Institutions:

Chamber of Hungarian Auditors (CHA)

Research on the Competence of Accountancy Professionals:

There is no relevant research report on the competence of accountancy professionals in Hungary.

Competence standards/Training Plans for Accountancy Professionals in Organizations:

There is no relevant mandatory training plan to accountancy professionals in Hungary.

Approaches to competence training of accountancy professionals in enterprises

The main approaches to training used in Hungary are:

- on-the-job education upgrading
- professional qualification training
- participation in external training and forums
- internal training
- on-the-job guidance by supervisor
- cross-departmental discussion
- moving between business departments to acquire in – depth understanding.

The respondents considered that these approaches are very effective to development.

Annual Performance Appraisal to Accountancy Professionals:

There is no mandatory annual performance appraisal for Accountancy professionals in Hungary.

CPD for accountancy Professionals in organisations.

There are specific training requirements to both auditors and accountants.

Generally, approximately 10 to 20 hours CPD are required annually, depending on the nature of their work.

The Importance of Accountancy Professionals to Corporate Performance:

The respondents considered that the accountancy professionals as "very important" (maximum five points) to a company's performance improvement.

The Importance of Competencies of Accountancy Professionals

(importance up to 5 points)

Capabilities / Skills	Importance (1 – 5 points)
Knowledge and Approaches to Financial Accounting	5
Knowledge and Approaches to Management Accounting	4
Knowledge of taxation	3
Capabilities of Data Analysis	4
Understanding in Application of Emerging Technologies and Related Software	4
Knowledge and Approaches to Risk Management	5
Knowledge and Approaches to Corporate Governance	3
Knowledge and Approaches to Audit and Assurance	5
Understanding of Organizations' Business Models	3
Capability of Evaluating Different Strategic Options	3
Capability of Grasping the Macroeconomic Impact to Organizations	3
Ability of Keeping Abreast of The latest development in accountancy	3

Thailand

Professional Institutions:

Federation of Accountancy Professions ("FAP") http://en. fap. or. th/

Research on the Competence of Accountancy Professionals:

There is no relevant research report on the competence of accountancy professionals in Thailand.

Competence standards/Training Plans for Accountancy Professionals in Organizations:

There is no specific skill requirement arose by companies in Thailand to accountancy professionals. However, a certified public accountant (CPA) holder must complete 20 hours of formal training and 20 hours of informal training annually as the completion of CPD requirement per year after CPA certificate has been obtained.

Approaches to competence tailandraining of accountancy professionals in enterprises

The main approaches to training used in Thailand are:

- on-the-job education upgrading
- professional qualification training
- participation in external training and forums
- internal training
- on-the-job self-exploration
- on-the-job guidance by supervisor
- external communication and studying
- cross-departmental discussion
- moving between business departments to acquire in-depth understanding.

It is mandatory for all employees to comply with talent development policies arose by companies in Thailand. The respondents considered that such development plans are effective, and will be enable to result better skills to employees as the company grows.

Annual Performance Appraisal to Accountancy Professionals in organisation.

There is annual performance appraisal to accountancy professionals in Thailand. A Thai respondent from Deloitte said that the company would conduct Mid-Year Performance Appraisal and Year End Performance Appraisal.

CPD of accountancy Professionals in Organisation.

FAP requires that all CPA holders must complete 20 hours of formal training and 20 hours of informal training annually as the completion of CPD requirement per year.

The Importance of Accountancy Professionals to Corporate Performance:

The respondents considered that the accountancy professionals as "very important" (Maximum five points) to a company's performance improvement.

The Importance of Competencies of Accountancy Professionals
(importance up to 5 points)

Capabilities / Skills	Importance (1 – 5 points)
Knowledge and Approaches to Financial Accounting	5
Knowledge and Approaches to Management Accounting	4
Knowledge of taxation	5
Capabilities of Data Analysis	5
Understanding in Application of Emerging Technologies and Related Software	5
Knowledge and Approaches to Risk Management	5
Knowledge and Approaches to Corporate Governance	5
Knowledge and Approaches to Audit and Assurance	4
Understanding of Organizations' Business Models	5
Capability of Evaluating Different Strategic Options	4
Capability of Grasping the Macroeconomic Impact to Organizations	4
Ability of Keeping Abreast of The latest development in accountancy	5

Vietnam

Professional Institutions:

Vietnam Association of Certified Public Accountants (VACPA)

The relevant information regarding the Vietnamese Professionals Training Program is temporarily unavailable to us, but VACPA has provided a large number of accountancy professionals to Vietnam.

Research on the Competence of Accountancy Professionals:

The relevant answers are not provided.

Competence standards/Training Plans for Accountancy Professionals in Organizations:

- The relevant requirements are clearly specified in Vietnamese accounting regulations, with the following exceptions referred from Accounting Law 2003:

- Article 50 Standards, rights and responsibilities of accountants

Accountants must satisfy standards as below:

1. Accountants must adhere to professional ethical standards, be honest and incorruptible, and comply with the laws

2. Accountants must have professional accounting certificates

3. Accountants shall be entitled to be independent during the process of professional accountancy work.

4. Accountants should comply with laws to carry out bookkeeping work and other assigned works, and should be responsible for all their professional works. When the accountant resigns, all accounting works and files must be handed over to successor, and the former accountant also needs to be responsible for all accounting works during the period of designation.

Approaches to competence training of accountancy professionals in enterprises

The main approaches to training used in Vietnam are:

- on-the-job education upgrading
- professional qualification training
- participation in external training and forums
- internal training
- job rotation
- on-the-job self-exploration
- cross-departmental discussion
- moving between business departments to acquire in-depth understanding.

The respondents considered that aforementioned training approaches are very appropriate and effective to accountancy professionals, so that aforementioned approaches are widely used in most of accountancy agencies.

Annual Performance Appraisal to Accountancy Professionals in organisation.

The financial and accounting personnel in the majority of Vietnamese companies shall be subject to annual performance appraisal.

Annual performance appraisal to accountancy professionals is implemented by most of companies in Vietnam.

CPD of Accountancy Professionals in enterprises

Vietnam has stipulated specific annual training to accountancy professionals what is minimal 40 hours per year generally.

The Importance of Accountancy Professionals to Corporate Performance:

The respondents considered that the accountancy professionals as "important" (four points out of five) to a company's performance improvement.

The Importance of Competencies of Accountancy Professionals
(importance up to 5 points)

Capabilities / Skills	Importance (1 – 5 points)
Knowledge and Approaches to Financial Accounting	5
Knowledge and Approaches to Management Accounting	2
Knowledge of taxation	3
Capabilities of Data Analysis	4
Understanding in Application of Emerging Technologies and Related Software	2

续表

Capabilities / Skills	Importance（1 – 5 points）
Knowledge and Approaches to Risk Management	4
Knowledge and Approaches to Corporate Governance	3
Knowledge and Approaches to Audit and Assurance	5
Understanding of Organizations' Business Models	3
Capability of Evaluating Different Strategic Options	2
Capability of Grasping the Macroeconomic Impact to Organizations	4
Ability of Keeping Abreast of The latest development in accountancy	4

Russia

Professional Institutions:

There is no specific organization to take charge of the development of accountancy professionals. The necessary qualifications can be obtained by passing the professional examinations organized by professional accountancy institutions, including:

- ACCA http: //www. accaglobal. com/gb/en. html
- CPA http: //www. cpa. org. ru/about/en/about-EICPA

Research on the Competence of Accountancy Professionals:

There is no relevant study and research report on the competence of accountancy professionals in Russia.

Competence Standards/Training Plans for Accountancy Professionals in Organizations:

The government started to introduce professional accountancy standards in 2016. According to these professional standards, employees engaged in accounting functions should have a range of knowledge and skills (such as the preparation of major documents statements, knowledge of the legislation, technical applications, etc.).

There is no specific training programme or division dedicated to developing talent in Russian companies.

Approaches of Competence Training to Accountancy Professionals in Enterprises.

The main approaches to training used in Russia are:

- on-the-job education upgrading
- professional qualification training
- participation in external training and forums
- internal training
- job rotation

- on-the-job self – exploration
- on-the-job guidance by supervisor
- external communication and studying
- cross-departmental discussion
- moving between business departments to acquire in-depth understanding.

Comments: All of aforementioned approaches are appropriate to Russia. Their effectiveness and popularity depend on the business scale and the sector of organization.

Annual Performance Appraisal to Accountancy Professionals in Enterprises: None.

CPD of Accountancy Professionals in Enterprises:

There is no mandatory requirement regarding CPD at government level.

The importance of Accountancy Professionals to Corporate Performance:

The respondents considered that the Accountancy professionals as "important" (four points out of five) to a company's performance improvement.

The Importance of Competencies of Accountancy Professionals
(importance up to 5 points)

Capabilities / Skills	Importance (1 – 5 points)
Knowledge and Approaches to Financial Accounting	5
Knowledge and Approaches to Management Accounting	5
Knowledge of taxation	5
Capabilities of Data Analysis	5
Understanding in Application of Emerging Technologies and Related Software	5
Knowledge and Approaches to Risk Management	3
Knowledge and Approaches to Corporate Governance	3
Knowledge and Approaches to Audit and Assurance	3
Understanding of Organizations' Business Models	4
Capability of Evaluating Different Strategic Options	3
Capability of Grasping the Macroeconomic Impact to Organizations	4
Ability of Keeping Abreast of The latest development in accountancy	5

Indonesia

Professional Institutions:

Universities are responsible for the development of accounting talents, mainly represented by University of Indonesia.

Website: http://www. feb. ui. ac. id/akuntansi/

Research on the Competence of Accountancy Professionals:

Please visit the FEB UI website for relevant researches.

Website: http://www. feb. ui. ac. id/akuntansi/

Approaches of Competence Training to Accountancy Professionals in Enterprises.

The main approaches to training used in Indonesia are:

- professional qualification training
- participation in external training and forums
- internal training

Comments: Highly effective.

Annual Performance Appraisal to Accountancy Professionals in Enterprises:

The respondents considered that there is annual performance appraisal in Indonesia.

CPD of Accountancy Professionals in Enterprises:

The respondents reported that 40 hours of CPD must be satisfied as the minimum level in Indonesia, and this requirement is also applicable to certified accountancy members.

The Importance of Accountancy Professionals to Corporate Performance:

The respondents considered that the Accountancy professionals as "very important" (Maximum five points) to a company's performance improvement.

The Importance of Competencies of Accountancy Professionals

(importance up to 5 points)

Capabilities / Skills	Importance (1 − 5 points)
Knowledge and Approaches to Financial Accounting	5
Knowledge and Approaches to Management Accounting	3
Knowledge of taxation	5
Capabilities of Data Analysis	5
Understanding in Application of Emerging Technologies and Related Software	5
Knowledge and Approaches to Risk Management	4
Knowledge and Approaches to Corporate Governance	3
Knowledge and Approaches to Audit and Assurance	5
Understanding of Organizations' Business Models	4
Capability of Evaluating Different Strategic Options	3
Capability of Grasping the Macroeconomic Impact to Organizations	3
Ability of Keeping Abreast of The latest development in accountancy	4

Kazakhstan

Professional Institutions:

There is no specific organization to take charge of the development of accountancy professionals in Kazakhstan. However, professional accountancy institutions in Kazakhstan provide accountancy education services. Additionally, qualified certificates also can be obtained through passing the professional examinations, include ACCA, Certified Accounting Practitioners ("CIP"), Certified International Professional Accountant ("CIPA"), Professional Accountant, etc.

Research on the Competence of Accountancy Professionals:

There is no relevant research report on the competence of accountancy professionals in Kazakhstan.

Competence standards/Training Plans for Accountancy Professionals in Organizations:

According to the regulation of the Republic of Kazakhstan on Accounting Reporting, professional accountants can be appointed as chief accountants of the public interest organizations (Article 9) since 1 January 2012. A professional accountant refers to an individual who has the certificate of professional accountant based upon the requirements of Regulation No. 455 promulgated by the Minister of Finance of The Republic of Kazakhstan on 13 December, 2007.

There is no requirement to companies in Kazakhstani to set up a training program or a special department to take charge of the development of accountancy professionals.

Approaches of Competence Training to Accountancy Professionals in Enterprises.

The main approaches to training used in Kazakhstan are:

- on-the-job education upgrading
- professional qualification training
- participation in external training and forums
- internal training
- job rotation
- on-the-job self-exploration
- on-the-job guidance by supervisor
- external communication and studying
- cross-departmental discussion
- moving between business departments to acquire in-depth understanding.

The respondents considered that all of aforementioned approaches are appropriate to Kazakhstani. Their effectiveness and popularity depend on the business scale and the sector of organization.

Annual Performance Appraisal to Accountancy professionals:

There is no annual performance appraisal to accountancy professionals in Kazakhstani.

CPD of Accountancy Professionals:

There is no mandatory CPD requirement at government level in Kazakhstan.

The Importance of Accountancy Professionals to Corporate Performance:

The respondents considered that the Accountancy professionals as "important" (four points out of five) to a company's performance improvement.

The Importance of Competencies of Accountancy Professionals
(importance up to 5 points)

Capabilities / Skills	Importance (1 – 5 points)
Knowledge and Approaches to Financial Accounting	5
Knowledge and Approaches to Management Accounting	5
Knowledge of taxation	5
Capabilities of Data Analysis	5
Understanding in Application of Emerging Technologies and Related Software	5
Knowledge and Approaches to Risk Management	3

续表

Capabilities / Skills	Importance (1 – 5 points)
Knowledge and Approaches to Corporate Governance	3
Knowledge and Approaches to Audit and Assurance	3
Understanding of Organizations' Business Models	4
Capability of Evaluating Different Strategic Options	3
Capability of Grasping the Macroeconomic Impact to Organizations	4
Ability of Keeping Abreast of The latest development in accountancy	5

India

Professional institution:

There is no specific institution or organization responsible for the development of the accounting personnel.

Research on the competence of accountancy pnofessienals.

Respondents are unaware of whether there is such research in India.

Competence standards / Training plans for accountancy professionals in enterprises.

There is no specific competence standard.

Approaches to competence training of accountancy professionals in enterprises

The main approaches to training used in India are:

- professional qualification training
- participation in external training and forums
- internal training
- job rotation
- on-the-job self-exploration
- on-the-job guidance by supervisor
- moving between business departments to acquire in-depth understanding.

Annual performance appraisal of accountancy professionals in enterprises.

In most companies, accountancy personnel are subject to annual appraisals.

CPE of accountancy professionals in enterprises.

The stipulations in http://www.cpeicai.org/? page _ id = 134 are as follows:

CPE hour's requirements for the block period of 3 years (1 January 2017 to 31 December 2019) to be complied with by different categories of members:

1. All the members (aged less than 60 years) who are holding Certificate of

Practice (except all those members who are residing abroad) are required to:

a. Complete at least 120 CPE credit hours in a rolling period of three-years.

b. Complete minimum 20 CPE credit hours of structured learning in each calendar year.

c. Balance 60 CPE credit hours (minimum 20 CPE credit hours in each calendar year) can be completed either through Structured or Unstructured learning (as per Member's choice).

2. All the members (aged less than 60 years) who are not holding Certificate of Practice; and all the members who are residing abroad (whether holding Certificate of Practice or not) are required to:

a. Complete at least 60 CPE credit hours either structured or unstructured learning (as per Member's choice) in rolling period of three years.

b. Complete minimum 15 CPE credit hours of either structured or unstructured learning (as per member's choice) in each calendar year.

3. All the members (aged 60 years & above) who are holding Certificate of Practice shall be subject to other specific requirements.

Importance of accountancy professionals. for corporate performance:

Respondents deem the accountancy professionals as "highly important" (Maximum five points) for a company's performance improvement.

The Importance of Competencies of Accountancy Professionals
(importance up to 5 points)

Capabilities / Skills	Importance (1 – 5 points)
Knowledge and Approaches to Financial Accounting	5
Knowledge and Approaches to Management Accounting	5
Knowledge of taxation	4
Capabilities of Data Analysis	5
Understanding in Application of Emerging Technologies and Related Software	3
Knowledge and Approaches to Risk Management	3
Knowledge and Approaches to Corporate Governance	3
Knowledge and Approaches to Audit and Assurance	4

续表

Capabilities / Skills	Importance （1 - 5 points）
Understanding of Organizations' Business Models	4
Capability of Evaluating Different Strategic Options	2
Capability of Grasping the Macroeconomic Impact to Organizations	1
Ability of Keeping Abreast of The latest development in accountancy	1

Pakistan

Professional Institutions:

● Local professional bodies involved in the development of accountancy professionals, include:

● The Institute of Chartered Accountants of Pakistan (ICAP) http://www. icap. org. pk/

● Pakistan Institute of Public Finance Accountants (PIPFA) http://pipfa. org. pk/

● Institute of Cost and Management Accountants of Pakistan (ICMAP) https://www. icmap. com. pk/

● International professional bodies involved in the development of accountancy professionals, include

● ACCA http://www. accaglobal. com/pk/en. html, etc.

● The most famous universities, which offer training programs for accountancy professionals, include

● Lahore University of Management Sciences (LUMS) https://lums. edu. pk/

● Institute of Business Administration (IBA) https://www. iba. edu. pk/

● University of Karachi (UoK) http://uok. edu. pk/

Accounting Education Providers:

Registered Accounting Education Tutors ("RAETs") approved by ICAP are authorized to conduct tutorial classes for ICAP and MFC students. These RAETs are treated as important elements for the development of local accountancy professionals. Go to https://goo. gl/WaMcu5 for the list of RAETs.

Training Institutions:

ICAP requires that students should be trained from approved training organizations outside practice ("TOOP") . These organizations also make contribution to the development of accountancy professionals in Pakistan. The list of approved institutions can be found in the link of https: //goo. gl/xxqgNR.

Research on the Competence of Accountancy Professionals:

Respondents are unaware of whether there is such research in Pakistan.

Competence standards / Training Plans for Accountancy Professionals in Organizations:

There is no overall guideline to organizations or enterprises in Pakistan, but different competencies or skills are defined according to different job descriptions.

In some special cases, there would have specific guidelines provided by the relevant authorities. For examples, the listing regulation of Pakistan Stock Exchange provides instructions regarding the appointment of internal audit directors and chief financial officers for listed companies. According to aforementioned instructions, a candidate should be a member of chartered professional bodies.

Large organizations usually have a learning and development department dedicated to the training programmes for accountancy professionals. For example, our organization's learning department takes charge of revising training contents, conducting promotional training, conducting software upgrade training, etc. , regularly.

Approaches of Competence Training to Accountancy Professionals in Pakistan:

The main approaches to training used in Pakistan are:

- professional qualification training
- internal training
- on-the-job self-exploration
- moving between business departments to acquire in-depth understanding.

The respondents considered that the selected development path to be highly effective, since you can learn from other professionals and get trained from your organization to get better feedback and learning applications. Using the trainer model and pass on what you have learned to the public will trigger a trickledown effect.

For internal training, an external professional trainer may be employed so that the trainees can be benefited from specific professional training.

Annual Performance Appraisal to Accountancy Professionals in enterprises.

The performance appraisal would be imposed to accountancy professionals in Pakistani according to the organization's policies.

CPD of Accountancy Professionals:

Enterprises in Pakistani generally do not have specific requirements for CPD hours, but there have other requirements based upon the different HR policies that vary with different enterprises.

Members of professional bodies must comply with the CPD requirements arose by professional bodies. For example, ICAP provides CPD guidance in accordance with its Directive 8.01, which is available at https://goo.gl/A7DzJa

The Importance of Accountancy Professionals to Corporate Performance:

The respondents considered that the accountancy professionals as "important" (four points out of five points) to a company's performance improvement.

The Importance of Competencies of Accountancy Professionals
(importance up to 5 points)

Capabilities / Skills	Importance (1 – 5 points)
Knowledge and Approaches to Financial Accounting	5
Knowledge and Approaches to Management Accounting	5
Knowledge of taxation	4
Capabilities of Data Analysis	5
Understanding in Application of Emerging Technologies and Related Software	5
Knowledge and Approaches to Risk Management	4
Knowledge and Approaches to Corporate Governance	5
Knowledge and Approaches to Audit and Assurance	4
Understanding of Organizations' Business Models	4
Capability of Evaluating Different Strategic Options	4
Capability of Grasping the Macroeconomic Impact to Organizations	4
Ability of Keeping Abreast of The latest development in accountancy	4

Afterword

The "Belt and Road Initiative" aroused great repercussion both at home and abroad after it was put forward by President Xi Jinping in 2013. Since then, many organizations have delved deep into the potential opportunities brought about by the Initiative, and have taken concrete actions to promote its development. Accounting plays a key and foundational role in the economic operation and international economic exchanges of a country. During the process of promoting the Belt and Road Initiative, it will certainly encounter a great many new problems and challenges in the accounting, taxation and financial areas. Therefore, enhancing our study of such issues, and promoting the communication and coordination on accounting and related issues among the Belt and Road countries will undoubtedly give an impetus to the construction of the Belt and Road Initiative. In November 2016, during my visit to ACCA headquarters and meeting with its chief executive Ms. Helen Brand, we found out that both sides had common concerns, so we promptly reached a consensus on establishing, by relying on our respective advantages, a joint research team to study the accounting issues related to the Belt and Road Initiative, and convening high-level symposiums based on these studies. The research team was quickly set up and grew stronger, as Deloitte joined it and brought along its international expert network. Gratifyingly, the research team has cleared away all sorts of stumbling blocks, and completed the industry's first systematic research report on accounting issues related to the Belt and Road Initiative on schedule. Despite there still can have further improvement, the report has won high appreciation from multiple parties for its research ideas and value.

In May 2017, the Belt and Road Forum for International Cooperation was successfully held in Beijing. Encouraged by the Forum and with the great support of leaders from the Ministry of Finance and its Accounting Department, ASC ("Accounting Society of China") became a co-organizer of the high-level symposium on "Accounting Infrastructure" Promotes "Belt and Road Initiative". Also, with the joining of Inspur Group, a company which has been successfully expanding its business into the Belt and Road countries, we grew even more confident in organizing a high-quality workshop. Thanks to the joint efforts made by various sides, particularly the substantial support of experts from the government departments, academia and business circles, the symposium held by SNAI in July 2017 turned out to be a huge success. We ascribe this success not only to the new concept of "accounting infrastructure" which gained unanimous recognition of all participants, but also to the deeply inspiring speeches delivered by many experts. In order to scale up the outcome of this symposium, we set up an editorial board and asked the experts to further revise and enrich their scripts. Meanwhile, we also translated their scripts into English for easy reference to our foreign readers. These efforts finally lead to what you are reading now, which is the fruit of continuous hard work by our symposium speakers and editorial board members over the past few months.

As this collection of essays is soon sent to the press, I would like to express my special gratitude to Assistant Finance Minister Zhao Mingji and Director Gao Yibin for their great support to our work. Mr. Zhao Mingji attended the symposium amid a tight schedule and delivered a strategically insightful speech. While reflecting the high attention given by the Ministry of Finance to accounting issues related to the Belt and Road Initiative, his speech also provided important guidance to our future work. Moreover, I also need to extremely appreciate my old friend Mr. Fu Junyuan, as Vice General Manager of China Communications Construction Company (CCCC), Mr. Noritaka Akamatsu, as Senior Advisor of OREI of Asian Development Bank (ADB), and Mr. Wang Xingshan, as Executive President of Inspur Group for their enlightening speeches. Whether it is the arrangements of research, the organization of symposium, or the editing and publishing of this essay collection, they are all the results of sincere cooperation and concerted efforts of the parties. In addition, I would also like to take this opportunity to express my heartfelt appreciations to the co-editors of this book: Mr. Wang Peng, as Vice Inspector of the Accounting Department in Ministry of Finance; Ms. Helen Brand, ACCA Chief Executive; and Mr. Patrick Tsang, Deloitte China CEO. I am also obliged to editors from the Economic Science Press for their arduous work. Last but not least, my gratitude must also go to those who made enormous efforts behind the scenes for the publishing of this book. They are: Ms. Liu Minghua and Ms. Ren Zheng from Deloitte China; Ms. Liang Shuping, Ms. Qian Yuyi and Ms. Zhu Xiaoyun from ACCA; and Dr. Ge Yuyu, Dr. Tong Chengsheng, Mr. Liu Xiaoqiang, Ms. Fu Qiulian, Mr. Lv Xiaolei and Dr. Li Xinning from SNAI.

Fruitful achievements have been received since the Belt and Road Initiative was brought forward, and even more good news is yet to come. Hence it requires more positive efforts from the accounting community to further promote the implementation of the Initiative. And we look forward to closely cooperating with friends from various circles on this grand project to strengthen the accounting infrastructure and work towards a better future.

Li Kouqing, SNAI President
October 21, 2017